Professional Developer's Guide

Constructing Intelligent Agents Using Java™, Second Edition

Joseph P. Bigus
Jennifer Bigus

Wiley Computer Publishing

John Wiley & Sons, Inc.

NEW YORK • CHICHESTER • WEINHEIM • BRISBANE • SINGAPORE • TORONTO

To Sarah Jo and Alexander,
who are definitely more important than Java.

Publisher: Robert Ipsen
Editor: Margaret Eldridge
Assistant Editor: Adaobi Obi
Managing Editor: Angela Smith
New Media Editor: Brian Snapp
Text Design & Composition: D&G Limited, LLC

This book is printed on acid-free paper. ∞

Library of Congress Cataloging-in-Publication Data:
Bigus, Joseph P.
    Constructing intelligent agents using JAVA/Joseph P. Bigus, Jennifer Bigus.—2nd ed.
      p. cm.—(Professional developer's guide series)
    ISBN: 0-471-39601-X
      1. Intelligent agents (Computer software) 2. Java (Computer program language) I. Bigus, Jennifer, 1960–II. Title. III. Series.

    QA76.76.I58 B563 2001
    006.3—dc21

                              2001017638

Printed in the United States of America.

10 9 8 7 6 5 4 3 2 1

Professional Developer's Guide Series

Other titles in the series:

Contents

Foreword to the Second Edition

In the three years since we wrote the first edition of this book, much has changed in the computing industry. Trends that were just emerging then are clearly established now. Our judgment that Java would become a major programming language was certainly right on. Today there are more than 2.5 million Java programmers, according to Sun's latest estimates. The commercialization of the Internet has continued unabated, with booms and busts in the valuation of the new dot.com businesses. And agents? Well, agents are everywhere, not always visible, but certainly playing their role in personalizing and automating the Web experience for millions of users. Java has clearly proven to be the language of choice for constructing agents and multiagent systems.

Many of the reasons for this second edition are due to the rapid evolution and maturing of the Java language and programming environment. When the first edition was published, Java applets appeared to be the *killer app* for Java, but instead Java has succeeded largely as an application programming language running on servers. Rather than downloading applets from Web browsers, Java is being embedded into Web pages and invoked on the server to provide dynamic Web content in Java Server Pages. The Java "write once, run everywhere" promise has evolved into the "write once, test everywhere" reality. No, Java isn't perfect. But its portability has been proven in hundreds of cross-platform applications. The original java.awt GUI framework has been supplanted by the more capable and lighter-weight Swing framework. The Java programming environment has moved from the immature JDK 1.1 to the more robust Java 2 platform.

Consequently, we have updated our code to use Swing and the latest JDK, changed our applets into applications to avoid the lingering browser compatibility issues, and strengthened our use of the JavaBean component model. We now provide UML diagrams of our class relationships and the major interactions among objects in the *CIAgent* framework, and we have added JavaDocs to the source code. We have updated the example applications to reflect more standard Java programming practices and to enhance the use of agent functionality in a Web context. In recognition of the use of this book as a college text, we have expanded the end-of-chapter exercises, expanded the on-line resource section, and almost doubled the number of bibliographic references.

We added genetic algorithms and fuzzy-rule system implementations to our collection of artificial intelligence algorithms. The ability to plug agents into our Personal Agent Manager should be a great addition to any applied AI or agents class. We have updated and greatly expanded our treatment of agents and multiagent systems in this edition. This edition's CD-ROM includes the new Java-based IBM Agent Building and Learning Environment (ABLE), which will provide a natural progression from the basic concepts and capabilities of the *CIAgent* framework presented in this book to the more capable and sophisticated ABLE platform.

In summary, we hope that we strengthened the book for those readers who found the first edition useful. We thank you for your support and hope that this book can play some small part in helping to move intelligent software agents along on their way to commercial success. If you have comments or suggestions, please e-mail us at support@bigusbooks.com.

Preface

The term artificial intelligence (AI) has gone in and out of style over the past forty years. At first, it represented the promise of computers and the ability of humankind to create intelligent machines with abilities comparable or possibly superior to those in humans. However, after years of unfulfilled expectations, it came to be associated with failed approaches. Although the term may have fallen out of favor, the basic desire to make computers act smarter or more intelligent has not gone away. Indeed, as we have built more and more complex systems out of layers of conventional software, the need for intelligence, whether real or artificial, has only increased.

In this book, we approach AI not as a holy grail requiring parity with human abilities in order to signal success, but as a set of techniques for making software that is more intuitive and easier to use, and which makes users more productive. In short, AI allows us to build software that is smarter than it otherwise would be, and that is qualitatively better than software that does not use AI techniques.

Whether it is viewed as a failure or a success, the fact remains that AI research has made major contributions to the design and development of mainstream commercial software. Perhaps the biggest impact has been in the area now known as object-oriented programming. The idea of software objects with associated data and procedures is a refinement of the AI concept of frames, which had slots or attributes for holding data related to a concept and attached procedures (methods) for processing that data. Smalltalk was the first "pure" object programming language, but Lisp, Pascal, and C also had object extensions. The C++ language was the most widely used object-oriented programming language, primarily because it was an extension of the extremely popular C language that already had thousands of fluent programmers.

Although it was once a topic of heated argument in software development circles, the object-oriented approach to commercial software design and development is clearly the preferred method today. The introduction of the Java programming language by Sun Microsystems in 1996 has not only confirmed this preference, but has shown how deeply this conviction is held. The industry interest and uptake of Java has been astounding to most experienced software developers, because it usually takes decades before new programming languages gain any significant following. However, with its C++-like syntax and Smalltalk-like semantics and run-time behavior, Java has received unprecedented buy-in from commercial software developers, even though it has been in commercial use for a relatively short time. Part of the reason for its popularity can be attributed to Java's "write once, run anywhere" cross-platform portability, built-in graphical user interface (GUI) framework, and strong support for both client/server and network-centered applications. As we describe later, this same collection of language features makes Java ideal for writing intelligent agent applications.

How to Use This Book

This book is targeted at Java programmers who are familiar with object-oriented design concepts and who are interested in learning how to make their programs behave more intelligently. Programmers with experience in other object-oriented languages such as C++ or Smalltalk should have no trouble following the Java examples presented in this book. Although we provide a brief introduction to the Java language and its programming environment, this book is not a Java primer. If you are completely new to Java programming, you should also get a book written explicitly for beginning Java programmers.

Readers can use this book to achieve two different but overlapping goals. For those who are mostly interested in the underlying AI programming techniques, we provide an introduction to the relevant AI concepts as well as concrete Java code examples. This material, presented in the first half of the book, could be used as a text for an undergraduate course in AI programming. People who are mostly interested in creating their own intelligent agents or in understanding the issues related to intelligent agent applications can focus on the second half of the book, where we present our design and implementation of a Java framework for constructing intelligent agents, along with several applications. Taken in its entirety, this book provides the background and fundamentals of AI programming techniques as a base, then builds on this foundation to construct a complete framework for developing intelligent agent applications, whether on the desktop or across the Internet.

In addition to providing a discussion of the technical issues related to intelligent agents, we provide citations to a number of related papers and articles. At the end of most chapters, a set of exercises is provided to test your understanding of the material. A set of Java applications is included for hands-on experimentation and for exploring (and possibly extending) the behavior of the various AI techniques.

Organization of the Book

This book is divided into two major parts. Part One focuses on the AI algorithms and techniques used to make applications and agents intelligent. Part Two builds on Part One by taking the AI algorithms and using them in an intelligent agent framework and example applications. All programs and examples are written entirely in Java.

In Chapter 1, we discuss some of the history of AI research and the basic premises of both the symbol-processing and neural-network (connectionist) schools. We explore the evolution of AI systems into today's intelligent agents and the simultaneous emergence of network computing and the Web. We discuss the many ways that AI can be used to add value to commercial software systems. We examine the Java programming language from an intelligent agent perspective in terms of its support for autonomy, intelligence, and mobility.

In Chapter 2, we show how to solve problems using search and state-based definitions of the world. We describe how problems can be mapped onto a state-space representation, and how common AI search strategies such as breadth-first, depth-first, and best-first search can be used to find solutions to problems. We implement these search techniques in Java and develop an application to help us examine their behavior on sample problems. We also discuss other, more advanced heuristic search techniques. We end the chapter with a discussion of genetic search algorithms and describe our implementation.

Chapter 3 deals with the major types of knowledge representation used in AI systems. We start with a general discussion of the types of knowledge we need to represent and then explore propositional and predicate logic, frames, and semantic networks. An emerging standard knowledge representation, the Knowledge Interchange Format (KIF), is described in detail. Finally, we discuss the issues that arise when building a domain-specific knowledge base. Knowledge representation is a key element in any AI application, so we pay particular attention to the strengths and weaknesses of the various techniques.

Reasoning systems, specifically rule-based systems, are the focus of Chapter 4. The basic elements of a rule are described, including antecedent and consequent clauses, certainty factors, and sensor and effector (action) rules. An example rule base is used throughout the chapter to illustrate the concepts related to forward chaining and backward chaining with rules. We develop a Java application and classes to implement rules and rule-based inferencing. Fuzzy-rule systems that combine rules and fuzzy logic are described and implemented in Java. We also explore the issues related to planning, a specialty in AI that is particularly relevant to intelligent agent systems.

In Chapter 5, we discuss learning and adaptive techniques and the advantages such behavior provides in intelligent agents. We describe the fundamental issues in building learning systems and the major paradigms, including supervised, unsupervised, and reinforcement learning. We introduce neural networks and describe the fundamentals of back-propagation networks and self-organizing feature maps. Next, we show how information theory is used to build decision trees using induction. These three learning algorithms are then implemented in Java, along with an application to serve as a test-bed for exploration.

Chapter 6 provides a bridge from the AI techniques described in Chapters 2–5 to the intelligent agents and the applications developed in the rest of the book. We look at the agent attributes of perception and action and how AI provides the solutions. The issues related to multiagent systems are also discussed. As an introduction to the general topic of communications between agents, we describe the classic blackboard agent architecture. We examine the Knowledge Query and Manipulation Language (KQML) as the leading approach for communicating between agents. Finally, we discuss how agents can cooperate and compete in the emerging electronic commerce world.

In Part Two, we change our focus from the underlying AI issues and techniques to their application in the major intelligent-agent paradigms. Part Two consists of a set of application chapters in which we design and build an intelligent agent architecture and then apply it to several common application domains. We build on the AI functions developed and described in Part One.

Chapter 7 is a key chapter in this book because here we develop the *CIAgent* intelligent agent architecture, going from requirements through specifications and design. We describe the major Java classes, the functions they provide, and their Java implementations. The JavaBeans software component model is evaluated as it relates to intelligent agent requirements. Finally, we extend the rule-based processing capabilities introduced in Chapter 4 by adding support for *Facts*, *Sensors*, and *Effectors* in rules.

Chapter 8 illustrates how we can use our *CIAgent* framework to construct an application that provides a simple agent platform, allowing users to develop and plug in their own agents. We develop several *CIAgent* intelligent agents: one to schedule work for other agents, one to watch file states, one to notify the user of events, and one to monitor airfares over the Internet. The airfare agent uses rules and forward-chaining reasoning to determine which flights might interest the user. The agents are all JavaBeans and provide their own **Customizer** dialogs to edit their properties. Multiagent system applications can be created in this application through the use of event notifications between agents.

The Internet is the focus of our intelligent agent application in Chapter 9. We design and develop an information filter application that uses several agents to download data from Internet news groups and Web pages and to intelligently filter that information using neural networks. The user can specify a set of keywords that are used to score news articles for their potential relevance to the user. Three different types of filtering are provided. Basic keyword filtering orders the articles based on the total number of keyword matches. Neural segmentation is used in cluster filtering, in which the article profiles are clustered and the scores in each cluster are averaged. In feedback filtering, articles are assigned a relevance value ranging from useless to interesting. These values are used as the target value to train a back-propagation neural network model to predict the relevance scores of new articles.

Chapter 10 focuses on the issues involved when autonomous agents interact in multiagent systems. We develop an electronic marketplace application with a *CIAgent*-based

Facilitator as the market manager. *BuyerAgents* and *SellerAgents* communicate with the Facilitator using KQML-like messages and the JavaBeans event framework. The sales negotiation strategies range from simple hardcoded logic to rule-based inferencing using action rules.

We conclude in Chapter 11 with an examination of several Java-based agent environments and applications. These include IBM's ABLE, Reticular Systems, Inc.'s Agent-Builder, IBM's Aglets, FIPA-OS, Tryllian Systems' Gossip, CSELT's JADE, Stanford University's JATLite, Sandia Lab's Jess, ObjectSpace's Voyager, and British Telecom's ZEUS. We close with a discussion of the state of the art of Java intelligent agents and expected future developments.

Appendix A provides the source code for several of the example rulebases used in Chapter 4. Appendix B contains the data sets used in the *Learn* application in Chapter 5. Appendix C contains information about the code on the CD-ROM. The Bibliography is a resource list of AI, intelligent agents, and Java papers, articles, and books.

Conventions Used in this Book

Italic is used to indicate filenames, file pathnames, and program names, and is used to identify important new terms as they are defined and introduced in the text. *Italic* is also used for packages, methods, variables, and HTML tags when they are referenced in the main text. **Boldface** is used for GUI buttons, menu items, user commands, and class names. A mono-spaced font such as `Courier` is used for Java and HTML code set off from the main body of the text.

Java Classes and Applications

This book includes a CD-ROM containing the Java code from the AI demonstration applications developed in Part One, as well as the *CIAgent* intelligent agent applications from Part Two. The code was developed and tested using Java 2 JDKs. The Sun 1.3 JRE is included on the CD-ROM, as well as the IBM Agent Building and Learning Environment (ABLE).

The code is organized into seven packages that correspond to seven directories. These include *search*, *rule*, and *learn* from Part One, and *ciagent*, *pamanager*, *infofilter*, and *marketplace* from Part Two. The source code and the compiled code are provided on the CD-ROM in this directory structure. It is also provided as a *jar* file for portability and easy integration into your Java environment.

The AI demonstration applications can be run by going to the root *ciagent* directory and running them from the command line, as follows:

```
> java search.SearchApp
> java rule.RuleApp
> java learn.LearnApp
```

The *CIAgent* applications can be run by going to the root *ciagent* directory and running them from the command line, as follows:

```
> java pamanager.PAManagerApp
> java infofilter.InfoFilterApp
> java marketplace.MarketplaceApp
```

NOTE

The code provided with this book is meant to be illustrative only. It is sample code. It has not been designed or tested for commercial use. We have tried our best to make sure the code works as designed in the context of the descriptions and examples presented in the book. From our experience with the first edition of this book, the vast majority of problems readers encountered were Java environment problems (including browser and applet problems). In order to rectify that, in this edition we have changed all of the Java applets to applications.

All you need to run the code in this book is a working Java 2 environment. So before you write to us, please make sure your Java environment is installed and working correctly. If so, and you still have problems getting one of the applications to run, or you encounter what you believe is a bug in the code—please contact us. We will be happy (maybe not happy, but willing) to investigate and fix any reports of problems in the code. Information and code fixes will be posted to the *BigusBooks* site at www.bigusbooks.com. Limited technical support will be provided via e-mail at support@bigusbooks.com.

Accessing On-Line Information

The Web and the Internet provide a large number of resources on the Java programming language and intelligent agents. The Sun Java Web site (http://java.sun.com) contains complete documentation of the Java language and the Java APIs. Development tool vendors such as IBM, Borland/Inprise, and Symantec also have sites devoted to Java.

The Java Tutorial. This site provides an on-line version of the excellent *Java Tutorial* book series produced by Sun. This is the place to go for code examples and documentation on everything related to Java programming including the *awt* and Swing GUI frameworks, networking, graphics, database access, applets, servlets, security, sound, internationalization, and more. The URL is www.java.sun.com/docs/books/tutorial/.

IBM developerWorks. The *developerWorks* site is a resource for programmers. It contains information on everything from Java to open source and XML. The technical articles are usually first-rate and it provides links to other Java-related sites. The URL is www.ibm.com/developer/.

Gamelan. The *Gamelan* site is part of the *EarthWeb* developer.com collection of sites. It contains Java information and articles including many contributed JavaBeans and source code examples. The URL is http://gamelan.earthweb.com/.

Intelligent agent information is easily obtained from one of several Web sites, as follows:

- **UMBC AgentWeb.** This academic site, sponsored by the University of Maryland, Baltimore County, contains many useful links to information about intelligent software agents. The material ranges from basic introductory level to contacts with advanced researchers. The URL is www.cs.umbc.edu/agents/.

- **MIT Software Agents Group.** This site, sponsored by the Massachusetts Institute of Technology's Media Lab, features a searchable database to other agent sites and agent conference information, as well as many on-line research papers. The URL is http://agents.www.media.mit.edu/groups/agents/.

- **Knowledge Sharing Effort.** This Web site at Stanford University features links to papers and code related to the Knowledge Sharing Effort that produced both the Knowledge Interchange Format (KIF) and Knowledge Query and Manipulation Language (KQML) specifications. The URL is http://hpdce.stanford.edu/knowledge.html.

- **SIGART.** The Association of Computing Machinery (ACM) Special Interest Group on Artificial Intelligence home page contains information on the International Joint Conferencc on AI as well as an excellent index based on AI and related subject areas. The main URL is http://sigart.acm.org/ai/ and the subject index page is http://sigart.acm.org/ai/ontology.html.

- **The American Association for Artificial Intelligence (AAAI).** This site contains information on AAAI-sponsored conferences and publications. The *AI Topics* site has a wealth of information on intelligent software, agents, and multiagent systems. The main URL is www.aaai.org/ and the topics are at www.aaai.org/Pathfinder/pathfinder.html.

- **Object Management Group (OMG).** The OMG is an open membership, not-for-profit consortium that produces and maintains standards for interoperable enterprise applications. They are best known for their CORBA, IIOP, and UML specifications. The URL is www.omg.org.

- **Foundation for Intelligent Physical Agents (FIPA).** FIPA is the leading international standards body working for the interoperability of heterogeneous intelligent agents. The membership includes a who's-who of computer and communications companies including Sun Microsystems, IBM Corp., Hewlett-Packard, Fujitsu, British Telecom, Nortel, and many others. The site contains information on the FIPA mission, specifications, and quarterly meetings. The URL is www.fipa.org/.

- **PC AI Magazine.** Providing "Intelligent technology for the real world," *PC AI's* site provides links to many AI topics and applications. Published since 1987, *PC AI* is one of the longest-running magazines focused on intelligent software. The URL is www.pcai.com/pcai/.

- **IBM alphaWorks.** This site, sponsored by IBM, contains much of the latest Internet technology developed by IBM. Packages are updated regularly and some products are removed when their status changes from research and product previews to commercial products. You can find information on the Agent Building and Learning Environment (ABLE) and other Java and XML technologies. The URL is http://alphaworks.ibm.com.

- **BigusBooks.** This site, provided by the authors, contains additional information about this book. It will provide FAQs, technical support, and code updates. The main URL is www.bigusbooks.com/. Limited technical support will be provided via e-mail at support@bigusbooks.com.

Acknowledgments

We would like to extend our thanks to the many people who helped make this book possible. First, thanks to our children, Sarah Jo and Alexander, who once again had to deal with not one, but both parents working on a book at the same time.

Next, we would like to thank the people who read through early drafts of the material, who reviewed our design and Java-coding practices, and who, through their feedback, helped improve the quality of the first edition. These include Cindy Hitchcock, Jeff Pilgrim, Don Schlosnagle, Rich Burr, Paul Coffman, and Paul Monday from IBM. Thanks again to Don Schlosnagle and Jeff Pilgrim for their comments on the second edition.

We would like to thank Ed Kay, Glenn Blank, and Don Hillman at Lehigh University for their education in AI techniques. Joe would also like to thank some of the people at IBM who worked on the Agent Builder Environment project (before it was ABE). These include Manny Aparicio, Benjamin Grosof, Joe Resnak, David Levine, and Don Gilbert. Discussions with Ted Selker and Rob Barret from IBM Almaden Research Center were also valuable. Joe would like to thank Don Schlosnagle and Jeff Pilgrim for all of their work on the ABLE project, and his manager at Watson Research, Nagui Halim, for his guidance and support.

It was our pleasure to work with the excellent staff at Wiley, including our editor, Margaret Eldridge, Angela Smith, and Brian Snapp.

And, finally, thanks to all of the readers of the first edition of this book. Without your positive feedback and support, this second edition would not have been possible.

About the Authors

Dr. Joseph P. Bigus is a senior technical staff member at the IBM T. J. Watson Research Center where he is the project leader on the ABLE research project. He is a member of the IBM Academy of Technology and an IBM Master Inventor, with over 20 U.S. patents on neural networks, data mining, and agent technologies. Joe was an architect of the IBM Neural Network Utility and Intelligent Miner for Data products. He received his M.S. and Ph.D. degrees in Computer Science from Lehigh University, and a B.S. in Computer Science from Villanova University. Joe has authored two books, *Data Mining with Neural Networks* (McGraw-Hill, 1996) and *Constructing Intelligent Agents with Java* (John Wiley & Sons, 1998). Dr. Bigus's current research interests include learning algorithms, intelligent agents, and multiagent teams and their applications to systems management, e-commerce, and knowledge management.

Jennifer Bigus is the principal consultant at Bigus Technologies Inc., where she designs and develops Java and e-business applications. She has over 20 years of experience in the computer industry, ranging from teaching business data processing on mainframe computers to programming embedded microprocessors, to providing e-business consulting services. She was a team leader for the first release of Java on the AS/400 System and wrote the initial whitepaper on Java for the AS/400. She has spoken at a number of AS/400 conferences and user-group meetings and co-authored the IBM redbook, *Introduction to Enterprise JavaBeans for the AS/400 System*. She has an M.S. degree in Computer Science from Lehigh University and a B.S. degree in Computer Science from Winona State University.

Introduction

In this chapter, we present an introduction to the two major topics covered in this book: artificial intelligence (AI) and intelligent agents. We trace the history of AI research and discuss the basic premises of both the symbol processing and neural network schools. We explore the evolution of AI systems from a promising but largely discredited technology into the basis for today's intelligent agent applications. The simultaneous emergence of network computing and the Web, and their requirements for intelligent software are also discussed. We present key attributes of intelligent agents such as autonomy, mobility, and intelligence and provide a taxonomy for classifying various intelligent agent applications. We also discuss the unique features of the Java programming language that support our agent requirements.

Artificial Intelligence

The science of AI is approximately forty years old, dating back to a conference held at Dartmouth in 1958. During the past forty years, the public perception of AI has not always matched the reality. In the early years, the excitement of both scientists and the popular press tended to overstate the real-world capabilities of AI systems. Early success in game playing, mathematical theorem proving, common-sense reasoning, and college mathematics seemed to promise rapid progress toward practical machine intelligence. During this time, the fields of speech recognition, natural language understanding, and image optical character recognition all began as specialties in AI research labs.

However, the early successes were followed by a slow realization that what was hard for people and easy for computers was more than offset by the things that were easy for people to do but almost impossible for computers to do. The promise of the early years has never been fully realized, and AI research and the term *artificial intelligence* have become associated with failure and over-hyped technology.

Nevertheless, researchers in AI have made significant contributions to computer science. Many of today's mainstream ideas about computers were once considered highly controversial and impractical when first proposed by the AI community. Whether it is the WIMP (windows, icon, mouse, pointer) user interface, which dominates human-computer interaction today, or object-oriented programming techniques, which are sweeping commercial software development, AI has made an impact. Today, the idea of intelligent software agents helping users do tasks across networks of computers would not even be discussed if not for the years of research in distributed AI, problem solving, reasoning, learning, and planning. So before we dive into the tools and tricks of the AI trade, let's take a brief look at the underlying ideas behind the intelligence in our intelligent agents.

Basic Concepts

Throughout its history, AI has focused on problems that lie just beyond the reach of what state-of-the-art computers could do at that time [Rich and Knight 1991]. As computer science and computer systems have evolved to higher levels of functionality, the areas that fall into the domain of AI research have also changed. Invented to compute ballistics charts for World War II-era weapons, the power and versatility of computers were just being imagined. Digital computers were a relatively new concept, and the early ideas of what would be useful AI functions included game playing and mathematics.

After 40 years of work, we can identify three major phases of development in AI research. In the early years, much of the work dealt with formal problems that were structured and had well-defined problem boundaries. This included work on math-related skills such as proving theorems, geometry, calculus, and playing games such as checkers and chess. In this first phase, the emphasis was on creating general "thinking machines" which would be capable of solving broad classes of problems. These systems tended to include sophisticated reasoning and search techniques.

A second phase began with the recognition that the most successful AI projects were aimed at very narrow problem domains and usually encoded much specific knowledge about the problem to be solved. This approach of adding specific domain knowledge to a more general reasoning system led to the first commercial success in AI: expert systems. Rule-based expert systems were developed to do various tasks including chemical analysis, configuring computer systems, and diagnosing medical conditions in patients. They utilized research in knowledge representation, knowledge engineering, and advanced reasoning techniques, and proved that AI could provide real value in commercial applications. At the same time, computer workstations were developed specifically to run Lisp, Prolog, and Smalltalk applications. These AI workstations featured powerful integrated development environments and were years ahead of other commercial software environments.

We are now well into a third phase of AI applications. Since the late 1980s, much of the AI community has been working on solving the difficult problems of machine vision and speech, natural language understanding and translation, common-sense reasoning, and robot control. A branch of AI known as connectionism regained popularity and expanded the range of commercial applications through the use of neural networks for data mining, modeling, and adaptive control. Biological methods such as genetic algorithms and alternative logic systems such as fuzzy logic have combined to reenergize the field of AI. Recently, the explosive growth in the Internet and distributed computing has led to the idea of agents that move through the network, interacting with each other and performing tasks for their users. Intelligent agents use the latest AI techniques to provide autonomous, intelligent, and mobile software agents, thereby extending the reach of users across networks.

When we talk about artificial intelligence or intelligent agents, the question often arises, what do we mean by *intelligence*? Do we mean that our agent acts like a human, that it thinks like a human, or that it acts or thinks rationally? While there are as many answers as there are researchers involved in AI work, we'll tell you what we think it means. To us, an intelligent agent acts rationally. It does the things we would do, but not necessarily the same way we would do them. Our agents may not pass the Turing test, proposed by Alan Turing in 1950 as a yardstick for judging computer intelligence. But our agents will perform useful tasks for us. They will make us more productive. They will allow us to do more work in less time, and see more interesting information and less useless data. Our programs will be qualitatively better using AI techniques than they would be otherwise. No matter how humble, that is our goal: to develop better, smarter applications.

Symbol Processing

There are many behaviors to which we ascribe intelligence. Being able to recognize situations or cases is one type of intelligence. For example, a doctor who talks with a patient and collects information regarding the patient's symptoms and then is able to accurately diagnose an ailment and the proper course of treatment exhibits this type of intelligence. Being able to learn from a few examples and then generalize and apply that knowledge to new situations is another form of intelligence.

Intelligent behavior can be produced by the manipulation of symbols. This is one of the primary tenets of AI techniques. Symbols are tokens that represent real-world objects or ideas and can be represented inside a computer by character strings or by numbers. In this approach, a problem must be represented by a collection of symbols, and then an appropriate algorithm must be developed to process these symbols.

The physical symbol systems hypothesis [Newell 1980] states that only a "physical symbol system has the necessary and sufficient means for general intelligent action." This idea, that intelligence flows from the active manipulation of symbols, was the cornerstone on which much of the subsequent AI research was built. Researchers constructed intelligent systems using symbols for pattern recognition, reasoning, learning, and planning [Russell and Norvig 1995]. History has shown that symbols may be appropriate for reasoning and planning, but that pattern recognition and learning may be best left to other approaches.

There are several typical ways of manipulating symbols that have proven useful in solving problems. The most common approach is to use the symbols in formulations of if-then rules that are processed using reasoning techniques called forward and backward chaining. Forward chaining lets the system deduce new information from a given set of input data. Backward chaining allows the system to reach conclusions based on a specific goal state. Symbol processing techniques may also include constructing a semantic network, in which the symbols and the concepts they represent are connected by links into a network of knowledge that can then be used to determine new relationships. Another formalism is a frame, in which related attributes of a concept are grouped together in a structure with slots and are processed by a set of related procedures called daemons or fillers. Changing the value of a single slot could set off a complex sequence of related procedures as the set of knowledge represented by the frames is made consistent. These reasoning techniques are described in more detail in Chapter 3, "Knowledge Representation," and Chapter 4, "Reasoning Systems."

Symbol processing techniques represent a relatively high level in the cognitive process. From a cognitive science perspective, symbol processing corresponds to conscious thought, where knowledge is explicitly represented, and the knowledge itself can be examined and manipulated. While symbol processing and conscious thought are clearly part of the story, another set of researchers is examining a nonsymbolic approach to intelligence modeled after the brain.

Neural Networks

An increasingly popular method in AI is called neural networks or connectionism. Neural networks have less to do with symbol processing, which is inspired by formal mathematical logic, and more to do with how human or natural intelligence occurs. Humans have neural networks in their heads, consisting of hundreds of billions of brain cells called neurons, connected by adaptive synapses that act as switching systems between the neurons. Artificial neural networks are based on this massively parallel architecture found in the brain. They process information not by manipulating symbols but by processing large amounts of raw data in a parallel manner. Different formulations of neural networks are used to segment or cluster data, to classify data, and to make predictive models using data. A collection of processing units that mimic the basic operations of real neurons is used to perform these functions. As the neural network learns or is trained, a set of connection weights among the processing units is modified based on the relationships perceived among the data.

Compared to symbol processing systems, neural networks perform relatively low-level cognitive functions. The knowledge they gain through the learning process is stored in the connection weights and is not readily available for examination or manipulation. However, the ability of neural networks to learn from and adapt to their surroundings is a crucial function for intelligent software systems. From a cognitive science perspective, neural networks are more like the underlying pattern recognition and sensory processing performed by the unconscious levels of the human mind. We discuss neural networks and learning in Chapter 5, "Learning Systems."

Whereas AI research was once dominated by symbol processing techniques, there is now a more balanced view in which the strengths of neural networks are used to counter the weaknesses of symbol processing. In our view, both are absolutely necessary in order to create intelligent applications and intelligent autonomous agents.

Turing and Connectionist Networks

Digital computers are based on a theoretical foundation laid out by the English scientist and mathematician Alan Turing in 1935. The Universal Turing Machine, an abstract device comprised of a tape with symbols (the program) and a read/write scanner (the computer), can match the behavior of a human, working with paper and pencil, following a mechanical process or algorithm. The Universal Turing Machine can simulate the behavior of any other processing machine. It defines the limits of computability using conventional computers.

In a paper written in 1948, a decade before Frank Rosenblatt's work on the Perceptron, Turing went outside the logical box of the Turing machine and described an extended machine that includes a black box or oracle providing the means for carrying out uncomputable tasks [Copeland and Proudfoot 1999]. In his definition of the O-machine, Turing introduced a type of neural network he called a B-type unorganized machine. His neural network contained a collection of neurons with arbitrary interconnection patterns. Connections pass through modifier devices that serve as dynamic switches, either allowing the signal to pass or blocking it. Each neuron has two inputs and a single output that computes the logical not-AND (NAND) function. He chose the NAND function because all other Boolean logical operations can be constructed using NAND gates. (Turing tended toward the most general solutions to computing problems.)

This is interesting because much of the tension between the mathematical logic school of AI and the more empirical soft computing school of AI is based on the heritage of Turing machines. And here was Alan Turing, extending his logical base with neural networks toward computing the uncomputable. His 1948 paper, titled "Intelligent Machinery," was not published until 1968, fourteen years after his death. Although his definition of artificial intelligence, the so-called Turing Test, is widely known throughout the field, his work on connectionist computing is relatively unknown. Connectionism is a natural, logical extension of his work on the Turing machine.

In his biography [Hodges 1983] Turing is quoted as saying "if a machine is expected to be infallible, it cannot also be intelligent" (page 361). It seems we want perfection from artificial intelligence, while we expect (and get) far less from human intelligence. People aren't perfect, yet they represent the highest form of intelligence on earth. Why do we expect machine intelligence to be perfect? So connectionists, take heart. You are following in the path of Alan Turing, the father of modern computing.

The Internet and the Web

The Internet grew out of government funding for researchers who needed to collaborate over great distances. As a byproduct of solving those problems, protocols that allowed different computers to talk to each other, exchange data, and work together were developed. This led to TCP/IP becoming the de facto standard networking protocol for the Internet. The growth in the Internet is astounding, with the number of sites increasing exponentially. Thousands of new sites are connected to the Internet each month, containing approximately 1 billion static Web pages with over 7 billion hyperlinks among them.

While electronic mail (e-mail) was once the primary service provided by the Internet, information publishing and software distribution are now of equal importance. The Gopher text information service, which gained popularity in the early 1990s, generated the first wave of information publishing on the net. The File Transfer Protocol (FTP) allowed users to download research papers and articles as well as retrieve software updates and even complete software products over the Internet. The Network News Transport Protocol (NNTP) allowed users to exchange ideas on a broad range of topics in Internet news groups. But it was the HyperText Transfer Protocol (HTTP) that brought the Internet from the realm of academia and computer technologists into the public consciousness. The development of the Mosaic browser at the University of Illinois transformed the Internet into a general-purpose communications medium, where computer novices and experts, consumers, and businesses can interact in entirely new ways.

The Web, with its publishing and broadcasting capabilities, has extended the range of applications and services that are available to users of the Internet. The now-ubiquitous Web browser provides a universal interface to applications regardless of which server platform is serving up the application. In the browsing or "pull" mode, the Web allows individuals to explore vast amounts of information in one relatively seamless environment. Knowing that all of the information is out there, but not knowing exactly how to find it, can make the Web-browsing experience quite frustrating. The popular search engines and Web index sites such as AltaVista, Excite, Yahoo, and Lycos provide an important service to users of the Web, by grouping information by topics and keywords. But even with the search engines and index sites, Web browsing is still a hit-or-miss proposition (with misses more likely than hits). In this environment, intelligent agents will emerge as truly useful personal assistants by searching, finding, and filtering information from the Web, then bringing it to a user's attention. Even as the Web evolves into "push" or broadcast mode, where users subscribe to sites which send out constant updates to their Web pages, this requirement for filtering information will not go away. Unless the broadcast sites are able to send out very personalized streams of information, the user will still have to separate the valuable information from the useless noise.

While the Internet and Web have captured the public's attention, businesses are quickly adapting the way they use information technology through their internal networks or intranets. Companies use intranets for internal and external e-mail, to post information, and to handle routine administrative tasks. Intranets allow a wide variety of client computers to connect to centralized servers, without the cost and complexity of developing client/server applications. Intranets serve the same purpose and have the same advantages for companies that the Internet has for individuals. A standardized client application, the Web browser, running on standard personal computers or low-cost network computers, can provide a single point of access to a collection of corporate-wide network-based applications.

The emergence of e-business has dramatically changed the Internet and expanded its use by businesses and consumers. The Business to Consumer (B2C) model, in which companies "go direct" to their customers, has lowered the cost of doing business and endangered middlemen in the supply chain. Companies such as Dell Computer and Amazon.com have transformed retailing and forced more traditional bricks-and-mortar companies to become net-savvy clicks-and-bricks businesses with a substantial on-line presence. The Business to Business (B2B) opportunities have spawned hundreds of vertical electronic marketplaces where buyers and suppliers in industries such as chemicals, metals, and electronics come together to do business. Both B2C and B2B require intelligent software to provide personalized information, to perform automated negotiations, and to perform planning and scheduling functions.

Intelligent Agents

As is often the case when a technical field provokes commercial interest, there has been a large movement and change of focus in the AI research community to apply the basic AI techniques to distributed computer systems, company-wide Intranets, the Internet, and the Web. Initially, the focus was limited to word searches, information retrieval, and filtering tasks. But as more and more commercial transactions are performed on networks, there is more interest in having smart agents that can perform specific actions. By taking a step back and looking at what the Internet has become, many researchers who had been looking at how intelligent agents could cooperate to achieve tasks on distributed computer systems have realized that there is finally a problem in search of a technology (as opposed to the other way around). Intelligent agents can provide real value to businesses and users in this new, interconnected world.

Up to this point, we have discussed AI and its evolution into software agents at an abstract level. In the following sections, we explore some of the technical facets of intelligent agents, how they work, and how we can classify them based on their abilities and underlying technologies.

Events, Conditions, and Actions

Suppose we have an intelligent agent, running autonomously, primed with knowledge about the tasks we require of it and ready to move out onto the network when the opportunity arises. Now what? How does the agent know that we want it to do something for us, or that it should respond to someone who is trying to contact us? This is where we have to deal with events, recognize conditions, and take actions.

Are They Agents or Distributed Objects?

For the skeptics in the audience, you may be asking, "What's the big deal with agents?" They're just distributed objects with a different name. CORBA has been around for years, Microsoft's (OLE, ActiveX, COM, DCOM, etc.) objects have been around for years. What's the difference?

To address this question, let's examine a distributed object application and a distributed multiagent system application. A distributed object application is defined by the objects, the data, and the behavior (methods) required to implement the functions needed. The interactions between objects are explicitly defined; the sequence of method calls is spelled out in gory detail. An object is a software entity that encapsulates state (data) and behavior (function) and exposes a set of methods or procedures to manipulate that state. Objects are *used* by other objects to perform actions. Objects don't initiate actions of their own volition.

In a multiagent system, we have a collection of software entities that autonomously perform actions. Each agent has a more complex internal state than an object, but even more importantly, they have internal goals. Agents decide what to do and when to do it. Agents can say "no" when requested to perform an action. Objects have fixed roles. Agents can change roles dynamically as the application runs.

In a distributed object application, every object is contributing a small piece of function in achieving a single application goal. In an agent system, a collection of goal-oriented software entities cooperate to achieve a single application goal. Objects invoke methods. Agents have conversations. Objects are data packets with buttons waiting to be pushed. Agents are actively deciding what buttons to push.

In the context of intelligent agents, an event is anything that happens to change the environment or anything of which the agent should be aware. For example, an event could be the arrival of a new piece of mail. Or it could be a change to a Web page. Or it could be a timer going off at midnight—time to start sending out the faxes that are queued up. Short of having our agent constantly running and checking or polling all the devices and computer systems we want it to monitor, having events signal important occurrences is the next best thing. Actually, it may be the best thing, because our agent can sleep, think about what has happened during the day, do housekeeping tasks, or do anything else useful while it is waiting for the next event to occur.

When an event does occur, the agent has to recognize and evaluate what the event means and then respond to it. This second step, determining what the condition or state of the world is, could be simple or extremely complex, depending on the situation. If mail has arrived, then the event will be self-describing: a new piece of mail has arrived.

The agent may then have to query the mail system to find out who sent the mail and what the topic is, or even scan the mail text to find keywords. All of this is part of the *recognize* component of the cycle. The initial event may wake up the agent, but the agent then has to figure out what the significance of the event is in term of its duties. In the mail example, suppose the agent recognizes that the mail is from your boss, and that the message is classified as URGENT. This brings us to the next and perhaps most useful aspect of intelligent agents: actions.

If intelligent agents are going to make our lives easier (or at least more interesting), they must be able to take action, to do things for us. Having computers do things for us is not a new idea. Computers were developed to help people do work. However, having the computer initiate an action on our behalf is something totally different from entering a command on the command line and pressing *Enter* to run the command. While the results of our typing the command and pressing ENTER may not always be exactly what we had in mind when we typed it in (it always seems that we realize what we should have typed after we press ENTER), we know that whatever happens, it is our doing. Having an agent (intelligent or not, human or computerized) take an action for us requires a certain leap of faith or at least some level of trust. We must trust that our intelligent agent is going to behave rationally and in our best interest. Like all situations in which we delegate responsibility to a third party, we have to weigh the risks and the rewards. The risk is that the agent will mess things up, and we will have to do even more work to set things right. The reward is that we are freed from having to worry about the details of getting that piece of work done.

So, events-conditions-actions define the workings of our agent. Some researchers feel that an agent must also be proactive. It must not only react to events, it must be able to plan and initiate actions on its own. We agree. However, in our view, this action (signaling some event, or calling some application interface) is the result of some earlier event that caused our agent to go into planning mode. We want our intelligent agents to be able to initiate transactions with other agents on our behalf, using all of the intelligence and domain knowledge they can bring to bear. But this is just an extension of the event-condition-action paradigm.

Taxonomies of Agents

While intelligent agents are still somewhat new in commercial computing environments, they have been the focus of researchers for years. During that time, many different ways of classifying or categorizing agents have been proposed. One way is to place the agent in the context of intelligence, agency, and mobility. Another approach is to focus on the primary processing strategy of the agent. A third is to categorize the agent by the function it performs. In the following sections we explore all three perspectives on viewing agent capabilities.

Agency, Intelligence, and Mobility

When we talk about software agents, there are three dimensions or axes that we use to measure their capabilities: agency, intelligence, and mobility [IBM 1996]. Agency deals with the degree of autonomy the software agent has in representing the user to other agents, applications, and computer systems. An agent represents the user, helps the user, guides the user, and in some cases, takes unilateral actions on the user's behalf. This progression from simple helper to full-fledged assistant takes us from agents that can be hard-coded, to those which, out of simple necessity, must contain more advanced intelligence techniques.

Intelligence refers to the ability of the agent to capture and apply application domain-specific knowledge and processing to solve problems. Thus our agents can be relatively dumb, using simple coded logic, or they can be relatively sophisticated, using complex AI-based methods such as inferencing and learning.

An agent is mobile if it can move between systems in a network. Mobility introduces additional complexity to an intelligent agent, because it raises concerns about security (the agent's and the target system's) and cost. Intranets are a particularly ripe environment for mobile intelligent agents to roam because they require less security than in the wide-open Internet.

Processing Strategies

One of the simplest types of agents is *reactive* or *reflex* agents, which respond in the event-condition-action mode. Reflex agents do not have internal models of the world. They respond solely to external stimuli and the information available from their sensing of the environment [Brooks 1986]. Like neural networks, reactive agents exhibit *emergent behavior*, which is the result of the interactions of these simple individual agents. When reactive agents interact, they share low-level data, not high-level symbolic knowledge. One of the fundamental tenets of reactive agents is that they are grounded in physical sensor data and are not operating in the artificial symbol space. Applications of these agents have been limited to robots, which use sensors to perceive the world.

Deliberative or *goal-directed* agents have domain knowledge and the planning capability necessary to take a sequence of actions in the hope of reaching or achieving a specific goal. Deliberative agents may proactively cooperate with other agents to achieve a task. They may use any and all of the symbolic AI reasoning techniques that have been developed over the past forty years.

Collaborative agents work together to solve problems. Communication between agents is an important element, and while each individual agent is autonomous, it is the synergy resulting from their cooperation that makes collaborative agents interesting and useful. Collaborative agents can solve large problems that are beyond the scope of any single agent and they allow a modular approach based on specialization of agent functions or domain knowledge. For example, collaborative agents may work as design assistants on large, complex engineering projects. Individual agents may be called upon to verify different aspects of the design, but their joint expertise is applied to ensure that the overall design is consistent. In a collaborative agent system, the agents must be able to exchange information about beliefs, desires, and intentions, and possibly even share their knowledge.

Agents with beliefs, desires, and intentions are known as BDI model agents in the AI research community [Bratman 1987]. There is some contention in the field as to whether BDI agents, which are quite heavyweight, are really necessary to build multi-agent systems. The beliefs represent knowledge about the state of the world. What the agent believes to be true about the world is its reality. It is the basis for all of its reasoning, planning, and subsequent actions. Beliefs are essential for an agent because it cannot ever have complete knowledge of the outside world. Things change. Some things can't be seen or known. Because the agent's beliefs can't be perfect, they must be able to model uncertainty and imprecision in the facts it knows. Desires are assignments of goodness to states of the world, from the agent's perspective. Desires turn into goals when the agent is reasoning about how it wants the world to be. When the agent reasons about the state of the world (beliefs) and its desires (goals) it must decide what course of action to take. These committed plans are called intentions. So, BDI agents have quite lofty requirements from an AI reasoning perspective. BDI agents are autonomous AI software components.

As mentioned earlier, a *mobile* agent is a software process (a running program's code and its state) that can travel across computer systems in a network doing work for its owner. An advantage of mobile agents is that the communications between the home system and the remote systems are reduced. By allowing the agent to go to the remote system and access data locally on that system, we enable a whole new class of applications. For example, mobile agents could provide an easy way to do load balancing in distributed systems. "Oh, the processor is heavily loaded here, better hop on over to System X for a while."

Danny Lange, who led the IBM Aglets development team, lists the following seven reasons for using mobile agents [Lange 1998]:

- They can reduce network load, because agents move to a system and do their work there rather than take up network bandwidth sending messages back and forth.
- They can overcome network latency because they are resident on the machine rather than remote.
- They can encapsulate protocols as they move around the network talking to other mobile agents.
- They can operate autonomously so that they keep working even when network connections go down.
- They can dynamically adapt to changes in system loading.
- They are heterogeneous.
- They are fault-tolerant because they can move from a system that is having difficulty or about to fail.

As Nwana (1996) says, "mobility is neither a necessary nor sufficient condition for agenthood." Sometimes it makes sense to have your agent go out on the network; other times it does not. For some people, the idea of sending a mobile agent off to work is comfortable and natural. For others, the lack of a familiar computing model (it is neither server-based nor client/server) makes mobile agents hard to fathom. For example, if your agent contains some exclusive domain knowledge or algorithms, then sending that intellectual property out on the network to reside on foreign hosts, may not be a good idea. Better to keep that agent at home in a safe, secure system, and send out messenger collaborative agents to do the traveling. Perhaps the biggest inhibitor to widespread use of mobile agents is security. We have a name for software that comes unbidden onto our systems and starts executing. We call them *viruses*. How do we make sure that only "good" mobile agents can run on our system, but not "bad" agents? And how can we tell the difference?

Processing Functions

Perhaps the most natural way of thinking about the different types of agents is based on the function they perform. Thus, we have user interface agents, which try to "do what you mean" rather than what you say when interacting with a piece of application or system software. We have search agents, which go out on the Internet and find documents for us. We have filter agents, which process incoming mail or news postings, ferreting out the stuff of interest from the more mundane or uninteresting rubbish. We have domain-specific assistants, which can book a business trip, schedule a meeting, or verify that our design does not violate any constraints. In short, any combination of intelligent agent attributes can be combined and applied to a specific domain to create a new, function-specific intelligent agent. All we need are the software tools and computing infrastructure to be able to add the domain knowledge and reasoning or learning capabilities to our agents, and the comfort level that is required to trust the agent to do our bidding.

Interface agents work as personal assistants to help a user accomplish tasks. Interface agents usually employ learning to adapt themselves to the work habits and preferences of the user. Patti Maes (1994) at MIT identifies four ways that learning can occur. First, an agent can learn by watching over the user's shoulder, observing what the user does and imitating the user. Second, the agent can offer advice or take actions on the user's behalf and then learn by receiving feedback or reinforcement from the user. Third, the agent can get explicit instructions from the user (if this happens, then do that). Finally, by asking other agents for advice, an agent can learn from their experiences. Note that interface agents collaborate primarily with the user, not with other agents (asking advice is the one exception). Using various learning mechanisms, interface agents offer the promise of customizing the user interface of a computer system or set of applications for a particular user and her unique working style. If interface agents can collaborate and share their knowledge about how to do a task, then when one person in a workgroup figures out how to do something, that skill can be transferred to all other users in that workgroup through their interface agents. The productivity gains could be enormous.

Another generic class of agents is *information* agents. In some ways, information agents are the Dr. Jekyll/Mr. Hyde of software programs. They seem harmless enough, providing information to you, but can quickly transform into the monster of *information overload*. Some information agents go out on the Internet or the Web and seek out information of interest to the user. Others filter streams of information coming in e-mail correspondence and newsgroup postings. But either way, information agents try to help with the core problem of getting the right information at the right time. The question is not whether there is too much information or too little, but making sure that you see the right information. Of course, what is "right" depends on the context in which you are working. This information overload problem is one of the prime factors in the emergence of intelligent software agents as viable commercial products. Whether routing particularly important e-mail messages, or actively constructing a personal newspaper (consisting only of interesting articles and advertisements), information agents promise relief from the overwhelming amount of data we are exposed to each day. Information agents called Spiders are already being used to index the Web. In general, information agents can be static, sitting on one system using search engines and Web indexes to gather information for the user, or they can be mobile, going out and actively searching for information. Either way, their function remains the same: to deliver useful information to the user.

In the preceding sections, we have described three of the major taxonomies for classifying agents, but there are others. Some feel that collaboration with other agents is a major distinction. Others feel that whether the agent interacts directly with a human user or not is important. Still others feel that learning ability should be a primary basis for classifying agents. Whether the agent works across a network or only locally on a PC or workstation is another distinguishing attribute. Because intelligent agents exist in a multidimensional space, characterizing agents by two or three of those dimensions is somewhat risky [Nwana 1996]. However, we feel that the loss of some precision is more than offset by the clarity of the two- or three-dimensional approach. People find it hard to think in six- or seven-dimensional space. In our opinion, agency and intelligence are the fundamental underlying capabilities on which agents should be classified. Mobility or some other characteristic could be used as the third axis, as required.

To be sure, there are software agents that are autonomous, but not intelligent. These agents often act as simple machine performance monitors in distributed system management applications. Simple Network Management Protocol (SNMP) agents are an example of this kind. On the other hand, there are programs or applications which use AI techniques such as learning and reasoning, but which have relatively little autonomy. Classic expert systems are an example. They are not intelligent agents in the sense used in this book. We are interested in programs at the intersection of two domains, intelligence and agency. All other characteristics are secondary and may or may not be present for us to use the term *intelligent agent*.

Intelligent agents are software programs, nothing more and nothing less. Sometimes this has a negative impact when someone new to the topic comes to the realization that there is no magic here, just programming. However, intelligent agents, at least as we define and refer to them, are software programs with an attitude. They exist to help users get their work done. You may say that that is what application software is supposed to do. This is true. However, many applications today assume a level of familiarity and sophistication in the users that many users are incapable of or unwilling to achieve. People just want to get their job done. Most don't care if the font is TrueType or Adobe, if the component model is COM, CORBA, or JavaBeans, or whether the code is client/server or Web-based. Toward this end, intelligent agent software is practical software. It just gets the job done. If intelligent agent software introduces another level of complexity that the user has to deal with, then it will be a failure. Intelligent agents must be enabling and automating, not frustrating or intrusive.

Agents and Human-Computer Interfaces

One of the perennial complaints of users and one of the sticking points between humans and computers has been the interface between them. A QWERTY keyboard and a mouse pointing device have become accepted as the way people interact with computers, but they are far from natural. The most natural way for people to interact is through language, facial expressions, and body language. After 30 years of research into speech processing, we are finally getting usable software that will allow us to talk to our computers. But recognition is not the same as understanding. Although a computer can display the words you just spoke, they can't necessarily figure out the reference to *him* or *her*, detect sarcasm, or catch literary references. But things are changing, fast.

The Blue Eyes project at IBM Almaden Research Center features a camera that can figure out where a user is looking on the screen (gaze identification) to determine what article they are reading. Gesture recognition software allows computers to respond to waves of the hand, and even understand facial expressions. And, no surprise here, intelligent software forms the basis for these types of applications.

The COLLAGEN project at Lotus Research and Mistubishi Reseach develops agents that can watch a user interact with an application and figure out the task that the user is trying to perform and give assistance [Rich and Sidner 1997]. The OpenSesame application on Macintosh watches a user, learns their behavior, and offers to automate repetitive tasks [Caglayan, et al. 1997].

Avatars, or on-line graphic persona, are becoming more important. Chat rooms and other on-line forums provide the ability for people to mix and exchange information. Avatars allow people to show (or hide) their true personality. Microsoft Agents provide a basic capability to develop avatars for applications running on Windows operating systems. For example, Microsoft Office has these little "Assistants" that appear on the screen to help you. These animated creatures change expression as you interact with the computer, blink their eyes, and straighten up at attention when you mouse over to them. They provide context-sensitive help. Some people love them, but others find that having movement on the periphery of the screen is quite annoying. But, like them or not, these Microsoft Agents are most likely the first wave of the future of human-computer interface agents (see http://msdn.microsoft.com/).

Using Java for Intelligent Agents

In this section, we talk about the Java language and the specific features of Java that support intelligent agent applications. These features will be explored in more detail in the remainder of the book.

Overview of the Java Language

Java is an object-oriented programming language. It was originally designed for programming real-time embedded software for consumer electronics, particularly set-top boxes that interface between cable providers or broadcasters, and televisions or television-like appliances. However, the effort was redirected to the Internet when the market for set-top boxes did not develop quickly enough, while the Internet exploded in popularity.

Originally the developers of Java intended to use C++ for their software development. But they needed a language that could execute on different sets of computer chips to accommodate the ever-changing consumer electronics market. So they decided to design their own language that would be independent of the underlying hardware.

It is this "architecture-neutral" aspect of Java that makes it ideal for programming on the Internet. It allows a user to receive software from a remote system and execute it on a local system, regardless of the underlying hardware or operating system. An interpreter and runtime called the Java Virtual Machine (JVM) insulates the software from the underlying hardware.

Unlike more traditional languages, Java source code does not get translated into the machine instructions for a particular computer platform. Instead, Java source code (.java) is compiled into an intermediate form called bytecodes which are stored in a *class* file. These bytecodes can be executed on any computer system that implements a JVM. This portability is perhaps one of the most compelling features of the Java language, from a commercial perspective. In the current era of cross-platform application development, any tool that allows programmers to write code once and execute it on many platforms is going to get attention.

The portable, interpreted nature of Java impacts its performance. While the performance of interpreted Java code is better than scripting languages and fast enough for interactive applications, it is slower than traditional languages whose source code is compiled directly into the machine code for a particular machine. To improve performance, Just-In-Time compilers (JITs) have been developed. A JIT compiler runs concurrently with the Java Virtual Machine and determines what pieces of Java code are called most often. These are compiled into machine instructions on-the-fly so that they do not need to be interpreted each time they are encountered within a program. Static compilers have also been developed to compile the Java source code into machine code that can be executed without interpretation (but with loss of portability).

The bytecode portability is what enables Java to be transported across a network and executed on any target computer system. Java applets are small Java programs designed to be included in an HTML (HyperText Markup Language) Web document. HTML tags specify the name of the Java applet and its Uniform Resource Locator (URL). The URL is the location on the Internet where the applet bytecodes reside. When a Java-enabled Web browser displays an HTML document containing an applet tag, the Java bytecodes are downloaded from the specified location and the Java Virtual Machine interprets or executes the bytecodes. Java applets enable Web pages to contain animated graphics and interactive content.

Because Java applets can be downloaded from any system, security mechanisms exist within the Java Virtual Machine to protect against malicious or errant applets. The Java runtime system verifies the bytecodes as they are downloaded from the network to ensure that they are valid bytecodes and checks that the code does not violate any of the inherent restrictions placed on applets. Java applets are restricted from communicating with any server other than the originating host, the one from which they were downloaded. They cannot run a local executable program or access local files. The restrictions are in place to prevent a Java applet from gaining access to the underlying operating system or data on the system. These restrictions can be eased, however, through the use of digital signatures and alternate **SecurityManager** implementations.

But Java can be used for more than programming applets to run within a browser. Java is a full-function programming language that can be used to write standalone applications. These applications are not placed under the same security restrictions as applets and therefore can access data and underlying operating system functions.

As an object-oriented programming language, Java borrows heavily from Smalltalk, Objective C, and C++. It is characterized by many as a better, safer C++. Java uses C/C++ syntax and is readily accessible to the large existing C++ development community. Java, however, does not drag along the legacy of C. It does not allow global variables, functions, or procedures. With the exception of a few primitive data types like integers and floating-point numbers, everything in Java is an object. Object references are not pointers, and pointer manipulation is not allowed. This contributes to the general robustness of Java programs since pointer operations tend to be particularly nasty and bug-prone. Java also manages memory itself, thereby avoiding problems with allocation and deallocation of objects. It does not allow multiple inheritance like C++ does, but supports another type of reuse through the use of formal *interface* definitions.

Java is similar enough to C and C++ that it already feels familiar to most of the existing programming community. But it is different enough in important ways (memory management and cross-platform portability) that it is worth it for programmers to switch to a new language.

Autonomy

For a software program to be autonomous, it must be a separate process or thread. Java applications are separate processes and as such can be long-running and autonomous. A Java application can communicate with other programs using sockets. In an application, an agent can be a separate thread of control. Java supports threaded applications and provides support for autonomy using both techniques.

Earlier, we described intelligent agents as autonomous programs or processes. As such, they are always waiting, ready to respond to a user request or a change in the environment. One question that comes to mind is "How does the agent know when something changes?" In our model, as with many others, the agent is informed by sending it an event. From an object-oriented design perspective, an event is nothing more than a method call or message, with information passed along on the method call that defines what happened or what action we want the agent to perform, as well as data required to process the event.

In Java there is an event-processing mechanism that is used in the Abstract Windowing Toolkit (AWT) to pass user-defined events such as mouse movements and menu selections to the underlying window components. Depending on the type of agent we are building, we may need to process these low-level events, such as when a GUI control gets focus, or a window is resized or moved, or the user presses a key. The *awt.event* package also supports higher-level semantic events such as user actions.

Intelligence

The intelligence in intelligent agents can range from hard-coded procedural or object-oriented logic to sophisticated reasoning and learning capabilities. While Prolog and Lisp are the two languages usually associated with AI programming, in recent years, much of the commercial AI work has been coded in C and C++. As a general-purpose, object-oriented programming language, Java provides all of the base functions needed to support these behaviors. In the past few years, Java has clearly become the favorite language for AI implementations.

There are two major aspects to AI applications, knowledge representation and algorithms that manipulate those representations. All knowledge representations are based on the use of slots or attributes that hold information regarding some entity, and links or references to other entities. Java objects can be used to encode this data and behavior as well as the relationships between objects. Standard AI knowledge representation such as frames, semantic nets, and if-then rules can all be easily and naturally implemented using Java.

Mobility

There are several different aspects to mobility in the context of intelligent agents and intelligent applications. Java's portable bytecodes and Java archive (JAR) files allow groups of compiled Java classes to be sent over a network and then executed on the target machine. Java applets provide a mechanism for running Java code remotely via a Web browser. Other environments, such as the IBM Aglets, allow Java processes to be started, suspended, and moved.

One of the prime requirements for mobile programs is the ability to save the state of the running process, ship it off, and then resume where the process left off, only now it is running on a different system. Computer science researchers have explored this topic in great detail in relation to load balancing on distributed computer systems such as networks of workstations. Having homogeneous machines was a crucial part of making this work. Once again, the Java Virtual Machine comes to the rescue. By providing a standard computing environment for a Java process to run in, the JVM provides a homogeneous virtual machine that allows Java agents to move between heterogeneous hardware systems (from a Palm device, to a PC or Macintosh computer, to a Sun workstation, to an IBM eServer iSeries 400) without losing a beat.

Other aspects of Java also enable mobility. The JavaBean delegation event model allows dynamic registration of **EventSources** and **EventListeners**. Thus a mobile Java agent could "plug in" to an already-running server environment when it arrives, and then "unplug" itself, when it is time to move on. The *java.net* package provides network communications capability that allows mobile agents or a mobile agent infrastructure to talk to other servers and send serialized Java code and process state data over sockets.

The Java remote method invocation (java.rmi) package allows Java objects to call methods on other objects across a network, creating distributed object applications. The *rmiregistry* can be used to locate remote objects by name, and RMI will even dynamically load the class bytecodes when they are needed. By implementing the *java.rmi.Remote* interface and by throwing *java.rmi.RemoteExceptions*, methods in any Java class can be extended to work in distributed applications. Agents using RMI could easily be spread out, and even move across a network, while communicating with each other using remote method calls.

Summary

In this chapter, we presented an introduction to artificial intelligence and intelligent agents. The major points include the following:

- The field of AI is approximately 40 years old. During that time, AI has evolved from trying to build general problem solvers using search, to building expert systems with deep but narrow domain knowledge, to combining knowledge, reasoning, and learning to solve difficult real-world problems.

- A software agent exhibits *intelligence* if it acts rationally. It uses knowledge, information, and reasoning to take reasonable actions in pursuit of a goal or goals.

- Most AI techniques are based on *symbol processing*. A set of tokens or symbols is used to represent knowledge and the state of the world, and algorithms manipulate those symbols to mimic high-level cognitive processing functions.

- *Neural networks* are another school of AI, based on a brain-like adaptive parallel computing model that does not use explicit symbols. Neural networks learn or adapt when exposed to data and correspond to cognitive functions such as low-level sensory processing and pattern recognition.

- The Internet, intranets, and the Web have caused an explosion in the amount of information available to people. The easy-to-use Web browsers have also attracted many new computer users to the on-line world. These factors have contributed to create a huge opportunity for *intelligent agents*, software that helps users do complex computing tasks.

- Intelligent agents must be able to recognize events, determine the meaning of those events, and then take actions on behalf of a user.

- Agents can be categorized by placing them in a three-dimensional space, where the axes are *agency*, the amount of autonomy an agent has; *intelligence*, the knowledge, reasoning, and learning capabilities of the agent; and *mobility*, the ability to move between systems in a network.

- *Reactive agents* are relatively simple agents that sense their world, and respond reflexively to external stimuli. *Deliberative agents* are more complex, using knowledge, reasoning, and even learning to plan and achieve their goals. *Collaborative agents* work together as a team, combining their knowledge and specialized skills to solve large problems. *BDI agents* have beliefs, desires, and intentions, with complex internal mental states and reasoning capabilities.

- Intelligent agents can also be classified by the functions they perform. *Interface agents* work as personal assistants to help users accomplish tasks. *Information agents* work to prevent information overload. They can either actively search out desired information on the Web, or filter out uninteresting or unwanted data as it arrives. *Domain-specific agents* can do on-line shopping, make travel arrangements, suggest a good book or CD, or help schedule a meeting.

- The Java language has many attributes that make it ideal for implementing agents and multiagent systems. These include its object-oriented style, support for threads, distributed objects, network-centric design and network access, and code portability.

- In the end, the success or failure of intelligent agents will depend on how much value they provide to their users.

CHAPTER 2

Problem Solving Using Search

In this chapter we explore the first major thrust of artificial intelligence (AI) research, problem solving using search. We discuss how problems can be represented as states and then solved using simple brute-force search techniques or more sophisticated heuristic search methods. A Java application is developed that implements five different search algorithms.

Defining the Problem

The focus of much AI research has been on solving problems. While, in the past, some critics have argued that AI has focused on unrealistically simple or toy problems, this is certainly not the case today. In hindsight, it is not clear that the "toy problem" criticisms were justified at all. Much of the point of the AI research was to understand "how" to solve the problem, not just to get a solution. So seemingly simple problems—puzzles, games, stacking wooden blocks—were the focus of AI programs. And one of the first areas of work, general problem-solving methods, highlighted a major barrier to artificial intelligence software. How do you represent a problem so that the computer can solve it? Even before that, how do you define the problem with enough precision so that you can figure out how to represent it?

While "knowing what business you are in" is one of the elementary business maxims, for artificial intelligence it is "knowing what problem you are trying to solve." For some people, solving the problem successfully is the only goal. Why use a computer unless it can help you solve business problems (and make money)? For others, the challenge is to reproduce human problem-solving techniques or, at least, gain a better understanding of how people solve complex problems. Today, very few people would claim that search-based methods demonstrate how our brain solves problems, but these methods have proven extremely useful and have a place in any discussion of practical AI techniques.

The first step in any problem-solving exercise is to clearly and succinctly define what it is we are trying to do. Do we want to find the best possible route for a trip or any one that will get us to our destination? Can we wait several hours or days for an answer, or do we need the best answer that can be computed in ten seconds? Someone once said that in AI the most important part of problem solving is "representation, representation, representation." In this chapter, we look at ways of representing our problem so that we can solve it using search techniques. We also examine which search techniques we should use. In the next section, we explore one of the primary problem representations, the state-space approach.

State Space

Suppose that the problem we want to solve deals with playing and winning a game. This game could be a simple one, such as tic-tac-toe, or a more complex one, such as checkers, chess, or backgammon. In any case, the key to approaching this problem with a computer is to develop a mapping from the game-space world of pieces and the geometric pattern on a board, to a data structure that captures the essence of the current game state. For tic-tac-toe, we could use an array with nine elements, or we could define a 3-by-3 matrix with 1s and 0s to denote the Xs and Os of each player.

We start with an *initial state*, which in the case of tic-tac-toe is a 3-by-3 matrix filled with spaces (or empty markers). For any state of our game board, we have a set of *operators* that can be used to modify the current state, thereby creating a new state. In our case, this is a player marking an empty space with either an X or an O. The combination of the initial state and the set of operators make up the *state space* of the problem. The sequence of states produced by the valid application of operators from the initial state is called the *path* in the state space. Now that we have the means to go from our initial state to additional valid game states, we need to be able to detect when we have reached our *goal* state. In tic-tac-toe, a goal state is when any row, column, or diagonal consists of all Xs or all Os. In this simple example, we can check the tic-tac-toe board to see if either player has won by explicitly testing for our goal condition. In more complicated problems, defining the *goal test* may be a substantial problem in itself.

In many search problems, we are not only interested in reaching a goal state, we would like to reach it with the lowest possible cost (or the maximum profit). Thus, we can compute the cost as we apply operators and transition from state to state. This *path cost* or *cost function* is usually denoted by g. Given a problem which can be represented by a set of states and operators and then solved using a search algorithm, we can compare the quality of the solution by measuring the path cost. In the case of tic-tac-toe we have a limited search space. However, for many real-world problems the search space can grow very large, so we need algorithms that can scale to handle a large search space.

Effective search algorithms must do two things: cause motion or traversal of the state space, and do so in a controlled, systematic manner. Random search may work in some problems, but, in general, we need to search in an organized, methodical way. If we have a systematic search strategy that does not use information about the problem to help direct the search, it is called a *brute-force, uninformed,* or *blind* search. The only difference between the different brute-force search techniques is the order in which the nodes are expanded. But even slight changes in the order can have a significant impact on the behavior of the algorithm. Search algorithms which use information about the problem, such as the cost or distance to the goal state, are called *heuristic, informed,* or *directed* searches. The primary advantage of heuristic search algorithms is that we can make better choices concerning which node to expand next. This substantially improves the efficiency of the search algorithms.

There are several aspects of the performance of a search algorithm that are important to recognize [Russell and Norvig 1995]. An algorithm is *optimal* if it will find the best solution from among several possible solutions. A strategy is *complete* if it guarantees that it will find a solution if one exists. The efficiency of the algorithm, in terms of *time complexity* (how long it takes to find a solution) and *space complexity* (how much memory it requires), is a major practical consideration. Having an optimal search algorithm, guaranteed to find the best solution, has little practical value if it takes hours to complete, when we only have minutes to make a decision. Similarly, having a complete algorithm that is a memory hog is useless if it runs out of memory just before it finds the solution to your problem.

Search Strategies

In this section we examine two basic search techniques used to solve problems in AI, breadth-first search and depth-first search. Later we will explore enhancements to these algorithms, but first we need to make sure we understand how these basic approaches work. We will work through several examples, using the map shown in Figure 2.1.

First, we need to define the problem we are trying to solve. In this case, it is quite simple. Given a starting point at any one of the cities on the map, can we find any other city on the map as long as there is a path from the start city to the end or goal city? At this time, we are not trying to find the shortest path or anything like that. We simply want to find whether the goal city is on the map.

Now that we have defined the problem, the next step is to decide how to represent the problem as a state space. A map like the one in Figure 2.1 can be naturally represented by a graph data structure, where the cities' names are the nodes, and the major roadways between cities are the links or edges of the graph. So, from a programming perspective, our problem is to traverse a graph data structure in a systematic way until we either find the goal city or exhaust all possibilities. Hopefully having the entire state space shown on a map will make understanding the operations of the search algorithms easier. In more complex problems, all we have is the single start state and a set of operators that are used to generate new states. The search algorithms work the same way,

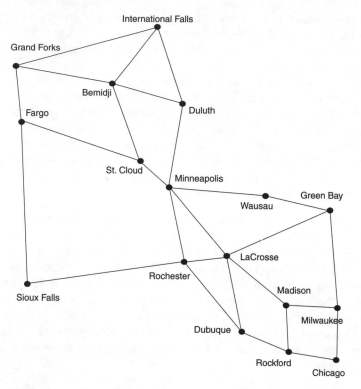

Figure 2.1 Map of midwestern U.S. cities.

but conceptually, we dynamically grow or expand the graph, instead of having it entirely specified at the start.

Breadth-First Search

The breadth-first search algorithm searches a state space by constructing a hierarchical tree structure consisting of a set of nodes and links. The algorithm defines a way to move through the tree structure, examining the values at nodes in a controlled and systematic way, so that we can find a node that offers a solution to the problem we have represented using the tree structure.

The algorithm is as follows:

1. Create a queue and add the first **SearchNode** to it.
2. Loop:
    a. If the queue is empty, quit.
    b. Remove the first **SearchNode** from the queue.

c. If the **SearchNode** contains the goal state, then exit with the **SearchNode** as the solution.

d. For each child of the current **SearchNode**, add the new **SearchNode** to the back of the queue.

The breadth-first algorithm spreads out in a uniform manner from the start node. From the start node, it looks at each node that is one edge away. Then it moves out from those nodes to all nodes two edges away from the start node. This continues until either the goal node is found or the entire tree is searched. Breadth-first search is complete; it will find a solution if one exists. But it is neither optimal in the general case (it won't find the best solution, just the first one that matches the goal state), nor does it have good time or space complexity (it grows exponentially in time and memory consumption).

Let's walk through an example to see how breadth-first search could find a city on our map. Our search begins in **Rochester**, and we want to know if we can get to **Wausau** from there. The **Rochester** node is placed on the queue in Step 1. Next we enter our search loop at Step 2. We remove **Rochester**, the first node, from the queue. **Rochester** does not contain our goal state (**Wausau**) so we expand it by taking each child node in **Rochester**, and adding them to the back of the queue. So we add **Sioux Falls**, **Minneapolis**, **LaCrosse**, and **Dubuque** to our search queue. Now we are back at the top of our loop. We remove the first node from the queue (**Sioux Falls**) and test it to see if it is our goal state. It is not, so we expand it, adding **Fargo** and **Rochester** to the end of our queue, which now contains [**Minneapolis**, **LaCrosse**, **Dubuque**, **Fargo**, **Rochester**]. We remove **Minneapolis**, the goal test fails, and we expand that node, adding **St. Cloud**, **Wausau**, **Duluth**, **LaCrosse**, and **Rochester** to the search queue, now holding [**LaCrosse**, **Dubuque**, **Fargo**, **Rochester**, **St. Cloud**, **Wausau**, **Duluth**, **LaCrosse**, **Rochester**]. We test **LaCrosse** and then expand it, adding **Minneapolis**, **Green Bay**, **Madison**, **Dubuque**, and **Rochester** to the list, which has now grown to [**Dubuque**, **Fargo**, **Rochester**, **St. Cloud**, **Wausau**, **Duluth**, **LaCrosse**, **Rochester**, **Minneapolis**, **Green Bay**, **Madison**, **Dubuque**, **Rochester**]. We remove **Dubuque** and add **Rochester**, **LaCrosse**, and **Rockford** to the search queue.

At this point, we have tested every node that is one level away in the tree from the start node (**Rochester**). Our search queue contains the following nodes: [**Fargo**, **Rochester**, **St. Cloud**, **Wausau**, **Duluth**, **LaCrosse**, **Rochester**, **Minneapolis**, **Green Bay**, **Madison**, **Dubuque**, **Rochester**, **Rochester**, **LaCrosse**, **Rockford**]. We remove **Fargo**, which is two levels away from **Rochester**, and add **Grand Forks**, **St. Cloud**, and **Sioux Falls**. Then we test and expand **Rochester** (**Rochester** to **Minneapolis** to **Rochester** is two levels away from our start). Next is **St. Cloud**; again we expand that node. Finally, we get to **Wausau**; our goal test succeeds and we declare success. Our search order was **Rochester**, **Sioux Falls**, **Minneapolis**, **LaCrosse**, **Dubuque**, **Fargo**, **Rochester**, **St. Cloud**, and **Wausau**.

Note that this trace could have been greatly simplified by keeping track of nodes that had been tested and expanded. This would have cut down on our time and space complexity, yet still would have been a complete algorithm because we would have searched every node before we stopped. However, in more realistic problems where each node is expanded using a list of operators and the states are more complex than just strings, it is not so easy to determine that two states are identical. This explosion of nodes and states is not unusual for a breadth-first search problem.

Depth-First Search

Depth-first search is another way to systematically traverse a tree structure to find a goal or solution node. Instead of completely searching each level of the tree before going deeper, the depth-first algorithm follows a single branch of the tree down as many levels as possible until it either reaches a solution or a dead end. The algorithm follows:

1. Create a queue and add the first **SearchNode** to it.

2. Loop:

   a. If the queue is empty, quit.

   b. Remove the first **SearchNode** from the queue.

   c. If the **SearchNode** contains the goal state, then exit with the **SearchNode** as the solution.

   d. For each child of the current **SearchNode**: Add the new **SearchNode** to the front of the queue.

This algorithm is identical to the breadth-first search with the exception of the last step in the loop. The depth-first algorithm searches from the start or root node all the way down to a leaf node. If it does not find the goal node, it backtracks up the tree and searches down the next untested path until it reaches the next leaf. If you imagine a large tree, the depth-first algorithm may spend a large amount of time searching the paths on the lower left when the answer is really in the lower right. But since depth-first search is a brute-force method, it will blindly follow this search pattern until it comes across a node containing the goal state, or until it searches the entire tree. Depth-first search has lower memory requirements than breadth-first search. For problems with extremely deep or infinite search trees, depth-first search can spend all of its time searching one deep branch of the tree, looping forever as it dynamically expands nodes. For this reason, depth-first search is neither complete nor optimal.

As we did earlier, let's walk through a simple example of how depth-first search would work if we started in **Rochester** and wanted to see if we could get to **Wausau**. Starting with **Rochester**, we test and expand it, placing **Sioux Falls**, then **Minneapolis**, then **LaCrosse**, then **Dubuque** at the front of the search queue: [**Dubuque**, **LaCrosse**, **Minneapolis**, **Sioux Falls**]. We remove **Dubuque** and test it; it fails, so we expand it adding **Rochester** to the front, then **LaCrosse**, then **Rockford**. Our search queue now looks like [**Rockford**, **LaCrosse**, **Rochester**, **LaCrosse**, **Minneapolis**, **Sioux Falls**]. We remove **Rockford**, and add **Dubuque**, **Madison**, and **Chicago** to the front of the queue in that order, yielding [**Chicago**, **Madison**, **Dubuque**, **LaCrosse**, **Rochester**, **LaCrosse**, **Minneapolis**, **Sioux Falls**]. We test **Chicago**, and place **Rockford** and **Milwaukee** on the queue. We take **Milwaukee** from the front and add **Chicago**, **Madison**, and **Green Bay** to the search queue. It is now [**Green Bay**, **Madison**, **Chicago**, **Rockford**, **Chicago**, **Madison**, **Dubuque**, **LaCrosse**, **Rochester**, **LaCrosse**, **Minneapolis**, **Sioux Falls**]. We remove **Green Bay** and add **Milwaukee**, **LaCrosse**, and

Wausau to the queue in that order. Finally, **Wausau** is at the front of the queue, our goal test succeeds, and our search ends. Our search order was **Rochester**, **Dubuque**, **Rockford**, **Chicago**, **Milwaukee**, **Green Bay, and Wausau**.

In this example, we again did not prevent tested nodes from being added to the search queue. As a result, we had duplicate nodes on the queue. In a depth-first search, this could be disastrous. We could have easily had a cycle or loop where we tested one city, then a second, then the first again, ad infinitum. In the next section, we show our Java implementation of these search algorithms, starting with a class for the node and one for the search graph. We include tests to avoid the duplication of nodes on the search queue.

The SearchNode Class

We define search problems using a hierarchical tree or graph structure, comprised of a set of nodes and links. Our search algorithms work on the node structure defined in the **SearchNode** class shown in Figure 2.2.

The first data member in our **SearchNode** class (see Figure 2.2) is the symbolic name or *label* of the node. Next is the *state*, which can be any **Object**. The *oper* is the definition of the operation that created the state of the object. This would be used in problems such as games where the state of a parent node would be expanded into multiple child nodes and states based on the application of the set of operators.

The *links* member is a **Vector** containing references to all other **SearchNode** objects to which this node is linked. **SearchNode** objects can be connected to form any graph including tree structures.

The *depth* member is an integer that defines the distance from the start or root node in any search. The two boolean flags, *expanded* and *tested*, are used by the search algorithms to avoid getting into infinite loops. The first, *expanded*, is set whenever the node is expanded during a search. The second, *tested*, is used whenever the state of the node is tested during a search. Depending on the search algorithm, this flag may or may not be used. The *cost* member can be used to represent the current accumulated cost or any other cost measure associated with the search problem. The static member *traceTextArea* is used to display trace information in our example application.

The constructor takes two parameters, the *name* and the initial object state. The constructor initializes the *depth*, *links*, and *oper* members and sets the boolean flags to false.

Once we have created an instance of a **SearchNode**, we specify the links to other nodes. The *addLink()* method adds a link to a single **SearchNode** object. For graphs with high connectivity, the *addLinks()* method is provided to add links to an arbitrary number of nodes by passing an array of **SearchNode** objects as a parameter to the method.

We provide a method for testing whether the node is a leaf node in a tree structure (i.e., it has no children) and methods to set and get the *depth*, *oper*, *expanded*, and *tested* data members.

The *reset()* method is used to reset the node depth and the boolean flags before starting a search. The *setDisplay()* method is used in our example application to register a

```
package search;

import java.util.*;
import javax.swing.*;

public class SearchNode extends Object {
  protected String label;
  protected Object state;
  protected Object oper;
  protected Vector links;
  protected int depth;
  protected boolean expanded;
  protected boolean tested;
  protected float cost = 0;
  private static JTextArea traceTextArea;
  public static final int FRONT = 0;
  public static final int BACK = 1;
  public static final int INSERT = 2;

  SearchNode(String label, Object state) {
    this.label = label;
    this.state = state;
    depth = 0;
    links = new Vector();
    oper = null;
    expanded = false;
    tested = false;
  }

  public void addLink(SearchNode node) {
    links.addElement(node);
  }

  public void addLinks(SearchNode[] nodes) {
    for(int i = 0; i < nodes.length; i++) {
      links.addElement(nodes[i]);
    }
  }

  public boolean leaf() {
    return (links.size() == 0);
  }

  public void setDepth(int depth) {
    this.depth = depth;
  }

  public void setOperator(Object oper) {
```

Figure 2.2 The SearchNode class listing.

```
    this.oper = oper;
}

public void setExpanded() {
  expanded = true;
}

public void setExpanded(boolean state) {
  expanded = state;
}

public boolean isExpanded() {
  return expanded;
}

public void setTested() {
  tested = true;
}

public void setTested(boolean state) {
  tested = state;
}

public boolean isTested() {
  return tested;
}

static public void setDisplay(JTextArea textArea) {
  traceTextArea = textArea;
}

public Object getState() {
  return state;
}

public void reset() {
  depth = 0;
  expanded = false;
  tested = false;
}

public void trace() {
  String indent = new String();

  for(int i = 0; i < depth; i++) {
    indent += "  ";
  }
```

(continues)

Figure 2.2   Continued.

```
      traceTextArea.append(indent + "Searching " + depth + ": " + label
         + " with state = " + state + "\n");
   }

   public void expand(Vector queue, int position) {
      setExpanded();
      for(int j = 0; j < links.size(); j++) {
        SearchNode nextNode = (SearchNode) links.elementAt(j);

        if(!nextNode.tested) {
          nextNode.setTested(true);
          nextNode.setDepth(depth + 1);
          switch(position) {
            case FRONT:
              queue.insertElementAt(nextNode, 0);
              break;
            case BACK:
              queue.addElement(nextNode);
              break;
            case INSERT:
              boolean inserted = false;
              float nextCost = nextNode.cost;

              for(int k = 0; k < queue.size(); k++) {
                if(nextCost < ((SearchNode) queue.elementAt(k)).cost) {
                  queue.insertElementAt(nextNode, k);
                  inserted = true;
                  break;
                }
              }
              if(!inserted) {
                queue.addElement(nextNode);
              }
              break;
          }
        }
      }
   }
}
```

Figure 2.2   The SearchNode class listing (Continued).

JTextArea component for displaying trace information during a search. The *trace()* method writes out an indented string indicating the depth of the node in the search tree along with its label and state. As written, it assumes that the state is a string.

The most complicated method in our **SearchNode** class is the *expand()* method, which is used by the various search algorithms to build a search tree from the initial search graph. The parameters are a *queue* (a **Vector** instance) and a parameter specifying where the child nodes should be placed on the *queue*. The options are *front*, *back*, or *insert*, based on the current cost in the **SearchNode**.

When expanding a node, we first mark the node as expanded. We then loop over all of the nodes to which the node has links. For each node, if it has not been *tested* (actually, this means placed on the *queue*, because the node states are tested only when they are removed from the front of the *queue*), we mark it as *tested*, set its *depth* in the search tree, and then place it on the *queue* in the specified position. For FRONT, we add at position 0. For BACK we simply *addElement()*, which places it at the end of the **Vector**.

For the INSERT case, we have a loop where we compare the cost of the node we are trying to insert, *nextNode*, to the cost of the nodes on the *queue*. If *nextCost* is lower, we place the *nextNode* on the *queue*. There are two cases where the *nextNode* will not be inserted in this loop: when the *queue* is empty, and when the *nextCost* is greater than the cost of all of the nodes already on the *queue*. In this case, the boolean flag, *inserted*, will not be set and *nextNode* will be added to the end of the *queue*.

Now that we have defined the **SearchNode** class, we can talk about the **SearchGraph** class, which contains the set of **SearchNode** objects that define our problem states. **SearchGraph** is a relatively simple class, as shown in Figure 2.3. It contains only two instance variables: the *graph* that is a **Hashtable** of (*label*, **SearchNode**) pairs and a *name* which is a **String** that identifies the **SearchGraph**. The constructor takes a single **String** parameter for the **SearchGraph** name. The *reset()* method uses the enumeration of the elements in the *graph* to iterate over the **SearchNode** objects and reset each one in turn. The *put()* method takes a **SearchNode** object as a single argument, and adds it to the *graph* with the *label* as the key and the **SearchNode** object as the value.

The remainder of the methods in the **SearchGraph** class define four of the five search methods that are described in more detail in the next section.

Search Application

In this section, we develop a Java application to illustrate the behavior of five search algorithms. The Search application classes are **SearchApp**, which contains our *main()*, and **SearchFrame**, which implements our main window. They were constructed using the Borland/Inprise JBuilder 3.0 Java interactive development environment. The visual builder allows us to create the complete GUI using Java Swing components in a drag and drop style. JBuilder automatically generates the Java code for creating the GUI controls and action event handlers in the **SearchFrame** class. We then added the logic for creating the **SearchGraph** and **SearchNodes** and invoking the search algorithms. The **SearchApp** code that invokes the **SearchFrame** is not presented here. It simply instantiates the **SearchFrame** class and displays it. Likewise, a substantial amount of the code in the **SearchFrame** class deals with GUI control logic and we will not present that

```
package search;

import java.util.*;

class SearchGraph extends Object {
  String name;
  Hashtable graph = new Hashtable();

  public SearchGraph(String name) {
    this.name = name;
  }

  public Hashtable getGraph() {
    return graph;
  }

  public SearchNode getNode(String nodeName) {
    return (SearchNode) graph.get(nodeName);
  }

  void reset() {
    Enumeration enum = graph.elements();

    while(enum.hasMoreElements()) {
      SearchNode nextNode = (SearchNode) enum.nextElement();

      nextNode.reset();
    }
  }

  void put(SearchNode node) {
    graph.put(node.label, node);
  }

  public SearchNode depthFirstSearch(SearchNode initialNode,
      Object goalState) {
    Vector queue = new Vector();

    queue.addElement(initialNode);
    initialNode.setTested(true);
    while(queue.size() > 0) {
      SearchNode testNode = (SearchNode) queue.firstElement();

      queue.removeElementAt(0);
      testNode.trace();
      if(testNode.getState().equals(goalState)) {
        return testNode;
```

Figure 2.3   The SearchGraph class listing.

```
      }
      if(!testNode.isExpanded()) {
        testNode.expand(queue, SearchNode.FRONT);
      }
    }
    return null;
}

public SearchNode breadthFirstSearch(SearchNode initialNode,
    Object goalState) {
  Vector queue = new Vector();

  queue.addElement(initialNode);
  initialNode.setTested(true);
  while(queue.size() > 0) {
    SearchNode testNode = (SearchNode) queue.firstElement();

    queue.removeElementAt(0);
    testNode.trace();
    if(testNode.getState().equals(goalState)) {
      return testNode;
    }
    if(!testNode.isExpanded()) {
      testNode.expand(queue, SearchNode.BACK);
    }
  }
  return null;
}

public SearchNode depthLimitedSearch(SearchNode initialNode,
    Object goalState, int maxDepth) {
  Vector queue = new Vector();

  queue.addElement(initialNode);
  initialNode.setTested(true);
  while(queue.size() > 0) {
    SearchNode testNode = (SearchNode) queue.firstElement();

    queue.removeElementAt(0);
    testNode.trace();
    if(testNode.getState().equals(goalState)) {
      return testNode;
    }
    if(testNode.depth < maxDepth) {
      if(!testNode.isExpanded()) {
        testNode.expand(queue, SearchNode.FRONT);
      }
```

(continues)

Figure 2.3 Continued.

```
          }
        }
        return null;
     }

     public SearchNode iterDeepSearch(SearchNode startNode,
         Object goalState) {
       int maxDepth = 10;

       for(int j = 0; j < maxDepth; j++) {
         reset();
         SearchNode answer = depthLimitedSearch(startNode, goalState, j);

         if(answer != null) {
           return answer;
         }
       }
       return null;
     }

     public SearchNode bestFirstSearch(SearchNode initialNode,
         Object goalState) {
       Vector queue = new Vector();

       queue.addElement(initialNode);
       initialNode.setTested(true);
       while(queue.size() > 0) {
         SearchNode testNode = (SearchNode) queue.firstElement();

         queue.removeElementAt(0);
         testNode.trace();
         if(testNode.getState().equals(goalState)) {
           return testNode;
         }
         if(!testNode.isExpanded()) {
           testNode.expand(queue, SearchNode.INSERT);
         }
       }
       return null;
     }
   }
```

Figure 2.3 The SearchGraph class listing (Continued).

material here. Instead, we will highlight only brief sections of the code that demonstrate how to use the underlying application classes. All of the classes discussed in this chapter are in the *search* package shown in Figure 2.4.

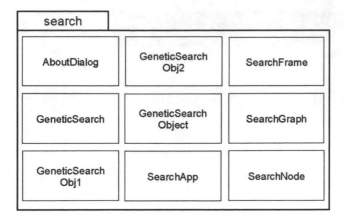

Figure 2.4 The *search* package UML diagram.

The user interface of our application is comprised of a single **JFrame**, shown in Figure 2.5. A user can select from one of five search techniques: depth-first, breadth-first, iterated-deepening, best-first, and genetic search. We have already presented the breadth-first and depth-first algorithms in some detail. We will discuss all five algorithms and their implementations in the following sections. The user can choose which algorithm to use by selecting the appropriate menu item under the **Algorithm** pull-down menu. For algorithms that use the **SearchGraph** class, the **Start node** and **Goal state** can be selected from the top two combo boxes. If the **Genetic search algorithm** is selected, the bottom four controls are enabled, allowing the user to specify the **Genetic object class name**, the **Population size**, the **Number of generations** to be processed, and the **Fitness threshold** used for early stopping. Pressing the **Start** menu item under the **File** pull-down menu will invoke the corresponding search algorithm with the specified parameters passed as arguments. As the search algorithms progress, trace information is displayed in the text area at the top of the dialog. Pressing the **Clear** menu item under the File pull-down menu will clear this area between runs, if desired.

A single static method *buildTestGraph()* is defined in the **SearchFrame** class which creates a **SearchGraph** used in our examples of the different search algorithms. This graph defines the set of midwestern U.S. cities as shown in Figure 2.1. First we instantiate the **SearchGraph** object and then create one **SearchNode** for each city. After each **SearchNode** object is created, it is added to the **SearchGraph** by using the *put()* method. Note that the node *name* and the *state* (also the city's name) are identical. This is for illustration purposes only. There is no reason why the node *label* and the *state* have to be the same. In fact, the second parameter on the **SearchNode** constructor can be any Java **Object**. So we could have an array or matrix for tic-tac-toe, or some other arbitrarily complex state-space representation, depending on the problem we are trying to solve.

```
public static SearchGraph buildTestGraph() {
  SearchGraph graph = new SearchGraph("test");
  SearchNode roch = new SearchNode("Rochester", "Rochester");
```

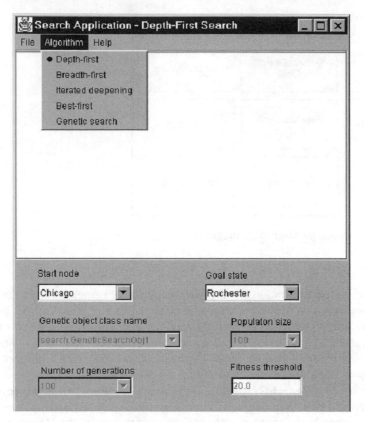

Figure 2.5 The search application window.

```
graph.put(roch);
SearchNode sfalls = new SearchNode("Sioux Falls", "Sioux Falls");

graph.put(sfalls);
SearchNode mpls = new SearchNode("Minneapolis", "Minneapolis");

graph.put(mpls);
SearchNode lacrosse = new SearchNode("LaCrosse", "LaCrosse");

graph.put(lacrosse);
SearchNode fargo = new SearchNode("Fargo", "Fargo");

graph.put(fargo);
SearchNode stcloud = new SearchNode("St.Cloud", "St.Cloud");

graph.put(stcloud);
SearchNode duluth = new SearchNode("Duluth", "Duluth");

graph.put(duluth);
SearchNode wausau = new SearchNode("Wausau", "Wausau");
```

```
graph.put(wausau);
SearchNode gforks = new SearchNode("Grand Forks", "Grand Forks");

graph.put(gforks);
SearchNode bemidji = new SearchNode("Bemidji", "Bemidji");

graph.put(bemidji);
SearchNode ifalls = new SearchNode("International Falls",
                    "International Falls");

graph.put(ifalls);
SearchNode gbay = new SearchNode("Green Bay", "Green Bay");

graph.put(gbay);
SearchNode madison = new SearchNode("Madison", "Madison");

graph.put(madison);
SearchNode dubuque = new SearchNode("Dubuque", "Dubuque");

graph.put(dubuque);
SearchNode rockford = new SearchNode("Rockford", "Rockford");

graph.put(rockford);
SearchNode chicago = new SearchNode("Chicago", "Chicago");

graph.put(chicago);
SearchNode milwaukee = new SearchNode("Milwaukee",
                        "Milwaukee");

graph.put(milwaukee);
roch.addLinks(new SearchNode[]{ mpls, lacrosse, sfalls, dubuque });
mpls.addLinks(new SearchNode[]{ duluth, stcloud, wausau });
mpls.addLinks(new SearchNode[]{ lacrosse, roch });
lacrosse.addLinks(new SearchNode[]{ madison, dubuque, roch });
lacrosse.addLinks(new SearchNode[]{ mpls, gbay });
sfalls.addLinks(new SearchNode[]{ fargo, roch });
fargo.addLinks(new SearchNode[]{ sfalls, gforks, stcloud });
gforks.addLinks(new SearchNode[]{ bemidji, fargo, ifalls });
bemidji.addLinks(new SearchNode[]{ gforks, ifalls, stcloud, duluth });
ifalls.addLinks(new SearchNode[]{ bemidji, duluth, gforks });
duluth.addLinks(new SearchNode[]{ ifalls, mpls, bemidji });
stcloud.addLinks(new SearchNode[]{ bemidji, mpls, fargo });
dubuque.addLinks(new SearchNode[]{ lacrosse, rockford });
rockford.addLinks(new SearchNode[]{ dubuque, madison, chicago });
chicago.addLinks(new SearchNode[]{ rockford, milwaukee });
milwaukee.addLinks(new SearchNode[]{ gbay, chicago });
gbay.addLinks(new SearchNode[]{ wausau, milwaukee, lacrosse });
wausau.addLinks(new SearchNode[]{ mpls, gbay });
roch.cost = 0;
sfalls.cost = 232;
mpls.cost = 90;
```

```
    lacrosse.cost = 70;
    dubuque.cost = 140;
    madison.cost = 170;
    milwaukee.cost = 230;
    rockford.cost = 210;
    chicago.cost = 280;
    stcloud.cost = 140;
    duluth.cost = 180;
    bemidji.cost = 260;
    wausau.cost = 200;
    gbay.cost = 220;
    fargo.cost = 280;
    gforks.cost = 340;
    return graph;
}
```

After the **SearchNode** objects are created, we define the connectivity between nodes using the *addLinks()* method. Next, we set the *cost* of each node as the distance from each city to Rochester, Minnesota. We use this in the best-first search example discussed later in this section. This cost value is set to a static value for this example. In most search problems, the cost would be computed as the search progresses. This is another simplification used to make the explanation clearer.

When the **Start** menu item is pressed, an **ActionEvent** is generated and the *StartMenuItem_actionPerformed()* method is invoked. The search algorithms are run on a separate thread from the GUI. We create a new thread, *runnit*, and start it. Because the **SearchFrame** implements the **Runnable** interface, the *run()* method is called. In *run()*, first we retrieve the *start* and *goal* **Strings** from the combo box controls. Next we clear all of the **SearchNode** objects in the graph by calling *reset()*. Then we call the selected search algorithm. Only one **Algorithm** radio button menu item can be selected at any time. When pressed, the menu item event handler methods set the *searchAlgorithm* data member value accordingly. The *run()* method invokes the corresponding search method based on the *searchAlgorithm* value. For the four graph-based search techniques this requires only a single method call. The genetic search algorithm, discussed in more detail later in this chapter, must retrieve the user settings from the four GUI controls first, and then invoke the search method.

```
void StartMenuItem_actionPerformed(ActionEvent e) {
    runnit = new Thread(this);
    runnit.start();
}

public void run() {
    int method = 0;
    SearchNode answer = null;
    SearchNode startNode;
    String start = (String) startComboBox.getSelectedItem();

    startNode = graph.getNode(start);
    String goal = (String) goalComboBox.getSelectedItem();
```

```
graph.reset();
switch(searchAlgorithm) {
  case DEPTH_FIRST: {
    traceTextArea.append("\n\nDepth-First Search for " + goal
        + ":\n\n");
    answer = graph.depthFirstSearch(startNode, goal);
    break;
  }
  case BREADTH_FIRST: {
    traceTextArea.append("\n\nBreadth-First Search for " + goal
        + ":\n\n");
    answer = graph.breadthFirstSearch(startNode, goal);
    break;
  }
  case ITERATED: {
    traceTextArea.append("\n\nIterated-Deepening Search for "    + goal
        + ":\n\n");
    answer = graph.iterDeepSearch(startNode, goal);
    break;
  }
  case BEST_FIRST: {
    traceTextArea.append("\n\nBest-First Search for " + goal
        + ":\n\n");
    goalComboBox.setSelectedItem("Rochester");
    answer = graph.bestFirstSearch(startNode, "Rochester");
    break;
  }
  case GENETIC_SEARCH: {
    traceTextArea.append("\n\nGenetic Search using... \n\n");
    geneticSearch.setGeneticObjectClassName(
      (String) GeneticObjClassComboBox.getSelectedItem());
    geneticSearch.setMaxNumPasses(
      ((Integer) NumGenerationsComboBox.getSelectedItem())
       .intValue());
    geneticSearch.setDebugOn(debugOn);
    geneticSearch.setPopulationSize(
      ((Integer) PopulationSizeComboBox.getSelectedItem())
       .intValue());
    try {
      geneticSearch.setFitnessThreshold(
        Double.valueOf( FitnessThresholdTextField.getText().trim())
         .doubleValue());
      } catch(Exception e) {
      geneticSearch.setFitnessThreshold(20.0);
      FitnessThresholdTextField.setText("20.0");
    }
    geneticSearch.init();
    geneticSearch.search();
    break;
  }
}
```

```
        if(searchAlgorithm != GENETIC_SEARCH) {
          if(answer == null) {
            traceTextArea.append("Could not find answer!\n");
          } else {
            traceTextArea.append("Answer found in node " + answer.label);
          }
        }
      }
```

Breadth-First Search

The Java implementation of the breadth-first search algorithm is shown in the following example. The *breadthFirstSearch()* method is part of the **SearchGraph** class. The parameters are the initial **SearchNode** and the goal state, which in our Search application is the object label. First we instantiate our queue of nodes to search, then add the *initialNode* to the queue and mark it as tested.

In a *while()* loop, we first check to see if there are any more nodes to expand. If so, we remove the first node, call *trace()* to print out a message, then test the node to see if it matches our goal state. Although in our example application we are using **Strings** to represent our goal state, this code should work for any state **Object** provided it implements the *equals()* method. If the goal test succeeds, we return with the node that matches the goal state. If the goal test fails and we haven't already expanded this node, we expand it by placing all of the nodes it has links to on the back of the queue. When the queue is empty we exit the *while()* loop.

```
public SearchNode breadthFirstSearch(SearchNode initialNode,
    Object goalState) {
  Vector queue = new Vector();

  queue.addElement(initialNode);
  initialNode.setTested(true);
  while(queue.size() > 0) {
    SearchNode testNode = (SearchNode) queue.firstElement();

    queue.removeElementAt(0);
    testNode.trace();
    if(testNode.getState().equals(goalState)) {
      return testNode;
    }
    if(!testNode.isExpanded()) {
      testNode.expand(queue, SearchNode.BACK);
    }
  }
  return null;
}
```

A breadth-first search performs a complete search of the state space. If there are multiple solutions, it will find a solution with the shortest number of steps because each node of length n is examined before the next layer of nodes is explored. In Figure 2.6 we show

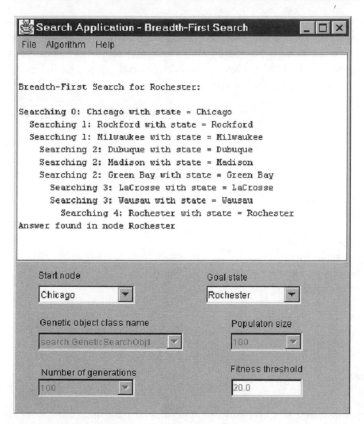

Figure 2.6 Breadth-first search algorithm example.

the output of a breadth-first search run against our *testGraph* with Chicago as the start node and Rochester as the destination. Note that the exact search order is affected by how we define the links in our *testGraph*.

Depth-First Search

The Java code for our depth-first search algorithm is similar to our breadth-first code, except the child nodes are added to the front of the queue instead of the back. This small change makes a big difference in the search behavior of the algorithm. Depth-first search requires less memory than breadth-first search but it can also spend lots of time exploring paths that lead to dead ends.

The *depthFirstSearch()* parameters are the starting **SearchNode** and the goal state. First we instantiate our *queue* of nodes to search, and add the *initialNode* to the queue and mark it as tested.

In a *while()* loop, we first check to see if there are any more nodes to expand. If so, we remove the first node, call *trace()* to print out a message, then test the node to see if it matches our goal state. Although in our example application we are using **Strings** to represent our goal state, this code should work for any state **Object** provided it implements the *equals()* method. If the goal test succeeds, we return with the node that matched the goal state. If the goal test fails and we haven't already expanded this node, we expand it by placing all of the nodes it has links to on the front of the *queue*. When the *queue* is empty we exit the *while()* loop.

```
public SearchNode depthFirstSearch(SearchNode initialNode,
    Object goalState) {
  Vector queue = new Vector();

  queue.addElement(initialNode);
  initialNode.setTested(true);
  while(queue.size() > 0) {
    SearchNode testNode = (SearchNode) queue.firstElement();

    queue.removeElementAt(0);
    testNode.trace();
    if(testNode.getState().equals(goalState)) {
      return testNode;
    }
    if(!testNode.isExpanded()) {
      testNode.expand(queue, SearchNode.FRONT);
    }
  }
  return null;
}
```

Figure 2.7 shows depth-first search results using our search application, with Chicago as the start node and Rochester as the destination.

Improving Depth-First Search

One easy way to get the best characteristics of the depth-first search algorithm along with the advantages of the breadth-first search is to use a technique called iterative-deepening search. In this approach, we first add a slight modification to the depth-first search algorithm by adding a parameter called *maxDepth*, to limit our search to a maximum depth of the tree. Then we add a control loop in which we continually deepen our depth-first search until we find the solution.

This algorithm, like standard breadth-first search, is a complete search and will find an optimal solution. But, like the depth-first algorithm, it has much lower memory requirements. Although we are retracing ground when we increase our depth of search, this approach is still more efficient than pure breadth-first or pure unlimited depth-first search for large search spaces [Russell and Norvig 1995].

Our Java implementation of the iterated-deepening search algorithm uses two methods. The *iterDeepSearch()* method performs the outer loop, repeatedly calling *depthLimitedSearch()* with the *maxDepth* increasing by one for each successive call. The *depthLimitedSearch()* method is essentially the same as our standard depth-first search

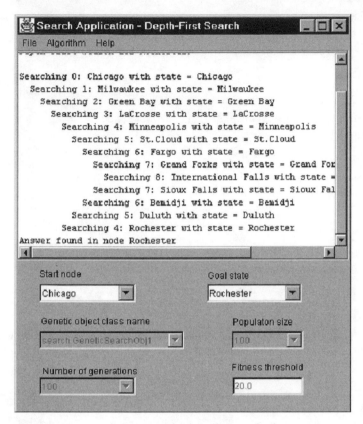

Figure 2.7 Depth-first search algorithm example.

algorithm, with the test against *maxDepth* used to short-circuit expansion of **Search-Node** once they get too deep.

```
public SearchNode depthLimitedSearch(SearchNode initialNode,
    Object goalState, int maxDepth) {
  Vector queue = new Vector();

  queue.addElement(initialNode);
  initialNode.setTested(true);
  while(queue.size() > 0) {
    SearchNode testNode = (SearchNode) queue.firstElement();

    queue.removeElementAt(0);
    testNode.trace();
    if(testNode.getState().equals(goalState)) {
      return testNode;
    }
    if(testNode.depth < maxDepth) {
      if(!testNode.isExpanded()) {
```

```
            testNode.expand(queue, SearchNode.FRONT);
        }
      }
    }
  return null;
}

public SearchNode iterDeepSearch(SearchNode startNode,
    Object goalState) {
  int maxDepth = 10;

  for(int j = 0; j < maxDepth; j++) {
    reset();
    SearchNode answer = depthLimitedSearch(startNode, goalState, j);

    if(answer != null) {
      return answer;
    }
  }
  return null;
}
```

In Figure 2.8 we show a trace of a search from Chicago to Rochester using the iterated-deepening algorithm. Notice how the algorithm recovers ground as it goes to each level.

Heuristic Search

The Traveling Salesman Problem (TSP), in which a salesman makes a complete tour of the cities on his route and visits each city exactly once while traveling the shortest possible distance, is an example of a problem that has a combinatorial explosion. As such, it cannot be solved using breadth-first or depth-first search for problems of any realistic size. TSP belongs to a class of problems known as NP-hard or NP-complete. Unfortunately, there are many problems which have this form and which are essentially intractable. In these cases, finding the best possible answer is not computationally feasible, and so we have to settle for a good answer. In this section we discuss several heuristic search methods that attempt to provide a practical means for approaching these kinds of search problems.

Heuristic search methods are characterized by the sense that we have limited time and space in which to find an answer to complex problems, and so we are willing to accept a good solution. As such, we apply heuristics or rules of thumb as we search the tree to try to determine the likelihood that following one path or another is more likely to lead to a solution. Note that this is in stark contrast to the brute-force methods, which chug along merrily regardless of whether a solution is anywhere in sight.

Heuristic search methods use objective functions called (surprise!) heuristic functions to try to gauge the value of a particular node in the search tree and to estimate the value of following down any of the paths from the node. In the next sections we describe four types of heuristic search algorithms.

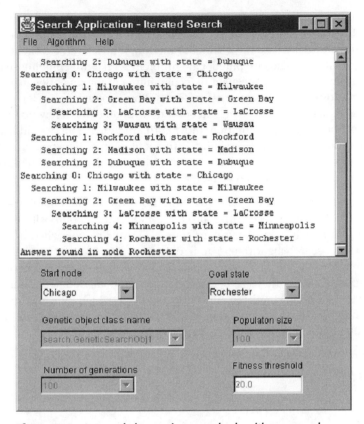

Figure 2.8   Iterated-deepening search algorithm example.

Generate-and-Test Algorithm

The generate-and-test algorithm is the most basic heuristic search function. The steps are as follows:

1. Generate a possible solution, either a new state or a path through the problem space.

2. Test to see if the new state or path is a solution by comparing it to a set of goal states.

3. If a solution has been found, return success; otherwise return to step 1.

This is a depth-first search procedure that performs an exhaustive search of the state space. If a solution is possible, the generate-and-test algorithm will find it. However, it may take an extremely long time. For small problems, generate-and-test can be an effective algorithm, but for large problems, the undirected search strategy leads to lengthy run times and is impractical. The major weakness of generate-and-test is that we get no feedback on which direction to search. We can greatly improve this algorithm by providing feedback through the use of heuristic functions.

Hill-climbing is an improved generate-and-test algorithm in which feedback from the tests is used to help direct the generation (and evaluation) of new candidate states. When a node state is evaluated by the goal test function, a measure or estimate of the distance to the goal state is also computed. One problem with a hill-climbing search in general is that the algorithm can get caught in local minima or maxima. Because we are always going in the direction of least cost, we can follow a path up to a locally good solution, while missing the globally excellent solution available just a few nodes away. Once at the top of the locally best solution, moving to any other node would lead to a node with lower goodness. Another possibility is that a plateau or flat spot exists in the problem space. Once the search algorithm gets up to this area all moves would have the same goodness and so progress would be halted.

To avoid getting trapped in sub-optimal states, variations on the hill-climbing strategy have been proposed. One is to inject noise into the evaluation function, with the initial noise level high and slowly decreasing over time. This technique, called *simulated annealing*, allows the search algorithm to go in directions that are not "best" but allow more complete exploration of the search space. Simulated annealing is analogous to annealing of metals, whereby they are heated and then gradually cooled. Thus a temperature parameter is used in simulated annealing, such that a high temperature allows continued searching, but as the temperature cools the search algorithm reverts to the more standard hill-climbing behavior [Kirkpatrick, Gelatt, and Vecchi 1983].

In the next section we describe best-first search, which is a more formal specification of a greedy, hill-climbing search algorithm.

Best-First Search

Best-first search is a systematic control strategy, combining the strengths of breadth-first and depth-first search into one algorithm. The main difference between best-first search and the brute-force search techniques is that we make use of an evaluation or heuristic function to order the **SearchNode** objects on the queue. In this way, we choose the **SearchNode** that appears to be best, before any others, regardless of their position in the tree or graph. Our implementation of best-first search uses the current value of the *cost* data member to order the **SearchNode** objects on the search queue. In our *buildTestGraph()* method, we set the cost of the nodes to be equal to the approximate straight-line distance from each city to Rochester, Minnesota.

The *bestFirstSearch()* parameters are the initial **SearchNode** and the goal state. To start, we instantiate our *queue* of nodes to search, and add the *initialNode* to the queue and mark it as tested.

In a *while()* loop, we first check to see if there are any more nodes to expand. If so, we remove the first node, call *trace()* to print out a message, then test the node to see if it matches our goal state. Although in our example application we are using **Strings** to represent our goal state, this code should work for any state **Object** provided it implements the *equals()* method. If the goal test succeeds, we return with the node that matched the goal state. If the goal test fails and we haven't already expanded this node, we expand the node by inserting each of the nodes it has links to on the *queue* based on the cost. When the *queue* is empty we exit the *while()* loop.

```
public SearchNode bestFirstSearch(SearchNode initialNode,
    Object goalState) {
  Vector queue = new Vector();

  queue.addElement(initialNode);
  initialNode.setTested(true);
  while(queue.size() > 0) {
    SearchNode testNode = (SearchNode) queue.firstElement();

    queue.removeElementAt(0);
    testNode.trace();
    if(testNode.getState().equals(goalState)) {
      return testNode;
    }
    if(!testNode.isExpanded()) {
      testNode.expand(queue, SearchNode.INSERT);
    }
  }
  return null;
}
```

Figure 2.9 shows an example of the best-first search algorithm applied to the problem of finding the best route from Chicago to Rochester, Minnesota.

Greedy Search

Greedy search is a best-first strategy in which we try to minimize the estimated cost to reach the goal (certainly an intuitive approach!). Since we are greedy, we always expand the node that is estimated to be closest to the goal state. Unfortunately, the exact cost of reaching the goal state usually can't be computed, but we can estimate it by using a cost estimate or heuristic function $h()$. When we are examining node **n**, then $h(\mathbf{n})$ gives us the estimated cost of the cheapest path from **n**'s state to the goal state. Of course, the better an estimate $h()$ gives, the better and faster we will find a solution to our problem. Greedy search has similar behavior to depth-first search. Its advantages are delivered via the use of a quality heuristic function to direct the search.

A* Search

One of the most famous search algorithms used in AI is the A* search algorithm, which combines the greedy search algorithm for efficiency with the uniform-cost search for optimality and completeness. In A* the evaluation function is computed by adding the two heuristic measures; the $h(\mathbf{n})$ cost estimate of traversing from **n** to the goal state, and $g(\mathbf{n})$ which is the known path cost from the start node to **n** into a function called $f(\mathbf{n})$.

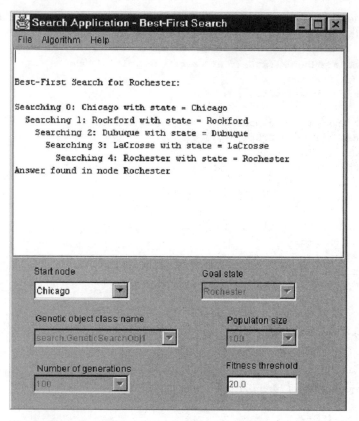

Figure 2.9 Best-first search algorithm example.

Again, there is nothing really new here from a search algorithm point of view; all we are doing is using better information (heuristics) to evaluate and order the nodes on our search queue. We know how much it cost to get where we are (node **n**) and we can guesstimate how much it will cost to reach the goal from **n**. Thus we are bringing all of the information about the problem we can to bear on directing our search. This combination of strategies turns out to provide A* with both completeness and optimality.

Constraint Satisfaction

Another approach to problem solving using search is called constraint satisfaction. All problems have some constraints that define what the acceptable solutions are. For example, if our problem is to load a delivery truck with packages, a constraint may be that the truck holds only 2000 pounds. This constraint could help us substantially reduce our search space by ignoring search paths that contain a set of items that weigh more than 2000 pounds. Constraint satisfaction search uses a set of constraints to define the space of acceptable solutions. Rather than a simple goal test, the search is complete when we have a set of bindings of values to variables, a state where the minimum set of constraints holds.

The role of constraints is to bind variables to values or limit the range of values that they may take on, thus reducing the number of combinations we need to explore. First, an initial set of constraints is applied and propagated through the problem, subject to the dependencies that exist. For example, if we set a limit of 2000 pounds for a particular delivery truck, that may immediately remove some items from consideration. Also, once we assign an object to the truck that weighs 800 pounds, we can infer that now the limit for additional items is 1200 pounds. If a solution is not found by propagating the constraints, then search is required. This may involve backtracking or undoing an assignment or variable binding.

Means-Ends Analysis

Means-ends analysis is a problem-solving process based on detecting differences between states and then trying to reduce those differences. First used in the General Problem Solver [Newell and Simon 1963], means-ends analysis uses both forward and backward reasoning and a recursive algorithm to systematically minimize the differences between the initial and goal states.

Like any search algorithm, means-ends analysis has a set of states along with a set of operators that transform that state. However, the operators or rules for transformation do not completely specify the before and after states. The left side or antecedent of the rule only contains the subset of conditions, the *preconditions*, which must be true in order for the operator to be applied. Likewise the right-hand side of the rule identifies only those parts of the state that the operator changes. Each operator has a before and after list of states and state changes that are only a subset of the whole problem space. A simplified version of the means-ends analysis is described here [Rich and Knight 1991].

Means-Ends Analysis (Current-State, Goal-State)

1. Compare the current-state to the goal-state. If states are identical then return success.

2. Select the most important difference and reduce it by performing the following steps until success or failure:

    a. Select an operator that is applicable to the current difference. If there are no operators that can be applied, then return failure.

    b. Attempt to apply the operator to the current state by generating two temporary states, one where the operator's preconditions are true (pre-state), and one that would be the result if the operator were applied to the current state (post-state).

    c. Divide the problem into two parts, a *first*part, from the current-state to the pre-state, and a *last*part, from the post-state to the goal state. Call means-ends analysis to solve both pieces. If both are true, then return success, with the solution consisting of the *first*part, the selected operator, and the *last*part.

Means-ends analysis is a powerful heuristic search algorithm. It has been applied in many artificial intelligence applications, especially in planning systems.

Genetic Algorithms

While most of the search algorithms presented to this point are examples of GOFAI (Good Old-Fashioned AI), more recent techniques have been developed to explore large state-spaces. One of the most successful is called genetic search, which uses a class of algorithms called genetic algorithms. In terms of blind or heuristic approaches, genetic algorithms are more heuristic, in that they use fitness functions to score the quality of the state. Another major difference is that genetic algorithms search the solution space in parallel, exploring tens or hundreds of alternate solutions at the same time.

Genetic algorithms use a biological process metaphor to derive solutions to problems. First, the problem state must be encoded into a string, called a chromosome, which is usually a binary string, but could be a string of real values. There must be an evaluation or objective function that takes that encoded string as input and produces a "goodness" or biological "fitness" score. This score is then used to rank a set of strings (individuals in the population of strings) based on their fitness. If you are familiar with Charles Darwin's "survival of the fittest" theory, you can probably see where this is going.

The strings (individuals) that are most fit are randomly selected to survive and even procreate into the next generation of strings. Genetically inspired operators are used to modify the selected string, in an attempt to improve its fitness and get even closer to the goal or optimum solution. The mutation operator, like biological mutation, performs random mutations or changes in the chromosome of the individual. In the usual binary string case, we randomly flip a few bits. The crossover operator takes two particularly fit individuals and combines their genetic material, forming two new children. The intuitive rationale for this operation is that because both parents were fit individuals, the chances are good that the offspring will also be well-endowed in terms of providing a good solution to the problem at hand.

Figure 2.10 shows two parent chromosomes, A and B, with examples of mutation and one-point crossover operators. We first mutate parent A's chromosome by flipping bits

Parent A:		0 0 1 0 0 1 0 0 1 1
Parent B:		1 1 0 0 0 0 1 0 1 0
Mutate(A)		0 0 1 1 0 1 0 0 0 1
Crossover(A,B)	Child 1:	0 0 1 0 0 0 1 0 1 0
	Child 2:	1 1 0 0 0 1 0 0 1 1

Figure 2.10   A genetic operator example.

at the fourth position (from 0 to 1) and the ninth position (from 1 to 0), counting from the left. Changed bits are indicated by underlines. Next, we apply the crossover operator to the parents at bit position three: We take the first three bits from parent A and the rightmost 7 bits from parent B to create child 1, and the first three bits from parent B with the rightmost 7 bits from parent A to create child 2.

Genetic algorithms are particularly suited to optimization problems because they are, in essence, performing a parallel search in the state space. The crossover operator injects large amounts of noise into the process to make sure that the entire search space is covered. The mutation operator allows fine-tuning of fit individuals in a manner similar to hill-climbing search techniques. Control parameters are used to determine how large the population is, how individuals are selected from the population, and how often any mutation and crossover is performed.

Genetic Search Implementation

In this section, we describe our implementation of a genetic search algorithm. Two major classes are used to define a genetic search. The **GeneticSearch** class contains the overall control logic for the algorithm and manipulates a collection of **Genetic-SearchObject**s that represent the population members. The **GeneticSearchObject**s contain the chromosome definition and the fitness function for the specific problem we are trying to solve.

```java
package search;

import java.util.*;
import javax.swing.*;

public class GeneticSearch extends Object {
  protected Class geneticObjectClass;
  protected Vector population;
  protected Hashtable operatorFitness = null;
  protected int chromosomeLength = 10;
  protected String vocabulary = "01";
  protected String geneticObjectClassName = "search.GeneticSearchObj1";
  protected int maxNumPasses = 50;
  protected double fitnessThreshold = 100000.0;
  protected int populationSize = 20;
  protected int replacementSize = 20;
  protected double crossoverRate = 0.65;
  protected double mutationRate = 0.008;
  protected double maxFitness = Double.MAX_VALUE;
  protected double minFitness = 0.0;
  protected double avgFitness = 0.0;
  protected double totalFitness = 0.0;
  protected double[] summedFitness;
  protected int numPasses = 0;
  protected JTextArea traceTextArea;
  protected boolean debugOn = false;
```

```
public GeneticSearch() {}

... ... ...

}
```

The **GeneticSearch** class is fairly complex, containing approximately 20 data members. These include the *geneticObjectClassName* **String** and corresponding *geneticObjectClass* **Class** instance; the *population*, a **Vector** of **GeneticSearchObject**s; and the *operatorFitness* **Hashtable**, which contains the operator definitions. The *chromosomeLength* and *vocabulary* members describe the number of characters and the alphabet used in the chromosome (the default is binary "0" and "1"). Parameters the user can set using the **SearchFrame** controls include the *maxNumPasses* and *fitnessThreshold*, which are used as alternate stopping conditions, and the *populationSize*, which defines how many **GeneticSearchObject** instances are created and held in the *population* **Vector**.

The *replacementSize* defines how many new population members are added each generation. In this implementation, the entire population is replaced each cycle so the *replacementSize* is set equal to the *populationSize*. The *crossoverRate* and *mutationRate* define the probabilities that those operators are applied. A set of fitness metrics, including the *maxFitness*, *minFitness*, *avgFitness*, and *totalFitness*, are provided, along with an array of doubles *summedFitness* used to improve computational performance. The *numPasses* member is used to count the number of generations processed.

The **GeneticSearch** *init()* method first sets the population fitness metrics to 0.0, allocates the *population* and *summedFitness* members, and sets the *replacementSize* equal to the *populationSize*. It then loads the specified **GeneticObjectClass** and creates a dummy instance. Note that this approach is very flexible; the user can specify any new class to be used as the **GeneticSearchObject** class, provided it is in the **Classpath** and can be found by the Java runtime. We use the *dummy* instance to get the list of operators and their corresponding probabilities of being selected, along with the *chromosomeLength* and *vocabulary* used by this particular **GeneticSearchObject** subclass. Next we generate the first population in a *while()* loop, asking the dummy instance to provide a random chromosome, creating the **GeneticSearchObject** instance in *createChild* (passing the chromosome in as an argument), and then inserting the new instance into the population. When *init()* completes, we have *populationSize* instances of the user specified **GeneticSearchObject** in our population, and we are ready to do a genetic search.

```
public void init() {
  numPasses = 0;
  maxFitness = 0.0;
  minFitness = 0.0;
  avgFitness = 0.0;
  totalFitness = 0.0;
  population = new Vector();
  summedFitness = new double[populationSize + 1];
  replacementSize = populationSize;
  try {
```

```
    geneticObjectClass = Class.forName(geneticObjectClassName);
    GeneticSearchObject dummy =
       (GeneticSearchObject) geneticObjectClass.newInstance();

    if(operatorFitness == null) {
       operatorFitness = dummy.getOperatorFitness();
    }
    chromosomeLength = dummy.getChromosomeLength();
    vocabulary = dummy.getVocabulary();
    while(population.size() < populationSize) {
       String chromosome = dummy.getRandomChromosome();
       GeneticSearchObject newOne = createChild(chromosome);

       if(newOne != null) {
          insertIntoPopulation(newOne, population);
       }
    }
} catch(ClassNotFoundException e1) {
    System.out.println("Error:" + e1.toString());
} catch(InstantiationException e2) {
    System.out.println("Error:" + e2.toString());
} catch(IllegalAccessException e3) {
    System.out.println("Error:" + e3.toString());
}
}
```

The *search()* method is called to perform the complex genetic search, starting from our initial population. It first initializes the population, then goes into a loop, calling the *processOneGeneration()* method (which processes one generation!) until the *maxNumPasses* has been reached, or the *maxFitness* reaches the *fitnessThreshold*. Note that this test, as coded, only allows for increasing fitness values to indicate goodness. A fitness function that decreases as population members get closer to a solution will not work correctly.

```
public void search() {
   init();
   trace("Starting genetic search\n");
   while((numPasses < maxNumPasses) && (maxFitness < fitnessThreshold)) {
      processOneGeneration();
      trace("Generation[" + numPasses + "] "
            + population.elementAt(0).toString() + "\n");
   }
   trace("Genetic search complete\n");
   displayPopulation();
}
```

The *processOneGeneration()* method does a single step in the genetic search. It calls *evaluatePopulation()* which evaluates each chromosome by getting its fitness value, finding the maximum and minimum fitness values, and summing them up for use by the *createNewMembers()* method. It then calls the *createNewMembers()* method to generate a completely new generation to replace the current one. Note that we could provide

---

a function to replace only a subset of the current population, but for simplicity, we replace the entire population here.

```
public void processOneGeneration() {
  evaluatePopulation();
  Vector newPopulation = createNewMembers();

  integratePopulation(newPopulation);
  numPasses++;
}
```

The *evaluatePopulation()* method walks through the population, incrementally sums up the *rawFitness* values for each member and stores it in the *summedFitness* array for use by the roulette wheel selection routine. As the values are summed, the minimum and maximum values are computed, along with the average fitness over the entire population.

The *createNewMembers()* method starts by using a technique called **elitism**. The best member of the current population (at population index 0 because they are sorted by fitness values) is copied over as the first member of the new population. Looping until the specified number of new members are created, two parents are selected at random from the current population (biased by their fitness values) using the *rouletteWheelSelection* algorithm. The chromosomes from the parents are retrieved and a genetic operator is selected at random (biased by the operator fitness values defined in the **GeneticSearchObject** class). Once selected, the operator is invoked, passing the parent chromosomes as parameters. The child chromosomes are returned and used to create the children **GeneticSearchObject** instances, which are then inserted into the new population.

```
protected void evaluatePopulation() {
  double rawFitness = 0.0;

  totalFitness = 0.0;
  for(int i = 0; i < populationSize; i++) {
    rawFitness =
      ((GeneticSearchObject) population.elementAt(i)).computeFitness();
    if(i == 0) {
      summedFitness[0] = rawFitness;
    } else {
      summedFitness[i] = rawFitness + summedFitness[i - 1];
    }
    if(rawFitness < minFitness) {
      minFitness = rawFitness;
    }
    if(rawFitness > maxFitness) {
      maxFitness = rawFitness;
    }
    totalFitness += rawFitness;
  }
  avgFitness = totalFitness / populationSize;
}
```

```
protected Vector createNewMembers() {
  Vector newPopulation = new Vector();

  newPopulation.addElement(population.elementAt(0));
  try {
    while(newPopulation.size() < replacementSize) {
      GeneticSearchObject[] parents = selectParents();
      String[] childChromosomes = null;
      String[] parentChromosomes = new String[2];

      parentChromosomes[0] = parents[0].getChromosome();
      parentChromosomes[1] = parents[1].getChromosome();
      String operatorName = selectOperator();

      childChromosomes = (String[]) invokeOperator(operatorName,
          parentChromosomes);
      if(childChromosomes != null) {
        GeneticSearchObject[] children =
          createChildren(childChromosomes);
        int count = children.length;

        if((count >= 1) && (children[0] != null)) {
          insertIntoPopulation(children[0], newPopulation);
        }
        if((count >= 2) && (children[1] != null)) {
          insertIntoPopulation(children[1], newPopulation);
        }
      }
    }
  } catch(Exception e) {
    System.out.println("Error: during creation of next generation " + e);
  }
  return newPopulation;
}

public GeneticSearchObject[] createChildren(String[] chromosome) {
  GeneticSearchObject[] children =
    new GeneticSearchObject[chromosome.length];
  GeneticSearchObject child1 = createChild(chromosome[0]);

  children[0] = child1;
  if(chromosome.length == 2) {
    GeneticSearchObject child2 = createChild(chromosome[1]);

    children[1] = child2;
  }
  return children;
}

public GeneticSearchObject createChild(String chromosome) {
  GeneticSearchObject child = null;
```

```
try {
  child = (GeneticSearchObject) geneticObjectClass.newInstance();
  child.setChromosome(chromosome);
  child.setCrossoverRate(crossoverRate);
  child.setMutationRate(mutationRate);
} catch(Exception e) {
  System.out.println("createChild: exception " + e);
}
return child;
}
```

The *integratePopulation()* method simply replaces the current population with the new population. The *insertIntoPopulation()* method takes a single new population member and inserts it into the population based on its fitness value.

```
protected void integratePopulation(Vector newPopulation) {
  population = newPopulation;
}


protected void insertIntoPopulation(GeneticSearchObject newMember,
    Vector list) {
  try {
    boolean inserted = false;
    int size = list.size();
    double fitness = newMember.getFitness();

    if(size == 0) {
      list.addElement(newMember);
    } else {
      for(int i = 0; i < size; i++) {
        GeneticSearchObject tmpMember =
          (GeneticSearchObject) list.elementAt(i);

        if(fitness > tmpMember.getFitness()) {
          list.insertElementAt(newMember, i);
          inserted = true;
          break;
        }
      }
      if(!inserted) {
        list.addElement(newMember);
      }
    }
  } catch(Exception e) {
    System.out.println("insertIntoPopulation exception " +
      e.toString());
  }
}
```

The *rouletteWheelSelection()* method chooses a single population member by rolling a die (selecting a new random number between 0 and the *totalFitness* of the population).

It then walks through the *summedFitness* array until it exceeds the *summedFitness* value. At that index value, the population member is chosen for reproduction.

```java
public GeneticSearchObject[] selectParents() {
  GeneticSearchObject[] parents = new GeneticSearchObject[2];

  parents[0] = rouletteWheelSelection();
  parents[1] = rouletteWheelSelection();
  return parents;
}

public String selectOperator() {
  int size = operatorFitness.size();
  double threshold = Math.random() * 100;
  Enumeration operators = operatorFitness.keys();
  double sum = 0.0;

  while(operators.hasMoreElements()) {
    String operatorName = (String) operators.nextElement();
    Double operator = (Double) operatorFitness.get(operatorName);
    double fitness = operator.doubleValue();

    sum += fitness;
    if(sum >= threshold) {
      return operatorName;
    }
  }
  return null;
}

public GeneticSearchObject rouletteWheelSelection() {
  double selectionThreshold = 0.0;
  double fitness = 0.0;

  selectionThreshold = Math.random() * totalFitness;
  for(int i = 0; i < populationSize; i++) {
    if(summedFitness[i] >= selectionThreshold) {
      GeneticSearchObject member =
        (GeneticSearchObject) population.elementAt(i);

      return member;
    }
  }
  return null;
}

public String[] invokeOperator(String operatorName, String[] parents) {
  if(operatorName.equals("onePointCrossoverAndMutate")) {
    return onePointCrossoverAndMutate(parents);
  } else if(operatorName.equals("onePointCrossover")) {
```

```
      return onePointCrossover(parents);
   } else if(operatorName.equals("mutate")) {
      return mutate(parents);
   }
   return parents;
}
```

The three genetic operators are provided in the **SearchGraph** class. They are implemented in the *onePointCrossoverAndMutate, onePointCrossover*, and *mutate* methods. Each operator takes a pair of **GeneticSearchObject** parents as inputs and returns two children **GeneticSearchObject**s.

The *onePointCrossover()* operator takes the genetic material from both parents, picks a single point in the chromosome to split the chromosomes and recombines them with material from each parent. First a random number is generated. If the random number is less than the *crossoverRate* parameter, the crossover operation takes place. If not, the parent chromosomes are just returned as is. If a crossover is to be performed, another random number is generated and scaled by the chromosome length to define a bit position where the split is to be made. Each parent chromosome is split into two substrings at the crossover point and reassembled with the left substring of parent[1] combined with the right substring of parent[2], and the right substring of parent[1] combined with the left substring of parent[2].

The *onePointCrossoverAndMutate()* operator performs the same operation as the *onePointCrossover()* operator but then mutates each child chromosome based on the current *mutationRate* parameter. The *mutate()* operator simply applies the *mutateChromosome()* operation to the parent chromosomes. The *mutateChromosome()* method takes a single chromosome and rolls the dice for each bit position in the chromosome. If the random number is less than the current *mutationRate* parameter, then another random number is used to select a new value from the vocabulary of the chromosome. This is a rather expensive operation as coded. Another implementation would be to do a single roll of the dice to decide whether to mutate and then mutate at only one bit position.

```
public String[] onePointCrossoverAndMutate(String[] parents) {
   String[] children = new String[2];
   String c1Chromosome = parents[0];
   String c2Chromosome = parents[1];
   double rand = Math.random();

   if(rand < crossoverRate) {
      String p1Left = c1Chromosome;
      String p1Right = "";
      String p2Left = c2Chromosome;
      String p2Right = "";
      int bitPosition = (int) (Math.random() * chromosomeLength);

      if((bitPosition > 0) && (bitPosition <= chromosomeLength)) {
         p1Left = c1Chromosome.substring(0, bitPosition);
         p1Right = c1Chromosome.substring(bitPosition, chromosomeLength);
         p2Left = c2Chromosome.substring(0, bitPosition);
```

```
            p2Right = c2Chromosome.substring(bitPosition, chromosomeLength);
        }
        c1Chromosome = p1Left + p2Right;
        c2Chromosome = p2Left + p1Right;
    }
    c1Chromosome = mutateChromosome(c1Chromosome);
    c2Chromosome = mutateChromosome(c2Chromosome);
    children[0] = c1Chromosome;
    children[1] = c2Chromosome;
    return children;
}

public String mutateChromosome(String chromosome) {
    StringBuffer buf = new StringBuffer(chromosome);
    int size = chromosome.length();
    int vocabSize = vocabulary.length();

    for(int i = 0; i < size; i++) {
        double rand = Math.random();
        int bitPos = 0;

        if(rand < mutationRate) {
            if(debugOn) {
                System.out.println("mutate bit position = " + i);
            }
            double rand2 = Math.random();

            bitPos = (int) (rand2 * vocabSize);
            if(bitPos == vocabSize) {
                bitPos = bitPos - 1;
            }
            char newValue = vocabulary.charAt(bitPos);

            buf.setCharAt(i, newValue);
        }
    }
    return buf.toString();
}

public String[] onePointCrossover(String[] parents) {
    String[] children = new String[2];
    String c1Chromosome = parents[0];
    String c2Chromosome = parents[1];
    double rand = Math.random();

    if(rand < crossoverRate) {
        String p1Left = c1Chromosome;
        String p1Right = "";
        String p2Left = c2Chromosome;
        String p2Right = "";
        int bitPosition = (int) (Math.random() * chromosomeLength);
```

```
         if((bitPosition > 0) && (bitPosition <= chromosomeLength)) {
           p1Left = c1Chromosome.substring(0, bitPosition);
           p1Right = c1Chromosome.substring(bitPosition, chromosomeLength);
           p2Left = c2Chromosome.substring(0, bitPosition);
           p2Right = c2Chromosome.substring(bitPosition, chromosomeLength);
         }
         c1Chromosome = p1Left + p2Right;
         c2Chromosome = p2Left + p1Right;
       }
       children[0] = c1Chromosome;
       children[1] = c2Chromosome;
       return children;
     }


     public String[] mutate(String[] parents) {
       String[] children = new String[2];

       children[0] = mutateChromosome(parents[0]);
       children[1] = mutateChromosome(parents[1]);
       return children;
     }
```

GeneticSearchObject Class

The **GeneticSearchObject** class, shown in Figure 2.11, defines the population members used by the **GeneticSearch** algorithm. The class defines the chromosome length and vocabulary, as well as the fitness function used to evaluate each instance of the class. It contains eight class data members. These include *searchAgent*, which is a reference to the parent **GeneticSearch** object, the *chromosome* **String**, the *vocabulary* used by the chromosome, and the length of the chromosome. The *fitness* of the population member is represented by a **double** value. A **boolean** *fitnessComputed* is used to avoid recomputation of the fitness in cases when it is expensive. Use of this feature is optional and is dependent on the implementation of the **GeneticSearchObject** subclass. The last two data members are the *crossoverRate* and *mutationRate* used by the standard genetic operators to influence reproduction.

The major methods in the **GeneticSearchObject** class include the *computeFitness()* method, which examines the chromosome and computes and returns a fitness value. The *getRandomChromosome()* method simply calls the *generateRandomChromosome* method to create a *chromosome* of the specified length using the alphabet defined in the vocabulary. The default operators are defined in the *getOperatorFitness()* method which lists the operator name and their probability of being selected by the *selectOperator* method in the **GeneticSearch** class. In this implementation, the genetic operators are predefined. This design could easily be extended to allow **GeneticSearchObject**s to define their own operators that are specifically meant to work on their chromosomes. For example, non-**String** chromosomes could be supported allowing real values to be part of the chromosome. The default **GeneticSearch** operators only work on strings.

```
package search;

import java.util.*;

public class GeneticSearchObject extends Object {
  protected GeneticSearch searchAgent;
  protected String chromosome;
  protected String vocabulary = "01";
  protected int chromosomeLength = 10;
  protected double fitness = 0.0;
  protected boolean fitnessComputed = false;
  protected double crossoverRate = 0.65;
  protected double mutationRate = 0.008;

  public GeneticSearchObject() {}

  public double getFitness() {
    return fitness;
  }

  public double computeFitness() {
    return fitness;
  }

  public String getRandomChromosome() {
    return generateRandomChromosome();
  }

  public void setChromosome(String chromosome) {
    this.chromosome = chromosome;
    computeFitness();
  }

  public String getChromosome() {
    return chromosome;
  }

  public int getChromosomeLength() {
    return chromosomeLength;
  }

  public String getVocabulary() {
    return vocabulary;
  }

  public void setCrossoverRate(double rate) {
```

(continues)

Figure 2.11 The GeneticSearchObject class listing.

```
      crossoverRate = rate;
    }

    public double getCrossoverRate() {
      return crossoverRate;
    }

    public void setMutationRate(double rate) {
      mutationRate = rate;
    }

    public double getMutationRate() {
      return mutationRate;
    }

    public String generateRandomChromosome() {
      String chromosome = new String(new char[chromosomeLength]);
      StringBuffer buf = new StringBuffer(chromosome);
      int size = chromosomeLength;
      int vocabSize = vocabulary.length();

      for(int i = 0; i < size; i++) {
        double rand = Math.random();
        int bitPos = (int) (rand * vocabSize);

        if(bitPos == vocabSize) {
          bitPos = bitPos - 1;
        }
        char newValue = vocabulary.charAt(bitPos);

        buf.setCharAt(i, newValue);
      }
      return buf.toString();
    }

    public Hashtable getOperatorFitness() {
      Hashtable operatorFitness = new Hashtable();

      operatorFitness.put("onePointCrossoverAndMutate", new Double(40));
      operatorFitness.put("onePointCrossover", new Double(30));
      operatorFitness.put("mutate", new Double(30));
      return operatorFitness;
    }

    public String toString() {
      return chromosome + " : " + String.valueOf(fitness);
    }
```

Figure 2.11   The GeneticSearchObject class listing (Continued).

```
public double binaryToInteger(String binCode) {
  double temp;
  double value = 0;
  int inLength = binCode.length();
  char bit;

  for(int i = 0; i < inLength; i++) {
    bit = binCode.charAt(i);
    if(bit == '1') {
      value += Math.pow((double) 2, (double) (inLength - 1 - i));
    }
  }
  return value;
  }
}
```

Figure 2.11   Continued.

The *binaryToInteger()* method is provided to interpret the chromosome bit string as an integer value.

GeneticSearchObj1 Class

The **GeneticSearchObj1** class, defined in Figure 2.12, extends the **GeneticSearchObject** class. It defines a binary string for the *chromosome* with a length of 20. The fitness function is very simple: it counts the number of binary 1s in the chromosome string. A perfect fitness would equal 20. Other than the constructor, the only base class method that is overridden is the *computeFitness()* method. Since the fitness value is inherent in the chromosome string, the value is only computed once and the *fitnessComputed* flag is used to avoid needlessly recomputing the fitness. Note that in more complex cases where the fitness must be computed relative to some outside object or an object that may have changed since the last time the value was computed, then this short-circuit may not be useable. While the short circuit may seem unnecessary here, in cases where the fitness function is more complex and if partial replacement of population is allowed, then the same population member may be asked for its fitness value tens or hundreds of times.

GeneticSearchObj2 Class

The **GeneticSearchObj2** class, defined in Figure 2.13, extends the **GeneticSearchObject** class. It defines a binary string for the chromosome with a length of 20. The fitness function is very simple: it counts the number of binary 0s in the chromosome string. A perfect fitness would equal 20. Other than the constructor, the only base class method that is overridden is the *computeFitness()* method. Like the **GeneticSearchObj1** class, it makes use of the *fitnessComputed* flag to avoid needless recomputation of the fitness value.

```
package search;

public class GeneticSearchObj1 extends GeneticSearchObject {
  public GeneticSearchObj1() {
    chromosomeLength = 20;
    vocabulary = "01";
  }

  public double computeFitness() {
    if(fitnessComputed) {
      return fitness;
    }
    int size = chromosomeLength;
    double sum = 0.0;

    for(int i = 0; i < size; i++) {
      if(((String) chromosome).charAt(i) == '1') {
        sum = sum + 1.0;
      }
    }
    fitness = sum;
    fitnessComputed = true;
    return fitness;
  }
}
```

Figure 2.12   The GeneticSearchObj1 class listing.

Using the **SearchApp** example application, select **Genetic Search** from the **Algorithm** menu. The bottom four GUI controls become enabled. Select either the **search.GeneticSearchObj1** or **search.GeneticSearchObj2** class. Use the default population size of 100, the number of generations of 100, and the fitness threshold value of 20. We know that the maximum fitness (the perfect individual having either all 1s or all 0s) will equal 20. Starting from a randomized population, we expect that each succeeding generation will improve toward our goal (perfection). Press the **Start** menu item under the **File** pull down menu. The genetic search algorithm will start producing generations of population members using a combination of our genetic operators. You should see the fitness level rise until it reaches 100 generations or the fitness reaches 20.

Summary

In this chapter we presented the major search algorithms used in artificial intelligence applications. The major points include the following:

■ The *state space* approach to problem representation requires a mapping from the real-world problem to a data structure (the state), an *initial state*, a set of

```
package search;

public class GeneticSearchObj2 extends GeneticSearchObject {
  public GeneticSearchObj2() {
    chromosomeLength = 20;
    vocabulary = "01";
  }

  public double computeFitness() {
    if(fitnessComputed) {
      return fitness;
    }
    int size = chromosomeLength;
    double sum = 0.0;

    for(int i = 0; i < size; i++) {
      if(((String) chromosome).charAt(i) == '0') {
        sum = sum + 1.0;
      }
    }
    fitness = sum;
    fitnessComputed = true;
    return fitness;
  }
}
```

Figure 2.13   The GeneticSearchObj2 class listing.

operators for changing the state, and the definition of a *goal test* to determine when we have reached a goal state. A *cost* may also be associated with a generated state.

■ Effective search algorithms must cause systematic motion through the state space. *Brute-force search* algorithms blindly search the state space, while *heuristic search* algorithms use feedback or information about the problem to direct the search.

■ A search algorithm is *optimal* if it is guaranteed to find the best solution from a set of possible solutions. An algorithm is *complete* if it will always find a solution if one exists. The *time complexity* defines how fast an algorithm performs and scales. The *space complexity* describes how much memory the algorithm requires to perform the search.

■ *Breadth-first search* is a complete algorithm with exponential time and space complexity. It examines each one step away from the initial state, then each state two steps away, and so on.

■ *Depth-first search* has lower memory requirements than breadth-first search, but it is neither complete (it can get stuck in loops) nor optimal. In depth-first search, a single path is chosen and followed until a solution is found, or a dead end (a leaf node) is reached. The algorithm then backs up and continues down another path.

- *Iterated-deepening search* uses a modified version of depth-first search to limit the depth of search. It does this with a control loop that increases the depth with every iteration. The approach combines the best of breadth-first and best-first search. It is complete and optimal, and it has much lower memory requirements than unlimited depth-first search.

- *Heuristic search* algorithms use information about the problem to help direct the path through the search space. This information is used to select which nodes to expand. *Best-first search* always expands the node that appears to be closest to the solution. *A* search* uses the known cost combined with an estimate of the distance from the state to the goal to choose a node to expand. A* is complete and optimal, and has memory requirements comparable to depth-first search.

- *Constraint satisfaction search* uses information about valid states to help limit or constrain the range of the search. *Means-ends analysis* solves problems by detecting differences between states and then trying to reduce those differences.

- *Genetic search* uses a biological metaphor that relies on problem solutions being represented by binary strings called chromosomes. The chromosomes are manipulated by genetic operators such as crossover and mutation. Genetic search performs parallel search, where the population size represents the degree of parallelism. The various genetic operators can force widespread exploration of the search space (crossover) or relatively localized hill-climbing behavior (mutation).

Exercises

1. Run the *SearchApp* Java application. Referring to Figure 2.1, select two cities and run the depth-first, breadth-first, and iterated-deepening search algorithms. Which algorithm finds the solution in the least time? Why? What if you selected two other cities?

2. In this chapter we developed a version of the best-first search algorithm in which the estimated cost from the current node to the goal state was the straight-line distance to the goal. The A* search algorithm combines this estimated cost with the current known cost from the start node to the current node. Extend the best-first implementation to perform A* search. How does it compare to best-first?

3. What is the major drawback to the search-based problem-solving approach? How do heuristics help overcome this weakness? How does constraint satisfaction search overcome this weakness?

4. Genetic algorithms are often used to find good solutions to difficult optimization problems. Pick a maximization problem and construct a binary chromosome to represent the solution. How many bits do you need to represent each value?

5. Create a **GeneticSearchObject** subclass to solve the problem defined in Exercise 2.4. In your *computeFitness()* method, you'll have to break the chromosome string into substrings, convert them to numbers, and plug them into the maximization formula.

CHAPTER 3

Knowledge Representation

I n this chapter we explore some of the techniques used to represent domain knowledge in artificial intelligence programs. We start with a discussion of several kinds of knowledge and the different demands that people and computers place on knowledge representations. We describe procedural and declarative knowledge representations and follow with an introduction to propositional and predicate logic. Next we discuss frames and semantic nets, two related artificial intelligence techniques for representing concepts and their relationships. The Knowledge Interchange Format (KIF) is presented as an emerging industry standard for knowledge representation. Finally, we discuss the knowledge acquisition process, in which expert domain knowledge is turned into a knowledge base for problem solving.

From Knowledge to Knowledge Representation

What is knowledge? Is knowledge the same thing as facts? *Webster's Dictionary* [Merriam-Webster 1988] defines knowledge as "the fact or condition of knowing something with familiarity gained through experience or association." People gain knowledge through experience—they see, hear, touch, feel, and taste the world around them. We can associate something we see with something we hear, thereby gaining new knowledge about the world. An alternate definition for knowledge is "the fact or condition of being aware of something." How do we make a computer aware of something? Suppose we know that the sun is hot, balls are round, and the sky is blue. These facts are knowledge about the world. How *do* we store this knowledge in our brain? How *could* we store this knowledge in a computer? This problem, called knowledge representation, is one of the first, most fundamental issues that researchers in artificial intelligence had to face. And the answer they found was *symbols*.

While psychologists and neuroscientists are still searching for the answer to how people store knowledge in their brains (we know it has something to do with the synapses), in the field of artificial intelligence, programmers use symbols to represent and manipulate knowledge in computers. What is a symbol? A symbol is a number or character string that represents an object or idea. Strings and numbers are used because computers are very good at processing them. This is called the internal representation of the knowledge. However, people are most comfortable using a natural language like English to represent knowledge. Thus, for practical reasons, we need mappings from facts to an internal computer representation and also to a form that people can understand.

Though natural language is perhaps the most easily understood knowledge representation for people, it is certainly not the best for computers, because natural language is inherently ambiguous. That is, two people can read the same statement and disagree as to what it means. This ambiguity is exactly why the languages of formal mathematics and logic were developed during the past two millennia. It should be no surprise that artificial intelligence was first applied to formal languages and mathematical theorem proving, and that one of the first knowledge representations was formal logic. For those mathematicians who were the first computer programmers, logic was a "natural" language to use.

There are many different kinds of knowledge we may want to represent: simple facts or complex relationships, mathematical formulas or rules for natural language syntax, associations between related concepts, inheritance hierarchies between classes of objects. As we will show, each type of knowledge places special requirements on both human comprehension and computer manipulation. Knowledge representation is not a one-size-fits-all proposition. Consequently, choosing a knowledge representation for any particular application involves tradeoffs between the needs of people and computers. In addition to being easy to use, a good knowledge representation also must be easily modified and extended, either by changing the knowledge manually or through automatic machine-learning techniques. Let's look at some common kinds of knowledge and the most popular approaches for storing that knowledge in computers.

Procedural Representation

Perhaps the most common technique for representing knowledge in computers is to use *procedural* knowledge. Procedural code not only encodes facts (constants or bound variables) but also defines the sequence of operations for using and manipulating those facts. Thus, program code is a perfectly natural way of encoding procedural knowledge. Whether data structures or objects are used to model the problem, the program is essentially one big knowledge representation. Programs written in scripting languages such as Visual Basic, JavaScript, and LotusScript are examples of a procedural knowledge representation. The knowledge of how to process data is encoded in the control structures and sequence of the program statements. This "hardcoded" logic is typically not considered to be part of AI per se, but few real AI programs exist which do not contain some amount of procedural control code.

In procedural code, the knowledge and the manipulation of that knowledge are inextricably linked. This weakness is overcome by the most popular knowledge representation approach, called *declarative*. In declarative knowledge representation, a user simply states facts, rules, and relationships. These facts, rules, and relationships stand by themselves and represent pure knowledge. Most of the knowledge representation techniques studied in artificial intelligence and discussed in the remainder of this chapter are declarative. However, declarative knowledge needs to be processed by some procedural code, so we never get too far from the need for explicit sequential instructions for the computer to follow. Still, the separation of knowledge from the algorithm used to manipulate or reason with that knowledge provides advantages over procedural code. Because the knowledge is explicitly represented, it can be more easily modified. Also, separating the control logic and reasoning algorithms from the knowledge allows us to write optimized and reusable inferencing procedures.

Relational Representation

Another way to represent information is in relational form, such as that used in relational database systems. Relational databases provide a powerful and flexible mechanism for storing knowledge, which is why they have almost completely taken over the business of storing information in commercial business systems. Knowledge is represented by tuples or records of information about an item, with each tuple containing a set of fields or columns defining specific attributes and values of that item. By storing a collection of information in a table, we can use relational calculus to manipulate the data, based on the relations defined, and query the information stored in the table. Structured Query Language (SQL) is the most popular language for manipulating relational data.

While relational database tables are flexible, they are not good at representing complex relationships between concepts or objects in the real world. This is where network and hierarchical database systems, such as IBM's IMS, are strong. Having links or pointers between related groups of data allows both hierarchical and complex network graphs to be built. The AI techniques of semantic nets and frames, discussed in more detail later in this chapter, use a similar approach for representing knowledge.

Hierarchical Representation

Another type of knowledge is inheritable knowledge, which centers on relationships and shared attributes between kinds or classes of objects. Hierarchical knowledge is best used to represent "isa" relationships, in which a general or abstract type (for example, ball) is linked to more specific types (rubber, golf, baseball, football) which inherit the basic properties of the general type. The strength of object inheritance allows for compact representation of knowledge and allows reasoning algorithms to process at different levels of abstraction or granularity. We could reason about sports and the common attributes of balls at one level, or we could delve into the details of a particular sport and its respective type of ball. The use of categories or types gives structure to the world by grouping similar objects together. Using categories or clusters simplifies reasoning by limiting the number of distinct things we have to deal with. A taxonomy or hierarchy of objects or concepts is a useful way to organize collections of categories, because it allows us to reduce complexity and think at higher levels of abstraction where possible.

Using objects to model the world and to represent knowledge is becoming increasingly popular. In addition to relational and network databases, object databases that store object data and methods are now being deployed. Besides mapping naturally onto the real world, objects can also be used to model abstract ideas and their relationships. Object-oriented programming languages such as Smalltalk, C++, and Java provide a natural framework for representing knowledge as objects, and for reasoning about and manipulating those objects. Inheritance and class hierarchies are fundamental concepts on which object programs are built, and basically come "for free" with object-oriented knowledge representations.

AI problem solving often requires capturing knowledge about objects in the real world and about nonphysical measurements such as time. Knowing what to expect based on the elapsed time from one event to another is often the hallmark of intelligent behavior. Knowing that a friend just threw a snowball at your head would be useful knowledge so that you could brace for possible impact. Knowing which friend threw the snowball could help you determine the likelihood of getting hit at all. But this knowledge would only apply for a short time (2–5 seconds after the throwing event). Time concepts such as *before*, *after*, and *during* are crucial to common-sense reasoning and planning. When we are trying to solve a problem, we often pretend that "time stands still" while we are doing our computation. However, in many problems we must deal explicitly with changes due to the passing of time or the movement of objects in the world. Special forms of logic, called temporal logic, have been developed to deal with representing time and reasoning about time.

Although there are as many different ways to represent knowledge as there are types of knowledge, only a handful of knowledge representations are widely used in artificial intelligence applications. In the remainder of this chapter, we explore formal logic, frames, and semantic nets, while in the next chapter we explore rule-based knowledge representations. We start our discussion with predicate logic.

Predicate Logic

The use of formal logic as a primary knowledge representation harkens back to the beginnings of artificial intelligence research. Mathematical deduction, based on logic, was a well-known method of generating new knowledge from existing knowledge. Early AI researchers, therefore, used what they knew. While a detailed discussion of formal logic is outside the scope of this book, we will give a brief introduction to this topic.

Formal logic is a language with its own *syntax*, which defines how to make sentences, and corresponding *semantics*, which describes the meaning of the sentences. The most basic form of logic representation is called boolean or propositional logic, in which each proposition or fact is represented by a symbol that evaluates to either **true** or

false. Sentences can be constructed using proposition symbols (**P**, **Q**, **R**, . . .) and boolean connectives, such as conjunction (**and**), disjunction (**or**), implication (**P implies Q**), and equivalence (**A is equivalent to B**). Using this simple syntax, we can write implications or rules, such as (**P and Q**) **implies R** or, more programmatically **if P and Q then R**. In the preceding rule, **P and Q** is called the premise or *antecedent*, and **R** is the conclusion or *consequent*. In addition to joining propositions with connectives, a proposition can be negated (**not**) so that if **P** is **true**, then **not P** is **false**. Common rules of inference can be used to reason and infer facts from propositional logic sentences. One of the most familiar is called *Modus Ponens*, in which given a rule, **A implies B**, and knowledge that the antecedent sentence **A** is true, we can infer that the sentence **B** is also true.

Boolean logic is used as the basis for designing digital computers and is quite suited and powerful for circuit design. However, it quickly runs out of steam as a knowledge representation language. So, *predicate logic*, which allows *predicates* on objects to define attributes and relations between objects, has become the preferred logic for knowledge representation in artificial intelligence systems. Using objects, attributes, and relations, we can represent almost any type of knowledge. In addition, predicate logic introduces the concept of *quantifiers*, which allow us to refer to sets of objects. The two types of quantifiers are *existential* (there exists some object that has the specified attribute) and *universal* (all objects of this type have this attribute). A statement such as "**Minnesota is cold in the winter**." could be represented in predicate logic in several ways. We could use a conjunction of functions (say that fast three times), in which functions are relations with a single parameter, as in **place(Minnesota) and temperature(cold) and season(winter)**. Or we could use a single relation, such as **cold(Minnesota, winter)**. Or we could even say **winter(Minnesota, cold)** to represent the same statement.

From these examples, you can see that predicate logic does not give any guidance as to what predicates we should use. It also does not explicitly say how time or events should be represented. That is not to say that we can't represent these types of knowledge in predicate logic. It can be done. The main point is to understand that even with the syntax and semantics defined, we still have a lot of decisions to make in how the knowledge is represented by predicates.

Having a good knowledge representation solves only half of the problem, because we also need to manipulate the knowledge to generate new facts and prove or refute assertions about the knowledge. Unfortunately, predicate logic does not provide a sure-fire way to derive new information. However, it still can be used to process knowledge in a useful way. Two techniques, called *resolution* and *unification*, are used to process predicate statements to prove whether a particular statement is true or not, based on the other known facts. Together these algorithms form the basis for Prolog (**Program**ming in **log**ic). Prolog and Lisp are the two programming languages traditionally used for artificial intelligence applications [Clocksin and Mellish 1981]. While we will not go into details here, a basic understanding of the capabilities and limitations of predicate logic as a basis for reasoning is necessary. Our discussion will focus on two basic mechanisms, resolution and unification.

Resolution

Resolution is an algorithm for proving facts true or false by virtue of contradiction [Robinson 1965]. If we want to prove a theorem **X** is true, we have to show that the negation of **X** is not true. For example, suppose that we know the following two facts:

1. **not feathers(Tweety) or bird(Tweety)**
2. **feathers(Tweety)**

Sentence 1 states that either Tweety does not have feathers or else Tweety is a bird. Sentence 2 states that Tweety has feathers. To prove that Tweety is a bird, we first add an assumption that is the negation of that predicate, giving sentence 3:

1. **not feathers(Tweety) or bird(Tweety)**
2. **feathers(Tweety)**
3. **not bird(Tweety)**

In sentences 1 and 2, **not feathers(Tweety)** and **feathers(Tweety)** cancel each other out. Resolving sentences 1 and 2 produces the resolvant, sentence 4, which is added to our fact set:

1. **not feathers(Tweety) or bird(Tweety)**
2. **feathers(Tweety)**
3. **not bird(Tweety)**
4. **bird(Tweety)**

It is clear that sentences 3 and 4 cannot both be true: either Tweety is a bird or it is not. Thus, we have a contradiction. We have just proved that our first assumption, **not bird(Tweety)**, is false, and the alternative, **bird(Tweety)**, must be true [Winston 1993]. If the clauses to be resolved are selected in systematic ways, then resolution is guaranteed to find a contradiction if one exists, although it may take a long time to find.

Unification

Unification is a technique for taking two sentences in predicate logic and finding a substitution that makes them look the same. This is a requirement for proving theorems using resolution, as discussed previously. If two predicates are identical, then they match, by definition. If one or both contains variables, then appropriate substitutions must be found using unification as follows:

- A variable can be replaced by a constant.
- A variable can be replaced by another variable.
- A variable can be replaced with a predicate, as long as the predicate does not contain that variable.

Given the following set of predicates, let's explore how they can be unified.

1. **hates(X, Y)**
2. **hates(George, broccoli)**
3. **hates(Alex, spinach)**

We could unify sentence 2 with 1 by binding George to variable X, and broccoli to variable Y. Similarly, we could bind Alex to X and spinach to Y. Note that if the predicate names were different, we could not unify these predicates. If we introduce a few more predicates, we can explore more complex unifications:

4. **hates(X, vegetable(Y))**
5. **hates(George, vegetable(broccoli))**
6. **hates(Z, broccoli)**

We could unify sentence 6 with sentence 1 by replacing variable X with variable Z and variable Y with the constant broccoli. Sentences 4 and 5 could be unified with George bound to X, and broccoli to variable Y.

A generalized version of the unification algorithm, called *match*, is used in Prolog. *Facts* are represented in Prolog by clauses, which look like standard predicates and declare things which are unconditionally true. *Rules* are clauses in which the conclusion may be true, provided that all of the clauses in the condition part are true. Prolog provides a built-in inferencing procedure, based on resolution, for processing rules and answering questions posed as goal clauses [Bratko 1986].

While predicates can be used to represent and reason with rules, all rule systems do not use predicate logic as their knowledge representation language. Early rule-based systems were developed using Prolog and Lisp, but most commercial implementations are now written in C and C++. In Chapter 4, "Reasoning Systems," we will describe a rule-based inferencing system developed using Java.

Frames

A frame is a collection of attributes that define the state of an object and its relationship to other frames (objects). But a frame is much more than just a record or data structure containing data. In AI, frames are called slot-and-filler data representations. The slots are the data values, and the fillers are attached procedures which are called *before*, *during* (to compute the value of), or *after* the slot's value is changed. Frames are often linked into a hierarchy to represent has-part and isa relationships.

If a sequence of actions is applied to a frame, then some of the attributes change while most remain the same. When sequences of operations are required, as in a search problem, a problem known as the *frame problem* arises. The problem is that if we copy the complete frame (state of the object) for each step in the sequence, then we may quickly use up the computer memory, as we duplicate the same unchanged knowledge over and over. The frame problem addresses the issue that when an action occurs, it is not always obvious which attributes in the frame should change. The solution is to only

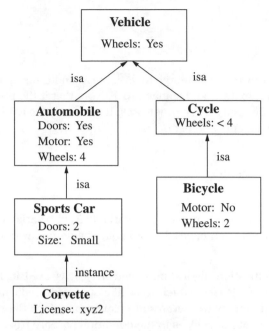

Figure 3.1 A frame example.

specify the parts of the state that must match for a condition to be true, and to only change those slots or attributes that change as a result of an operator.

Figure 3.1 shows an example of a frame representation for a subset of the domain of vehicles. Notice that each frame has a set of slots, and the frames are linked together to show their relationships. For example, the automobile frame has three slots. It is a subset of vehicles as indicated by the isa link. Our definition says that an automobile must have doors, a motor, and four wheels. A sports car is a subset or type of automobile. It has two doors and is small. Notice that sports car inherits several attributes from automobile. Finally, Corvette is an instance of a sports car, and each instance has a unique license number.

To anyone familiar with object-oriented programming, a frame sounds very much like an object, whose data members are the slots, and whose methods are the attached procedures or daemons. In some sense, any Java program is a frame-based mechanism for knowledge representation. Object-oriented programs also make use of inheritance for isa relationships, and containment or references for has-part relationships. In fact, an instance of a Java object with data members to hold the state and methods to test and change the object state provides a solution to the frame problem described previously.

Semantic Nets

Semantic nets are used to define the meaning of a concept by its relationships to other concepts. A graph data structure is used, with nodes holding concepts and links with

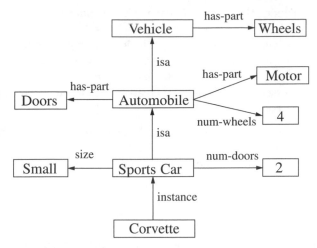

Figure 3.2 A semantic net example.

natural language labels showing the relationships. A portion of a semantic net representation of the vehicle domain is shown in Figure 3.2.

Again, the standard relationships such as isa, has-part, and instance should be familiar to readers with object-oriented design experience. Much of the object modeling work was anticipated by the semantic net research done in the 1960s [Quillian 1968]. Once the semantic net is constructed, a technique called *spreading activation* is used to see how two concepts or nodes are related.

While not obvious at first glance, both frames and semantic nets are very closely related to predicate logic. Russell and Norvig (1995) provide an algorithm for transforming both representations into first-order logic. The major difference between these knowledge representations is their syntax. Some people prefer formal logic, while others can relate more easily to graphical representations.

Representing Uncertainty

In almost any real-world application, a reasoning system will not have all of the relevant information it needs to solve a problem *a priori*. We have uncertainty. In most cases, there will be some information available, but the rest will have to be inferred or collected as the inferencing proceeds. Fortunately, we have a statistical theory which works well under conditions of uncertainty, called Bayes' Rule or Bayes' Theorem.

The probability of something can range from a probability of 0.0 (no chance) to a probability of 1.0 (certainty). Statisticians differentiate between two kinds of probabilities. First, there are unconditional (or prior) probabilities that represent the chance that something will happen. For example, we can look in a weather almanac and see that, on average, it has rained 10 days in March in Minnesota over the last hundred years. So the probability that it will rain on any given day in March is roughly 33 percent. This is the prior or unconditional probability. However, suppose we know that a big storm is blowing in from South Dakota, and it will reach Minnesota tomorrow. Given that knowledge, we may say there is an 80 percent chance of rain. Did the long-term probability change? No; but we have evidence that tomorrow could be a rainy day, so we make use of that evidence to update our forecast. Statisticians call this type of probability estimate a conditional probability, expressed as $P(H|E)$, that is read as the probability of hypothesis H given that we have observed evidence E.

Bayes' Theorem states that we can compute the conditional probability that event Y will occur given that event X already occurred, providing we know the prior probabilities that X and Y could happen, and the conditional probability that X will occur when we know that Y has already occurred.

$$P(Y|X) = P(X|Y)\frac{P(Y)}{P(X)}$$

A Bayesian network (also called a belief network, causal network, or probabilistic network) is a data structure (a directed acyclic graph) that is used to represent dependence between variables. Each variable has a corresponding node with a conditional probability table defining the relationships between its parent nodes. The primary use of Bayesian networks is to use probability theory to reason with uncertainty.

Knowledge Interchange Format

So far, we have discussed predicate logic, frames, and semantic nets, and have shown how they can represent knowledge. Because proponents of the various techniques could not agree on one knowledge representation format for their AI applications, a clear need was identified for a common language to bridge the gaps.

The Knowledge Interchange Format (KIF) is a language that was expressly designed for the interchange of knowledge between agents [Gensereth and Fikes 1992]. Based on predicate logic, KIF is a flexible knowledge representation language that supports the definition of objects, functions, relations, rules, and metaknowledge (knowledge about knowledge). In the past few years, KIF has emerged as the preferred language in efforts to have a standard knowledge representation format for use between a variety of intelligent agents.

The KIF language syntax is reminiscent of Lisp, which is not surprising given its predicate logic basis. Unlike Lisp, however, KIF is not meant to be a programming language. Nor is it meant to be used as an internal knowledge representation. KIF was explicitly designed to provide a common format for exchanging information. KIF is powerful and expressive enough to support the requirements of a wide variety of AI programs. Regardless of the internal knowledge representations, as long as every program can read and write KIF, the knowledge is portable and reusable in many different contexts. KIF is formally defined and is the result of several years of effort by the Defense Advanced Research Projects Agency (DARPA) Knowledge Sharing Environment workgroup. The KIF syntax can be split into three major groups: variables, operators, and constants.

KIF supports two types of variables: individual variables which begin with the ? character, and sequence variables which begin with an @ character. The four types of operators include term operators, rule operators, sentence operators, and definition operators. If a token is not a variable or an operator, then it must be a constant. KIF provides distinctions for several different types of constants. All numbers, characters, and strings are basic constants in KIF. Object constants denote objects, function constants denote functions over objects, relation constants denote relations, and logical constants express boolean conditions about the world which must be either true or false.

The language supports four types of expressions: terms, sentences, rules, and definitions. Terms denote objects, sentences represent facts, rules represent legal steps of inferencing, and definitions are used to define constants. Sentences are made up of constants, terms, and other sentences. KIF defines both forward (premise followed by consequent) and reverse (consequent followed by premise) rules.

A form in KIF is either a sentence, a rule, or a definition. And finally, a KIF knowledge base is a finite set of forms. The order of the forms in a knowledge base is not important.

An example rule in KIF is

```
(=> (EventName "AGENT:STARTING")
    (SetIdentifiedIntervalAlarm "NETSCAPE" 20 "minutes"))
```

which translates to "If we receive an AGENT:STARTING event, then start a named interval alarm (a timer) identified by the string "NETSCAPE" to go off every 20 minutes." The KIF rule

```
(GetStockPrice ?price) (IntegerCompare ?price ">" 150)
```

means "get the stock price and place it in variable *?price*, then test to see if the price is greater than 150." A complex rule can be almost unreadable (no offense intended to Lisp programmers), as follows:

```
(=> (AND (AND (EventName "StockAdapter:StockPriceEvent")
    (GetStockEventCount ?count)) (IntegerCompare ?count "=" 2))
    (AND (AND ( AND (TurnOffIdentifiedIntervalAlarm "IBM")
    (StockAdapterShow "Turned off the alarm." " " " "))
    (SetIdentifiedIntervalAlarm "HSY" 20 "minutes"))
    (StockAdapterShow "Started an alarm for Hershey." " " " ")))
```

This means "If this is a *StockPriceEvent* and this is the second *StockPriceEvent* event sent from the *StockAdapter*, then turn off the IBM stock watch timer, display a message, start a timer for Hershey foods, and display another message." Keep in mind that KIF is not a programming language. By using KIF as a knowledge representation, we could use multiple rule editors with nice (but very different) graphical environments for authoring rules. As long as they all write out the rules in KIF format, they would be interchangeable. Likewise, if one agent could write out its knowledge in KIF format and another one could read it, they could share their knowledge, even though their internal representations may be totally incompatible. Unfortunately, there is more to agent interaction than just having a common interchange format for knowledge. We discuss some of those issues in Chapter 6, "Agents and Multiagent Systems."

This brings us to the end of our discussion of knowledge representation formats. We can use procedural code, predicate logic, if-then rules, semantic nets, or frames to represent facts, rules, relationships, and complex transformations. These various kinds of knowledge representations can encode knowledge about almost any problem domain. When combined with a reasoning system or inference engine, a knowledge base becomes a part of a knowledge-based system, the last topic in this chapter.

Building a Knowledge Base

Now that we have described many types of knowledge we want to represent, we need to group it all together in one place, in our knowledge base. The knowledge base is the central repository of information containing the facts we know about objects and their relationships. It was only after several years of AI research that it became clear that knowledge was the key to building successful AI systems. All of the work on search algorithms and general problem-solving methods showed that without deep knowledge of the problem domain, any realistic problem soon exceeded the limits of standard search techniques.

The process of mapping the set of knowledge in a particular problem domain and converting it into a knowledge base is called *knowledge engineering* or *knowledge acquisition*. These terms grew out of the development of early expert systems, in which several unique roles were identified. First, there is the *domain expert*, who, through years of experience, has gathered the knowledge about how things work and relate to one another, and how to solve problems in his or her specialty. A *knowledge engineer* is a person who can take that domain knowledge and represent it in a form for use by the reasoning system. As an intermediary between the human expert and the expert system, the knowledge engineer must have good people skills as well as good technical skills. A combination of questionnaires, interviews, and first-hand observations are used to give the knowledge engineer the deep understanding required to transform the expert's knowledge into facts and rules for the knowledge base.

While essential, it soon became clear that knowledge acquisition was a difficult and costly process. Sometimes the experts weren't so keen on having their expertise captured and turned into a computer application that could put them out of a job. Sometimes the experts couldn't really explain "how" they came up with those incredible insights into problems. Sometimes, the problem was that the experts were, well, experts, and so their time was valuable. They needed to solve the problems, not spend hours talking to a knowledge engineer. A third word was soon associated with knowledge acquisition, and that word was *bottleneck*. Several major expert system projects failed in the mid- to late 1980s, and the *knowledge acquisition bottleneck* was identified as the major culprit.

At the same time, artificial intelligence researchers became interested in machine learning techniques. Using historical data from databases or examples generated by experts, neural networks could be trained to perform classification and prediction tasks without going through the expensive knowledge acquisition process. These expert networks, as they are called, performed as well as the painstakingly crafted rule-based systems in many cases. This spurred a renewed interest in adaptive systems that continues today.

Neural networks are more than a solution to the knowledge acquisition problem; they offer an alternative to symbol processing. Neural networks do not manipulate symbols, or anything that can be easily related to symbols. As a data or knowledge representation, neural networks are essentially a "black box." The topology and values of the interconnection weights define the neural network and the knowledge it encodes. This representation doesn't easily lend itself to examination or understanding at the symbolic level. Only the input fields and the output fields are identifiable. The internal states and processing are the result of an adaptive "learning" or "training" process in which data is presented to the neural network and the connection weights are automatically adjusted via a learning algorithm.

However, even though neural networks may not be easily converted to a symbolic form, they most definitely are a knowledge base, because they encode the knowledge implicit in the training data. We look at neural networks and learning in more detail in Chapter 5, "Learning Systems."

Summary

In this chapter we talked about knowledge and knowledge representation techniques commonly used in artificial intelligence programs. The main points are as follows:

- There are many types of *knowledge*, including facts and relationships, which may be organized by categories, associations, and hierarchies. The process of taking knowledge and putting it into a computer so we can use it to solve problems is called *knowledge representation*.

- A good knowledge representation must be easily understood by people. It should also be unambiguous and easily manipulated by computers and reasoning algorithms.

- There are two primary types of knowledge representations, *procedural* and *declarative*. An example of a procedural knowledge representation is program code. Most knowledge representations used in artificial intelligence are declarative.

- *Propositional* and *predicate logic* can be used to represent objects, functions, and relationships. *Resolution* and *unification* are techniques used to prove theorems and infer new facts using logic.

- *Frames* are comprised of *slots* for data values, and *fillers*, procedures for computing values and enforcing constraints between the slots. Each frame represents a concept and can be linked to other frames to form hierarchical and inheritance relationships.

- *Semantic nets* are graphs used to define relationships between concepts. Natural language labels on links show the relationships between the nodes.

- *Bayes' Rule* is the basis for Bayesian or *causal networks*, which represent probabilistic relationships between variables and allow reasoning under conditions of *uncertainty*.

- *Knowledge Interchange Format* (*KIF*) is a language designed to allow intelligent agents to exchange knowledge. KIF is based on predicate logic and supports object definitions, functions over objects, relationships between objects, and rules.

- A *knowledge base* is a collection of knowledge related to a specific problem domain. A *knowledge engineer* translates an expert's knowledge into a computer knowledge representation.

- *Machine learning* can be used to overcome the *knowledge acquisition bottleneck*. *Neural networks* can encode knowledge in their connection weights, but as a knowledge representation they are a "black box."

Exercises

1. Write a set of rules using propositional logic that represents the following knowledge:

   Intelligent agents have three major attributes: agency, intelligence, and mobility. Agency measures agent autonomy. Intelligence indicates agent reasoning or learning capabilities. Mobility means the agent can move across the network.

2. Rewrite the set of rules in Exercise 3.1 using predicate logic.

3. Create a semantic net for the domain of pizza pies or ice cream (your choice).

4. What are some of the strengths and weaknesses of the Bayesian reasoning approach? What is the basic underlying assumption concerning the relationships between variables when using Bayes' nets?

5. In this chapter, we presented KIF as one of the candidates for a standard knowledge representation for agents. Recently XML has been proposed as the standard data representation for many applications. What are some advantages and disadvantages of using XML as a knowledge representation language?

4

Reasoning Systems

In this chapter, we focus on how the various knowledge representations introduced in Chapter 3 can be used for reasoning. We implement a Java application that uses both forward- and backward-chaining algorithms to process if-then rules. We also implement a forward-chaining algorithm using fuzzy logic. Finally, we explore several artificial intelligence (AI) techniques used for planning, including goal stack planning, nonlinear planning, and hierarchical planning.

Reasoning with Rules

If-then rules have become the most popular form of declarative knowledge representation used in AI applications. There are several reasons for this. Knowledge represented as if-then rules is easily understandable. Most people are comfortable reading rules, in contrast to knowledge represented in predicate logic. Each rule can be viewed as a standalone piece of knowledge or unit of information in a knowledge base. New knowledge can be easily added, and existing knowledge can be easily changed by creating or modifying individual rules.

Rules are easily manipulated by reasoning systems. Forward chaining can be used to produce new facts (hence the term "production" rules), and backward chaining can deduce whether statements are true or not. Rule-based systems were among the first large-scale commercial successes of AI research. An *expert system* or *knowledge-based system* is the common term used to describe a rule-based processing system. It consists of three major elements: a *knowledge base* (the set of if-then rules and known facts); a *working memory* or database of derived facts and data; and an *inference engine*, which contains the reasoning logic used to process the rules and data.

Before we get into the details of reasoning with rules, let's look at the following simple rule:

```
if num_wheels = 4 and motor = yes then vehicleType = automobile
```

This rule has two *antecedent* clauses joined by a conjunction (*num_wheels* = 4 and *motor* = yes) and has a single *consequent* clause (*vehicleType* = automobile). A rule states a relationship between clauses (assertions or facts) and, depending on the situation, can be used to generate new information or prove the truth of an assertion. For example, if we know that a vehicle has four wheels and a motor, then, using the previously described rule, we can conclude that the *vehicleType* is an automobile and add that fact to our knowledge base. On the other hand, if we are trying to prove that the *vehicleType* is an automobile, we need to find out whether the vehicle has four wheels and a motor. In the first case, we are forward chaining, using facts and rules to derive new facts. In the second case, we are backward chaining, trying to prove an assertion in the consequence of a rule by showing that the antecedent clauses are true.

A rule whose antecedent clauses are all true is said to be *triggered* or *ready to fire*. We *fire* a triggered rule by asserting the consequent clause and adding it as a fact to our working memory. At any time, a rule base may contain several rules that are ready to fire. It is up to the control strategy of the inference engine to decide which one gets fired. We will discuss this point in more detail later in this chapter.

Most rule-based systems allow rules to have names or labels such as **Rule1:** or **Automobile:** to easily identify rules for editing or for tracing during inferencing. Some systems allow disjunctions (**or**) between antecedent clauses. This is a shorthand that reduces the size of a rule base. For example,

```
Rule 1: if num_wheels = 2 then vehicleType = cycle
Rule 2: if num_wheels = 3 then vehicleType = cycle
Rule 3: if (num_wheels = 2 or num_wheels = 3) then vehicleType = cycle
```

Rule 3: could replace **Rule 1:** and **Rule 2:** in the rule base. Most rule systems also allow boolean condition operators such as <, >, and != , in addition to equality. We could rewrite **Rule 3:** without using disjunctions:

```
Rule 4: if (num_wheels > 1) and (num_wheels < 4) then vehicleType = cycle
```

Another common enhancement to rule syntax is the addition of a confidence or certainty factor. If we only wrote rules that applied 100 percent of the time with 100 percent confidence, we would have a very small knowledge base. In general, we write rules that apply most of the time. These *heuristics* or "rules of thumb" are often sufficient to produce reasonable behavior from a rule-based system. However, in some cases, we must deal with uncertainty in the data, as well as our uncertainty concerning the applicability of the rule. For example, we could write a rule for weather prediction:

```
Rule 5: if (weather_forecast = rain) and (weather_probability > 80%)
then (chance_of_rain = high) with CF: 90.
```

That means if the weather forecast says rain is likely with a probability above 80 percent, then we are 90 percent certain that it will rain. If we have little confidence in our local weather prediction service, we may lower the certainty factor of the rule to 50 percent.

Many rule-based systems allow functions to be called from the antecedent clauses. These functions are called *sensors*, because they go out of the inference engine and test some condition in the environment. Sensors usually return boolean values, but they may also return data or facts to the working memory. When functions are allowed in the consequent, they are called *effectors*, which greatly expand the capability of the rule-based system. An effector turns a rule from a fact-generating mechanism into an action-generating device. These action rules allow intelligent agents to do things for us. For example, an intelligent agent that processes e-mail might contain the following rule:

```
Rule 6: if sensor(mailArrived) then effector(processMail)
```

where *mailArrived* and *processMail* are defined as functions which interface with the e-mail system, and *sensor()* and *effector()* are methods provided by the inferencing system for invoking those functions.

In small numbers, rules can adequately represent many types of domain knowledge. However, as the number of rules grows, the intuitive aspects of if-then rules are diminished, and they lose their effectiveness from a readability perspective. Commercial rule-based systems often allow grouping or partitioning of rules so that they can be treated as logical blocks of knowledge in an attempt to overcome this weakness.

Another common problem in rule-based systems is that as more complete information comes in, or as things change in the outside world, rules that may have been true before become false. The consequence is that we may have to "take back" some of the "facts" which were generated by the rules. For example, if we see that the grass is wet, we may fire a rule that concludes it is raining. However, we may then get information that the sprinkler system is on. This may cause us to retract our assertion that it is raining or at least lower our confidence or certainty in making that conclusion. This problem of dealing with changes and retracting facts or assertions is called non-monotonic reasoning. Keeping a rule base consistent by managing dependencies between inferred facts requires a truth maintenance system. Most reasoning systems, such as predicate logic, are monotonic, that is, they add information but do not retract information from the knowledge base.

In the next two sections we explore forward and backward reasoning with rules. In both sections, we will be using a simple rule base as an example. This rule base should be familiar. We described some of the relations in Chapter 3, "Knowledge Representation," when we discussed frames and semantic nets. We call it the *Vehicles Rule Base* (Figure 4.1). It has only nine rules and seven variables, with one intermediate variable. Seven of the rules define the kind of vehicle, and two are used to determine if the vehicle is a cycle or an automobile. The brevity and clarity of this small rule base will help us focus on the issues related to rule-based inferencing, and hopefully not get distracted by the details of a more complex problem domain.

Our *vehicles* domain can identify three types of cycles (one with a motor and two without) and seven types of automobiles. We differentiate cycles as having less than four

```
Vehicles Rule Base:

Bicycle: IF vehicleType=cycle
    AND num_wheels=2
    AND motor=no
    THEN vehicle=Bicycle
Tricycle: IF vehicleType=cycle
    AND num_wheels=3
    AND motor=no
    THEN vehicle=Tricycle
Motorcycle: IF vehicleType=cycle
    AND num_wheels=2
    AND motor=yes
    THEN vehicle=Motorcycle
SportsCar: IF vehicleType=automobile
    AND size=small
    AND num_doors=2
    THEN vehicle=Sports_Car
Sedan: IF vehicleType=automobile
    AND size=medium
    AND num_doors=4
    THEN vehicle=Sedan
MiniVan: IF vehicleType=automobile
    AND size=medium
    AND num_doors=3
    THEN vehicle=MiniVan
SUV: IF vehicleType=automobile
    AND size=large
    AND num_doors=4
    THEN vehicle=Sports_Utility_Vehicle
Cycle: IF num_wheels<4
    THEN vehicleType=cycle
Automobile: IF num_wheels=4
    AND motor=yes
    THEN vehicleType=automobile
```

Figure 4.1 The Vehicles Rule Base.

wheels, and automobiles as having exactly four wheels and a motor. The various types of automobiles are identified by their relative size and the number of doors they have.

Forward Chaining

Forward chaining is a data-driven reasoning process in which a set of rules is used to derive new facts from an initial set of data. It does not use the resolution algorithm used in predicate logic. The forward-chaining algorithm generates new data by the simple and straightforward application or firing of the rules. As an inferencing procedure, forward chaining is very fast. Early expert system applications of forward chaining include R1/XCON, an expert system used to build configurations for Digital Equipment Corporation's VAX computer systems [McDermott 1982], and PROSPECTOR, a system used to predict the location of mineral deposits from prospecting data [Duda, et al. 1977]. Forward chaining is also used in real-time monitoring and diagnostic systems where quick identification and response to problems are required.

Several commercial tools were developed primarily to do forward-chaining reasoning. The OPS5 language and the later, enhanced OPS83 were developed at Carnegie-Mellon University. OPS5 was used to implement the R1 system. IBM developed KnowledgeTool and TIRS (The Integrated Reasoning System), which were primarily forward-chaining tools. In addition to providing the reasoning capabilities, these commercial systems also provided several different control strategies and the ability to mix in procedural program code, effectively giving sensor and effector capabilities.

Later in this chapter, we are going to implement a forward-chaining system, but first, let's look at the reasoning process in more detail. As mentioned before, any expert system requires three basic elements, a knowledge base of rules and facts, a working memory for storing data during inferencing, and an inference engine. The following steps are part of the forward-chaining cycle:

1. Load the rule base into the inference engine and load any facts from the knowledge base into the working memory.
2. Add any additional initial data into the working memory.
3. *Match* the rules against the data in the working memory and determine which rules are triggered, meaning that all of their antecedent clauses are true. This set of triggered rules is called the *conflict set*.
4. Use the *conflict resolution* procedure to select a single rule from the conflict set.
5. *Fire* the selected rule by evaluating the consequent clause(s); either update the working memory if it is a fact-generating rule, or call the effector procedure, if it is an action rule. This is referred to as the *act* step.
6. Repeat steps 3, 4, and 5 until the conflict set is empty.

During the match phase of forward chaining the inference system compares the known facts or working memory against the antecedent clauses in the rules to determine which rule or rules could fire. In a knowledge base with many facts and rules, the match phase can take an enormous amount of processing time. Thus, we would like to only test those rules whose antecedent clauses refer to facts that have been updated by the prior rule's firing. The *Rete* algorithm, developed for the OPS5 language, builds a network data structure to manage the dependencies between the data, condition tests, and rules, and minimizes the number of tests required for each match operation [Forgy 1982]. While the *Rete* algorithm is the Cadillac of match algorithms, many forward-chaining systems use methods that are less efficient but easier to implement.

Once we have completed the match phase and produced the conflict set, we move to the conflict resolution step. Conflict resolution is perhaps the most important step in terms of the behavior of the forward-chaining inferencing system. When the conflict set is empty or contains only a single rule, the problem is trivial. However, in many cases, there will be more than one rule that is triggered. Which rule do we select to fire? Several alternatives are available, as follows:

- Select the first rule in the conflict set. This is certainly simple, and for some domains it works.

- Select the rule with the highest specificity or number of antecedent clauses. The idea here is to select the rule that is the most specific (has the most test conditions on the *if* part of the rule) before we fire more general rules that have fewer antecedent clauses.

- Select the rule that refers to the data that has changed most recently. This method requires that changes to the working memory are time-stamped or somehow tagged to show when they were last modified.

- If the rule has fired on the previous cycle, do not add it to the conflict set. This strategy is sometimes extended to limit rules so they can only fire once.

- In cases where there is a tie, select a rule randomly from this subset of the original conflict set.

In addition to match and conflict resolution, forward-chaining systems often utilize one of several control strategies to help guide the inferencing process. Note that this practice is a diversion from the pure declarative approach of if-then rules. However, to build practical working forward-chaining expert systems these control strategies are required. This is a case of real-world pragmatism versus academic idealism.

A common control strategy in rule-based systems is to assign priorities to rules that can be used to aid in the selection process. If we have a process that proceeds in three phases, we can assign priority 1 to the set of rules that contribute to the first phase, priority 2 to the rules in the second phase, and likewise for the third subset of rules. The advantage of using priorities is that it greatly reduces the number of rules that have to be searched and tested in the match phase.

Another approach that can be used to achieve the same results, even if the inferencing system doesn't formally support priorities, is to use guard clauses. For example, we could add a clause priority = 1 to the antecedents of all rules in group one, priority = 2 in group two and so on. While less efficient than if the inferencing system supports priorities, it does produce the desired behavior.

A Forward-Chaining Example

In this section, we take a look at a simple example of forward chaining in our vehicle domain. To start, we load our Vehicles rule base into the inference engine and define a set of initial values for variables in the working memory, as follows:

```
num_wheels=4
motor=yes
num_doors = 3
size=medium
```

Next, we do a match phase in which we examine the antecedent clauses of each rule to determine which ones can be triggered. We have no value for *vehicleType*, so the first seven rules are not triggered. The last two rules require values for *num_wheels* and *motor*, so they are candidates. The *num_wheels < 4* clause in the **Cycle:** rule is false, so that is not triggered, but *num_wheels = 4* and *motor = yes* are both true and so the **Automobile:** rule is triggered. Our conflict set from our first match cycle contains a single rule, the **Automobile:** rule.

```
Automobile: IF num_wheels=4
  AND motor=yes
  THEN vehicleType=automobile
```

Conflict resolution is easy: We select the single rule and fire it in the act cycle. Firing the **Automobile:** rule causes us to bind the value "automobile" to the *vehicleType* variable, and add it to our working memory:

```
num_wheels=4
motor=yes
num_doors = 3
size=medium
vehicleType=automobile
```

Now we are ready for our next inferencing cycle. We do a match against the rules to determine which ones could be fired. Now that *vehicleType* has a value, the first seven rules are candidates. However, the first three rules require that *vehicleType* = cycle, which is false. This leaves the next four rules: **SportsCar:**, **Sedan:**, **MiniVan:**, and **SUV:**. Only a single rule has all of its antecedent clauses satisfied, the **MiniVan:** rule with *num_doors = 3* and *size = medium*. Once again, our conflict set has only a single rule in it.

```
MiniVan: IF vehicleType=automobile
  AND size=medium
  AND num_doors=3
  THEN vehicle=MiniVan
```

We fire the **MiniVan:** rule and add the new information that *vehicle = MiniVan* to the working memory.

```
num_wheels=4
motor=yes
num_doors = 3
size=medium
vehicleType=automobile
vehicle=MiniVan
```

We do yet another match phase and find that only one rule is triggered again, the **Mini-Van:** rule. However, because it has already fired, we do not add it to the conflict set. Our conflict set is now empty, so we halt our forward-chaining inferencing. In this example, we started with four facts and computed two new facts, determining that the *vehicle* is a *MiniVan*.

Backward Chaining

Backward chaining is often called goal-directed inferencing, because a particular consequence or goal clause is evaluated first, and then we go backward through the rules. Unlike forward chaining, which uses rules to produce new information, backward chaining uses rules to answer questions about whether a goal clause is true or not. Backward chaining is more focused than forward chaining, because it only processes rules that are relevant to the question. It is similar to how resolution is used in predicate logic. However, it does not use contradiction. It simply traverses the rule base trying to prove that clauses are true in a systematic manner.

Backward chaining is used for advisory expert systems, where users ask questions and get asked leading questions to find an answer. A famous early expert system, Mycin, used backward chaining to perform diagnoses of bacterial infections in medical patients [Shortliffe 1976].

One advantage of backward chaining is that, because the inferencing is directed, information can be requested from the user when it is needed. Some reasoning systems also provide a trace capability that allows the user to ask the inference engine why it is asking for some piece of information, or why it came to some conclusion.

We are going to implement a backward-chaining system later in this chapter. Now, let's look at the steps that are part of the backward-chaining cycle.

1. Load the rule base into the inference engine and load any facts from the knowledge base into the working memory.

2. Add any additional initial data into the working memory.

3. Specify a goal variable for the inference engine to find.

4. Find the set of rules that refer to the goal variable in a consequent clause. That is, find all rules which set the value of the goal variable when they fire. Put each rule on the goal stack.

5. If the goal stack is empty, halt.

6. Take the top rule off the goal stack.

7. Try to prove the rule is true by testing all antecedent clauses to see if they are true. We test each antecedent clause, in turn, as follows:

   a. If the clause is true, go on to the next antecedent clause.

   b. If the clause is false, then pop the rule off the goal stack; go to step 5.

   c. If the truth value is unknown because the antecedent variable is unknown, go to step 4, with the antecedent variable as the new goal variable.

   d. If all antecedent clauses are true, fire the rule, setting the consequent variable to the consequent value, pop the rule off the goal stack, and go to 5.

Let's look more closely at how the backward-chaining algorithm works using a rule from our Vehicles rule base as an example. Suppose we want to find out whether the *vehicle* we have is a *MiniVan*. This is the rule that must be satisfied:

```
MiniVan: IF vehicleType=automobile
  AND size=medium
  AND num_doors=3
THEN vehicle=MiniVan
```

We start with an empty working memory. No facts are known about the vehicle attributes. The first thing we would do is check working memory to see if *vehicle = MiniVan* is already true. If not, then all of the antecedent clauses of the **MiniVan:** rule must be true to safely conclude that the *vehicle* is a *MiniVan*. Consequently, we must try to prove each antecedent clause in turn. The first thing we do is test if *vehicleType = automobile* is true. The *vehicleType* variable has no value, so we look for a rule that has *vehicleType = automobile* in its consequent clause, and find the **Automobile:** rule below:

```
Automobile: IF num_wheels=4
  AND motor=yes
  THEN vehicleType=automobile
```

This is an example of backward chaining. We start with the **MiniVan:** rule, and, in the course of proving that true, we have chained to another rule, the **Automobile:** rule. These rules are linked by the *vehicleType = automobile* clause that they both share. Focused now on the **Automobile:** rule, we need to know if *num_wheels = 4*. We look in the working memory and see that *num_wheels* has no value. We look for a rule that has *num_wheels = 4* as a consequent. There are none. Now, we could either give up, or we could ask the user to provide an answer. We ask the user, who says there are four wheels on the vehicle. The first antecedent clause is true, so we move onto the second clause, *motor = yes*. We check the working memory, and *motor* has no value. We again search the rule base for a rule with *motor = yes* in the consequent and can find none. We ask the user to provide a value. The user answers that the vehicle has a motor, so *motor = yes* is true. Both of the antecedent clauses are now true. We have proved that the **Automobile:** rule is true, and we can set *vehicleType = automobile*. Our working memory now contains the following facts:

```
num_wheels=4
motor=yes
vehicleType=automobile
```

Going back to our original rule, we now know that the first antecedent clause is true. We next need to find values for *size* and *num_doors*. Using the same process described previously, we end up asking the user for these values. The user indicates that *size = medium* and *num_doors = 3*. All the antecedent clauses have been satisfied, so we can conclude that the *vehicle* is a *MiniVan*. Our final working memory contains:

```
num_wheels=4
motor=yes
vehicleType=automobile
size=medium
num_doors=3
vehicle=MiniVan
```

While our little example worked out, in many cases the rule we are trying to prove is not true. We may need to search other paths through alternate rules in order to answer the user's question. The backward-chaining algorithm performs what amounts to a depth-first search through the rule base while trying to prove a goal clause.

Fuzzy Rule Systems

In the rich history of rule-based reasoning in AI, the inference engines almost without exception were based on Boolean or binary logic. However, in the same way that neural networks have enriched the AI landscape by providing an alternative to symbol processing techniques, fuzzy logic has provided an alternative to Boolean logic-based systems [Bigus 1996].

Fuzzy logic is not just probability in a different guise. Probability theory deals with the chance or *likelihood* that an event will occur,

Tomorrow there is a 50% chance that it will rain,

while fuzzy logic deals with the *degree* to which an event occurs,

Tomorrow it will rain hard.

What does that mean? People talk that way all of the time. Does it mean that it will rain half an inch or a tenth of an inch per hour for a 30-minute period? The degree that something occurs is a fuzzy, ill-defined condition. If water drops into the rain gauge, then it rained. That's a fact. Whether it rained hard is a matter of degree (and opinion).

Unlike Boolean logic, which has only two states, true or false, fuzzy logic deals with truth values which range continuously from 0.0 to 1.0. Thus something could be *half true* (0.5) or *very likely true* (0.9) or *probably not true* (0.1). The use of fuzzy logic in reasoning systems impacts not only the inference engine, but the knowledge representation itself [Zadeh 1994]. Instead of making arbitrary distinctions between variables and states, as is required with Boolean logic systems, fuzzy logic allows one to express knowledge in a rule format that is close to a natural language expression. For example, if we had a set of fuzzy rules to control the speed of the motor on a fan (see Figure 4.2), we could say

if temperature is hot and humidity is sticky then motor is fast

The difference between this fuzzy rule and the Boolean-logic rules we used in our forward- and backward-chaining examples is that the clauses "temperature is hot" and "humidity is sticky" are not strictly true or false. Clauses in fuzzy rules are real-valued functions called *membership functions* that map the fuzzy set *hot* onto the domain of the fuzzy variable *temperature* and produce a truth-value that ranges from 0.0 to 1.0 (a continuous output value). Fuzzy variables are also called *linguistic* variables, because they map naturally to concepts we use in everyday language.

Reasoning in fuzzy rule systems is a forward-chaining procedure. The initial numeric data values are *fuzzified*, that is, turned into fuzzy values using the membership functions. Instead of a match and conflict resolution phase where we select a triggered rule to fire, in fuzzy systems, all rules are evaluated, because every fuzzy rule can be true to some degree (ranging from 0.0 to 1.0). The antecedent clause truth values are com-

```
Motor Fuzzy Rule Base:

SlowRule: IF temp is cold
    AND humidity is pleasant
    THEN motor is slow.
MediumRule: IF temp is medium
    AND humidity is comfortable
    THEN motor is medium.
FastRule: IF temp is hot
    AND humidity is sticky
    THEN motor is fast.
VeryFastRule: IF temp is very hot
    AND humidity is very sticky
    THEN motor is very fast.
```

Figure 4.2 The motor fuzzy rule base.

bined using fuzzy logic operators; a fuzzy conjunction (**and** operation) takes the minimum value of the two fuzzy clauses. Next, the fuzzy sets specified in the consequent clauses of all rules are combined, using one of the fuzzy compositional rules of inference. The result is a single output fuzzy set, which is then *defuzzified* to return a crisp output value.

There are two major methods for inferencing in fuzzy rule systems, the *min-max* approach and the *fuzzy additive* approach. In min-max, each rule's consequent fuzzy set is limited to the minimum of the antecedent truth values. The output fuzzy set is computed by taking the maximum of the minimized consequent fuzzy set from each rule [Cox 1994]. The other method, fuzzy additive, also limits the consequent fuzzy set to the minimum truth value of the antecedent. Instead of taking the maximum of the resulting consequent fuzzy sets, the two truth values are summed (hence, fuzzy additive) and limited to a maximum value of 1.0. This slight modification over the min-max method insures that all of the rules in a fuzzy set can contribute something to the final result set. Using min-max, only rules that have a truth value greater than the output fuzzy set truth value can contribute to the result.

Both min-max and fuzzy additive inferencing techniques reduce the truth of the consequent fuzzy set before the output fuzzy set is updated. These approaches are based on the idea that the truth of the fuzzy consequent can't be greater than the truth of the antecedent. There are two methods of correlating or limiting the height of the consequent based on the antecedents: *minimum correlation* and *product correlation*. The minimum correlation technique truncates the consequent fuzzy set to the minimum of the antecedent's truth value. The effect is to clip the consequent fuzzy set and create a plateau. This distorts the consequent fuzzy set shape, and some information is lost as a result. The product correlation method maintains the shape of the consequent fuzzy set by simply scaling it by the truth value of the antecedent [Cox 1994].

Once the output fuzzy set is computed using one of the correlation and inferencing techniques described previously, the fuzzy set must be defuzzified or converted back to a crisp numeric value. There are two common techniques for defuzzification, centroid and maximum height. In centroid defuzzification, the center of gravity of the fuzzy set is found by computing a weighted mean of the fuzzy set. This means that approximately half of the area under the membership function is above the centroid point, while half is below it. The centroid approach is the most widely used technique because the defuzzified values change smoothly as the shape of the fuzzy set changes, and it is relatively easy to calculate. The maximum height finds the center point in the region with the maximum truth value. Conceptually, if the fuzzy set came to a point, the maximum height would be the domain value at that point. If it came to a plateau, the defuzzified value would be the center of the plateau.

Fuzzy membership functions can be defined as having any shape over the domain or range of discourse of the linguistic variable that maps to values between 0.0 and 1.0. Typical fuzzy sets are made up of line segments forming triangles and trapezoids, or Gaussian-shaped functions. In this book, we use three basic fuzzy sets: triangle, trapezoid, and a shoulder set that is like one half of a trapezoid, with a plateau of 1.0 to the left or right and a slope down to a value of 0.0 at some point in the domain. Figure 4.3 shows examples of these fuzzy sets.

The Rule Application

In this section, we present a Java application that implements both Boolean and fuzzy logic-based inferencing and demonstrates the two major types of reasoning algorithms used with rule-based systems: forward and backward chaining.

The *Rule* application classes, **RuleApp**, which contains our *main()*, and **RuleFrame**, which implements our main window, were constructed using the Borland/Inprise JBuilder 3.0 Java interactive development environment. The visual builder allows us to

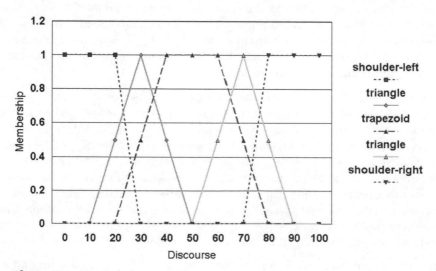

Figure 4.3 Example fuzzy sets.

create the complete GUI using Java **Swing** components in a drag-and-drop style. JBuilder automatically generates the Java code for creating the GUI controls and action event handlers in the **RuleFrame** class. We then added the logic for creating the sample **RuleBases** and invoking the reasoning algorithms. The **RuleApp** code that invokes the **RuleFrame** is not presented here. It simply instantiates the **RuleFrame** class and displays it. Likewise, a substantial amount of the code in the **RuleFrame** class deals with GUI control logic and we will not present that material here. Instead, we will highlight only brief sections of the GUI code that demonstrate how to use the underlying application classes. All of the classes discussed in this chapter are in the **rule** package, shown in Figure 4.4.

The **RuleFrame** class uses two sets of classes, one for the standard Boolean forward- and backward-chaining inference engine, and another for the fuzzy logic-based forward-chaining inference engine. A **RuleBase** interface is defined along with the **BooleanRuleBase** and **FuzzyRuleBase** classes.

The *Rule* application features a set of controls for selecting **Forward chain** or **Backward chain** inferencing, the **Goal** variable and **Result** when backward chaining is

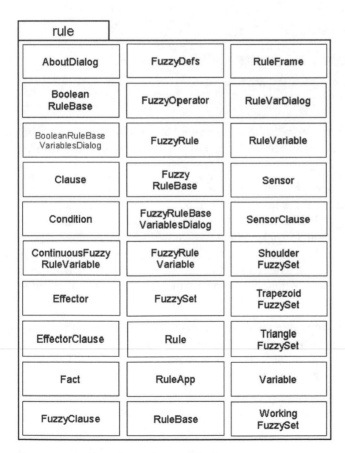

rule

AboutDialog	FuzzyDefs	RuleFrame
Boolean RuleBase	FuzzyOperator	RuleVarDialog
BooleanRuleBase VariablesDialog	FuzzyRule	RuleVariable
Clause	Fuzzy RuleBase	Sensor
Condition	FuzzyRuleBase VariablesDialog	SensorClause
ContinuousFuzzy RuleVariable	FuzzyRule Variable	Shoulder FuzzySet
Effector	FuzzySet	Trapezoid FuzzySet
EffectorClause	Rule	Triangle FuzzySet
Fact	RuleApp	Variable
FuzzyClause	RuleBase	Working FuzzySet

Figure 4.4 The rule package UML diagram.

Figure 4.5 The *Rule* application window.

selected, and a text area for displaying the rule base, the variables, and their current values, and a trace of the inferencing process. Figure 4.5 shows the *Rule* application window.

At the top of the window, you can choose one of the four sample rule bases provided by selecting them from the **RuleBase** pull-down menu. Under the **Data** pull-down menu, you can select either to **Use default values**, or **Set values . . .** to bring up a dialog that allows you to set individual variables to user-specified values. Four example rule bases are provided: the Vehicles rule base already discussed, a bugs rule base, a plants rule base, and a motor rule base. The rules of the selected rule base are displayed in the text area in the main window. Whenever variable values are changed, the new values are shown in the text area.

Near the top of the **RuleFrame** window, two radio button controls allow you to specify whether forward or backward chaining should be used. If backward chaining is specified, the name of the goal variable must be entered in the **Goal** text field to the right of the **Backward chaining** radio button.

There are two menu items under the **File** pull-down menu. To start an inferencing cycle with the currently selected rule base and current variable values, select the **Start** menu item. If forward chaining is specified, the rule base will be evaluated and the results will be displayed in the text area. If backward chaining is specified, then the *Goal* variable must be selected. Only the **BooleanRuleBase** supports backward chaining. When the backward chaining completes, the result will be displayed in the **Results** text field at the top of the window. After a **Start** inferencing cycle is performed, the user can press the **Reset** menu item on the **File** pull-down menu to set all of the rule-based variables to null values. After a **Reset**, you must go to the **Data** menu and select either the **Use default values** menu item, or select the **Set values . . .** menu item to set the variables to custom values.

We start our examination of the *Rule* application by looking at the classes that make up the Boolean rule base. These include the **Rule** class, the **RuleVariable** class, and the **RuleBase** class, as well as several support classes such as **Clause**. We start our discussion with the **Rule** class.

Rules

The **Rule** class is used to define a single rule and also contains methods that support the inferencing process. Each **Rule** has a *name* data member, a reference to the owning **BooleanRuleBase** object (described later), an array of antecedent **Clauses**, and a single consequent **Clause**. The **Rule**'s truth value is stored in the **Boolean** *truth*. Note, this is a **Boolean** object, not an elementary boolean variable. This allows us to use a null value to indicate that the rule's truth cannot be determined (because one of the variables referenced in a clause is also null or undefined). The *fired* boolean member indicates whether this rule has been fired or not.

There are several **Rule** constructors, each requiring a reference to the **BooleanRule-Base** instance, the **Rule** name, one or more antecedent or left-hand-side (LHS) clauses, and the single consequent or right-hand-side (RHS) clause. Each constructor allocates the correct number of entries in the *antecedents* array, and also registers itself with the **Clause** objects. It also adds the clauses to its data members. The *truth* is initialized to null, meaning undefined or unknown, and the **Rule** registers itself with the owning **BooleanRuleBase**.

```
package rule;

import java.util.*;
import java.io.*;
import java.awt.*;
import javax.swing.*;

public class Rule {
  BooleanRuleBase rb;
  String name;
  Clause antecedents[];
  Clause consequent;
  Boolean truth;
  boolean fired = false;

  public Rule(BooleanRuleBase rb, String name, Clause lhs, Clause rhs) {
    this.rb = rb;
    this.name = name;
```

```
        antecedents = new Clause[1];
        antecedents[0] = lhs;
        lhs.addRuleRef(this);
        consequent = rhs;
        rhs.addRuleRef(this);
        rhs.setConsequent();
        rb.ruleList.addElement(this);
        truth = null;
    }

    public Rule(BooleanRuleBase rb, String name, Clause[] lhsClauses,
                Clause rhs) {
        this.rb = rb;
        this.name = name;
        antecedents = new Clause[lhsClauses.length];
        for(int i = 0; i < lhsClauses.length; i++) {
            antecedents[i] = lhsClauses[i];
            antecedents[i].addRuleRef(this);
        }
        consequent = rhs;
        rhs.addRuleRef(this);
        rhs.setConsequent();
        rb.ruleList.addElement(this);
        truth = null;
    }
    ...   ...   ...
}
```

Clauses

Clauses are used both in the antecedent and consequent parts of a **Rule**. A **Clause** is usually made up of a **RuleVariable** on the left-hand side; a **Condition**, which tests equality, greater than, or less than; and the right-hand side, which in our implementation is a **String** (symbolic or numeric) value. For example, the rule

```
Automobile: IF num_wheels=4
  AND motor=yes
  THEN vehicleType=automobile
```

contains three clauses. The first antecedent clause is made up of the **RuleVariable** *num_wheels*, the **Condition** "=", and the **String** *4*. The other clauses are similarly composed. A **Clause** also contains a **Vector** of the **Rules** which contain this **Clause**; a *consequent* **boolean** which indicates whether the clause appears in the antecedent or the consequent of the rule; and a *truth* **Boolean** which indicates whether the clause is true, false, or unknown (null).

As shown in Figure 4.6, the **Clause** constructor takes a **RuleVariable** for the left-hand side, a **Condition** object, and a **String** for the right-hand side. The **Clause** registers itself with the **RuleVariable** so that whenever the variable's value is changed, the

```
package rule;

import java.util.*;
import java.io.*;

public class Clause {
  Vector ruleRefs;
  RuleVariable lhs;
  String rhs;
  Condition cond;
  boolean consequent;
  Boolean truth;

  public Clause(RuleVariable lhs, Condition cond, String rhs) {
    this.lhs = lhs;
    this.cond = cond;
    this.rhs = rhs;
    lhs.addClauseRef(this);
    ruleRefs = new Vector();
    truth = null;
    consequent = false;
  }

  public Clause() {}

  public String toString() {
    return lhs.name + cond.toString() + rhs + " ";
  }

  public void addRuleRef(Rule ref) {
    ruleRefs.addElement(ref);
  }

  public Boolean check() {
    if(consequent == true) {
      return truth = null;
    }
    if(lhs.value == null) {
      return truth = null;
    } else {
      Double lhsNumericValue = null;
      Double rhsNumericValue = null;
      boolean bothNumeric = true;

      try {
        lhsNumericValue = Double.valueOf(lhs.value);
```

(continues)

Figure 4.6   The Clause class listing.

```
            rhsNumericValue = Double.valueOf(rhs);
        } catch(Exception e) {
        bothNumeric = false;
        }
    switch(cond.index) {
        case 1:
            if(bothNumeric) {
                truth = new Boolean(lhsNumericValue.compareTo
                (rhsNumericValue)
                    == 0);
            } else {
                truth = new Boolean(lhs.value.equalsIgnoreCase(rhs));
            }
            break;
        case 2:
            if(bothNumeric) {
                truth = new Boolean(lhsNumericValue.compareTo
                (rhsNumericValue)
                    > 0);
            } else {
                truth = new Boolean(lhs.value.compareTo(rhs) > 0);
            }
            break;
        case 3:
            if(bothNumeric) {
                truth = new Boolean(lhsNumericValue.compareTo
                (rhsNumericValue)
                    < 0);
            } else {
                truth = new Boolean(lhs.value.compareTo(rhs) < 0);
            }
            break;
        case 4:
            if(bothNumeric) {
                truth = new Boolean(lhsNumericValue.compareTo
                (rhsNumericValue)
                    != 0);
            } else {
                truth = new Boolean(lhs.value.compareTo(rhs) != 0);
            }
            break;
        }
    return truth;
    }
}

public void setConsequent() {
```

Figure 4.6 The Clause class listing (Continued).

```
    consequent = true;
  }

  public Rule getRule() {
    if(consequent == true) {
      return (Rule) ruleRefs.firstElement();
    } else {
      return null;
    }
  }
}
```

Figure 4.6 Continued.

Clause can be automatically retested. The *consequent* **boolean** is set to false initially, because most clauses are antecedent clauses.

The **Clause** class contains four methods. The *addRuleRef()* method is used by the **Rule** constructor to register the **Rule** with this **Clause**. The *check()* method performs a test of the clause. If the clause is used as a consequent clause, then testing its truth value makes no sense; we return a null value. If the variable on the left-hand side is unbound, we also return null, because a truth value cannot be determined. If the variable is bound, we use the switch statement to test the specified logical condition and return the resulting truth value. The *setConsequent()* method sets the *consequent* **boolean** to true and the *getRule()* method returns a reference to the owning **Rule** instance.

The **Condition** class, listed in Figure 4.7, is a helper class to **Clause**. It takes a **String** representation of a conditional test and converts that into a code for use in the *switch* statement in the *Clause.check()* method.

Variables

We define an abstract base class for variables that support the function we need for rule processing and for learning in the next chapter. The **Variable** class, listed in Figure 4.8, has a *name* member to identify the variable, and a **String** *value* member (which could be an **Object** in a more general-purpose application). The *labels* member is used to hold discrete symbols for categorical variables. The *column* is used to specify the position of the variable in a data file. There is a default constructor, as well as one where the name is specified. Two accessor methods are provided to set the *value* and get the *value* of the **Variable**. The *setLabels()* method is used to define the valid symbolic values for categorical variables. The *getLabel()* method returns the symbolic value for the specified index and the inverse method *getIndex()* returns the index given a symbolic value. An example of how these methods are used is shown in the section on the *Vehicles Rule Base* implementation where the **Variables** are defined.

```
package rule;

import java.util.*;
import java.io.*;

public class Condition {
  int index;
  String symbol;

  public Condition(String symbol) {
    this.symbol = symbol;
    if(symbol.equals("=")) {
      index = 1;
    } else if(symbol.equals(">")) {
      index = 2;
    } else if(symbol.equals("<")) {
      index = 3;
    } else if(symbol.equals("!=")) {
      index = 4;
    } else {
      index = -1;
    }
  }

  public String toString() {
    return symbol;
  }
}
```

Figure 4.7 The Condition class listing.

Rule Variables

For rule processing, we subclass the **Variable** class and add some rule-specific behavior. The **RuleVariable** class, defined in Figure 4.9, provides the support necessary for variables used in inferencing. The constructor takes the *name* of the variable as the only parameter. **RuleVariables** inherit the discrete symbolic behavior of the base **Variable** class. A new data member is the **Vector** *clauseRefs*, which holds references to all **Clause**s that refer to this variable. Instances of **Clause** register themselves by calling the *addClauseRef()* method. There are several methods that are overridden as well as some new ones added for rule processing. The *setValue()* method not only sets the *value* of the variable, it also calls the *updateClauses()* method, which iterates through every **Clause** that refers to this **RuleVariable** and retests its *truth* value via its *check()* method.

The *promptString* holds the text that is displayed when the user is prompted to provide a value for this variable during backward chaining. The *ruleName* holds the name of the

```
package rule;

import java.util.*;
import java.io.*;

public abstract class Variable {
  protected String name;
  protected String value;
  protected Vector labels;
  protected int column;

  public Variable() {}

  public Variable(String name) {
    this.name = name;
    value = null;
  }

  public String getName() {
    return name;
  }

  public void setValue(String value) {
    this.value = value;
  }

  public String getValue() {
    return value;
  }

  public void setLabels(String newLabels) {
    labels = new Vector();
    StringTokenizer tok = new StringTokenizer(newLabels, " ");

    while(tok.hasMoreTokens()) {
      labels.addElement(new String(tok.nextToken()));
    }
  }

  public String getLabel(int index) {
    return (String) labels.elementAt(index);
  }

  public Vector getLabels() {
    return (Vector) labels.clone();
  }
```

(continues)

Figure 4.8   The Variable class listing.

```java
public String getLabelsAsString() {
  String labelList = new String();
  Enumeration enum = labels.elements();

  while(enum.hasMoreElements()) {
    labelList += enum.nextElement() + " ";
  }
  return labelList;
}

public int getIndex(String label) {
  int index = -1;

  if(labels == null) {
    return index;
  }
  for(int i = 0; i < labels.size(); i++) {
    if(label.equals((String) labels.elementAt(i))) {
      index = i;
      break;
    }
  }
  return index;
}

public boolean categorical() {
  if(labels != null) {
    return true;
  } else {
    return false;
  }
}

public String toString() {
  return name;
}

public void setColumn(int column) {
  this.column = column;
}

public abstract void computeStatistics(String inValue);

public abstract int normalize(String inValue, float[] outArray,
  int inx);

public int normalizedSize() {
```

Figure 4.8 The Variable class listing (Continued).

```
      return 1;
   }

   public String getDecodedValue(float[] act, int index) {
     return String.valueOf(act[index]);
   }
}
```

Figure 4.8 Continued.

```
package rule;

import java.util.*;
import java.awt.*;
import javax.swing.*;

public class RuleVariable extends Variable {
  protected BooleanRuleBase rb;
  protected Vector clauseRefs;
  protected String promptText;
  protected String ruleName;

  public RuleVariable(BooleanRuleBase rb, String name) {
    super(name);
    this.rb = rb;
    rb.addVariable(this);
    clauseRefs = new Vector();
  }

  public void setValue(String value) {
    this.value = value;
    updateClauses();
  }

  public String askUser() {
    String answer = null;
    JFrame frame = new JFrame();
    RuleVarDialog dlg = new RuleVarDialog(frame, "Ask User for Value",
                          true);

    dlg.setLocation(200, 200);
    dlg.setData(this);
    dlg.show();
    answer = dlg.getData();
```

(continues)

Figure 4.9 The RuleVariable class listing.

```
      setValue(answer);
      return value;
   }

   public void addClauseRef(Clause ref) {
      clauseRefs.addElement(ref);
   }

   public void updateClauses() {
      Enumeration enum = clauseRefs.elements();

      while(enum.hasMoreElements()) {
         ((Clause) enum.nextElement()).check();
      }
   }

   public void setRuleName(String ruleName) {
      this.ruleName = ruleName;
   }

   public void setPromptText(String prompText) {
      this.promptText = prompText;
   }

   public String getPromptText() {
      return promptText;
   }

   public void computeStatistics(String inValue) {}
   ;

   public int normalize(String inValue, float[] outArray, int inx) {
      return inx;
   }
}
```

Figure 4.9   The RuleVariable class listing (Continued).

rule which set this **RuleVariable**'s value. When the rule fires, it calls the *setRuleName()* method. The *askUser()* method instantiates a **RuleVarDialog** to prompt the user to supply a value (because it cannot be inferred). The dialog is modal, so control will only return after the user responds to the **RuleVarDialog**. The answer is then passed in as the **RuleVariable** value via the *setValue()* method call. This, in turn, updates all clauses that reference this **RuleVariable**. This method is used only by the backward-chaining algorithm.

```
package rule;

import java.util.*;
import javax.swing.*;

public interface RuleBase {
  public void setDisplay(JTextArea txtArea);

  public void trace(String text);

  public void displayVariables(JTextArea textArea);

  public void displayRules(JTextArea textArea);

  public void reset();

  public void backwardChain(String goalVarName);

  public void forwardChain();

  public Vector getGoalVariables();
}
```

Figure 4.10   The RuleBase Interface listing.

Boolean Rule Base

The **BooleanRuleBase** class, listed in Figure 4.10, defines a set of **RuleVariable**s and **Rule**s, along with the high-level methods for forward and backward chaining. The **BooleanRuleBase** has a *name*, a *variableList* that contains all of the **RuleVariable**s referenced by the **Rule**s, and the *ruleList*, which contains all of the **Rule**s. The *forwardChain()* and *backwardChain()* methods as well as other **BooleanRuleBase** data members that are used by the inferencing algorithms are described in their respective sections later in this chapter.

```
package rule;

import java.util.*;
import java.io.*;
import java.awt.*;
import javax.swing.*;

public class BooleanRuleBase implements RuleBase {
  String name;
  Hashtable variableList = new Hashtable();
  Clause clauseVarList[];
  Vector ruleList = new Vector();
```

```
      Vector conclusionVarList;
      Rule rulePtr;
      Clause clausePtr;
      Stack goalClauseStack = new Stack();
      Hashtable effectors;
      Hashtable sensors;
      Vector factList;
      JTextArea textArea1;

      public BooleanRuleBase(String name) {
        this.name = name;
      }
      ... ... ...
    }
```

The **BooleanRuleBase** class implements the **RuleBase** interface. This interface defines common behavior so that the **RuleFrame** can manage both Boolean and Fuzzy rule bases. It defines a set of GUI-oriented methods such as *setDisplay()*, *displayVariables()*, *displayRules()*, and *getGoalVariables()* and a set of common processing methods including *reset()*, *backwardChain()*, and *forwardChain()*.

Forward-Chaining Implementation

The forward-chaining implementation uses methods in both the **BooleanRuleBase** class and the **Rule** class. The *forwardChain()* method in the **BooleanRuleBase** class contains the main control logic for forward chaining. The method first allocates the *conflictRuleSet* vector. The *match()* method is called with a boolean true parameter to force an initial test of all rules in the rule base. This returns with the initial *conflictRuleSet*, a **Vector** of the rules that are triggered and could be fired. We then enter a *while()* loop, which runs until we have an empty *conflictRuleSet*. Inside the loop, we first call the *selectRule()* method, passing the *conflictRuleSet* as a parameter. The *selectRule()* method performs the conflict resolution strategy and returns with a single rule to fire. We call the **Rule** *fire()* method to perform the consequent clause assignment, and then retest all **Clause**s and **Rule**s which refer to the updated **Variable**. While not a *Rete* implementation, this approach limits the amount of clause testing that needs to be performed. With the updated *variableList*, we call *match()* again, but this time we pass in a boolean false parameter value. This tells *match()* to only look at the rule truth values, not to test each rule.

```
    public void forwardChain() {
      Vector conflictRuleSet = new Vector();

      conflictRuleSet = match(true);
      while(conflictRuleSet.size() > 0) {
        Rule selected = selectRule(conflictRuleSet);

        selected.fire();
        conflictRuleSet = match(false);
      }
    }
```

Now let's look at the individual methods in more detail. The **BooleanRuleBase** *match()* method takes a single boolean parameter. It walks through the *ruleList*. If the *test* parameter is true, it calls the **Rule** *check()* method to test all rule antecedent clauses and set the rule's truth value. If *test* is false, *match()* simply looks at the current rule's truth value. If the rule is true, and it hasn't already been fired, it will add it to the *matchList* **Vector**. If not, we just continue on to the next **Rule** on the *ruleList*. For tracing purposes, we display the conflict set.

```
public Vector match(boolean test) {
   Vector matchList = new Vector();
   Enumeration enum = ruleList.elements();

   while(enum.hasMoreElements()) {
     Rule testRule = (Rule) enum.nextElement();

     if(test) {
       testRule.check();
     }
     if(testRule.truth == null) {
       continue;
     }
     if((testRule.truth.booleanValue() == true)
         && (testRule.fired == false)) {
       matchList.addElement(testRule);
     }
   }
   displayConflictSet(matchList);
   return matchList;
}
```

The **BooleanRuleBase** *selectRule()* method takes a **Vector** of rules, the conflict set, as an input parameter. Our implementation is fairly simple. We use specificity, that is, the number of antecedent clauses, as our primary method for selecting a rule to fire. If two or more rules have the same number of antecedent clauses, we select the first rule we encounter. We start by taking the first rule off the list and designate it as our *bestRule*, also taking the number of antecedents as the current best or *max* value. In a *while()* loop, we walk through the rest of the conflict set. If we encounter a rule that has more antecedent clauses than our previous *max*, we set that rule as our current *bestRule* and corresponding *max* value. After looking at all of the rules in the conflict set, we return the final *bestRule* to be fired.

```
public Rule selectRule(Vector ruleSet) {
   Enumeration enum = ruleSet.elements();
   long numClauses;
   Rule nextRule;
   Rule bestRule = (Rule) enum.nextElement();
   long max = bestRule.numAntecedents();

   while(enum.hasMoreElements()) {
     nextRule = (Rule) enum.nextElement();
```

```
      if((numClauses = nextRule.numAntecedents()) > max) {
        max = numClauses;
        bestRule = nextRule;
      }
    }
    return bestRule;
  }
```

The **Rule** *check()* method is used during forward chaining to test the antecedent clauses of the rule. If any of the clauses has an undefined truth value, then a null value is returned by *check()*. If any of the clauses is false, then the rule's truth value is set to false and a false value is returned. If all of the antecedent clauses are true, then the rule's truth value is set to true, and a true value is returned. Note that only conjunctions (**and**) are supported, not disjunctions (**or**) between clauses.

```
Boolean check() {
  rb.trace("\nTesting rule " + name);
  for(int i = 0; i < antecedents.length; i++) {
    if(antecedents[i].truth == null) {
      return truth = null;
    }
    if(antecedents[i].truth.booleanValue() == true) {
      continue;
    } else {
      return truth = new Boolean(false);
    }
  }
  return truth = new Boolean(true);
}
```

The **Rule** *fire()* method is used during forward chaining when a rule with a true truth value is selected to be fired. The *fired* boolean flag is set to show that the rule has fired. The **RuleVariable** on the left-hand side of the consequent clause is set to the value of the right-hand side. The *checkRules()* method is then called to retest those rules which refer to the consequent variable.

```
void fire() {
  rb.trace("\nFiring rule " + name);
  truth = new Boolean(true);
  fired = true;
  if(consequent.lhs == null) {
    ((EffectorClause) consequent).perform(rb);
  } else {
    consequent.lhs.setValue(consequent.rhs);
    checkRules(consequent.lhs.clauseRefs);
  }
}
```

The **Rule** *checkRules()* method retests every clause which refers to the **RuleVariable** which was changed by the firing of the rule. Because the **RuleVariable** now has a value, all of the antecedent clauses which referred to it and had undefined or null truth values can now be set to either true or false. This means that **Rules** that referred to those clauses may now evaluate as either true or false.

```java
public static void checkRules(Vector clauseRefs) {
  Enumeration enum = clauseRefs.elements();

  while(enum.hasMoreElements()) {
    Clause temp = (Clause) enum.nextElement();
    Enumeration enum2 = temp.ruleRefs.elements();

    while(enum2.hasMoreElements()) {
      ((Rule) enum2.nextElement()).check();
    }
  }
}
```

The **Rule** *display()* method writes the rule out in a text format in the upper text area of the **RuleFrame**. This allows the user to examine the **BooleanRuleBase** to follow a chain of inference.

```java
void display(JTextArea textArea) {
  textArea.append(name + ": IF ");
  for(int i = 0; i < antecedents.length; i++) {
    Clause nextClause = antecedents[i];

    textArea.append(nextClause.toString());
    if((i + 1) < antecedents.length) {
      textArea.append("\n     AND ");
    }
  }
  textArea.append("\n     THEN ");
  textArea.append(consequent.toString() + "\n");
}
```

Backward-Chaining Implementation

The **BooleanRuleBase** *backwardChain()* method takes a single parameter, a **String** which is the name of the goal variable. This variable name is used to retrieve the goal's **RuleVariable** instance. All clauses which refer to the goal variable are enumerated and a *while()* loop is used to process each **Clause** object. If it is not a consequent clause, it is ignored and we continue through the loop to examine the next *goalClause*. If it is a consequent clause, we push it onto our *goalClauseStack*. We then get a reference to the **Rule** that contains this clause as its consequent. We call the *backChain()* on that rule to see if it is true or not. **Rule** *backChain()* will make recursive calls to **BooleanRuleBase** *backwardChain()*, if necessary, to follow a chain of inferences through the rule base in order to find out whether the original *goalClause* is true or false. **Rule** *backChain()* will return the **Rule**'s truth value.

- If the rule's truth value is null, we cannot determine whether the current *goalClause* is true or not. Either the rule base is incomplete, or the user provided an invalid value when prompted to provide one.

- If the rule was proven true, we fire the rule by setting the current goal variable to the value on the right-hand side of the *goalClause;* we add a reference to the variable to tell it what rule produced its value; we pop the clause off the *goalClauseStack* and display a success message. If the *goalClauseStack* is empty, we are done backward chaining, so we display a victory message and break out of the loop.

- If the rule was false, we pop the *goalClause* from the *goalClauseStack*, display a failure message, and continue through the *while()* loop to process the next *goalClause.*

```java
public void backwardChain(String goalVarName) {
  RuleVariable goalVar = (RuleVariable) variableList.get(goalVarName);
  Enumeration goalClauses = goalVar.clauseRefs.elements();

  while(goalClauses.hasMoreElements()) {
    Clause goalClause = (Clause) goalClauses.nextElement();

    if(goalClause.consequent.booleanValue() == false) {
      continue;
    }
    goalClauseStack.push(goalClause);
    Rule goalRule = goalClause.getRule();
    Boolean ruleTruth = goalRule.backChain();

    if(ruleTruth == null) {
      trace("\nRule " + goalRule.name
          + " is null, can't determine truth value.");
    } else if(ruleTruth.booleanValue() == true) {
      goalVar.setValue(goalClause.rhs);
      goalVar.setRuleName(goalRule.name);
      goalClauseStack.pop();
      trace("\nRule " + goalRule.name + " is true, setting "
          + goalVar.name + ": = " + goalVar.value);
      if(goalClauseStack.empty() -- true) {
        trace("\n +++ Found Solution for goal: " + goalVar.name);
        break;
      }
    } else {
      goalClauseStack.pop();
      trace("\nRule " + goalRule.name + " is false, can't set "
          + goalVar.name);
    }
  }
  if(goalVar.value == null) {
    trace("\n +++ Could Not Find Solution for goal: " + goalVar.name);
```

```
        }
    }
```

The **Rule** *backChain()* method will try to prove a rule either true or false by recursively calling **BooleanRuleBase** *backwardChain()* until the truth value can be determined. The method consists of a *for()* loop in which each antecedent clause is evaluated in turn. If the variable in an antecedent clause is undefined, then **BooleanRuleBase** *backwardChain()* is called to determine its value. If a value cannot be inferred, the user is prompted for a value using the **RuleVariable** *askUser()* method. Once the user provides a value, the clause is tested using the **Clause** *check()* method. If the clause is true, we continue through the loop to evaluate the next clause. If it is false, we exit, reporting that the rule's truth value is false because one of the antecedent clauses is false. If we get through the entire loop, then all of the antecedent clauses are true, so we set and return true as the **Rule**'s truth value.

```
Boolean backChain() {
    rb.trace("\nEvaluating rule " + name);
    for(int i = 0; i < antecedents.length; i++) {
        if(antecedents[i].truth == null) {
            rb.backwardChain(antecedents[i].lhs.name);
        }
        if(antecedents[i].truth == null) {
            antecedents[i].lhs.askUser();
            truth = antecedents[i].check();
        }
        if(antecedents[i].truth.booleanValue() == true) {
            continue;
        } else {
            return truth = new Boolean(false);
        }
    }
    return truth = new Boolean(true);
}
```

The FuzzyRuleBase Classes

The **FuzzyRuleBase** implementation is made up of several classes that roughly parallel the **BooleanRuleBase** design. These include **FuzzyRule**, **FuzzyClause**, **FuzzyRuleVariable**, **FuzzySet, and FuzzyRuleBase**. Because the overall structure of the classes is similar, we will focus primarily on the unique aspects of the fuzzy reasoning code.

FuzzyRule

The **FuzzyRule** class is used to define a single rule and also contains methods that support the inferencing process. Each **FuzzyRule** has a *name* data member, a reference to the owning **FuzzyRuleBase** object (described later), a **Vector** of antecedent **Fuzzy-Clause**s, and a single consequent **FuzzyClause**. The *firedFlag* **boolean** member indicates whether this rule has been fired or not. Each **FuzzyVariable** defined in the **FuzzyRuleBase** has a unique integer *id* value assigned. These *id* values are used in **BitSet** instances, *rdRefs*, and *wrRefs* to keep track of which variables have been assigned a value and to decide which rules to fire.

There are several **FuzzyRule** constructors, each requiring a reference to the **FuzzyRuleBase** instance, the **FuzzyRule** name, one or more **FuzzyAntecedentClause** objects, and the single **FuzzyConsequentClause** object. Each constructor allocates the correct number of entries in the *antecedents* **Vector**, and also registers each variable's *id* with the **Bitset** objects as it adds them to its data members. The **FuzzyRule**, unlike the Boolean **Rule** class, has no *truth* value. The **FuzzyRule** registers itself with the owning **FuzzyRuleBase**. The first two constructors are conditional rules that contain antecedent clauses and a consequent clause. The third constructor is an unconditional rule or assertion because it contains a consequent clause only.

```
package rule;

import java.util.*;

public class FuzzyRule extends Object {
  private FuzzyRuleBase rb;
  private String name;
  private BitSet rdRefs;
  private BitSet wrRefs;
  private boolean firedFlag;
  private Vector antecedents;
  private FuzzyClause consequent;

  FuzzyRule(FuzzyRuleBase rb, String name, FuzzyClause lhs,
            FuzzyClause rhs) {
    this.rb = rb;
    this.name = name;
    rdRefs = new BitSet();
    wrRefs = new BitSet();
    firedFlag = false;
    antecedents = new Vector();
    antecedents.addElement(lhs);
    consequent = rhs;
    if(consequent != null) {
      addWrReference(consequent.getLhsReferent());
      addRdReference(consequent.getRhsReferent());
    }
    rb.addConditionalRule(this);
  }

  FuzzyRule(FuzzyRuleBase rb, String name, FuzzyClause[] lhsClauses,
            FuzzyClause rhs) {
```

```
          this.rb = rb;
          this.name = name;
          rdRefs = new BitSet();
          wrRefs = new BitSet();
          firedFlag = false;
          antecedents = new Vector();
          for(int i = 0; i < lhsClauses.length; i++) {
            antecedents.addElement(lhsClauses[i]);
          }
          consequent = rhs;
          if(consequent != null) {
            addWrReference(consequent.getLhsReferent());
            addRdReference(consequent.getRhsReferent());
          }
          rb.addConditionalRule(this);
        }

        FuzzyRule(FuzzyRuleBase rb, String name, FuzzyClause rhs) {
          this.rb = rb;
          this.name = name;
          rdRefs = new BitSet();
          wrRefs = new BitSet();
          firedFlag = false;
          antecedents = new Vector();
          consequent = rhs;
          if(consequent != null) {
            addWrReference(consequent.getLhsReferent());
            addRdReference(consequent.getRhsReferent());
          }
          rb.addUnconditionalRule(this);
        }
        ...   ...   ...
      }
```

FuzzyClauses

FuzzyClauses are used both in the antecedent and consequent parts of a **FuzzyRule**. A **FuzzyClause** is made up of a **FuzzyRuleVariable** on the left-hand side; a **FuzzyOperator**, which implements fuzzy comparison or assignment; and the right-hand side, which is a **FuzzySet** value. For example the rule:

```
VeryFastRule: IF temp is very hot
      AND humidity is very sticky
      THEN motor is very fast.
```

contains three clauses. The first antecedent clause is made up of the **FuzzyRuleVariable** *temp*, the **FuzzyOperator is**, the linguistic hedge *very*, and the **FuzzySet** *hot*. The other clauses are similarly composed. A **FuzzyClause** also contains a *consequent* **boolean** which indicates whether the clause appears in the antecedent or the consequent of the rule.

The **FuzzyClause** constructor takes a **FuzzyRuleVariable** for the left-hand side; an **int** value representing the desired fuzzy comparison or assignment operator; and a hedged **FuzzySet** value for the right-hand side. The *eval()* method performs either the fuzzy comparison, if it is an antecedent clause, or a fuzzy assignment if it is a consequent clause. They are presented later in our discussion of fuzzy forward chaining.

```
package rule;

public class FuzzyClause extends Object {
  FuzzyRuleVariable lhs;
  int op;
  FuzzySet rhs;
  boolean consequent;

  protected FuzzyClause(FuzzyRuleVariable lhs, int op, FuzzySet rhs) {
    this.lhs = lhs;
    this.op = op;
    this.rhs = rhs;
    if(op == FuzzyOperator.AsgnIs) {
      consequent = true;
    } else {
      consequent = false;
    }
  }
  ... ... ...
}
```

The **FuzzyOperator** class implements two primary fuzzy logic operations between a **FuzzyRuleVariable** and a **FuzzyLiteral** (a **FuzzySet**) value. These operators are shown later during our trace through the fuzzy forward-chaining process. The assignment **is** operator sets the variable to the specified fuzzy set value. The comparison **is** operator tests the membership of the current left-hand side **FuzzyRuleVariable** value against the right-hand side **FuzzySet** and returns a value between 0.0 and 1.0.

ContinuousFuzzyRuleVariable

For fuzzy rule processing, we define the base **FuzzyRuleVariable** class (not shown) and the **ContinuousFuzzyRuleVariable** subclass that supports the use of **FuzzySets** in inferencing. The **ContinuousFuzzyRuleVariable** constructor takes a reference to the owning **FuzzyRuleBase**, the *name* of the variable, and the minimum and maximum values of the domain (called discourse) of the linguistic variable. A collection of getter and setter methods is provided for the data members but is not shown here. The *setList* **Hashtable** holds all of the fuzzy sets and linguistic hedges defined for the variable. Two **WorkingFuzzySet** instances are used. One *valFzy* holds the current fuzzy value of the variable, while the other *valFzyTmp* is used as a temporary fuzzy set during inferencing.

```
package rule;

import java.beans.*;
import java.util.*;
```

```
public class ContinuousFuzzyRuleVariable extends FuzzyRuleVariable {
  double discourseLo;
  double discourseHi;
  Hashtable setList;
  double valCrisp;
  WorkingFuzzySet valFzy;
  boolean valKnown;
  WorkingFuzzySet valFzyTmp;

  ContinuousFuzzyRuleVariable(FuzzyRuleBase base, String name,
      double discourseLo, double discourseHi) {
    super(FuzzyDefs.ContinuousVariable, base, name);
    this.discourseLo = discourseLo;
    this.discourseHi = discourseHi;
    setList = new Hashtable();
    valKnown = false;
    valCrisp = 0.0;
    valFzy = new WorkingFuzzySet(this, name + " Fuzzy Solution Space",
        rb.getAlphaCut(), discourseLo, discourseHi);
    valFzyTmp = new WorkingFuzzySet(this, name + " Fuzzy Work Space",
        rb.getAlphaCut(), discourseLo, discourseHi);
  }
... ... ...
}
```

To get or set a new value on the **ContinuousFuzzyRuleVariable**, two *setFuzzyValue()* methods are defined. The first simply calls *setRawValue()* which does an unconditional assignment to the variable's *valFzy* **FuzzySet**, and then defuzzifies it so that the numeric or crisp value (*valCrisp*) is available. During inferencing, the other *setFuzzyValue()* method is used, taking a new **FuzzySet** and an associated *truthValue* as input arguments.

```
public FuzzySet getFuzzyValue() {
  return valFzy;
}

public void setFuzzyValue(FuzzySet newValue) {
  setRawValue(newValue);
}

void setRawValue(FuzzySet newSet) {
  valFzy.copyOrAssertFzy(newSet);
  valCrisp = valFzy.defuzzify(rb.getDefuzzifyMethod());
}

void setFuzzyValue(FuzzySet newSet, double truthValue) {
  valFzyTmp.correlateWith(newSet, rb.getCorrelationMethod(),
      truthValue);
  valFzy.implicateTo(valFzyTmp, rb.getInferenceMethod());
  valCrisp = valFzy.defuzzify(rb.getDefuzzifyMethod());
}
```

The *getOrAddHedgedFuzzySet()* method first constructs the hedged set name by concatenating the *setName* with the hedges. Then, in a two-step process, it first creates a duplicate of the original fuzzy set (but with the hedged set name) and then applies the hedges to that set, thereby creating the hedged fuzzy set *truthVector*.

```
FuzzySet getOrAddHedgedSet(String setName, String hedges) {
  String hedgeName = setName + " " + hedges;

  if(!setExist(setName)) {
    System.out.println("Error: Unknown Set " + name + " " + setName);
  }
  if(setExist(hedgeName)) {
    return getSet(hedgeName);
  }
  ((FuzzySet) (setList.get(setName))).addClone(hedgeName);
  ((FuzzySet) (setList.get(hedgeName))).applyHedges(hedges);
  return getSet(hedgeName);
}
```

The *addSet . . . ()* methods are used to both create and then add instances of **ShoulderFuzzySet**, **TrapeziodFuzzySet**, and **TriangleFuzzySet** to the **ContinuousFuzzyRuleVariable**. All methods take the *setName* **String**, the *alphaCut* parameter, and then a set of parameters used on the respective **FuzzySet** constructors. In *addSetShoulder()* the beginning and end point and the set directions are specified. In the *addSetTrapezoid()* method, we specify the left and right end points and the left and right core points. In the *addSetTriangle()* method, we specify the left, center, and right points. All of these values must lie within the universe of discourse of the **ContinuousFuzzyRuleVariable**.

```
synchronized void addSetShoulder(String setName, double alphaCut,
    double ptBeg, double ptEnd, int setDir) {
  setList.put(setName,
             new ShoulderFuzzySet(this, setName, alphaCut, ptBeg,
               ptEnd, setDir));
}


synchronized void addSetTrapezoid(String setName, double alphaCut,
    double ptLeft, double ptLeftCore, double ptRightCore,
    double ptRight) {
  setList.put(setName,
             new TrapezoidFuzzySet(this, setName, alphaCut, ptLeft,
               ptLeftCore, ptRightCore, ptRight));
}


synchronized void addSetTriangle(String setName, double alphaCut,
    double ptLeft, double ptCenter, double ptRight) {
  setList.put(setName,
             new TriangleFuzzySet(this, setName, alphaCut, ptLeft,
               ptCenter, ptRight));
}
```

To reset a **ContinuousFuzzyRuleVariable**, the *reset()* method sets *valKnown* to false, *valCrisp* to 0.0, and then resets the *valFzy* and *valFzyTmp* FuzzySets.

```
void reset() {
  valKnown = false;
  valCrisp = 0.0;
  valFzy.reset();
  valFzyTmp.reset();
}
```

FuzzySet

The **FuzzySet** class is the base class for the triangle, trapezoid, shoulder, and working fuzzy sets used in this book. It contains an **int** *setType*; a **String** *setName*; *alphaCut*, *domainLo* and *domainHi* parameters; and an array of doubles called the *truthVector* that defines the shape of the fuzzy set at 256 points (*MAXVALUES*) over the discourse. In addition to getters and setters on these parameters, the **FuzzySet** class defines the *applyHedges()* method that modifies the base fuzzy set shape by concentrating and diluting it using the *applyHedgeConDil()* method. The supported linguistic hedges include *extremely*, *slightly*, *somewhat*, and *very*.

```
package rule;

import java.util.*;

public abstract class FuzzySet {
  protected int setType;
  protected String setName;
  protected double alphaCut;
  protected double domainLo;
  protected double domainHi;
  protected double[] truthVector;
  protected ContinuousFuzzyRuleVariable parentVar;

  protected FuzzySet(int setType, String setName,
                     ContinuousFuzzyRuleVariable parentVar,
                     double alphaCut, double domainLo, double domainHi) {
    this.setType = setType;
    this.setName = setName;
    this.parentVar = parentVar;
    this.alphaCut = alphaCut;
    this.domainLo = domainLo;
    this.domainHi = domainHi;
    this.truthVector = new double[FuzzyDefs.MAXVALUES];
    for(int i = 0; i < FuzzyDefs.MAXVALUES; i++) {
      truthVector[i] = 0.0;
    }
  }
}
```

```
protected FuzzySet(int setType, String setName,
                    ContinuousFuzzyRuleVariable parentVar,
                    double alphaCut) {
  this(setType, setName, parentVar, alphaCut, 0.0, 0.0);
}

public double getNumericValue() {
  return defuzzify((parentVar.getRuleBase()).getDefuzzifyMethod());
}

abstract void addClone(String setName);

void applyHedges(String hedges) {
  for(int i = (hedges.length()) - 1; i >= 0; -i) {
    char hedge = hedges.charAt(i);

    switch(hedge) {
      case FuzzyDefs.HedgeNull:
        break;
      case FuzzyDefs.HedgeExtremely:
        applyHedgeConDil(3.0);
        break;
      case FuzzyDefs.HedgeSlightly:
        applyHedgeConDil(0.3);
        break;
      case FuzzyDefs.HedgeSomewhat:
        applyHedgeConDil(0.5);
        break;
      case FuzzyDefs.HedgeVery:
        applyHedgeConDil(2.0);
        break;
    }
  }
}

void applyHedgeConDil(double exp) {
  for(int i = 0; i < FuzzyDefs.MAXVALUES; i++) {
    truthVector[i] = (double) Math.pow(truthVector[i], exp);
  }
}

void normalise() {
  double maxTruthValue = getSetHeight();

  if(maxTruthValue == 0.0) {
    return;
  }
  if(maxTruthValue == 1.0) {
    return;
  }
  for(int i = 0; i < FuzzyDefs.MAXVALUES; i++) {
```

```
        truthVector[i] = truthVector[i] / maxTruthValue;
      }
    }
... ... ...
}
```

The defuzzify method first calls the *applyAlphaCut()* method to zero out all *truthVector* values that are less than or equal to the *alphaCut* parameter. If *getSetHeight()* returns 0, then all 256 elements in the *truthVector* were below the *alphaCut* threshold and a defuzzified value of 0.0 is returned. Otherwise, we can apply one of our defuzzification methods, *CENTROID* or *MAXHEIGHT*, to the FuzzySet.

```
double defuzzify(int defuzzMethod) {
    double defuzzedNumber = 0.0;
    int j = 0;
    int k = 0;
    int m = 0;
    double truthValue1;
    double truthValue2;

    applyAlphaCut();
    if(getSetHeight() == 0) {
      defuzzedNumber = 0.0;
      return defuzzedNumber;
    }
    switch(defuzzMethod) {
    case FuzzyDefs.CENTROID:
      truthValue1 = 0.0;
      truthValue2 = 0.0;
      for(int i = 0; i < FuzzyDefs.MAXVALUES; ++i) {
        truthValue1 = truthValue1 + truthVector[i] * (double) i;
        truthValue2 = truthValue2 + truthVector[i];
      }
      if(truthValue2 == 0.0) {
        defuzzedNumber = 0.0;
      } else {
        j = (int) (truthValue1 / truthValue2);
        defuzzedNumber = getScalar(j);
      }
      break;
    case FuzzyDefs.MAXHEIGHT:
      truthValue1 = truthVector[0];
      j = 0;
      for(int i = 0; i < FuzzyDefs.MAXVALUES; ++i) {
        if(truthVector[i] > truthValue1) {
          truthValue1 = truthVector[i];
          k = i;
        }
      }
      for(m = k + 1; m < FuzzyDefs.MAXVALUES; ++m) {
```

```
          if(truthVector[m] != truthValue1) {
            break;
          }
        }
        j = (int) (((double) m - (double) k) / 2);
        if(j == 0) {
          j = k;
        }
        defuzzedNumber = getScalar(j);
        break;
      default:
        defuzzedNumber = 0.0;
    }
    return defuzzedNumber;
}


void applyAlphaCut() {
  for(int i = 1; i < FuzzyDefs.MAXVALUES; i++) {
    if(!aboveAlphaCut(truthVector[i])) {
      truthVector[i] = 0.0;
    }
  }
}


boolean aboveAlphaCut(double truthValue) {
  if(truthValue > alphaCut) {
    return true;
  } else {
    return false;
  }
}


double getScalar(int index) {
  double range = domainHi - domainLo;
  double width = range / FuzzyDefs.MAXVALUES;
  double scalar = (index * width) + domainLo;

  return scalar;
}


double getSetHeight() {
  double truthValue = truthVector[0];

  for(int i = 0; i < FuzzyDefs.MAXVALUES; i++) {
    if(truthVector[i] > truthValue) {
      truthValue = truthVector[i];
    }
  }
  return truthValue;
}
```

The membership method maps the scalar input value onto the **FuzzySet** membership function as represented by the 256-element *truthVector*. If the scalar value is below the domain of the **FuzzySet**, it is set to the height of the left-most element (at index 0). If the scalar value is above the domain, then it is set to the height of the right-most element (at index *MAXVALUES=256*). If the *scalar* falls between the *domainLo* and *domainHi*, it is linearly scaled to an index position in the *truthVector* and assigned the height at that index.

```
double membership(double scalar) {
  double truthValue = 0.0;
  int index;
  double range;

  if(scalar < domainLo) {
    truthValue = truthVector[0];
  } else if(scalar > domainHi) {
    truthValue = truthVector[FuzzyDefs.MAXVALUES];
  } else {
    range = domainHi - domainLo;
    index = (int) (((scalar - domainLo) / range)
                   * (FuzzyDefs.MAXVALUES - 1));
    truthValue = truthVector[index];
  }
  return truthValue;
}
```

The *segmentCurve()* and *vectorInterpret()* methods are used to fill in the shape of the *truthVector* of a **FuzzySet** once the key points are set. For example, in a trapezoid fuzzy set, four points are specified in the constructor. Then the *segmentCurve()* method is called to set the other 252 values in the *truthVector*.

```
int[] segmentCurve(int numberOfValues, double[] scalarVector,
                   double[] aTruthVector) {
  boolean normalSet = false;
  int point = 256;
  double[] tmpTruthVector = new double[FuzzyDefs.MAXVALUES + 1];
  double widthDomain = domainHi - domainLo;
  int[] tmpSegs = new int[]{ -1, FuzzyDefs.MAXVALUES };

  for(int i = 0; i < FuzzyDefs.MAXVALUES; ++i) {
    tmpTruthVector[i] = -1;
  }
  for(int i = 0; i < numberOfValues; ++i) {
    point = (int) (((scalarVector[i] - domainLo) / widthDomain)
                   * FuzzyDefs.MAXVALUES);
    tmpTruthVector[point] = aTruthVector[i];
    if(tmpSegs[0] == -1) {
      tmpSegs[0] = point;
    }
    if(aTruthVector[i] == 1.0) {
```

```
          normalSet = true;
        }
      }
      tmpSegs[1] = point;
      if(tmpTruthVector[0] == -1) {
        tmpTruthVector[0] = 0.0;
      }
      vectorInterpret(tmpTruthVector);
      for(int i = 0; i < FuzzyDefs.MAXVALUES; ++i) {
        truthVector[i] = tmpTruthVector[i];
      }
      return tmpSegs;
    }


    void vectorInterpret(double[] aTruthVector) {
      int i, j, k;
      int point1, point2;
      double factor;
      double seg1, seg2;

      i = 0;
      j = 0;
      skipIt:
      for(;;) {
        j++;
        if(j > FuzzyDefs.MAXVALUES) {
          return;
        }
        if(aTruthVector[j] == -1) {
          continue skipIt;
        }
        point1 = i + 1;
        point2 = j;
        for(k = point1; k < point2 + 1; ++k) {
          seg1 = k - i;
          seg2 = j - i;
          factor = seg1 / seg2;
          if(k > FuzzyDefs.MAXVALUES) {
            return;
          }
          aTruthVector[k] = aTruthVector[i]
                          + (factor * (aTruthVector[j] -
                            aTruthVector[i]));
        }
        i = j;
        if(i >= FuzzyDefs.MAXVALUES) {
          return;
        }
        continue skipIt;
      }
    }
```

Trapezoid Fuzzy Set Class

The **TrapezoidFuzzySet** defines a fuzzy membership function whose shape resembles a trapezoid. This fuzzy set takes four parameters, *ptLeft*, *ptLeftCore*, *ptRightCore*, and *ptRight*, to describe the base (left and right) and top (left and right) of the fuzzy set.

```
package rule;

public class TrapezoidFuzzySet extends FuzzySet {
   private double ptLeft;
   private double ptLeftCore;
   private double ptRightCore;
   private double ptRight;

   TrapezoidFuzzySet(ContinuousFuzzyRuleVariable parentVar, String name,
                     double alphaCut, double ptLeft, double ptLeftCore,
                     double ptRightCore, double ptRight) {
     super(FuzzyDefs.TRAPEZOID, name, parentVar, alphaCut);
     this.ptLeft = ptLeft;
     this.ptLeftCore = ptLeftCore;
     this.ptRightCore = ptRightCore;
     this.ptRight = ptRight;
     domainLo = parentVar.getDiscourseLo();
     domainHi = parentVar.getDiscourseHi();
     int numberOfValues = 6;
     double[] lclScalarVector = new double[7];
     double[] lclTruthVector = new double[7];

     lclScalarVector[0] = domainLo;
     lclTruthVector[0] = 0.0;
     lclScalarVector[1] = ptLeft;
     lclTruthVector[1] = 0.0;
     lclScalarVector[2] = ptLeftCore;
     lclTruthVector[2] = 1.0;
     lclScalarVector[3] = ptRightCore;
     lclTruthVector[3] = 1.0;
     lclScalarVector[4] = ptRight;
     lclTruthVector[4] = 0.0;
     lclScalarVector[5] = domainHi;
     lclTruthVector[5] = 0.0;
     segmentCurve(numberOfValues, lclScalarVector, lclTruthVector);
   }
   ... ... ...
   }
```

TriangleFuzzySet Class

The **TriangleFuzzySet** defines a fuzzy membership function whose shape resembles a triangle. This fuzzy set takes three parameters, *ptLeft*, *ptCenter*, and *ptRight*, to describe the base (left and right) and top (center) of the fuzzy set.

```
        package rule;

        public class TriangleFuzzySet extends FuzzySet {
          private double ptLeft;
          private double ptCenter;
          private double ptRight;

          TriangleFuzzySet(ContinuousFuzzyRuleVariable parentVar, String name,
                           double alphaCut, double ptLeft, double ptCenter,
                           double ptRight) {
            super(FuzzyDefs.TRIANGLE, name, parentVar, alphaCut);
            this.ptLeft = ptLeft;
            this.ptCenter = ptCenter;
            this.ptRight = ptRight;
            domainLo = parentVar.getDiscourseLo();
            domainHi = parentVar.getDiscourseHi();
            int numberOfValues = 5;
            double[] lclScalarVector = new double[7];
            double[] lclTruthVector = new double[7];

            lclScalarVector[0] = domainLo;
            lclTruthVector[0] = 0.0;
            lclScalarVector[1] = ptLeft;
            lclTruthVector[1] = 0.0;
            lclScalarVector[2] = ptCenter;
            lclTruthVector[2] = 1.0;
            lclScalarVector[3] = ptRight;
            lclTruthVector[3] = 0.0;
            lclScalarVector[4] = domainHi;
            lclTruthVector[4] = 0.0;
            segmentCurve(numberOfValues, lclScalarVector, lclTruthVector);
          }
        ... ... ...
        }
```

ShoulderFuzzySet Class

The **ShoulderFuzzySet** defines a fuzzy membership function whose shape resembles a line sloping up to a plateau. This fuzzy set takes three parameters, *ptBeg*, *ptEnd*, and the direction of the shoulder, either right or left.

```
        package rule;

        public class ShoulderFuzzySet extends FuzzySet {
          private double ptBeg;
          private double ptEnd;
          private int setDir;

          ShoulderFuzzySet(ContinuousFuzzyRuleVariable parentVar, String name,
                           double alphaCut, double ptBeg, double ptEnd,
```

```
                            int setDirection) {
        super(FuzzyDefs.SHOULDER, name, parentVar, alphaCut);
        this.ptBeg = ptBeg;
        this.ptEnd = ptEnd;
        this.setDir = setDirection;
        domainLo = parentVar.getDiscourseLo();
        domainHi = parentVar.getDiscourseHi();
        int numberOfValues = 4;
        double[] lclScalarVector = new double[5];
        double[] lclTruthVector = new double[5];

        if(setDirection == FuzzyDefs.LEFT) {
          lclScalarVector[0] = domainLo;
          lclTruthVector[0] = 1.0;
          lclScalarVector[1] = ptBeg;
          lclTruthVector[1] = 1.0;
          lclScalarVector[2] = ptEnd;
          lclTruthVector[2] = 0.0;
          lclScalarVector[3] = domainHi;
          lclTruthVector[3] = 0.0;
        } else {
          lclScalarVector[0] = domainLo;
          lclTruthVector[0] = 0.0;
          lclScalarVector[1] = ptBeg;
          lclTruthVector[1] = 0.0;
          lclScalarVector[2] = ptEnd;
          lclTruthVector[2] = 1.0;
          lclScalarVector[3] = domainHi;
          lclTruthVector[3] = 1.0;
        }
        segmentCurve(numberOfValues, lclScalarVector, lclTruthVector);
      }
    ...   ...   ...
    }
```

WorkingFuzzySet Class

The **WorkingFuzzySet**, shown in Figure 4.11, is one of the major classes in the **FuzzyRuleBase**. It is used to combine the fuzzy sets as we are inferencing with the *correlateWith()* and *implicateTo()* methods. These methods are described later when we look at fuzzy inferencing in more detail.

FuzzyRuleBase

The **FuzzyRuleBase** class implements the **RuleBase** interface and defines a set of **FuzzyRuleVariables** and **FuzzyRules**, along with the high-level methods for forward chaining. The **FuzzyRuleBase** has a *name*, a *variableList* that contains all of the **FuzzyRuleVariables** referenced by the **FuzzyRules**, and the *ruleList*, which contains

```
package rule;

public class WorkingFuzzySet extends FuzzySet {
  boolean setEmpty;

  WorkingFuzzySet(ContinuousFuzzyRuleVariable parentVar, String
                  setName, double alphaCut, double discourseLo,
                  double discourseHi) {
    super(FuzzyDefs.WORK, setName, parentVar, alphaCut, discourseLo,
        discourseHi);
    setEmpty = true;
  }

  void addClone(String cloneName) {}

  public boolean isEmpty() {
    return setEmpty;
  }

  void copyOrAssertFzy(FuzzySet inputSet) {
    if(setEmpty) {
      copy(inputSet);
    } else {
      assert(inputSet);
    }
  }

  void correlateWith(FuzzySet inputSet, int corrMethod,
                     double truthValue) {
    switch(corrMethod) {
      case FuzzyDefs.MINIMISE:
        for(int i = 0; i < FuzzyDefs.MAXVALUES; ++i) {
          if(truthValue <= inputSet.getTruthValue(i)) {
            truthVector[i] = truthValue;
          } else {
            truthVector[i] = inputSet.getTruthValue(i);
          }
        }
        break;
      case FuzzyDefs.PRODUCT:
        for(int i = 0; i < FuzzyDefs.MAXVALUES; ++i) {
          truthVector[i] = (inputSet.getTruthValue(i) * truthValue);
        }
        break;
    }
  }
```

Figure 4.11 The WorkingFuzzySet class listing.

```
void implicateTo(WorkingFuzzySet inputSet, int inferMethod) {
  switch(inferMethod) {
    case FuzzyDefs.FUZZYADD:
      for(int i = 0; i < FuzzyDefs.MAXVALUES; ++i) {
        double sum = truthVector[i] + inputSet.getTruthValue(i);

        if(sum < 1.0) {
          truthVector[i] = sum;
        } else {
          truthVector[i] = 1.0;
        }
      }
      break;
    case FuzzyDefs.MINMAX:
      for(int i = 0; i < FuzzyDefs.MAXVALUES; ++i) {
        if(truthVector[i] < inputSet.getTruthValue(i)) {
          truthVector[i] = inputSet.getTruthValue(i);
        }
      }
      break;
  }
}

void reset() {
  setEmpty = true;
  for(int i = 0; i < FuzzyDefs.MAXVALUES; ++i) {
    truthVector[i] = 0.0;
  }
}

void assert(FuzzySet inputSet) {
  for(int i = 0; i < FuzzyDefs.MAXVALUES; ++i) {
    if(truthVector[i] > inputSet.getTruthValue(i)) {
      truthVector[i] = inputSet.getTruthValue(i);
    }
  }
}

void copy(FuzzySet inputSet) {
  for(int i = 0; i < FuzzyDefs.MAXVALUES; ++i) {
    truthVector[i] = inputSet.getTruthValue(i);
  }
  setEmpty = false;
}
}
```

Figure 4.11 Continued.

all of the **FuzzyRules**. The key parameters that control inferencing are the *alphaCut*, *inferenceMethod, correlationMethod,* and *defuzzificationMethod* members. The *back-wardChain()* method, which is part of the **RuleBase** interface, is stubbed out to display a message indicating that **FuzzyRuleBase** does not support backward chaining.

```java
package rule;

import java.beans.*;
import java.util.*;
import javax.swing.*;

public class FuzzyRuleBase implements RuleBase {
  static int nextId = 0;
  private String name = "";

  private double alphaCut = FuzzyDefs.AlphaCutDefault;
  private int correlationMethod = FuzzyDefs.CorrelationMethodDefault;
  private int defuzzifyMethod = FuzzyDefs.DefuzzifyMethodDefault;
  private int inferenceMethod = FuzzyDefs.InferenceMethodDefault;

  private int varId = FuzzyDefs.VarIdInitial;
  private Hashtable variableList = new Hashtable();
  private int ruleId = FuzzyDefs.RuleIdInitial;

  private Vector ruleList = new Vector();
  private Vector cndRuleList = new Vector();
  private Vector uncRuleList = new Vector();
  private BitSet fbInitial = new BitSet();
  private JTextArea textArea;

  public FuzzyRuleBase(String name) {
    this.name = name;
  }

  public void displayVariables(JTextArea textArea) {
    Enumeration enum = variableList.elements();

    while(enum.hasMoreElements()) {
      FuzzyRuleVariable temp = (FuzzyRuleVariable) enum.nextElement();

      textArea.append("\n" + temp.getName() + " value = "
                      + temp.getNumericValue());
    }
  }

  public void displayRules(JTextArea textArea) {
    textArea.append("\n" + name + " Fuzzy Rule Base: " + "\n");
    Enumeration enum = ruleList.elements();

    while(enum.hasMoreElements()) {
      FuzzyRule temp = (FuzzyRule) enum.nextElement();
```

```
          textArea.append("\n" + temp.toString());
      }
      textArea.append("\n");
    }

    public void reset() {
      Enumeration enum = variableList.elements();

      while(enum.hasMoreElements()) {
        ((FuzzyRuleVariable) (enum.nextElement())).reset();
      }
      enum = ruleList.elements();
      while(enum.hasMoreElements()) {
        ((FuzzyRule) (enum.nextElement())).reset();
      }
    }

    public void backwardChain(String goalVarName) {
      textArea.append(
        "\nBackward Chaining is not supported in fuzzy rule base");
    }

    public Vector getGoalVariables() {
      return new Vector();
    }
  ...   ...   ...
  }
```

Next, we show the setters and getters for the main fuzzy inferencing control parameters. The *setAlphaCut()* method ensures that the *alphaCut* threshold (*truthValues* below this value are set to 0.0) is in the range of 0.0 and 1.0. Typical values are under 0.25 and the default is 0.1.

```
public void setAlphaCut(double alphaCut) {
  if((alphaCut > 0.0) && (alphaCut < 1.0)) {
    this.alphaCut = alphaCut;
  }
}

public double getAlphaCut() {
  return alphaCut;
}
```

The *setCorrelationMethod()* method insures that either *PRODUCT* or *MINIMISE* is selected for correlation. The *setDefuzzifyMethod()* makes sure that either *CENTROID* or *MAXHEIGHT* is used when defuzzifying **FuzzySets**. The *setInferenceMethod()* parameter can be either *FUZZYADD* or *MINMAX*.

```
public void setCorrelationMethod(int correlationMethod) {
  switch(correlationMethod) {
    case FuzzyDefs.PRODUCT:
```

```
        case FuzzyDefs.MINIMISE:
          this.correlationMethod = correlationMethod;
          break;
    }
  }

  public int getCorrelationMethod() {
    return correlationMethod;
  }

  public void setDefuzzifyMethod(int defuzzifyMethod) {
    switch(defuzzifyMethod) {
      case FuzzyDefs.CENTROID:
      case FuzzyDefs.MAXHEIGHT:
        this.defuzzifyMethod = defuzzifyMethod;
        break;
    }
  }

  public int getDefuzzifyMethod() {
    return defuzzifyMethod;
  }

  public void setInferenceMethod(int inferenceMethod) {
    switch(inferenceMethod) {
      case FuzzyDefs.FUZZYADD:
      case FuzzyDefs.MINMAX:
        this.inferenceMethod = inferenceMethod;
        break;
    }
  }

  public int getInferenceMethod() {
    return inferenceMethod;
  }
```

The *createClause()* and *getFuzzySet()* methods in the **FuzzyRuleBase** class are used when constructing new **FuzzyRule**s. This indirect method of constructing **FuzzyRules** is used so that the fuzzy sets and their hedges can be looked up by the **FuzzyRuleBase** instance. In *createClause()*, the **FuzzySet** is retrieved, based on its name and any hedges. Next, a **FuzzyClause** instance is created and returned to the caller. This method is shown in the *Motor* **FuzzyRuleBase** example later in this chapter.

```
public FuzzyClause createClause(ContinuousFuzzyRuleVariable lhs,
    int oper, String hedges, String setName) {
  FuzzySet rhs = getFuzzySet(lhs, setName, hedges);
  FuzzyClause clause = new FuzzyClause(lhs, oper, rhs);

  return clause;
}
```

```
private FuzzySet getFuzzySet(ContinuousFuzzyRuleVariable lhs,
    String setName, String hedges) {
  FuzzySet rhs = null;
  String value = setName.trim();
  String tmpHedges = hedges.trim();

  if(lhs.setExist(value)) {
    if(tmpHedges.length() == 0) {
      rhs = lhs.getSet(value);
    } else {
      rhs = lhs.getOrAddHedgedSet(value, tmpHedges);
    }
  } else {
    System.out.println("Error: Invalid fuzzy set name " + value);
  }
  return rhs;
}
```

Fuzzy Forward-Chaining Implementation

The forward-chaining implementation uses methods in the **FuzzyRuleBase**, **FuzzyRule**, **FuzzyClause**, **FuzzyOperator**, and **WorkingFuzzySet**. The **FuzzyRuleBase** *forward-Chain()* method automatically resets the rules (but not the variables which may have had their values set by the user). The *factBase* is initialized to a **BitSet** with all bits clear. The *factBase* is used to keep track of variables that have been computed or assigned values. Next the unconditional (assertion) rules are processed. Having assertion rules is one way to initialize variable values. Finally, the fuzzy forward inferencing logic is performed in the *processConditionalRules()* method. In the next few pages we trace through this code to give a feel for how it all works.

```
public void forwardChain() {
    Enumeration enum = ruleList.elements();

    while(enum.hasMoreElements()) {
      ((FuzzyRule) (enum.nextElement())).reset();
    }
    BitSet factBase = (BitSet) fbInitial.clone();

    factBase.set(0);
    processAssertionRules(factBase);
    processConditionalRules(factBase);
}
```

The *processAssertionRules()* method simply walks through the unconditional rules list and fires each rule. Since each rule has no antecedent clause, the effect of firing the rule is to perform the right-hand side assignment of the fuzzy set to the **ContinuousFuzzyRuleVariable** on the left-hand side.

```
private void processAssertionRules(BitSet factBase) {
  trace("\nProcessing unconditional fuzzy rules ");
  Enumeration enum = uncRuleList.elements();

  while(enum.hasMoreElements()) {
    FuzzyRule rule = (FuzzyRule) (enum.nextElement());
    rule.fire(alphaCut, factBase);
  }
}
```

The *processConditionalRules()* method is a bit more complex. The **FuzzyRuleBase** can handle multi-step forward inferencing. This means that in a given set of rules, we may have one subset that computes the value of a variable *X*, which is then referred to in the antecedent clause of another rule, *C*. Obviously, in this case, we have to process the rules that compute *X* before we can process rule *C*. In order to manage this process, we use a Java **BitSet**. A **BitSet** is an object that can sparsely represent a large bit string. We assigned a unique integer *Id* value to each variable in our **FuzzyRuleBase**. As soon as we do an assignment to the variable, we set its bit in the **BitSet**. This lets us know what variables have been computed. We use this mechanism to determine a series of subsets of rules to process. We use the **boolean** *moreRules* to indicate that we have another subset of **FuzzyRules** waiting to be processed. It controls when we exit the inferencing loop. We enter the loop with *moreRules* set to true.

Next we grab an **Enumeration** of all of the conditional rules in the rule base. For each rule that has not yet fired, we extract the *Id* bits for all left-hand side variable references (using the *getRdReferences()* method) and place them into two working **BitSet**s. We logically **and** the set of currently known variables (the *factBase*) with the variables required by the rule *lhs* (*tempFacts*). If the result equals the same bits required by the rule (*ruleTempFacts*), then we can add the rule to our list of rules to process (*tmpRuleSet*). After we have processed every rule in the rule base, we have our first subset of rules to process. If the *tmpRuleSet* is empty we are done, so we set the *moreRules* **boolean** to false, which forces us to exit the outermost loop. But if we have rules to process, we loop over the list and *fire()* each rule. A side effect of firing the rules is that our known variables, represented by the *factBase* member, has more bits set. Also all of the rules we just processed have their *fired* flags set. So the next time through the *while()* loop, we have fewer rules to examine and more bits set in the *factBase*. When we exit, we will have fired every rule that we could.

```
private void processConditionalRules(BitSet factBase) {
  boolean moreRules = true;
  Vector tmpRuleSet = new Vector();

  trace("\nProcessing conditional fuzzy rules ");
  while(moreRules) {
    Enumeration enum = cndRuleList.elements();

    while(enum.hasMoreElements()) {
      FuzzyRule rule = (FuzzyRule) (enum.nextElement());
```

```
                        if(!rule.isFired()) {
                          BitSet tmpRuleFacts = rule.getRdReferences();
                          BitSet tempFacts = rule.getRdReferences();

                          tempFacts.and(factBase);
                          if(tempFacts.equals(tmpRuleFacts)) {
                            tmpRuleSet.addElement(rule);
                          }
                        }
                      }
                      if(tmpRuleSet.isEmpty()) {
                        moreRules = false;
                        break;
                      }
                      for(int i = 0; i < tmpRuleSet.size(); i++) {
                        FuzzyRule rule = (FuzzyRule) tmpRuleSet.elementAt(i);

                        trace("\nFiring fuzzy rule: " + rule.getName());
                        rule.fire(alphaCut, factBase);
                      }
                      tmpRuleSet.removeAllElements();
                    }
                  }
```

Let's look at what happens in the **FuzzyRule** *fire()* method. There are two cases handled in this method. In the first case there are no antecedent clauses (it is an unconditional rule) and we just *eval()* the consequent clause and **or** it into our *workingSet*. In the second case it is a conditional rule with antecedents and consequents to process. We loop over the antecedent clauses, calling *eval()* on each. If the *truthValue* is less than the current *alphaCut* threshold, we set a flag *skipConsequent* so that we don't actually fire the consequent of the rule. Also, we keep track of the minimum truth value of all the antecedent clauses. If *skipConsequent* is still not true, we *eval()* the consequent clause (which does a fuzzy assignment) and **or** the results into our *workingSet*. Let's follow the code into the **FuzzyClause** *eval()* methods.

```
   void fire(double alphaCut, BitSet workingSet) {
     if(antecedents.isEmpty()) {
       if(consequent != null) {
         consequent.eval();
         workingSet.or(wrRefs);
         return;
       } else {
         System.out.println("Error: FuzzyRule cannot fire" + name);
       }
     }
     FuzzyClause clause;
     double truthValue;
     double truthValueMin = 1.0;
     boolean skipConsequent = false;
```

```
      for(int i = 0; i < antecedents.size(); i++) {
        clause = (FuzzyClause) (antecedents.elementAt(i));
        truthValue = clause.eval();
        firedFlag = true;
        if(truthValue <= alphaCut) {
          skipConsequent = true;
          break;
        }
        if(truthValue < truthValueMin) {
          truthValueMin = truthValue;
        }
      }
    if(!skipConsequent) {
      if(consequent != null) {
        consequent.eval(truthValueMin);
        workingSet.or(wrRefs);
      }
    }
  }
```

The **FuzzyClause** *eval()* methods are used in the **FuzzyRule** *fire()* methods to evaluate the clauses as we are inferencing. The no-argument version of *eval()* is called for antecedent clauses. This performs the fuzzy comparison. The *eval()* with the minimum truth value is called for the consequent clause when the rule fires. This does a fuzzy assignment. Next we look at the **FuzzyOperator** methods that perform the comparison or assignment.

```
protected double eval() {
  if(consequent == false) {
    return FuzzyOperator.cmpIs(lhs, rhs);
  } else {
    FuzzyOperator.asgnIs(lhs, rhs);
    return 0.0;
  }
}


protected double eval(double truthValue) {
  FuzzyOperator.asgnIs(lhs, rhs, truthValue);
  return 0.0;
}
```

The **FuzzyOperator** class fuzzy assignment *asgnIs()* and fuzzy comparison *cmpIs()* are used in the *eval()* methods described previously. The *asgnIs()* method with three parameters is called when the consequent clause is evaluated. This method does an assignment of the *rhs* **FuzzySet** subject to the *truthValue* to the *lhs* **FuzzyRuleVariable**. For antecedent clauses, we use the *cmpIs()* method. We get the current numeric value of the *lhs* **FuzzyRuleVariable** and test its membership in the *rhs* **FuzzySet**. This value between 0.0 and 1.0 is returned as the *truthValue* in the **FuzzyRule** *fire()* method.

```
static void asgnIs(FuzzyRuleVariable lhs, FuzzySet rhs) {
  lhs.setFuzzyValue(rhs);
```

```
        }

        static void asgnIs(FuzzyRuleVariable lhs, FuzzySet rhs,
                           double truthValue) {
          ((ContinuousFuzzyRuleVariable) lhs).setFuzzyValue(rhs, truthValue);
        }

        static double cmpIs(FuzzyRuleVariable lhs, FuzzySet rhs) {
          return (rhs.membership(lhs.getNumericValue()));
        }
```

Rule Application Implementation

The *Rule* application uses two main classes, **RuleApp** and **RuleFrame**, to manage instances of **BooleanRuleBase** and **FuzzyRuleBase** classes, and it provides a graphical interface for experimentation. The main application GUI was designed using Borland JBuilder 3.0 but this code could have been implemented manually or with some other Java GUI builder tool. The **RuleFrame** class is a subclass of the **JFrame Swing** class.

The **RuleFrame** constructor instantiates and initializes three example **BooleanRuleBase** objects and one **FuzzyRuleBase** object. This code is shown in the following example:

```
        static BooleanRuleBase bugs;
        static BooleanRuleBase plants;
        static BooleanRuleBase vehicles;
        static FuzzyRuleBase motor;
        static RuleBase currentRuleBase;

          vehicles = new BooleanRuleBase("Vehicles Rule Base");
          vehicles.setDisplay(traceTextArea);
          initVehiclesRuleBase(vehicles);
          currentRuleBase = vehicles;
          bugs = new BooleanRuleBase("Bugs Rule Base");
          bugs.setDisplay(traceTextArea);
          initBugsRuleBase(bugs);
          plants = new BooleanRuleBase("Plants Rule Base");
          plants.setDisplay(traceTextArea);
          initPlantsRuleBase(plants);
          motor = new FuzzyRuleBase("Motor Fuzzy Rule Base");
          motor.setDisplay(traceTextArea);
          initMotorRuleBase(motor);
```

When the **Start** menu item is selected from the **File** pull-down menu, the *StartMenuItem_actionPerformed()* method is called. In that method we first get the *goalVar* from the *GoalComboBox*. Then we check if we are in forward-chaining or backward-chaining mode. We invoke the *forwardChain()* or *backwardChain()* methods on the *currentRuleBase*. The current settings of the rule base variables are used as inputs to the inferencing cycles. As the inferencing progresses, trace messages are used to display intermediate results in the **RuleFrame**'s text area. When the **Reset** menu item is selected, *reset()* on the *currentRuleBase* is called.

```
void StartMenuItem_actionPerformed(ActionEvent e) {
  String goal = null;
  RuleVariable goalVar =
    (RuleVariable)GoalComboBox.getSelectedItem();

  traceTextArea.append("\n --- Starting Inferencing Cycle --- \n");
  currentRuleBase.displayVariables(traceTextArea);
  if(forwardChainRadioButton.isSelected() == true) {
    currentRuleBase.forwardChain();
  }
  if(backChainRadioButton.isSelected() == true) {
    if(currentRuleBase instanceof BooleanRuleBase) {
      if(goalVar == null) {
        traceTextArea.append("Goal variable is not defined!");
      } else {
        goal = goalVar.getName();
      }
    }
    currentRuleBase.backwardChain(goal);
  }
  currentRuleBase.displayVariables(traceTextArea);
  traceTextArea.append("\n --- Ending Inferencing Cycle --- \n");
  if(goalVar != null) {
    Object result = goalVar.getValue();

    if(result == null) {
      result = "null";
    }
    resultTextField.setText((String) result);
  }
}
```

While backward chaining, the **BooleanRuleBase** can get to a point where it needs a value for a variable but cannot determine the value through inferencing. It therefore opens a dialog and uses the **RuleVariable** *promptString* to ask the user to supply a value. This **RuleVarDialog** is shown in Figure 4.12.

The **RuleFrame** class uses the **BooleanRuleBaseVariablesDialog** (see Figure 4.13) or the **FuzzyRuleBaseVariablesDialog** (see Figure 4.14) to allow the user to set variable values, depending on which **RuleBase** is selected for processing. These dialogs feature a similar design. A list box displays the variable names and their current values. An additional GUI control, either a text field or a combo box, is provided to allow the user to choose or enter a new value for the variable.

The Vehicles RuleBase Implementation

The *Vehicles* rule base is defined using the **RuleFrame** *initVehiclesBooleanRuleBase()* method. The *vehicles* **BooleanRuleBase** instance is passed in as the only argument. In this method, each **RuleVariable** is defined by creating an instance with the *rb* reference

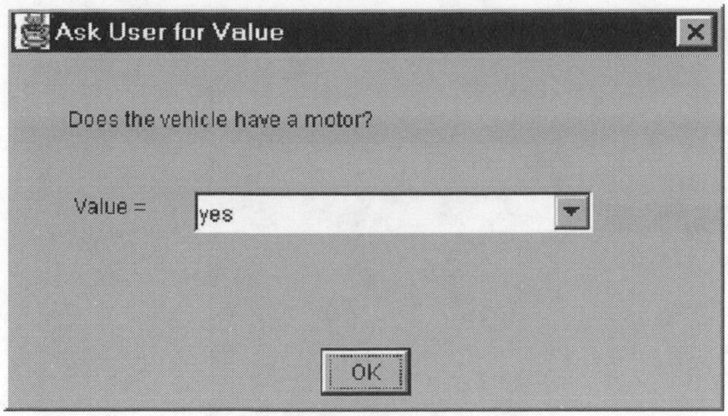

Figure 4.12 The RuleVar dialog.

and variable name as arguments on the constructor. The valid variable values are set using the *setLabels()* method, and the prompt text, used in the **RuleVarDialog** during backward chaining, is set using the *setPromptText()* method.

After all the variables are defined, a few condition instances are created for equals, not-equals, and less-than operators, and each **Rule** in the **BooleanRuleBase** is instantiated. The **Rule** constructors take a **BooleanRuleBase** reference, the rule *name* **String**, one or more antecedent **Clause**s, and a single consequent **Clause**.

```
public void initVehiclesRuleBase(BooleanRuleBase rb) {
    RuleVariable vehicle = new RuleVariable(rb, "vehicle");
```

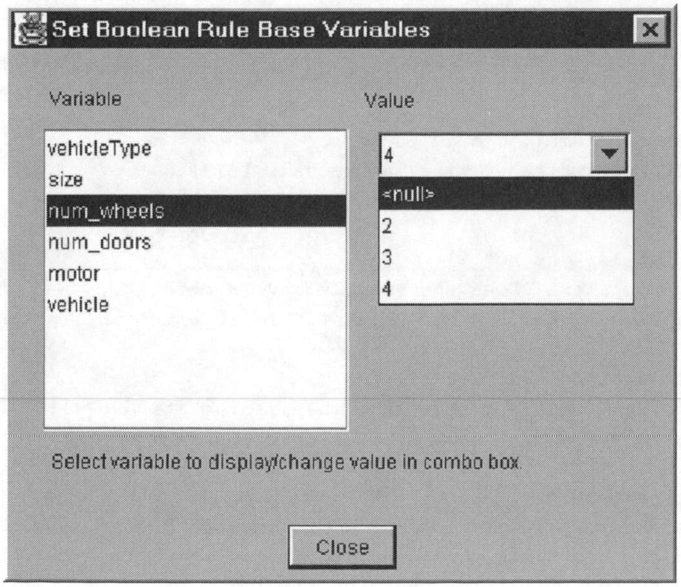

Figure 4.13 The BooleanRuleBaseVariablesDialog dialog.

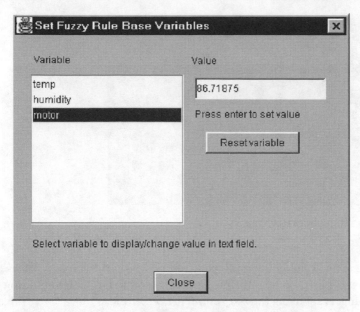

Figure 4.14 The FuzzyRuleBaseVariablesDIalog dialog.

```
vehicle.setLabels(
  "Bicycle Tricycle MotorCycle Sports_Car Sedan MiniVan
  Sports_Utility_Vehicle");
vehicle.setPromptText("What kind of vehicle is it?");
RuleVariable vehicleType = new RuleVariable(rb, "vehicleType");

vehicleType.setLabels("cycle automobile");
vehicleType.setPromptText("What type of vehicle is it?");
RuleVariable size = new RuleVariable(rb, "size");

size.setLabels("small medium large");
size.setPromptText("What size is the vehicle?");
RuleVariable motor = new RuleVariable(rb, "motor");

motor.setLabels("yes no");
motor.setPromptText("Does the vehicle have a motor?");
RuleVariable num_wheels = new RuleVariable(rb, "num_wheels");

num_wheels.setLabels("2 3 4");
num_wheels.setPromptText("How many wheels does it have?");
RuleVariable num_doors = new RuleVariable(rb, "num_doors");

num_doors.setLabels("2 3 4");
num_doors.setPromptText("How many doors does it have?");
Condition cEquals = new Condition("=");
Condition cNotEquals = new Condition("!=");
```

```
Condition cLessThan = new Condition("<");
Rule Bicycle =
  new Rule(rb, "bicycle",
    new Clause[]{
      new Clause(vehicleType, cEquals, "cycle"),
      new Clause(num_wheels, cEquals, "2"),
      new Clause(motor, cEquals, "no") },
    new Clause(vehicle, cEquals, "Bicycle"));
Rule Tricycle =
  new Rule(rb, "tricycle",
    new Clause[]{
      new Clause(vehicleType, cEquals,"cycle"),
      new Clause(num_wheels, cEquals, "3"),
      new Clause(motor, cEquals, "no") },
    new Clause(vehicle, cEquals, "Tricycle"));
Rule Motorcycle =
  new Rule(rb, "motorcycle",
    new Clause[]{
      new Clause(vehicleType, cEquals, "cycle"),
      new Clause(num_wheels, cEquals, "2"),
      new Clause(motor, cEquals, "yes") },
    new Clause(vehicle, cEquals, "Motorcycle"));
Rule SportsCar =
  new Rule(rb, "sportsCar",
    new Clause[]{
      new Clause(vehicleType, cEquals, "automobile"),
      new Clause(size, cEquals, "small"),
      new Clause(num_doors, cEquals, "2") },
    new Clause(vehicle, cEquals, "Sports_Car"));
Rule Sedan =
  new Rule(rb, "sedan",
    new Clause[]{
      new Clause(vehicleType, cEquals, "automobile"),
      new Clause(size, cEquals, "medium"),
      new Clause(num_doors, cEquals, "4") },
    new Clause(vehicle, cEquals, "Sedan"));
Rule MiniVan =
  new Rule(rb, "miniVan",
    new Clause[]{
      new Clause(vehicleType, cEquals, "automobile"),
      new Clause(size, cEquals, "medium"),
      new Clause(num_doors, cEquals, "3") },
    new Clause(vehicle, cEquals, "MiniVan"));
Rule SUV =
  new Rule(rb, "SUV",
    new Clause[]{
      new Clause(vehicleType, cEquals,"automobile"),
      new Clause(size, cEquals, "large"),
      new Clause(num_doors, cEquals, "4") },
    new Clause(vehicle, cEquals, "Sports_Utility_Vehicle"));
```

```
      Rule Cycle =
        new Rule(rb, "Cycle",
          new Clause(num_wheels, cLessThan, "4"),
          new Clause(vehicleType, cEquals, "cycle"));
      Rule Automobile =
        new Rule(rb, "Automobile",
          new Clause[]{
            new Clause(num_wheels, cEquals, "4"),
            new Clause(motor, cEquals, "yes") },
          new Clause(vehicleType, cEquals, "automobile"));
  }
```

The **RuleFrame** *demoVehiclesFC()* method is called when the *Vehicles* rule base and the forward-chaining radio button are selected and the **Use defaults . . .** menu item is selected. The *vehicle* and *vehicleType* variables are set to null, and the other variables are set to indicate that the *vehicle* is a *MiniVan*. After the variable values are set, they are displayed in the trace text area.

```
public void demoVehiclesFC(BooleanRuleBase rb) {
  traceTextArea.append(
    "\n --- Setting Values for Vehicles ForwardChain Demo ---\n ");
  rb.setVariableValue("vehicle", null);
  rb.setVariableValue("vehicleType", null);
  rb.setVariableValue("size", "medium");
  rb.setVariableValue("num_wheels", "4");
  rb.setVariableValue("num_doors", "3");
  rb.setVariableValue("motor", "yes");
  rb.displayVariables(traceTextArea);
}


public void demoVehiclesBC(BooleanRuleBase rb) {
  traceTextArea.append(
    "\n --- Setting Values for Vehicles BackwardChain Demo ---\n ");
  rb.setVariableValue("vehicle", null);
  rb.setVariableValue("vehicleType", null);
  rb.setVariableValue("size", "medium");
  rb.setVariableValue("num_wheels", "4");
  rb.setVariableValue("num_doors", "3");
  rb.setVariableValue("motor", "yes");
  rb.displayVariables(traceTextArea);
}
```

The **RuleFrame** *demoVehiclesBC()* method is called when the *Vehicles* rule base and the backward-chaining radio button are selected and the **Use defaults . . .** menu item is selected. The *vehicle* and *vehicleType* variables are set to null, and the other variables are set to indicate that the *vehicle* is a *MiniVan*. The variable values are set and are displayed in the trace text area.

Implementations of the other two Boolean rule bases provided with the **Rule App**, the bugs and plants rule bases, are listed in Appendix A.

The Motor RuleBase Implementation

The *motor* rule base is defined using the **RuleFrame** *initMotorRuleBase()* method. The *motor* **FuzzyRuleBase** instance is passed in as the only argument. The method first initializes the fuzzy inferencing parameters. Each **ContinuousFuzzyRuleVariable** is then defined by creating an instance with a rule base reference, the variable name, and the low and high values for the discourse as the arguments on the constructor. The **FuzzySets** are then defined and added to the variables.

After all the **ContinuousFuzzyRuleVariables** and associated **FuzzySets** are defined, each **FuzzyRule** in the **FuzzyRuleBase** is instantiated. The **FuzzyRule** constructors take a **FuzzyRuleBase** reference; the rule *name* **String**; one or more antecedent **FuzzyClauses** that use the fuzzy comparison (*cmpIs*) operator; and one consequent **FuzzyClause** that uses the fuzzy assignment (*asgnIs*) operator.

```
public void initMotorRuleBase(FuzzyRuleBase rb) {
   rb.setCorrelationMethod(FuzzyDefs.PRODUCT);
   rb.setInferenceMethod(FuzzyDefs.FUZZYADD);
   rb.setDefuzzifyMethod(FuzzyDefs.CENTROID);
   ContinuousFuzzyRuleVariable temp =
      new ContinuousFuzzyRuleVariable(rb,"temp", 0, 100);

   temp.addSetShoulder("cold", 0.1, 0, 25, FuzzyDefs.LEFT);
   temp.addSetTriangle("cool", 0.1, 10, 30, 50);
   temp.addSetTrapezoid("medium", 0.1, 25, 40, 60, 75);
   temp.addSetTriangle("warm", 0.1, 50, 70, 90);
   temp.addSetShoulder("hot", 0.1, 75, 100, FuzzyDefs.RIGHT);
   ContinuousFuzzyRuleVariable humidity =
      new ContinuousFuzzyRuleVariable(rb, "humidity", 0, 100);

   humidity.addSetShoulder("dry", 0.1, 0, 25, FuzzyDefs.LEFT);
   humidity.addSetTriangle("pleasant", 0.1, 10, 30, 50);
   humidity.addSetTrapezoid("comfortable", 0.1, 25, 40, 60, 75);
   humidity.addSetTriangle("sticky", 0.1, 50, 70, 90);
   humidity.addSetShoulder("sweltering", 0.1, 75, 100, FuzzyDefs.RIGHT);
   ContinuousFuzzyRuleVariable motor = new ContinuousFuzzyRuleVariable
      (rb, "motor", 0, 100);

   motor.addSetShoulder("slow", 0.1, 0, 40, FuzzyDefs.LEFT);
   motor.addSetTrapezoid("medium", 0.1, 25, 40, 60, 75);
   motor.addSetShoulder("fast", 0.1, 60, 100, FuzzyDefs.RIGHT);
   int compareIs = FuzzyOperator.CmpIs;
   int assignIs = FuzzyOperator.AsgnIs;

   FuzzyRule slowRule =
      new FuzzyRule(rb, "slowRule",
         new FuzzyClause[]{
            rb.createClause(temp, compareIs, "", "cold"),
            rb.createClause( humidity, compareIs, "", "pleasant") },
```

```
                    rb.createClause( motor, assignIs, "", "slow"));
      FuzzyRule mediumRule =
        new FuzzyRule(rb, "mediumRule",
          new FuzzyClause[]{
            rb.createClause(temp, compareIs, "","medium"),
            rb.createClause(humidity, compareIs, "", "comfortable") },
            rb.createClause(motor, assignIs, "", "medium"));
      FuzzyRule fastRule =
        new FuzzyRule(rb, "fastRule",
          new FuzzyClause[]{
            rb.createClause(temp, compareIs, "", "hot"),
            rb.createClause(humidity, compareIs, "", "sticky") },
            rb.createClause(motor, assignIs, "", "fast"));
      FuzzyRule veryFastRule =
        new FuzzyRule(rb, "veryFastRule",
          new FuzzyClause[]{
            rb.createClause(temp, compareIs, "V","hot"),
            rb.createClause(humidity, compareIs, "V", "sticky") },
            rb.createClause(motor, assignIs, "V", "fast"));
  }
```

The **RuleFrame** *demoMotorFC()* method is called when the *motor* fuzzy rule base and the forward-chaining radio button are selected and the **Use defaults . . .** menu item is selected. The *temp* and *humidity* **FuzzyRuleVariable**s are retrieved from the **Fuzzy-RuleBase** and then we set the values on each. The *demoMotorBC()* method simply informs the user that backward chaining is not supported by the **FuzzyRuleBase** class.

```
public void demoMotorFC(FuzzyRuleBase rb) {
  traceTextArea.append(
    "\n --- Setting Values for Motor ForwardChain Demo ---\n");
  ContinuousFuzzyRuleVariable temp =
    (ContinuousFuzzyRuleVariable) rb.getVariable("temp");
  ContinuousFuzzyRuleVariable humidity =
    (ContinuousFuzzyRuleVariable) rb.getVariable("humidity");

  temp.setNumericValue(90.0);
  humidity.setNumericValue(70.0);
  rb.displayVariables(traceTextArea);
}


public void demoMotorBC(FuzzyRuleBase rb) {
  traceTextArea.append(
    "\n --- Setting Values for Motor BackwardChain Demo ---");
  traceTextArea.append(
    "\n  Fuzzy Rule Base does not support backward inferencing!");
}
```

That brings to a close our discussion of the *Rule* application. All of the code described in this chapter is included on the CD-ROM. The application and its underlying **Boolean-RuleBase** and **FuzzyRuleBase** classes provide basic functionality. Some obvious enhancements come to mind, including support for **Objects** on both the left-hand and right-hand sides of **Clause**s. In the **Rule** class, it would be nice to provide support for sensors and effectors (which could be useful in Part Two of this book). Support for multiple instances of variables and tagging or time-stamping of data would greatly extend the forward-chaining capabilities. Adding rule priorities would also be useful for larger rule bases. Adding enhanced tracing and how-and-why support for the backward-chaining algorithm would be a nice touch. Although there is much more we could do, it is important to recognize that even this level of functionality is capable of producing useful behavior in applications or, as we will see, in intelligent agents.

In the remainder of this chapter, we change our focus from implementation to a more high-level discussion of planning. Planning is an interesting topic, because for anything other than simple tasks, intelligent agents need to build plans and execute them in order to perform useful work for us.

Planning

Planning is one of the most complex problems that AI has attempted to solve. However, it is one of the most useful in that most nontrivial problems require some ordered sequence of operations and a variety of techniques to solve. Planning involves several aspects of problem solving. First is the decomposition of a big problem into smaller, more easily solved subproblems. Second is taking into account the constraints on the order of solution of the subproblems so that we do not undo work we did in the previous step. Last is the challenge of keeping track of the state of the world as we progress toward a solution [Russell and Norvig 1995].

An important point to remember is that planning is not search. We are not simply trying to traverse a graph in search of a single goal node or to find a path to a goal node. In planning, we compute several steps of a problem-solving approach without executing them. Also, it is sometimes not possible to start at the beginning and proceed linearly to a solution. There may be discontinuities or breaks in our plan which we cannot overcome. For example, how do we get from A to B when there is no path between those points? In order to plan, we must have an internal model of the world so that we can propose operations and predict what the outcome will be, and whether it will bring us closer to the goal or not.

As with any search algorithm, a planning system must be able to select the best action or operation to perform for a given situation. It must be able to model or predict what the consequence of taking that action will be. It must detect when it has reached the goal, or realize when it has reached a dead end and needs to try a new plan of attack.

Perhaps the biggest difference between a planning problem and a simple search problem is that the state space is so large that you cannot carry the complete state along with you at each decision node. The sheer size of the space requires that we only keep track of the things that explicitly change due to some action we take. This problem is called the *frame problem* in AI literature.

There are three major approaches to planning that we will discuss briefly. First is goal stack planning, which is a linear problem-solving technique; next is a nonlinear method; and finally we'll look at a hierarchical planning algorithm.

Goal stack planning was an early attempt at solving problems that could be broken up into smaller problems, where there were constraints or interactions between steps in the plan. The research problem focused on a blocks world, where the goal was simply to arrange the blocks in a specified order. While seemingly trivial (any two-year-old can do the task), this toy problem illustrated essential requirements for successful planning strategies.

Given an initial configuration of blocks stacked on each other, or lying on a table, we specify a desired goal configuration. We have a defined set of operators for moving blocks. We can pick them up, move them, or stack them on other blocks. Our plan is to develop the sequence of operators that goes from our initial state to our goal state. Goal stack planning, as the name implies, uses a stack to hold subgoals or intermediate goals we solve as subproblems. A major problem with goal stack planning is that we can expend a lot of effort solving parts of the problem while making other parts more difficult, if not impossible, to solve. The major weakness is that goal stack planning tries to solve the problem and subproblems linearly, in order, and does not take into account how the sequence of actions can impact progress toward the ultimate goal.

Several nonlinear techniques were developed in order to avoid the problems with linear planning techniques such as goal stack planning. Nonlinear planning approaches can account for the interactions between operators and subgoals. They construct a plan where two or more subgoals can proceed simultaneously. Famous nonlinear AI planning systems include NOAH [Sacerdoti 1974] and MOLGEN [Stefik 1981]. A technique called constraint posting allows nonlinear plans to be constructed incrementally with a set of operators having incompletely specified order and variable bindings. Rather than apply a single operator and then update the space, as in state-space planning or search, constraint posting allows multiple operators and variable bindings to be specified in a single node.

Means-ends analysis is used to select operations along the way. Each operator has a set of preconditions that must hold in order for the operator to be applicable, and a set of postconditions that specify the changes to the state once the operator is applied. This pre/post condition list gets around the frame problem because it explicitly states what subset of conditions must hold and what conditions will be changed.

The third major class of planning algorithms, hierarchical planning, allows plans to proceed at higher levels of abstraction in order to sketch out feasible solutions without going immediately into the details. The ABSTRIPS system [Sacerdoti 1974] used criticality values to rank the importance of various preconditions on operators. The idea is to first solve the entire planning problem, taking into account only those preconditions at the highest levels of criticality, and then to proceed to finer and finer granularity by adding additional operators to satisfy the preconditions at the lower levels. Although the proper setting of the criticality values is crucial, hierarchical planners have proven it to be one of the most practical techniques for planning systems.

A more recent example of a nonlinear hierarchical planner is the PRODIGY planning algorithm developed at Carnegie-Mellon University [Veloso, Carbonell, et al. 1995]. PRODIGY uses means-ends analysis and backward-chaining search to reason about multiple goals and potential operators at the same time. Several learning algorithms are used to reduce the planning time and to improve the quality of the solutions. The operators can be defined to represent different levels of abstraction, which allows PRODIGY to also perform hierarchical planning.

Planning has become a major requirement for creating effective multiagent teams in dynamic environments. Coordinating the actions of a group of autonomous agents brings additional constraints and headaches to planners used for this purpose. We discuss this in more detail in Chapter 6, "Agents and Multiagent Systems."

Summary

In this chapter we focused on reasoning techniques used with if-then rules. The main points include the following:

- *If-then rules* are the most successful form of knowledge representation. They are easy for people to create and understand.

- A rule has two parts, an *if* or *antecedent* part, and a *then* or *consequent* part. A condition in the rule is called a *clause*. If all of the antecedent clauses of a rule are true, it is *triggered* to fire. When a rule *fires*, its consequent clause is made true and a new fact is added to the knowledge base.

- *Certainty* or *confidence factors* are used as rule modifiers in situations where either the validity of the data or the applicability of the rule is uncertain.

- Reasoning systems are either *monotonic*, meaning they only ever add new facts to the working memory, or *nonmonotonic*, where they can retract facts when provided with new evidence. Nonmonotonic reasoning systems must deal with *truth maintenance*, and track dependencies between facts in the working memory.

- *Forward chaining* is a data-driven inferencing method using rules. Starting with an initial set of facts in *working memory*, the *match* phase selects the *conflict set* of rules that are ready to fire. *Conflict resolution* selects a single rule to fire. The *act* phase fires the rule and adds a new fact to the working memory. This process is repeated until the conflict set is empty.

- *Backward chaining* is a goal-driven inferencing method using rules. Starting with a goal variable or clause, the algorithm chains through the rules from consequent clauses to antecedent clauses, trying to prove the rule true.

- *Fuzzy systems* are rule systems that use fuzzy logic rather than Boolean logic to make decisions. As a knowledge representation, fuzzy rules are more like natural language: they use linguistic variables and hedges such as *very* and *extremely* to modify conceptual variables.

- We implemented a *Rule application* that uses **BooleanRuleBase**, **Rule**, and **RuleVariable** classes to perform forward and backward chaining in Java. We also implemented a **FuzzyRuleBase** that uses fuzzy logic to perform forward inferencing.

- *Planning* is a fundamental requirement for intelligent agents. Planning is difficult because there are sometimes interactions between subproblems or pieces of the plan. Three major types of planning algorithms have been studied: *linear*, *nonlinear*, and *hierarchical*.

Exercises

1. Using the *Vehicles* rule base, manually walk through a backward-chaining inference cycle with the goal of *vehicles = sedan*. How many times did you have to ask the user to provide a value for an unknown variable while inferencing?

2. Run the **RuleApp** application program. Select the *Vehicles* rule base and set the variables so that the vehicle is recognized as a sedan. Do this using forward chaining and backward chaining. What were the differences between the two? For backward chaining, do the trace results compare to Exercise 4.1?

3. How could you extend the **Clause** class to support sensors and effectors? What other classes would have to be modified or extended to support these functions?

4. Early expert systems used confidence factors with boolean rules to reason about uncertainty. How do fuzzy rule systems overcome this issue, or do they? What is the difference between a probability and a fuzzy number?

5. The *Motor* fuzzy rule base uses four rules to cover the input space of temperature and humidity. Use the **RuleApp** to enter values over the entire range 0–100 for these variables and plot the motor output value. Does the output change smoothly or jump abruptly as the input values change? Add more rules to the motor rule base, and check the effect on the motor variable. Would adding more fuzzy sets or using other linguistic hedges help to smooth the output response?

6. You have to create a system to diagnose problems with an engine. A mechanic is available to act as the expert. Your job is to take his knowledge and turn it into rules. The application must make a best-guess diagnosis based on the available data. As more information is available, the diagnosis should be more accurate. Would you choose boolean or fuzzy rules for this application? Why?

CHAPTER 5

Learning Systems

I n this chapter, we focus on adaptive software and machine learning techniques. We start with an overview of the different paradigms for performing machine learning, including supervised, unsupervised, and reinforcement learning. We provide a general introduction to neural networks and then a more detailed discussion of back propagation and Kohonen maps. Next, we explore the use of information theory to construct decision trees from data. We design and implement a Java application and the corresponding Java classes for back propagation, Kohonen maps, and decision tree algorithms.

Overview

One central element of intelligent behavior is the ability to adapt or learn from experience. For all of the sophisticated knowledge representation and reasoning algorithms that we develop, there is no way that we can know *a priori* all of the situations that our intelligent agent will encounter. Thus, being able to adapt to changes in the environment or to get better at tasks through experience becomes a significant differentiator for any software system. Any agent that can learn has an advantage over one that cannot. Adding learning or adaptive behavior to an intelligent agent elevates it to a higher level of ability. A learning agent can adapt to your likes and dislikes. It can learn which agents to trust and cooperate with, and which ones to avoid. A learning agent can recognize situations it has been in before and improve its performance based on prior experience.

There are many forms of learning. First, there is rote learning, in which an example is given and the student (intelligent agent) copies the example and exactly reproduces the behavior. Although rote learning is a very simple form of learning, it still can be powerful.

For example, we could run a simulation 24 hours a day, 7 days a week, to generate new situations and the desired behavior, then present these examples to our agent. Our agent would be better able to respond to situations one week after we started the training and would be even better one month later (assuming the additional knowledge didn't slow down its response time).

Another form of learning is parameter or weight adjustment. In this case, we may know *a priori* what factors are important in a decision, but we do not know how to weight their contribution to the answer. We can adjust the weighting factors over time so that we improve the likelihood of a correct decision or output. This technique is the basis for neural network learning.

Induction is a process of learning by example in which we try to extract the important characteristics of the problem, thereby allowing us to generalize to novel situations or inputs. Decision trees and neural networks both perform induction and can be used for classification or regression (prediction) problems. The key aspect of inductive methods is that the examples are processed and automatically transformed into an internal form (knowledge representation) that captures the essence of the problem.

Another type of learning is called clustering, chunking, or abstraction of knowledge. Although people learn from very specific examples or situations, the ability to detect common patterns and generalize to new situations is a type of learning. By chunking ten cases into one more general case, we cut down on the amount of storage we need and also on the search or processing time. By thinking at higher or more abstract levels, we can think "great thoughts" without getting caught in the muddle of a million little details.

Clustering is another learning algorithm that is a type of chunking. Clustering algorithms look at high-dimensional data (data with many attributes) and score them for similarity based on some criterion. The result is that each sample is assigned to a cluster or group with other examples deemed to be "similar." This similarity could be used as a way of assigning meaning to that group of samples. For example, clustering data of business customers may result in four distinct clusters. Examination of the customers who fell into each cluster may show that they are being grouped based on their interests (types of product they buy) or by their purchasing patterns (number of visits, sales totals, profitability) or some other criterion that may not have been apparent when looking at the original data. Another example would be clustering documents we found particularly useful. This could provide valuable information to improve the performance of a document search engine the next time we make a query.

All of these learning techniques, including induction (for classification and prediction) and clustering, are used in data mining tools. Data mining is a process of extracting valuable, non-obvious information from large collections of data [Bigus 1996]. The main contribution of data mining is to find patterns which were not known to exist, that is, to discover new information or knowledge (some people refer to data mining as *knowledge discovery*). So learning, as applied to data mining, can be thought of as a way for intelligent agents to automatically discover knowledge rather than having it predefined using predicate logic, rules, or some other knowledge representation.

Learning Paradigms

There are several major paradigms, or approaches, to machine learning. These include supervised, unsupervised, and reinforcement learning. In addition, many researchers and application developers combine two or more of these learning approaches into one system. How the training data is processed is a major aspect of these learning paradigms.

Supervised learning is the most common form of learning and is sometimes called *programming by example*. The learning agent is trained by showing it examples of the problem state or attributes along with the desired output or action. The learning agent makes a prediction based on the inputs and if the output differs from the desired output, then the agent is adjusted or adapted to produce the correct output. This process is repeated over and over until the agent learns to make accurate classifications or predictions. Historical data from databases, sensor logs, or trace logs is often used as the training or example data. We describe two implementations of supervised learning algorithms later in this chapter: a back propagation neural network and a decision tree.

Unsupervised learning is used when the learning agent needs to recognize similarities between inputs or to identify features in the input data. The data is presented to the agent, and it adapts so that it partitions the data into groups. The clustering or segmenting process continues until the agent places the same data into the same group on successive passes over the data. An unsupervised learning algorithm performs a type of feature detection where important common attributes in the data are extracted. Later in this chapter, we present a neural network implementation of an unsupervised learning technique called a Kohonen map.

Reinforcement learning is a type of supervised learning used when explicit input/output pairs of training data are not available. It can be used in cases where there is a sequence of inputs and the desired output is only known after the specific sequence occurs. This process of identifying the relationship between a series of input values and a later output value is called temporal credit assignment. Because we provide less specific error information, reinforcement learning usually takes longer than supervised learning and is less efficient. However, in many situations, having exact prior information about the desired outcome is not possible. In many ways, reinforcement learning is the most realistic form of learning. Examples of reinforcement learning algorithms include temporal difference learning [Sutton 1988] and Q-learning [Watkins 1989].

Another important distinction in learning agents is whether the learning is done on-line or off-line. On-line learning means that the agent is sent out to perform its tasks and that it can learn or adapt after each transaction is processed. On-line learning is like on-the-job training and places severe requirements on the learning algorithms. It must be very fast and very stable (we don't want a brain-dead agent in the middle of a big sales negotiation). Off-line learning, on the other hand, is more like a business seminar. You take your salespeople off the floor and place them in an environment where they can focus on improving their skills without distractions. After a suitable training period, they are sent out to apply their newfound knowledge and skills. In an intelligent agent context, this means that we would gather data from situations that the agents have experienced.

We could then augment this data with information about the desired agent response to build a training data set. Once we have this database we can use it to modify the behavior of our agents.

Neural Networks

Neural networks provide an easy way to add learning ability to agents. There are many different types of neural networks, some which train quickly and some that require many passes over the data before they learn the assigned tasks. Neural networks can be used in supervised, unsupervised, and reinforcement learning scenarios. They can be used for classification, clustering, and prediction. In many applications, neural networks can replace expert systems, especially where sufficient data is available for training.

Not simply another learning algorithm or regression technique, neural networks actually represent a new and different computing model from the serial von Neumann computers we all know and love (and use every day). Borrowing heavily from the metaphor of the human brain, neural networks have hundreds or thousands of simple processors (called processing units, processing elements, or neurons) connected by hundreds or thousands of adaptive weights, as illustrated in Figure 5.1. This network of processors and connections forms a parallel computer that can adaptively rewire itself when it is exposed to data. The adaptive weights are adjusted and form the memory of the neural network computer, playing the role that the synapse has in the human brain. Another difference between neural networks and traditional digital computers is that neural network processors are analog, not digital. They don't spit out binary 1s and 0s, they produce a continuous range of outputs, usually from 0.0 to 1.0. The infinite number of real values between 0 and 1 can be used to our advantage.

The new parallel computing model notwithstanding, most neural network implementations today are simply programs running on serial computers. We can simulate the behavior of the neural network computer on our extremely flexible and powerful (and cheap) PCs and workstations. And while they could do wondrous things if implemented

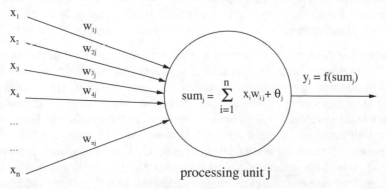

Figure 5.1 A neural processing unit.

in parallel hardware, neural networks have proven useful in many commercial applications even when simulated on standard computers.

Back Propagation

Back propagation is the most popular neural network architecture for supervised learning. It features a feed-forward connection topology, meaning that data flows through the network in a single direction, and uses a technique called the *backward propagation of errors* to adjust the connection weights [Rumelhart, Hinton, and Williams 1986]. In addition to a layer of input and output units, a back-propagation network can have one or more layers of hidden units, which receive inputs only from other units, not the external environment. A back-propagation network with a single hidden layer of processing units can learn to model any continuous function when given enough units in the hidden layer. The primary applications of back-propagation networks are for prediction and classification.

Figure 5.2 shows a diagram of a back-propagation neural network and illustrates the three major steps in the training process. First, input data is presented to the input layer of units on the left, and flows through the network until it reaches the network output units on the right. This is called the forward pass. The *activations* or values of the output units represent the actual or predicted output of the network. The desired output value is also presented to the network, because this is supervised learning. Next, the difference between the desired and actual output is computed, producing the network error. This error term is then passed backwards through the network to adjust the connection weights. This process is described in gory detail later in this section. These formulas are used as the basis for our Java implementation, described later in this chapter.

Each network input unit takes a single numeric value, x_i, which is usually scaled or normalized to a value between 0.0 and 1.0. This value becomes the input unit activation. Next, we need to propagate the data forward, through the neural network. For each unit in the hidden layer, we compute the sum of the products of the input unit activations and the weights connecting those input layer units to the hidden layer. This sum is the inner product (also called the dot or scalar product) of the input vector and the weights in the hidden unit. Once this sum is computed, we add a threshold value and then pass

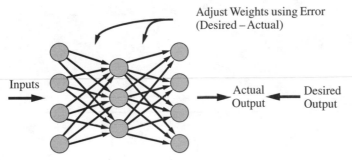

Figure 5.2   Back propagation neural network.

this sum through a nonlinear activation function, **f**, producing the unit activation y_j as shown in Figure 5.1. The formula for computing the activation of any unit in a hidden or output layer in the network is

$$y_j = \mathbf{f}\left(\text{sum}_j = \sum x_i w_{ij} + \theta_j \right),$$

where i ranges over all units leading into unit j, and the activation function is

$$\mathbf{f}(\text{sum}_j) = \frac{1}{1 + e^{-\text{sum}_j}}.$$

As mentioned earlier, we use the S-shaped sigmoid or logistic function for **f**. As shown in Figure 5.3, for a range of sums from -5 to $+5$ we get a y value ranging from 0 to 1. Extremely large positive or negative sums get squashed (that's a technical term) into that same range. The effect of the threshold θ is to shift the S-shaped curve left or right. For example, if the threshold is $+5$, then the sum would have to be -5 in order to produce an output value of 0.5.

The formula for calculating the changes to the weights is

$$\Delta w_{ij} = \eta \delta_j y_i$$

where w_{ij} is the weight connecting unit i to unit j, η is the learn rate parameter, δ_j is the error signal for that unit, and y_i is the output or activation value of unit i. For units in the output layer, the error signal is the difference between the target output t_j and the actual output y_j multiplied by the derivative of the logistic activation function.

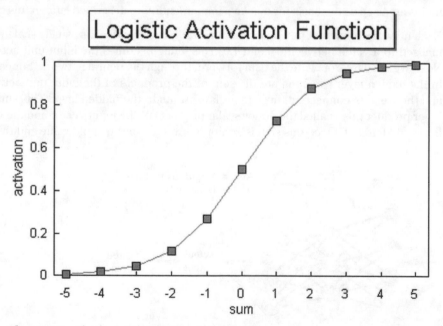

Figure 5.3 The logistic activation function.

$$\delta_j = (t_j - y_j)f'_j(\mathrm{sum}_j) = (t_j - y_j)y_j(1 - y_j)$$

For each unit in the hidden layer, the error signal is the derivative of the activation function multiplied by the sum of the products of the outgoing connection weights and their corresponding error signals. So for hidden unit j

$$\delta_j = f'_j(\mathrm{sum}_j)\sum \delta_k w_{jk}$$

where k ranges over the indices of the units receiving unit j's output signal.

A common modification of the weight update rule is the use of a momentum term α, to cut down on oscillation of the weights. So, the weight change becomes a combination of the current weight change, computed as before, plus some fraction (α ranges from 0 to 1) of the previous weight change. This complicates implementation because we now have to store the weight changes from the prior step.

$$\Delta w_{ij}(n + 1) = \eta\delta_j y_i + \alpha\Delta w_{ij}(n)$$

The mathematical basis for backward propagation is described in detail in Rumelhart, Hinton, and Williams (1986). When the weight changes are summed up (or batched) over an entire presentation of the training set, the error minimization function performed is called gradient descent. In practice, most people immediately update the network weights after each input vector is presented. While pattern updates, as this is called, can sometimes produce undesirable behavior, it usually results in faster training than using the batch updates.

Kohonen Maps

The self-organizing feature maps developed by Tuevo Kohonen have become one of the most popular and practical neural network models [Kohonen 1990]. A Kohonen map is a single-layer neural network comprised of an input layer and an output layer. Unlike back propagation, which is a supervised learning paradigm, feature maps perform unsupervised learning. Each time an input vector is presented to the network, its distance to each unit in the output layer is computed. Various distance measures have been used. The most common and the one used here is just the Euclidean distance. The output unit with the smallest distance to the input vector is declared the "winner." The winning unit and a set of units in the neighborhood weights are adjusted by moving the weights toward the input vector. Initially, the neighborhood and the learning rate are quite large and therefore many units are moved around in the input space to match the set of training vectors. As training progresses, the neighborhood shrinks and the learning rate is decreased. The Kohonen map self-organizes over time, and at the end of a successful training run, a topographic map is created. One attribute of such a map is that inputs that are near each other in the input space map onto output units that are in close proximity in the output layer of the neural network.

In Figure 5.4, we show a schematic diagram of a Kohonen map. First the inputs are presented to the input layer. Second, the distance of the input pattern to the weights to each output unit is computed using the Euclidean distance formula

$$y_j = \|\mathbf{x} - w_j\|^2$$

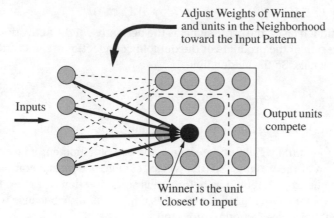

Figure 5.4 Kohonen map neural network.

where $\mathbf{x}$ is the input vector, w_j is the weight vector into output unit j, and y_j is the resulting distance. The output unit j with the minimum value y_j is declared the winner. The weights of the winner and the units in its neighborhood are then adjusted using:

$$w_j(t + 1) = w_j(t) + \beta(k)C_{ij}(k)y_j(t)$$

where w_j is the weight vector into unit j at previous time t and current time $t + 1$; $\beta(k)$ is the learn rate at iteration k; $C_{ij}(k)$ is the value of the neighborhood function for units i and j at iteration k; and y_j is the Euclidean distance between input vector $\mathbf{x}$ and weight vector w_j at time t. This neighborhood function $C_{ij}(k)$ is called a Gaussian function and is shaped like a Mexican hat or sombrero. It is defined as follows:

$$C_{ij}(k) = \exp\left(-\frac{\|i - j\|^2}{\sigma(k)^2}\right)$$

where i and j are the coordinates of the units in the two-dimensional map, and k is the iteration number. The width of the neighborhood function is $\sigma(k)^2$, which starts out as wide as the map when k is small and decreases to a final value encompassing a single unit when k is at its maximum value. The $\beta(k)$ parameter is the learn rate for iteration k. This is computed as follows:

$$\beta(k) = \beta_{\text{initial}}\left(\frac{\beta_{\text{final}}}{\beta_{\text{initial}}}\right)^{\frac{k}{k_{\text{max}}}}$$

where the k_{max} term is the maximum number of iterations to be performed. The learn rate $\beta(k)$ exponentially decreases as the iteration number k gets larger. We start at iteration $k = 0$ with the β_{initial} learn rate and end at iteration $k = k_{\text{max}}$ with the β_{final} value. Typical values for β_{initial} and β_{final} are 1.0 and 0.05 respectively. These formulas are used as the basis for our Java implementation, described later in this chapter.

Decision Trees

Decision trees perform induction on example data sets, generating classifiers and prediction models. A decision tree examines the data set and uses information theory to determine which attribute contains the most information on which to base a decision. This attribute is then used in a decision node to split the data set into two groups, based on the value of that attribute. At each subsequent decision node, the data set is split again. The result is a decision tree, a collection of nodes. The leaf nodes represent a final classification of the record. Examples of decision tree algorithms are ID3 [Quinlan 1986] and the C4.5 systems [Quinlan, 1993]. A generic term for the class of decision tree algorithms is Classification And Regression Trees (CART).

Information Theory

Decision trees are based on information theory, a mathematical concept first introduced by Shannon and Weaver (1949). The unit of information is a bit, and the amount of information in a single binary answer is $\log_2 P(v)$, where $P(v)$ is the probability of event v occurring. The *information* content is based on the prior probabilities of getting the correct answer to a question or classification [Russell and Norvig 1995]. Suppose we are trying to classify customers who will either renew their Internet service accounts or will cancel and switch to a competitor. Let's assume we had 1000 customers last year, 800 that renewed and 200 that canceled. We would have a training set with 1000 records, containing some set of attributes of those customers (their age, sex, income, average monthly connect time, years as customers, etc.) as well as the information on whether they renewed or canceled their service. Those who renewed we consider positive examples, p. Those who canceled we consider negative examples, n. If we had information on a customer and had to try to predict whether that customer would renew or cancel, how much information would be contained in a correct answer? The formula used is

$$\mathbf{I}\left(\frac{p}{(p + n)}, \frac{n}{(p + n)}\right) = -\left(\frac{p}{(p + n)}\right)\log_2\left(\frac{p}{(p + n)}\right) - \left(\frac{n}{(p + n)}\right)\log_2\left(\frac{n}{(p + n)}\right)$$

Notice that the denominator in all terms is the total number of records. The first term is the probability that the positive case occurs, $(p / (p + n))$, multiplied by the information content of that event, $\log_2 (p / (p + n))$. The second term is an equivalent expression applied to the negative examples. In our Internet service example, the chance that any single factor (for example, age) would completely divide the group into those who would renew or cancel is small. We need to measure how much information we still need after the test. Any attribute A which has v distinct values divides the data set into v subsets according to the values of A. Each resulting subset of the training data has its own makeup of p and n outcomes. On average, after testing attribute A, we still need

$$\text{Remainder}(A) = \sum \frac{(p_i + n_i)}{(p + n)} \mathbf{I}\left(\frac{p_i}{(p_i + n_i)}, \frac{n_i}{(p_i + n_i)}\right)$$

bits of information where i goes from 1 to v, the number of discrete values that attribute A can take. The difference between the information needed before the attribute test and the remainder is called the *information gain* of the test.

$$\text{Gain}(A) = \mathbf{I}\left(\frac{p}{(p+n)}, \frac{n}{(p+n)}\right) - \text{Remainder}(A)$$

As an example, suppose that men renew 90 percent of the time, and women renew 70 percent, and that our customer set is half men and half women. How much information gain would we get simply by testing whether a customer is male or female?

$$\begin{aligned} \text{Gain}(\text{Sex}) &= 1 - \left[\left(\frac{500}{1000}\right)\mathbf{I}\left(\frac{450}{500}, \frac{50}{500}\right) + \left(\frac{500}{1000}\right)\mathbf{I}\left(\frac{350}{500}, \frac{150}{500}\right)\right] \\ &= 1 - [(.5)\mathbf{I}(.9, .1) + (.5)\mathbf{I}(.7, .3)] \\ &= 1 - [(.5)0.468996 + (.5)0.881291] \\ &= 0.324857 \end{aligned}$$

Suppose that we had grouped the customers' usage habits into 3 groups: under 4 hours a month, from 4 to 10 hours, and over 10. Assume also that they were evenly split among all customers. When we look at their renewal rates, we see that the first group renews at 50 percent, the second at 90 percent, and the third at 100 percent. What information would we gain by testing on this attribute?

$$\begin{aligned} \text{Gain}(\text{Usage}) &= 1 - \left[(.333)\mathbf{I}\left(\frac{166}{333}, \frac{166}{333}\right) + (.333)\mathbf{I}\left(\frac{300}{333}, \frac{33}{333}\right) + (.333)\mathbf{I}(1, 0)\right] \\ &= 1 - [(.333)\mathbf{I}(.5, .5) + (.333)\mathbf{I}(.9, .1) + (.333)\mathbf{I}(1, 0)] \\ &= 1 - [(.333)1.0 + (.333)0.466133 + (.333)0.0] \\ &= 0.511778 \end{aligned}$$

You can see that in this example, the second case gives us more information gain than the first. So, if we were building a decision tree, we would want to first split the data based on how much connect-time they used, and then on whether the customer was male or female. This process of splitting the data, based on the attribute-value pair containing the most information, is continued until we can classify the data to our desired degree of accuracy.

Learn Application

In this section we describe an application that demonstrates three learning techniques, two types of neural networks and a tree classifier. Figure 5.5 shows the layout of our learning application window. It features two text display areas, one for the data used to train the neural networks or tree classifier, and one for trace information from the models themselves.

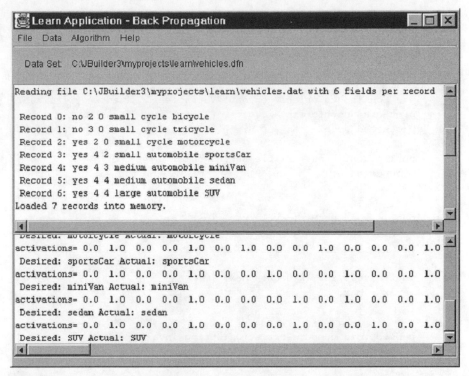

Figure 5.5 The *Learn* application.

Before we get into the implementation details of the *Learn* application, we need to introduce two subclasses of the **Variable** class for use in the learning algorithms. These classes deal specifically with discrete and continuous variables and support the behavior required for data normalization required by the neural network algorithms.

Continuous Variables

The **ContinuousVariable** class, shown in Figure 5.6, is a subclass of **Variable**. It provides the support necessary for variables that can take on a continuous real value ranging from some predefined minimum to a maximum value. The constructor takes the name of the variable as the only parameter. The *min* and *max* members can be set using the *setMin()* and *setMax()* methods directly, or they can be computed automatically if the **ContinuousVariable** is used as part of a **DataSet** by calling the *computeStatistics()* method. The *normalize()* method is used by the **DataSet** class when it is creating an all-numeric version of a data set. The **DataSet** class is used to load an entire training data file into memory and is described later in this chapter. This method does a simple linear scaling of the input value to a value in the range of 0.0 to 1.0. The **ContinuousVariable** class inherits the *normalizedSize()* method from the **Variable** class, because the normalized size is always 1.

```
package learn;

import java.util.*;
import java.io.*;

class ContinuousVariable extends Variable implements Serializable {
  protected double min = 0.0;
  protected double max = 0.0;

  public ContinuousVariable(String name) {
    super(name);
  }

  public void setMin(double min) {
    this.min = min;
  }

  public void setMax(double Max) {
    max = Max;
  }

  public void computeStatistics(String inValue) {
    double val = new Double(inValue).doubleValue();

    if(val < min) {
      min = val;
    }
    if(val > max) {
      max = val;
    }
  }

  public int normalize(String inStrValue, double[] outArray,
    int inx) {
    double outValue;
    double inValue = Double.valueOf(inStrValue).doubleValue();

    if(inValue <= min) {
      outValue = min;
    } else if(inValue >= max) {
      outValue = max;
    } else {
      double factor = max - min;

      outValue = inValue / factor;
    }
```

Figure 5.6 The ContinuousVariable class listing.

```
        outArray[inx] = outValue;
        return inx + 1;
    }
}
```

Figure 5.6   Continued.

Discrete Variables

The **DiscreteVariable** class, listed in Figure 5.7, is also a subclass of **Variable**. It provides the support necessary for variables that can take on a predefined set of numeric or symbolic values. The constructor takes the name of the variable as the only parameter. The minimum and maximum values can be set using the *setMin()* and *setMax()* methods directly, or they can be computed automatically if the **DiscreteVariable** is used as part of a **DataSet** by calling the *computeStatistics()* method. The value is assumed to be symbolic. If the symbol is already in the *labels* **Vector**, then it is ignored; otherwise, it is added to the list. The *normalize()* method is used by the **DataSet** class when it is creating an all-numeric version of a data set. This method converts each symbol to its index value and then converts that into a one-of-N code. The *normalizedSize()* method returns the number of unique discrete values the variable can take on, which is also the size of the one-of-N code when the variable is normalized. The *getDecoded-Value()* method is used to transform the output of a neural network back into a **String** value for display.

The DataSet Class

We provide multiple data sets for use with the three learning techniques. These include the exclusive-OR data set, a *vehicles* data set that mirrors the *vehicles* rule base used in Chapter 4, "Reasoning Systems," a restaurant data set, a linear ramp data set, and a clustering data set. The complete data sets are listed in Appendix B. Each data set is used to point out specific aspects of our learning algorithms. Because all three algorithms make use of a training data set, we have designed and implemented a common Java class called **DataSet**. The **DataSet** class definition is shown below. It makes use of the *java.io* package for loading the data from flat text files into memory, and also uses a text area for displaying the data and for trace information. Each **DataSet** instance has a name, a member for storing the file name, and a boolean flag, *allNumericData*, that indicates whether there is symbolic data in the file. Two **Vectors** are used to store the raw data read from the file along with a normalized all-numeric-data set, which we will discuss later. The *variableList* **Hashtable** holds a set of **Variables** that define the logical data types for each field in the file. The *fieldList* member holds references to the same **Variables** as the *variableList*, but the variables are added to the **Vector** in the order they are added to the **DataSet**, as shown in the *addVariable* method. This allows us to

```
package learn;

import java.util.*;
import java.io.*;

class DiscreteVariable extends Variable implements Serializable {
  protected int min;
  protected int max;

  public DiscreteVariable(String name) {
    super(name);
    labels = new Vector();
  }

  public void setMin(int min) {
    this.min = min;
  }

  public void setMax(int max) {
    this.max = max;
  }

  public void computeStatistics(String inValue) {
    if(labels.contains(inValue)) {
      return;
    } else {
      labels.addElement(inValue);
    }
  }

  public int normalize(String inValue, double[] outArray, int inx) {
    int index = getIndex(inValue);
    double code[] = new double[labels.size()];

    if(index < code.length) {
      code[index] = 1.0;
    }
    for(int i = 0; i < code.length; i++) {
      outArray[inx++] = code[i];
    }
    return inx;
  }

  public int getNormalizedSize() {
    return labels.size();
  }
```

Figure 5.7 The DiscreteVariable class listing.

```
public String getDecodedValue(double[] act, int start) {
  int len = labels.size();
  String value;
  double max = -1.0;

  value = String.valueOf(0);
  for(int i = 0; i < len; i++) {
    if(act[start + i] > max) {
      max = act[start + i];
      value = getLabel(i);
    }
  }
  return value;
}
}
```

Figure 5.7 Continued.

have a one-to-one correspondence between the fields in the file and the variables that define the data. The *numRecords* member is equivalent to the size of the *fieldList* and is provided for convenience. *NumRecords* is set to the number of records in the file.

There is a single constructor for the **DataSet** class. It takes as parameters the object name and the file name.

```
package learn;

import java.util.*;
import java.io.*;
import java.awt.*;
import javax.swing.*;

public class DataSet extends Object implements Serializable {
  protected String name;
  protected String fileName;
  protected boolean allNumericData;
  protected Vector data;
  protected Vector normalizedData;
  protected Hashtable variableList;
  protected Vector fieldList;
  protected int fieldsPerRec = 0;
  protected int normFieldsPerRec = 0;
  protected int numRecords = 0;
  transient public JTextArea textArea1;

  public DataSet(String name, String fileName) {
    this.name = name;
```

```
      if(fileName.endsWith(".dfn") || fileName.endsWith(".dat")) {
        int inx = fileName.indexOf('.');

        this.fileName = fileName.substring(0, inx);
      } else {
        this.fileName = fileName;
      }
      fieldsPerRec = 0;
      allNumericData = true;
      data = new Vector();
      variableList = new Hashtable();
      fieldList = new Vector();
    }
    ... ... ...
  }
```

The data file definition is a simple text file that contains a list of the field data types and their names. A single field must be designated as the *ClassField*. The data types can be *continuous*, *discrete*, or *categorical*. In the current implementation, *discrete* and *categorical* are treated the same. As each field type is read from the data definition file in the *loadDataFileDefinition()* method, a **Variable** of that type is instantiated with the specified name, and the **Variable** is added to the **DataSet** using the *addVariable()* method. The fields are assumed to be defined in the same order as the corresponding data in the data file. The data file definitions are included with the data set listings in Appendix B.

```
public void loadDataFileDefinition() {
  String tempRec[] = null;
  String line = null;

  trace("\nReading file definition " + fileName + ".dfn\n ");
  BufferedReader in = null;

  try {
    in = new BufferedReader(
      new InputStreamReader(new FileInputStream(fileName + ".dfn")));
  } catch(FileNotFoundException exc) {
    trace("Error: Can't find definition file " + fileName + ".dfn");
  }
  int recInx = 0;
  int token = 0;
  StringTokenizer input = null;

  do {
    try {
      line = in.readLine();
      if(line != null) {
        input = new StringTokenizer(line);
      } else {
        break;
      }
```

```
      } catch(IOException exc) {
        trace("Error reading file: " + fileName + ".dfn");
      }
      trace("\n Record " + recInx + ": ");
      String varType = input.nextToken();
      String varName = input.nextToken();

      if(varType.equals("continuous")) {
        addVariable(new ContinuousVariable(varName));
      } else if(varType.equals("discrete")) {
        addVariable(new DiscreteVariable(varName));
      } else if(varType.equals("categorical")) {
        addVariable(new DiscreteVariable(varName));
      }
      trace(varType + " " + varName);
      recInx++;
    } while(token != StreamTokenizer.TT_EOF);
    fieldsPerRec = fieldList.size();
    trace("\nCreated " + fieldsPerRec + " variables.\n");
}
```

One of the major methods in the **DataSet** class is the *loadDataFile()* method. This method takes no parameters because all the information necessary to read the file into memory is provided on the *DataSet()* constructor. Before we load the data file, we first read the file format definition using the *loadDataFileDefinition()* method. We use a **FileInputStream** to read data from the file. We use the *readLine()* method to read a line at a time and a **StringTokenizer** to parse out each field value. We instantiate a new **String** array to hold each record, and add it to the *data* **Vector**. As we are reading the file, we keep track of the size of the file and store this information in the *numRecords* member.

```
public void loadDataFile() {
  String tempRec[] = null;

  loadDataFileDefinition();
  fieldsPerRec = fieldList.size();
  String line = null;

  trace("\nReading file " + fileName + ".dat with " + fieldsPerRec
        + " fields per record\n ");
  BufferedReader in = null;

  try {
    in = new BufferedReader(
      new InputStreamReader(new FileInputStream(fileName + ".dat")));
  } catch(FileNotFoundException exc) {
    trace("Error: Can't find file " + fileName + ".dat");
  }
  int recInx = 0;
  int token = 0;
```

```
        StringTokenizer input = null;

        do {
          try {
            line = in.readLine();
            if(line != null) {
              input = new StringTokenizer(line);
              tempRec = new String[fieldsPerRec];
              data.addElement(tempRec);
            } else {
              break;
            }
          } catch(IOException exc) {
            trace("Error reading file: " + fileName + ".dat");
          }
          trace("\n Record " + recInx + ": ");
          for(int i = 0; i < fieldsPerRec; i++) {
            tempRec[i] = input.nextToken();
            ((Variable) fieldList.elementAt(i)).computeStatistics(tempRec[i]);
            trace(tempRec[i] + " ");
          }
          recInx++;
        } while(token != StreamTokenizer.TT_EOF);
        numRecords = recInx;
        trace("\nLoaded " + numRecords + " records into memory.\n");
        normalizeData();
        displayVariables();
        displayNormalizedData();
      }
```

The following members are part of the **Variable** class introduced in the preceding chapter, and are used by the **DataSet** class.

```
public abstract class Variable {
... ... ...

  public void setColumn(int column) {
    this.column = column;
  }

  public abstract void computeStatistics(String inValue);

  public abstract int normalize(String inValue, float[] outArray, int
inx);

  public int normalizedSize() { return 1; }
... ... ...
}
```

The next three methods deal with normalized data. Neural networks require all-numeric input data, so any data sets that contain symbols must be preprocessed. Also, neural networks usually require that the input data be scaled to a specific range, in our case, from

0.0 to 1.0. This conversion of symbolic data and scaling of continuous data is called *normalization*. We use the variable definitions to determine how to normalize the data. When we have a **DiscreteVariable**, we take the symbol or number and get its index value. This index value is then converted into a one-of-N vector. For example, if we have {yes, no, maybe} as three possible strings in a field defined as **DiscreteVariable**, we would convert each symbol into a code of 1s and 0s whose length is equal to the number of discrete values. So "yes" would map to 1 0 0, "no" to 0 1 0, and "maybe" to 0 0 1. Also note that we have an expansion here. An input record with 10 **DiscreteVariable** fields, each having three possible values, would expand into a thirty-element array for presentation to the neural network.

Another conversion we need to do is to scale continuous data that is out of the 0.0-to-1.0 range. We do a simple linear scaling here. There are more sophisticated techniques that could be used. For example, the IBM ABLE, described in Appendix C, uses a bilinear scaling technique in which the midpoint of the input data range is mapped to the midpoint (0.5) of the output data range. This tends to "center" the data around 0.5 in cases having outliers or other abnormalities. Notice that our one-of-N scaling used for discrete data is already in the 0.0-to-1.0 range, so no additional scaling is necessary.

The method *getNormalizedRecordSize()* computes the expansion that occurs during this normalization process. The *normalizeData()* method performs the actual scaling and translation to one-of-N codes. The *rawData* is the data read in from the file. The *normNumRec* is the array of **double**s that results after the preprocessing. When all is complete, the *normalizedData* vector holds a complete normalized data set corresponding to the original data set, ready for use by the neural networks.

```
public int getNormalizedRecordSize() {
    int sum = 0;
    Enumeration vars = variableList.elements();

    while(vars.hasMoreElements()) {
      Variable thisVar = (Variable) vars.nextElement();

      sum += thisVar.getNormalizedSize();
    }
    return sum;
}

public void normalizeData() {
    String tempRec[] = null;

    normalizedData = new Vector();
    normFieldsPerRec = getNormalizedRecordSize();
    Enumeration rawData = data.elements();

    while(rawData.hasMoreElements()) {
      int inx = 0;
      double normNumRec[] = new double[normFieldsPerRec];
      Enumeration fields = fieldList.elements();
```

```
          tempRec = (String[]) rawData.nextElement();
          for(int i = 0; i < fieldsPerRec; i++) {
            Variable thisVar = (Variable) fields.nextElement();

            inx = thisVar.normalize(tempRec[i], normNumRec, inx);
          }
          normalizedData.addElement(normNumRec);
        }
    }

    public void displayNormalizedData() {
      double tempNumRec[];
      int recInx = 0;

      trace("\n\nNormalized data:");
      Enumeration rawData = normalizedData.elements();

      while(rawData.hasMoreElements()) {
        trace("\n Record " + recInx++ + ": ");
        tempNumRec = (double[]) rawData.nextElement();
        int numFields = tempNumRec.length;

        for(int i = 0; i < numFields; i++) {
          trace(String.valueOf(tempNumRec[i]) + " ");
        }
      }
      trace("\n");
    }
  }
```

The *getClassFieldValue()* methods are used to display the results after a neural network training run. The first method takes the record index and returns the original "Class-Field" value. The second method takes an array of floats and the starting index of the output unit. The *DiscreteVariable.getDecodedValue()* method is used to select the array element with the maximum value, convert it into a discrete variable index, and then retrieve the corresponding **String** value. This is essentially the inverse of the steps performed in *normalizeData()* when a discrete value is turned into a one-of-N code.

```
public String getClassFieldValue(int recIndex) {
  Variable classField = (Variable) variableList.get("ClassField");

  return ((String[]) data.elementAt(recIndex))[classField.column];
}

public String getClassFieldValue(double[] activations, int index) {
  String value;
  Variable classField = (Variable) variableList.get("ClassField");

  if(classField.isCategorical()) {
    value = classField.getDecodedValue(activations, index);
```

```
    } else {
      value = String.valueOf(activations[index]);
    }
    return value;
}
```

In the following sections, we present our Java implementations of back propagation and Kohonen map neural network models. They are object-oriented, but not slavishly so. We would like these algorithms to run in a reasonable amount of time on standard PC hardware, so we don't have objects for each processing unit or layer. Our experience shows that we can have the advantages of object-oriented design and the performance of optimized algorithmic code.

BackProp Implementation

In this section, we describe our implementation of back propagation. The **BackProp** class, as shown in Figure 5.8, has four different sets of data members or parameters. First is a set that is used to manage the data. We have a reference to a **DataSet** object, *dataset*; the *data* **Vector**, which holds the training data; the current record index, *recInx*; the total number of records in the data set, *numRecs*; and the number of fields per record, *fieldsPerRec*. Next is a set of network architecture parameters. These include *numInputs*, *numHid1*, and *numOutputs*, which define the number of units in each of the three network layers. Some implementations support multiple hidden layers. This design can be easily extended to provide this support. *NumUnits* is the sum of the three layers of units, and *numWeights* is the total number of weights in the network.

In our implementation, we provide the following control parameters: *mode*, *learnRate*, *momentum*, and *tolerance*. When the *mode* parameter is set to a value of 0, the network is in training mode and the connection weights are adjusted. When the *mode* is set to 1, the network weights are locked. The *learnRate* and *momentum* parameters are used to control the size of the weight updates as described earlier. The *tolerance* parameter is used to specify how close the predicted output value has to be to the desired output value before the error is considered to be 0. For example, if our desired output value is 1.0, with a *tolerance* of 0.1, any predicted output value greater than 0.9 would result in 0 error.

Next, we have a set of data and error arrays. The primary arrays are the *activations*, the *weights*, and the *thresholds*. These specify the current state of the network. The *teach* array holds the desired or target output values. The other arrays are used in the computation of the error and weight changes.

To define a back propagation neural network, we provide the *createNetwork()* method. This method is provided instead of using the constructor so that the network's architecture can be changed without creating a new object. The *createNetwork()* method takes three parameters, the number of inputs, the number of hidden elements, and the number of output units. We compute some convenience data members, initialize the control parameters, and allocate all of the arrays. We then call the *reset()* method to initialize the network arrays.

```
package learn;

import java.awt.*;
import javax.swing.*;
import java.util.*;
import java.lang.Math;
import java.io.*;

public class BackProp extends Object implements Serializable {
  private String name;
  private DataSet dataset;
  private Vector data;
  private int recInx = 0;
  private int numRecs = 0;
  private int fieldsPerRec = 0;

  private double sumSquaredError;
  private double aveRMSError;
  private int numPasses;

  private int numInputs;
  private int numHid1;
  private int numOutputs;
  private int numUnits;
  private int numWeights;

  private int mode;
  private double learnRate;
  private double momentum;
  private double tolerance;

  private double activations[];
  private double weights[];
  private double wDerivs[];
  private double thresholds[];
  private double tDerivs[];
  private double tDeltas[];
  private double teach[];
  private double error[];
  private double deltas[];
  private double wDeltas[];
  transient public JTextArea textArea1;

  public BackProp(String name) {
    this.name = name;
    data = new Vector();
  }
```

Figure 5.8 The BackProp class listing.

```
public void setDataSet(DataSet dataset) {
  this.dataset = dataset;
}

public DataSet getDataSet() {
  return dataset;
}

public void setNumRecs(int numRecs) {
  this.numRecs = numRecs;
}

public int getNumRecs() {
  return numRecs;
}

public void setFieldsPerRec(int fieldsPerRec) {
  this.fieldsPerRec = fieldsPerRec;
}

public int getFieldsPerRec() {
  return fieldsPerRec;
}

public void setData(Vector data) {
  this.data = data;
}

public Vector getData() {
  return data;
}

public void setMode(int mode) {
  this.mode = mode;
}

public int getMode() {
  return mode;
}

public double getAveRMSError() {
  return aveRMSError;
}

public double getLearnRate() {
  return learnRate;
```

(continues)

Figure 5.8 Continued.

```
  }

  public double getMomentum() {
    return momentum;
  }

  public void show_array(String name, double[] arr) {
    if(textArea1 != null) {
      textArea1.append("\n" + name + "= ");
      for(int i = 0; i < arr.length; i++) {
        textArea1.append(arr[i] + "  ");
      }
    }
  }

  public void display_network() {
    show_array("activations", activations);
    String desired = dataset.getClassFieldValue(recInx - 1);
    String actual = dataset.getClassFieldValue(activations,
                        numInputs + numHid1);

    if(textArea1 != null) {
      textArea1.append("\n Desired: " + desired + " Actual: " +
        actual);
    }
  }

  public double logistic(double sum) {
    return 1.0 / (1 + Math.exp(-1.0 * sum));
  }

  public void readInputs() {
    recInx = recInx % numRecs;
    int inx = 0;
    double[] tempRec = (double[]) data.elementAt(recInx);

    for(inx = 0; inx < numInputs; inx++) {
      activations[inx] = tempRec[inx];
    }
    for(int i = 0; i < numOutputs; i++) {
      teach[i] = tempRec[inx++];
    }
    recInx++;
  }

  public void computeOutputs() {
    int i, j;
```

Figure 5.8 The BackProp class listing (Continued).

```
    int firstHid1 = numInputs;
    int firstOut = numInputs + numHid1;
    int inx = 0;

  for(i = firstHid1; i < firstOut; i++) {
    double sum = thresholds[i];

    for(j = 0; j < numInputs; j++) {
      sum += activations[j] * weights[inx++];
    }
    activations[i] = logistic(sum);
  }
  for(i = firstOut; i < numUnits; i++) {
    double sum = thresholds[i];

    for(j = firstHid1; j < firstOut; j++) {
      sum += activations[j] * weights[inx++];
    }
    activations[i] = logistic(sum);
  }
}

public void computeError() {
  int i, j;
  int firstHid1 = numInputs;
  int firstOut = numInputs + numHid1;

  for(i = numInputs; i < numUnits; i++) {
    error[i] = 0.0;
  }
  for(i = firstOut; i < numUnits; i++) {
    error[i] = teach[i - firstOut] - activations[i];
    sumSquaredError += error[i] * error[i];
    if(Math.abs(error[i]) < tolerance) {
      error[i] = 0.0;
    }
    deltas[i] = error[i] * activations[i] * (1 - activations[i]);
  }
  int winx = numInputs * numHid1;

  for(i = firstOut; i < numUnits; i++) {
    for(j = firstHid1; j < firstOut; j++) {
      wDerivs[winx] += deltas[i] * activations[j];
      error[j] += weights[winx] * deltas[i];
      winx++;
    }
```

(continues)

Figure 5.8 Continued.

```
        tDerivs[i] += deltas[i];
      }
    for(i = firstHid1; i < firstOut; i++) {
      deltas[i] = error[i] * activations[i] * (1 - activations[i]);
    }
    winx = 0;
    for(i = firstHid1; i < firstOut; i++) {
      for(j = 0; j < firstHid1; j++) {
        wDerivs[winx] += deltas[i] * activations[j];
        error[j] += weights[winx] * deltas[i];
        winx++;
      }
      tDerivs[i] += deltas[i];
    }
}


public void adjustWeights() {
  int i;

  for(i = 0; i < weights.length; i++) {
    wDeltas[i] = (learnRate * wDerivs[i]) + (momentum * wDeltas[i]);
    weights[i] += wDeltas[i];
    wDerivs[i] = 0.0;
  }
  for(i = numInputs; i < numUnits; i++) {
    tDeltas[i] = learnRate * tDerivs[i] + (momentum * tDeltas[i]);
    thresholds[i] += tDeltas[i];
    tDerivs[i] = 0.0;
  }
  if(recInx == numRecs) {
    numPasses++;
    aveRMSError = Math.sqrt(sumSquaredError / (numRecs *
      numOutputs));
    sumSquaredError = 0.0;
  }
}


public double getPrediction(double[] inputRec) {
  int firstOut = numInputs + numHid1;

  for(int inx = 0; inx < numInputs; inx++) {
    activations[inx] = inputRec[inx];
  }
  computeOutputs();
  return activations[firstOut];
}
```

Figure 5.8   The BackProp class listing (Continued).

```
public void process() {
  readInputs();
  computeOutputs();
  computeError();
  if(mode == 0) {
    adjustWeights();
  }
}

public void reset() {
  int i;

  for(i = 0; i < weights.length; i++) {
    weights[i] = 0.5 - (Math.random());
    wDeltas[i] = 0.0;
    wDerivs[i] = 0.0;
  }
  for(i = 0; i < numUnits; i++) {
    thresholds[i] = 0.5 - (Math.random());
    tDeltas[i] = 0.0;
    tDerivs[i] = 0.0;
  }
}

public void createNetwork(int numIn, int numHidden, int numOut) {
  numInputs = numIn;
  numHid1 = numHidden;
  numOutputs = numOut;
  numUnits = numInputs + numHid1 + numOutputs;
  numWeights = (numInputs * numHid1) + (numHid1 * numOutputs);
  learnRate = 0.2;
  momentum = 0.7;
  tolerance = 0.1;
  mode = 0;
  aveRMSError = 0.0;
  numPasses = 0;
  activations = new double[numUnits];
  weights = new double[numWeights];
  wDerivs = new double[numWeights];
  wDeltas = new double[numWeights];
  thresholds = new double[numUnits];
  tDerivs = new double[numUnits];
  tDeltas = new double[numUnits];
  teach = new double[numOutputs];
  deltas = new double[numUnits];
```

(continues)

Figure 5.8 Continued.

```
        error = new double[numUnits];
        reset();
        return;
    }
}
```

Figure 5.8 The BackProp class listing (Continued).

For the forward pass, three methods are used. The *readInputs()* method takes a record from the data set and copies the input values into the *activations* of the input units. It also copies the target values into the *teach* array. The *computeOutputs()* method does the complete forward pass through the network. Starting with the first layer, it computes the sum of the threshold and each input unit activation multiplied by the corresponding weight, and then calls the *logistic()* method to compute and set the activation value.

To compute the errors, we start at the output layer and work back toward the input. First, the output errors are computed by taking the difference between the *activations* produced by *computeOutputs()* and the *teach* values. Note that we also sum the squared errors here for computing the average root-mean-squared (RMS) error. The *deltas* are then computed using the derivative of the activation function.

To adjust the *weights*, the *adjustWeights()* method first computes the current weight deltas, *wDeltas*, and then adds those deltas to the weights. Notice that we use the *wDerivs* array to hold the accumulated set of weight changes that should be made to the *weights*. In pattern update, *wDerivs* holds only the changes from the current pattern. However, if we wanted to use batch updating, this array would hold the changes from all of the patterns in the data set. After we adjust the weights, we zero out the *wDerivs* array. Next we adjust the threshold weights for each unit in the hidden and output layer. The computations are similar to those for the regular weights. Note: It is not necessary to have a separate threshold array. Some implementations just add additional weights to the weight arrays and add a single additional unit that has a constant activation value of 1 to each layer.

To see how our back propagation network works, we can use our *Learn* application. Run the **LearnApp** *main()* from the command line by going to the root *ciagent* directory and entering the following:

```
>java learn.LearnApp
```

The Learn application window as shown in Figure 5.5 appears. Select **Back prop** as the learning method under the Algorithm pull-down menu and the load the **XOR** data set by selecting the **Load** menu item under the **Data** pull-down. The File Dialog will appear. Select the *xor.dfn* file and click on the Open button. The *xor.dfn* file and the data will be loaded into the **DataSet** and displayed in the top text area. The **Data Set** field should indicate that *xor.dfn* is the current data set. To train the back propagation network, select the **Start** menu item under the **File** pull-down menu. A message indicating that training is started should appear, along with the network architecture and the training parameters. A series of asterisks will appear on the bottom text area. When 2500 passes are complete, the network will be locked and a single pass through the data in test mode will be performed. The desired and actual values, the contents of the activations array, and the final average RMS error will be displayed in the bottom text area.

You can select other data sets to work with back prop, including the Vehicles and Animals for classification, and the Linear ramp to see an example of a prediction problem. The contents of each data set are listed in Appendix B. You can use your own training data sets by creating a data definition (*.dfn) file and corresponding data (*.dat) file. Whenever you select a different data set, its contents will be displayed in the top text area and indicated on the top of the **LearnFrame** panel. The **Reset** button will clear the bottom text area and reset the weights in the back prop network.

Kohonen Map Implementation

For our implementation of the Kohonen map neural network, we define a class named **KmapNet** shown in Figure 5.9. The structure of this class is similar to that of the **Back-Prop** class already presented in this chapter. The major difference between the **KMap-Net** and the **BackProp** class is the unsupervised versus supervised learning paradigm. The Kohonen map performs unsupervised learning, so there is no notion of a desired output; there are only inputs.

The **KMapNet** class has four different sets of data members or parameters. First is a set that is used to manage the data. We have a reference to a data set, *dataset*, the current record index, *recInx*, the total number of records in the data set, *numRecs*, and the number of fields per record, *fieldsPerRec*. Next is a set of network architecture parameters. These include *numInputs*, *numRows*, and *numCols*, which define the number of units in the input layer and the dimensions of the two-dimensional output layer. *NumUnits* is the sum of these two layers, and *numWeights* is the total number of weights in the network. In our relatively simple implementation, our control parameters consist of the *initialLearnRate*, *finalLearnRate*, and the current *learnRate*. The network *mode* is either train (0) or test (1). The *sigma* parameter is used in the computation of the neighborhood function.

Next we have a set of data and error arrays. The primary arrays are the *activations* and the *weights*, which specify the current state of the network. The *distance* array is a precomputed grid that defines the distances between units on the two-dimensional output grid. For example, in a network with a 4-by-4 output, the distances from unit 0,0 (top left) would be:

0	1	16	81
1	2	17	82
16	17	32	97
81	82	97	162

As you can see, the distance from a unit to itself is 0, to those units horizontally and vertically adjacent it is 1, and the distances grow as you move away from the unit. The *distance* array is used in the *adjustNeighborhood()* method.

```
package learn;

import java.awt.*;
import javax.swing.*;
import java.util.*;
import java.lang.Math;
import java.io.*;

public class KMapNet extends Object implements Serializable {
  private String name;
  private DataSet dataset;
  private Vector data;
  private int recInx = 0;
  private int numRecs = 0;
  private int fieldsPerRec;
  private int numPasses = 0;

  private int numInputs;
  private int numRows;
  private int numCols;
  private int numOutputs;
  private int numUnits;

  private int mode;
  private double learnRate;
  private double initLearnRate = 1.0;
  private double finalLearnRate = 0.05;
  private double sigma;
  private int maxNumPasses = 20;
  private int winner;

  private double activations[];
  private double weights[];
  private int distance[];
  transient public JTextArea textArea1;

  public KMapNet(String name) {
    this.name = name;
    data = new Vector();
  }

  public void setDataSet(DataSet dataset) {
    this.dataset = dataset;
  }

  public DataSet getDataSet() {
    return dataset;
```

Figure 5.9 The KMapNet class listing.

```
}

public void setNumRecs(int numRecs) {
  this.numRecs = numRecs;
}

public int getNumRecs() {
  return numRecs;
}

public void setFieldsPerRec(int fieldsPerRec) {
  this.fieldsPerRec = fieldsPerRec;
}

public int getFieldsPerRec() {
  return fieldsPerRec;
}

public void setData(Vector data) {
  this.data = data;
}

public Vector getData() {
  return data;
}

public void setMode(int mode) {
  this.mode = mode;
}

public int getMode() {
  return mode;
}

public void show_array(String name, double[] arr) {
  if(textArea1 != null) {
    textArea1.append("\n" + name + "= ");
    for(int i = 0; i < arr.length; i++) {
      textArea1.append(arr[i] + "   ");
    }
  }
}

public void display_network() {
  show_array("activations", activations);
  if(textArea1 != null) {
```

(continues)

Figure 5.9 Continued.

```
        textArea1.append("\nWinner = " + winner + "\n");
    }
}

public void readInputs() {
    recInx = recInx % numRecs;
    int inx = 0;
    double[] tempRec = (double[]) data.elementAt(recInx);

    for(inx = 0; inx < numInputs; inx++) {
        activations[inx] = tempRec[inx];
    }
    if(recInx == 0) {
        numPasses++;
        adjustNeighborhood();
    }
    recInx++;
}

public void computeDistances() {
    int i, j, xi, xj, yi, yj;

    distance = new int[numOutputs * numOutputs];
    for(i = 0; i < numOutputs; i++) {
        xi = i % numCols;
        yi = i / numRows;
        for(j = 0; j < numOutputs; j++) {
            xj = j % numCols;
            yj = j / numRows;
            distance[i * numOutputs + j] =
                (int) Math.pow(((xi - xj) * (xi - xj)), 2.0)
                + (int) Math.pow(((yi - yj) * (yi - yj)), 2.0);
        }
    }
}

public void adjustNeighborhood() {
    double ratio = (double) numPasses / maxNumPasses;

    learnRate = initLearnRate
        * Math.pow(finalLearnRate / initLearnRate, ratio);
    sigma = (double) numCols * Math.pow((0.20 / (double) numCols),
        ratio);
}

public void computeOutputs() {
    int index, i, j;
```

Figure 5.9 The KMapNet class listing (Continued).

```
    int lastOut = numUnits - 1;
    int firstOut = numInputs;

    for(i = firstOut; i <= lastOut; i++) {
      index = (i - firstOut) * numInputs;
      activations[i] = 0.0;
      for(j = 0; j < numInputs; j++) {
        activations[i] += (activations[j] - weights[index + j])
                          * (activations[j] - weights[index + j]);
      }
    }
  }

  public void selectWinner() {
    winner = 0;
    double min = activations[numInputs];

    for(int i = 0; i < numOutputs; i++) {
      if(activations[i + numInputs] < min) {
        min = activations[i + numInputs];
        winner = i;
      }
    }
  }

  public void adjustWeights() {
    int i, j, inx, base;
    int numOutputs = numRows * numCols;
    double dist, range, sigma_squared;

    sigma_squared = sigma * sigma;
    for(i = 0; i < numOutputs; i++) {
      dist = Math.exp((distance[winner * numOutputs + i] * -1.0)
        / (2.0 * sigma_squared));
      base = i * numInputs;
      range = learnRate * dist;
      for(j = 0; j < numInputs; j++) {
        inx = base + j;
        weights[inx] += range * (activations[j] - weights[inx]);
      }
    }
  }

  public int getCluster(double[] inputRec) {
    for(int inx = 0; inx < numInputs; inx++) {
      activations[inx] = inputRec[inx];
```

(continues)

Figure 5.9 Continued.

```
      }
      computeOutputs();
      selectWinner();
      return winner;
    }

    public void cluster() {
      readInputs();
      computeOutputs();
      selectWinner();
      if(mode == 0) {
        adjustWeights();
      }
    }

    public void reset() {
      int i;

      for(i = 0; i < weights.length; i++) {
        weights[i] = 0.6 - (0.2 * Math.random());
      }
    }

    public void createNetwork(int NumIn, int NumRows, int NumCols) {
      numInputs = NumIn;
      numRows = NumRows;
      numCols = NumCols;
      numOutputs = numRows * numCols;
      numUnits = numInputs + numOutputs;
      learnRate = 0.1;
      mode = 0;
      activations = new double[numUnits];
      weights = new double[numInputs * numOutputs];
      computeDistances();
      adjustNeighborhood();
      reset();
    }
  }
```

Figure 5.9 The KMapNet class listing (Continued).

To define a Kohonen map neural network, we provide the *createNetwork()* method. This method is provided instead of using the constructor so that we can change the network's architecture without creating a new object. The *createNetwork()* method takes three parameters: the number of inputs, the number of rows, and the number of columns. We compute some convenience data members, initialize the control parameters, and then allocate the activations and weights arrays. The *computeDistances()* method initializes the distance array. We then call the *adjustNeighborhood()* method to set the initial learn rate and *reset()* to initialize the weight array.

To process an input pattern, three methods are used. The *readInputs()* method takes a record from the data set and copies the input values into the *activations* of the input layer units. Because Kohonen maps use unsupervised learning, there are no target values. The *computeOutputs()* method computes the Euclidean distance between the input vector and the weight vectors. The *computeWinner()* method chooses the output with the minimum activation (closest to the input vector) as the *winner*. Note, we could do this function in our *computeOutputs()* method in this case. However, if we add more sophisticated winner selection techniques, such as learning with a conscience, we would want this broken out into a separate step.

The *adjustNeighborhood()* method computes two crucial values as training progresses, the learn rate and the neighborhood width or *sigma*. First, a *ratio* is computed which tells how far along we are in the training. This *ratio* increases over time. Then, the current *learnRate* is computed, decreasing over time. Finally, the neighborhood value, *sigma*, is computed.

Once the *winner* is selected, the *weights* are adjusted. In the *adjustWeights()* method, we use the neighborhood, the distance from the winning unit, and the *learnRate* to adjust the weights of units in the neighborhood of the winner.

Now we look at an example of Kohonen map training using our Learn application. Run the **LearnApp** *main()* from the command line by going to the *ciagent* root directory and entering:

```
>java learn.LearnApp
```

The Learn application window shown in Figure 5.5 appears. Select **Kohonen map** as the learning method under the **Algorithm** pull-down menu and load the **Cluster** data set by selecting the load menu item under the Data pull-down menu. The *kmap1.dfn* file and the data will be loaded into the **DataSet** and displayed in the top text area. To train the Kohonen map network, select the **Start** menu item under the **File** pull-down menu. A message appears in the bottom text area to indicate that training is starting. An asterisk is displayed after each pass through the training data. When training is complete, the total number of passes, the *winner* output unit index, and the contents of the *activations* array will be displayed for each record in the bottom text area.

Decision Tree Implementation

Now, let's turn to our implementation of a decision tree algorithm that handles discrete variables. There are two main classes: a **Node** that represents a decision tree node and the **DecisionTree** class itself. As defined in Figure 5.10, the **Node** has a name or *label*, a **Vector** of links to other **Nodes** in the **DecisionTree**, a reference to the parent node, and a **Vector** containing references to children nodes.

The **DecisionTree** class, listed in Figure 5.11, has a *name*, a reference to a **DataSet** object, as in the neural network classes; the goal **Variable**, *classVar*; and a list of all of

```java
package learn;

import java.awt.*;
import javax.swing.*;
import java.util.*;
import java.lang.Math;
import java.io.*;

public class KMapNet extends Object implements Serializable {
  private String name;
  private DataSet dataset;
  private Vector data;
  private int recInx = 0;
  private int numRecs = 0;
  private int fieldsPerRec;
  private int numPasses = 0;
  private int numInputs;
  private int numRows;
  private int numCols;
  private int numOutputs;
  private int numUnits;
  private int mode;
  private double learnRate;
  private double initLearnRate = 1.0;
  private double finalLearnRate = 0.05;
  private double sigma;
  private int maxNumPasses = 20;
  private int winner;
  private double activations[];
  private double weights[];
  private int distance[];
  transient public JTextArea textArea1;

  public KMapNet(String name) {
    this.name = name;
    data = new Vector();
  }

  public void setDataSet(DataSet dataset) {
    this.dataset = dataset;
  }

  public DataSet getDataSet() {
    return dataset;
  }

  public void setNumRecs(int numRecs) {
```

Figure 5.10 The Node class listing.

```
    this.numRecs = numRecs;
  }

  public int getNumRecs() {
    return numRecs;
  }

  public void setFieldsPerRec(int fieldsPerRec) {
    this.fieldsPerRec = fieldsPerRec;
  }

  public int getFieldsPerRec() {
    return fieldsPerRec;
  }

  public void setData(Vector data) {
    this.data = data;
  }

  public Vector getData() {
    return data;
  }

  public void setMode(int mode) {
    this.mode = mode;
  }

  public int getMode() {
    return mode;
  }

  public void show_array(String name, double[] arr) {
    if(textArea1 != null) {
      textArea1.append("\n" + name + "= ");
      for(int i = 0; i < arr.length; i++) {
        textArea1.append(arr[i] + "  ");
      }
    }
  }

  public void display_network() {
    show_array("activations", activations);
    if(textArea1 != null) {
      textArea1.append("\nWinner = " + winner + "\n");
    }
  }
```

(continues)

Figure 5.10   Continued.

```
public void readInputs() {
  recInx = recInx % numRecs;
  int inx = 0;
  double[] tempRec = (double[]) data.elementAt(recInx);

  for(inx = 0; inx < numInputs; inx++) {
    activations[inx] = tempRec[inx];
  }
  if(recInx == 0) {
    numPasses++;
    adjustNeighborhood();
  }
  recInx++;
}

public void computeDistances() {
  int i, j, xi, xj, yi, yj;

  distance = new int[numOutputs * numOutputs];
  for(i = 0; i < numOutputs; i++) {
    xi = i % numCols;
    yi = i / numRows;
    for(j = 0; j < numOutputs; j++) {
      xj = j % numCols;
      yj = j / numRows;
      distance[i * numOutputs + j] =
        (int) Math.pow(((xi - xj) * (xi - xj)), 2.0)
        + (int) Math.pow(((yi - yj) * (yi - yj)), 2.0);
    }
  }
}

public void adjustNeighborhood() {
  double ratio = (double) numPasses / maxNumPasses;

  learnRate = initLearnRate
              * Math.pow(finalLearnRate / initLearnRate, ratio);
  sigma = (double) numCols * Math.pow((0.20 / (double) numCols),
    ratio);
}

public void computeOutputs() {
  int index, i, j;
  int lastOut = numUnits - 1;
  int firstOut = numInputs;

  for(i = firstOut; i <= lastOut; i++) {
```

Figure 5.10 The Node class listing (Continued).

```
      index = (i - firstOut) * numInputs;
      activations[i] = 0.0;
      for(j = 0; j < numInputs; j++) {
        activations[i] += (activations[j] - weights[index + j])
                        * (activations[j] - weights[index + j]);
      }
    }
  }

  public void selectWinner() {
    winner = 0;
    double min = activations[numInputs];

    for(int i = 0; i < numOutputs; i++) {
      if(activations[i + numInputs] < min) {
        min = activations[i + numInputs];
        winner = i;
      }
    }
  }

  public void adjustWeights() {
    int i, j, inx, base;
    int numOutputs = numRows * numCols;
    double dist, range, sigma_squared;

    sigma_squared = sigma * sigma;
    for(i = 0; i < numOutputs; i++) {
      dist = Math.exp((distance[winner * numOutputs + i] * -1.0)
                    / (2.0 * sigma_squared));
      base = i * numInputs;
      range = learnRate * dist;
      for(j = 0; j < numInputs; j++) {
        inx = base + j;
        weights[inx] += range * (activations[j] - weights[inx]);
      }
    }
  }

  public int getCluster(double[] inputRec) {
    for(int inx = 0; inx < numInputs; inx++) {
      activations[inx] = inputRec[inx];
    }
    computeOutputs();
    selectWinner();
    return winner;
```

(continues)

Figure 5.10   Continued.

```
      }

      public void cluster() {
        readInputs();
        computeOutputs();
        selectWinner();
        if(mode == 0) {
          adjustWeights();
        }
      }

      public void reset() {
        int i;

        for(i = 0; i < weights.length; i++) {
          weights[i] = 0.6 - (0.2 * Math.random());
        }
      }

      public void createNetwork(int NumIn, int NumRows, int NumCols) {
        numInputs = NumIn;
        numRows = NumRows;
        numCols = NumCols;
        numOutputs = numRows * numCols;
        numUnits = numInputs + numOutputs;
        learnRate = 0.1;
        mode = 0;
        activations = new double[numUnits];
        weights = new double[numInputs * numOutputs];
        computeDistances();
        adjustNeighborhood();
        reset();
      }
    }
```

Figure 5.10   The Node class listing (Continued).

the **Variable** definitions for the data set. The **Vector** of examples holds the set of training records, which is the result of a partitioning of the original training set, based on an attribute test. The **DecisionTree** has a simple constructor allowing the name to be set.

The *buildDecisionTree()* method is the major method in this class. It takes three parameters: a **Vector** of examples (the data set), a list of the field definitions, and the default value that should be returned in case the decision tree fails. The first thing we do is instantiate a root **Node** for the decision tree. If the training set is empty, then we return the default value. Otherwise, if all of the records in the training set have an identical value for the class field, we return a leaf **Node** with that value. If neither of these two conditions is true, we must build a decision tree. The first step is to select the best

```
package learn;

import java.util.*;
import java.io.*;
import java.awt.*;
import javax.swing.*;
import java.lang.Math;

public class DecisionTree implements Serializable {
  protected String name;
  protected DataSet ds;
  protected Variable classVar;
  protected Hashtable variableList;
  protected Vector examples;
  protected static JTextArea textArea1;
  protected String record[];

  public DecisionTree(String Name) {
    name = Name;
  }

  public static void appendText(String text) {
    if(textArea1 != null) {
      textArea1.append(text);
    }
  }

  public boolean identical(Vector examples, Variable variable) {
    int index = variable.column;
    Enumeration enum = examples.elements();
    boolean same = true;
    String value = ((String[]) examples.firstElement())[index];

    while(enum.hasMoreElements()) {
      if(value.equals(((String[]) enum.nextElement())[index])) {
        continue;
      } else {
        same = false;
        break;
      }
    }
    return same;
  }

  public String majority(Vector examples) {
    int index = classVar.column;
```

(continues)

Figure 5.11 The DecisionTree class listing.

```
      Enumeration enum = examples.elements();
      int counts[] = new int[classVar.labels.size()];

      while(enum.hasMoreElements()) {
        String value = ((String[]) enum.nextElement())[index];
        int inx = ((Variable) classVar).getIndex(value);

        counts[inx]++;
      }
      int maxVal = 0;
      int maxIndex = 0;

      for(int i = 0; i < classVar.labels.size(); i++) {
        if(counts[i] > maxVal) {
          maxVal = counts[i];
          maxIndex = i;
        }
      }
      return classVar.getLabel(maxIndex);
  }

  public int[] getCounts(Vector examples) {
      int index = classVar.column;
      Enumeration enum = examples.elements();
      int counts[] = new int[classVar.labels.size()];

      while(enum.hasMoreElements()) {
        String value = ((String[]) enum.nextElement())[index];
        int inx = ((Variable) classVar).getIndex(value);

        counts[inx]++;
      }
      return counts;
  }

  double computeInfo(int p, int n) {
      double total = p + n;
      double pos = p / total;
      double neg = n / total;
      double temp;

      if((p == 0) || (n == 0)) {
        temp = 0.0;
      } else {
        temp = (-1.0 * (pos * Math.log(pos) / Math.log(2)))
             - (neg * Math.log(neg) / Math.log(2));
      }
```

Figure 5.11 The DecisionTree class listing (Continued).

```
      return temp;
   }

double computeRemainder(Variable variable, Vector examples) {
   int positive[] = new int[variable.labels.size()];
   int negative[] = new int[variable.labels.size()];
   int index = variable.column;
   int classIndex = classVar.column;
   double sum = 0;
   double numValues = variable.labels.size();
   double numRecs = examples.size();

   for(int i = 0; i < numValues; i++) {
     String value = variable.getLabel(i);
     Enumeration enum = examples.elements();

     while(enum.hasMoreElements()) {
       String record[] = (String[]) enum.nextElement();

       if(record[index].equals(value)) {
         if(record[classIndex].equals("yes")) {
           positive[i]++;
         } else {
           negative[i]++;
         }
       }
     }
     double weight = (positive[i] + negative[i]) / numRecs;
     double myrem = weight * computeInfo(positive[i], negative[i]);

     sum = sum + myrem;
   }
   return sum;
}

Vector subset(Vector examples, Variable variable, String value) {
   int index = variable.column;
   Enumeration enum = examples.elements();
   Vector matchingExamples = new Vector();

   while(enum.hasMoreElements()) {
     String[] record = (String[]) enum.nextElement();

     if(value.equals(record[index])) {
       matchingExamples.addElement(record);
     }
```

(continues)

Figure 5.11 Continued.

```
      }
      textArea1.append("\n Subset - there are " +
                       matchingExamples.size() + " records with " +
                       variable.name + " = " + value);
      return matchingExamples;
  }


  Variable chooseVariable(Hashtable variables, Vector examples) {
      Enumeration enum = variables.elements();
      double gain = 0.0, bestGain = -1.0;
      Variable best = null;
      int counts[];

      counts = getCounts(examples);
      int pos = counts[0];
      int neg = counts[1];
      double info = computeInfo(pos, neg);

      textArea1.append("\nInfo = " + info);
      while(enum.hasMoreElements()) {
        Variable tempVar = (Variable) enum.nextElement();

        gain = info - computeRemainder(tempVar, examples);
        textArea1.append("\n" + tempVar.name + " gain = " + gain);
        if(gain > bestGain) {
          bestGain = gain;
          best = tempVar;
        }
      }
      textArea1.append("\nChoosing best variable: " + best.name);
      return best;
  }

  public Node buildDecisionTree(Vector examples, Hashtable variables,
      Node defaultValue) {
    Node tree = new Node();

    if(examples.size() == 0) {
      return defaultValue;
    } else if(identical(examples, classVar)) {
      return new Node(
        ((String[]) examples.firstElement())[classVar.column]);
    } else if(variables.size() == 0) {
      return new Node(majority(examples));
    } else {
      Variable best = chooseVariable(variables, examples);
```

Figure 5.11   The DecisionTree class listing (Continued).

```
      tree = new Node(best.name);
      Enumeration enum = best.labels.elements();
      int numValues = best.labels.size();

      for(int i = 0; i < numValues; i++) {
        Vector examples1 = subset(examples, best, best.getLabel(i));
        Hashtable variables1 = (Hashtable) variables.clone();

        variables1.remove(best.getName());
        Node subTree = buildDecisionTree(examples1, variables1,
                          new Node(majority(examples1)));

        tree.addChild(subTree, best.name + "=" + best.getLabel(i));
      }
    }
    return tree;
  }
}
```

Figure 5.11 Continued.

attribute or variable on which to split. The *chooseVariable()* method does this selection using information theory. We assign the root of this tree to a **Node** for that variable. Now that we have decided which **Variable** to split on, we must determine which discrete value of that attribute we should use for the split. The *for()* loop does this by taking each possible value of the variable, subsetting the training data (examples) into groups where all records have the desired value of that attribute, and computing the information gain for that value of the variable. We recursively call *buildDecisionTree()* to fill out branches until we have built a complete decision tree that starts with our root **Node**.

The *chooseVariable()* method takes two parameters: the list of variables to consider and a subset of the training data. First we call *getCounts()* to compute the number of positive and negative examples of our class variable, which are returned as elements of an integer array. Next we call *computeInfo()* to compute the information value of this data set using the p and n returned by *getCounts()*. Note that in this implementation, we have only binary class variables. Finally, we compute the remainder for each variable and select the one that results in the largest information gain.

The *computeInfo()* method takes two integer parameters, p and n, as inputs. It computes the information value as previously defined in the formula for **I**. The only tricky part is the computation of the **log2 n**, which uses the mathematical fact that the log of any base can be computed using the natural log of n divided by the natural log of the base 2. The *computeRemainder()* method takes a single variable and a data set as inputs. It computes the number of positive and negative cases for each unique value the discrete variable can take on. It sums the information value for each distinct value weighted by the prior probability of that value and returns it as the remainder.

Finally, we have several utility methods. The *subset()* method takes a data set, a variable definition, and a value for that variable and returns the subset of data which contains that value in every record. The *identical()* method takes the data set and a single variable as input and returns a **boolean** value indicating whether all of the training records contain the same value for the specified variable. The *majority()* method examines a data set and returns the label which has the most examples for the specified variable.

We use the **XORTREE** data set and our *Learn* application to show an example of a decision tree. Run the **LearnApp** *main()* by going to the *ciagent* root directory and entering the following:

```
>java learn.LearnApp
```

The *Learn* application window shown in Figure 5.5 appears. Select **Decision Tree** as the learning method from the **Algorithm** pull-down menu and load the **XORTREE** data set by selecting the **Load** menu item from the **Data** pull-down. The *xortree.dfn* file and the data will be loaded into the **DataSet** and displayed in the top text area control. To build the decision tree, select the **Start** menu item from the **File** pull-down menu. When training is complete, the structure of the decision tree will be displayed in the bottom text area.

The Learn Application Implementation

The *Learn* application was developed using the Borland JBuilder 3.0 interactive development tool. The *Learn* application uses two classes: the **LearnApp** class, which contains our *main()*, and the **LearnFrame** class, which extends **JFrame** and implements the main window and GUI logic. The visual builder allows us to create the complete GUI using Java Swing components in a drag-and-drop style. JBuilder automatically generates the Java code for creating the GUI controls and action event handlers in the **LearnFrame** class. We then added the logic for creating and invoking the learning algorithms. The **LearnApp** code that invokes the **LearnFrame** is not presented here. It simply instantiates the **LearnFrame** class and displays it. Likewise, a substantial amount of the code in the **LearnFrame** class deals with GUI control logic and we will not present that material here. Instead, we will highlight only brief sections of the code that demonstrate how to use the underlying application classes. All of the classes discussed in this chapter are in the *learn* package, as shown in Figure 5.12.

The **LearnFrame** window consists of two text area controls, for displaying the **DataSet** and training information; three radio button menu items under the **Algorithm** menu for selecting the learning algorithm; a **Load** menu item under the **Data** menu for selecting and loading the **DataSet**; and **Start** and **Reset** menu items under the **File** menu. The **LearnFrame** window is shown in Figure 5.5. When the **Start** menu item is selected, a new thread is created and started. The **LearnFrame** *run()* method is called, which in turn simply invokes a corresponding *test()* method, depending on the selected algorithm.

```
public void run() {
  traceTextArea.setText("");
  if(BackPropRadioButtonMenuItem.isSelected()) {
    testBackProp(dataSet, traceTextArea);
```

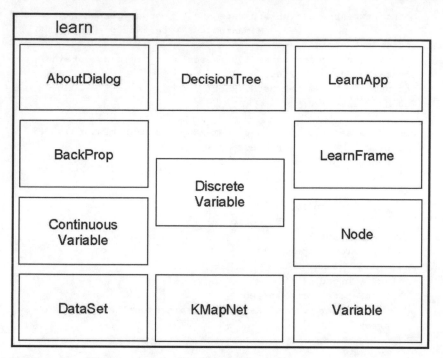

learn

AboutDialog	DecisionTree	LearnApp
BackProp		LearnFrame
	Discrete Variable	
Continuous Variable		Node
DataSet	KMapNet	Variable

Figure 5.12 The *Learn* package UML diagram.

```
    }
    if(KohonenRadioButtonMenuItem.isSelected()) {
      testKMapNet(dataSet, traceTextArea);
    }
    if(DecisionTreeRadioButtonMenuItem.isSelected()) {
      testDecisionTree(dataSet, traceTextArea);
    }
}

public void testBackProp(DataSet dataset, JTextArea bottomText) {
  BackProp testNet = new BackProp("Test Back Prop Network");

  bottomText.append("Training Back Prop network...");
  testNet.textArea1 = bottomText;
  testNet.setDataSet(dataset);
  testNet.setNumRecs(dataset.numRecords);
  testNet.setFieldsPerRec(dataset.normFieldsPerRec);
  testNet.setData(dataset.normalizedData);
  int numOutputs = dataset.getClassFieldSize();
  int numInputs = testNet.getFieldsPerRec() - numOutputs;

  testNet.createNetwork(numInputs, numInputs, numOutputs);
  bottomText.append("\nNetwork architecture = " + numInputs + "-"
                  + numInputs + "-" + numOutputs);
```

```java
bottomText.append("\nLearn rate = " + testNet.getLearnRate()
                  + ",  Momentum = " + testNet.getMomentum());
bottomText.append(
  "\n\nEach '*' indicates 100 passes over training data\n");
int maxNumPasses = 2500;
int numRecs = testNet.getNumRecs();
int numPasses = 0;

for(numPasses = 0; numPasses < maxNumPasses; numPasses++) {
  for(int j = 0; j < numRecs; j++) {
    testNet.process();
  }
  try {
    Thread.sleep(10);
  } catch(InterruptedException e) {}
  if((numPasses % 100) == 0) {
    bottomText.append("*");
  }
  if(exitThread) {
    testNet.textArea1.append(
      "\n\nUser pressed Reset ... training halted!\n\n");
    break;
  }
}
testNet.textArea1.append("\n Passes Completed: " + numPasses
    + "  RMS Error = " + testNet.getAveRMSError() + " \n");
testNet.setMode(1);
for(int i = 0; i < testNet.getNumRecs(); i++) {
  testNet.process();
  testNet.display_network();
}
}

public void testKMapNet(DataSet dataset, JTextArea bottomText) {
  KMapNet testNet = new KMapNet("Test Kohonen Map Network");

  bottomText.append("Training Kohonen map network...");
  bottomText.append("\nEach '*' indicates 1 pass over training
    data.\n");
  testNet.textArea1 = bottomText;
  testNet.setDataSet(dataset);
  testNet.setNumRecs(dataset.numRecords);
  testNet.setFieldsPerRec(dataset.fieldsPerRec);
  testNet.setData(dataset.normalizedData);
  testNet.createNetwork(testNet.getFieldsPerRec(), 4, 4);
  int maxNumPasses = 20;
  int numRecs = testNet.getNumRecs();
  int numPasses = 0;

  for(numPasses = 0; numPasses < maxNumPasses; numPasses++) {
    for(int j = 0; j < numRecs; j++) {
```

```
        testNet.cluster();
      }
      try {
        Thread.sleep(10);
      } catch(InterruptedException e) {}
      bottomText.append("*");
      if(exitThread) {
        testNet.textArea1.append(
          "\n\nUser pressed Reset ... training halted!\n\n");
        break;
      }
    }
    testNet.textArea1.append("\n Passes Completed: " + numPasses + " \n");
    testNet.setMode(1);
    for(int i = 0; i < testNet.getNumRecs(); i++) {
      testNet.cluster();
      testNet.display_network();
    }
  }

  public void testDecisionTree(DataSet dataSet, JTextArea bottomText) {
    DecisionTree tree = new DecisionTree("\n Test Decision Tree ");

    tree.textArea1 = bottomText;
    tree.ds = dataSet;
    tree.textArea1.append("Starting DecisionTree ");
    tree.fieldsPerRec = dataSet.fieldsPerRec;
    tree.examples = dataSet.data;
    tree.variableList = dataSet.variableList;
    boolean allCategorical = true;
    Enumeration enum = tree.variableList.elements();

    while(enum.hasMoreElements()) {
      Variable var = (Variable) enum.nextElement();

      if(!var.isCategorical()) {
        allCategorical = false;
        break;
      }
    }
    if(!allCategorical) {
      tree.textArea1.append(
        "\nDecision Tree cannot process continuous data\n");
      tree.textArea1.append("\nPlease select a different data set\n");
      return;
    }
    tree.classVar = (Variable) tree.variableList.get("ClassField");
    tree.variableList.remove("ClassField");
    Node root = tree.buildDecisionTree(tree.examples, tree.variableList,
                new Node("default"));
```

```
        tree.textArea1.append("\n\nDecisionTree -- classVar = "
            + tree.classVar.name);
      Node.displayTree(root, "   ");
      tree.textArea1.append("\nStopping DecisionTree - success!");
    }
```

Summary

In this chapter, we discussed machine learning techniques such as neural networks and decision trees. The main points include the following:

- There are several different forms of learning. *Rote learning* is based on memorization of examples. *Feature extraction* and *induction* are used to find important characteristics of a problem and to build a model that can be used for prediction in new situations. *Clustering* is a way to organize similar patterns into groups.

- *Supervised learning* relies on a teacher that provides the input data as well as the desired solution. *Unsupervised learning* depends on input data only and makes no demands on knowing the solution. *Reinforcement learning* is a kind of supervised learning, where the feedback is more general.

- *On-line learning* means that the agent is adapting while it is working. *Off-line learning* involves saving data while the agent is working and using that data later to train the agent.

- *Neural networks* are parallel computing models that adapt when presented with training data. They operate in supervised, unsupervised, and reinforcement learning modes. A neural network is comprised of a set of simple processing units and a set of adaptive, real-valued connection weights. Learning in neural networks is accomplished through the adjustment of the connection weights.

- *Back propagation networks* are supervised, feedforward neural networks that use the *backward propagation of errors* algorithm to adjust the connection weights. They are used for classification and prediction problems.

- *Kohonen map networks* are unsupervised, feedforward neural networks that self-organize and learn to map similar inputs onto output units that are in close proximity to each other. The inputs are measured using Euclidean distance in a high-dimensional input space and are mapped onto a two-dimensional output space. Kohonen maps perform clustering of input data.

- *Decision trees* use *information theory* to determine where to split data sets in order to build classifiers and regression trees.

Exercises

1. Given the following situations, which learning paradigm (supervised, unsupervised, or reinforcement) is most appropriate and why?

- Ranking articles based on specific user feedback
- Splitting customers into groups with similar preferences
- Playing tic-tac-toe or checkers

2. Add a new data set to the **LearnApp** for classifying coins by their attributes. This means a new data definition file must also be created. Use the **XOR** data set in the **LearnApp** as an example. Train a back propagation network to classify the coins. How many examples did you need to get satisfactory results?

3. Use the data set from Exercise 5.2 and cluster the data with a Kohonen feature map. How many clusters were identified?

4. Add a new data set to the **LearnApp** for classifying people as good or bad credit risks. What attributes should you use (age, sex, marital status, income, etc.)? What attributes should not be used for personal privacy or legal reasons? Build a decision tree to classify this data. Remember that the decision tree algorithm requires all variables to be discrete. Now train a back propagation network on this data set. Compare the classification accuracy of the decision tree and the back propagation network. How did the training time compare?

5. Use the data set from Exercise 5.4 and cluster the data with a Kohonen feature map. How many clusters were identified?

6. Name some of the advantages of decision tree learning algorithms over neural networks. What are some disadvantages?

7. What are the differences among back propagation, decision tree classifiers, and Kohonen map clustering? What is required of the training data?

CHAPTER 6

Agents and Multiagent Systems

In this chapter we explore the relationship between artificial intelligence (AI) and intelligent agents in detail. We show how artificial intelligence topics such as knowledge representation, reasoning, and learning can be combined to construct intelligent agents. We discuss the requirements for autonomous intelligent agents, including perception, reasoning, and the ability to take actions. We next examine the issues raised by multiagent systems, and give an example of the current state-of-the-art using the RoboCup example. We describe one of the earliest multiagent architectures, blackboard systems, and then discuss requirements for agent communications, specifically the Knowledge Query and Manipulation Language (KQML). We then focus on standards for agent interoperability and look at systems where multiple intelligent agents communicate, cooperate, and compete. Finally, we examine multiagent system software engineering issues.

Transition from AI to IA

In the preceding chapters, we have explored the major topics in artificial intelligence, search techniques, knowledge representations, reasoning algorithms, and learning. In the introductory chapter, we described how intelligent agents may be used to enhance the capabilities of applications and to help users get their work done. In this section, we point out the explicit links between the basic AI technologies and the corresponding intelligent agent (IA) behaviors. We also point out the features of the Java language that are applicable or important for implementing these behaviors.

In Chapter 2, "Problem Solving Using Search," we discussed state-based problem-solving using search. In Chapter 3, "Knowledge Representation," we explored several forms of knowledge representation. For our intelligent agents, knowledge representation is a crucial issue. As in any AI application, what our agent is expected to do, and in what domain, will have a significant impact on the type of knowledge representation we should use. If our agent has a limited number of situations it needs to respond to, maybe hard-coding the intelligence into procedural program code is the solution. If our agent has to build or use sophisticated models of the problem domain and solve problems at different levels of abstraction, then frames or semantic nets are the answer. However, if the agent has to answer questions or generate new facts from the existing data, then predicate logic or if-then rules should be considered. If our agent is going to interact with other agents and must share knowledge, then it should probably be able to read and write KIF data. In many applications, we'll need to use a mixture of these knowledge representations.

The amount of intelligence required by our agent, in terms of both domain knowledge and the power of the reasoning algorithms, is related to the degree of autonomy and, to a lesser extent, the degree of mobility it has. If our agent has to deal with a wide range of situations, then it needs a broad knowledge base and a flexible inference engine. If it is mobile, there may be a premium on having a small, compact knowledge representation and a lightweight reasoning system in terms of code size. At the same time, mobility can introduce security concerns that may make explicit if-then rules less desirable than other knowledge representations. For example, a neural network's "black-box" attributes, which are seen as a disadvantage from a traditional symbolic AI perspective, become a distinct advantage when viewed from a knowledge-security vantage point.

Whether learning is a desirable function depends on the domain the intelligent agent will work in, as well as the environment. If the agent is long-lived and will perform similar tasks many times during its lifetime, then learning can be used to improve its performance. But adding learning would be overkill if the agent will be used only occasionally. If we know the major rules of thumb, why not just program them into the agent and have it be capable of performing well from the start, instead of adding the complexity and costs associated with learning algorithms? But there are many domains, such as personal assistants, in which we do not know the user's preferences beforehand. One option is to ask the user to explicitly state what her preferences are. But this may be tedious for the user and, depending on the domain, may be impossible. Often, people know what they like but can't readily express it in words. That is where the advantage of a learning agent surfaces. By watching what the user does in certain situations, the intelligent agent can learn what the user prefers in a much less obtrusive way than by playing a game of "20 Questions."

If there will be a large amount of uncertainty in the problem domain, then using Bayesian networks or if-then rules with certainty factors may be appropriate. If the agent must find an optimal answer, then state-based search techniques or biologically based genetic algorithms should be used. Planning methods, such as those discussed in Chapter 4, "Reasoning Systems," would be called for if the agent has to execute a complex series of actions that are highly dependent on the situation. Reinforcement learning could be used to learn the sequence of operations required to achieve a goal.

To summarize, all of the AI techniques discussed in this book are applicable to intelligent agents. But, they are just tools which must be used by a skilled designer to craft a solution that meets the needs of a specific application. In the example code from the earlier chapters, we provide the simple building blocks to start your exploration of intelligent agents. In the following chapters, we will combine these basic elements into a framework for producing more powerful behavior. In the next sections, we look at specific agent capabilities, perceptions, and actions, and we discuss the requirements they place on IA implementations.

Perception

In order for a software agent to take some intelligent action, it first has to be able to perceive what is going on around it, to have some idea of the state of the world. For animals, this problem is solved by the senses of touch, smell, taste, hearing, and sight. The next problem is to not get overwhelmed by the constant stream of information. Because of the large amount of raw sensory input we get, one of the first things we learn is to filter out and ignore inputs that are expected or usual. We develop an internal model of the world, of what the expected consequences are when we take an action. As long as things are going as expected, we can get by without paying too much attention (for example, someone driving a car while talking on a cellular phone). But we also have learned to focus immediately on unexpected changes in the environment, such as if a car suddenly appears in our peripheral vision when we enter an intersection.

An intelligent agent must have an equivalent source of information about the world in which it lives. This information comes in through its *sensors*, which may or may not be grounded in the physical world. Our intelligent agent does not need to have senses in the same way we do, but it still has to be able to gather information about its environment. This could be done actively by sending query messages to other agents, or it could be done passively by receiving a stream of event messages from the system, the user, or other agents. Just like people, the software agent must be able to distinguish the normal events (mouse movements) from the significant events (double-click on an action icon). In a modern GUI environment such as Windows or Macintosh, the user generates a constant stream of events to the underlying windowing system. Our agents can monitor this stream and must recognize sequences of basic user actions (mouse movement, pause, click, mouse movement, pause, double-click) as signaling some larger-scale semantic event or user action.

If our agent works in the e-mail or newsgroup monitor domain, it will have to recognize when new documents arrive, whether the user is interested in the subject matter or not, and whether to interrupt the user at some other task to inform him of the newly available information. All of this falls into the realm of perception. Being able to notice or recognize information hidden in data is not easy. It requires intelligence and domain knowledge. Thus, being called "perceptive" is a compliment usually reserved for intelligent people. To be useful personal assistants, agents must be perceptive.

Of course, we can design our agents and their messages in such a way that they don't have to be *very* perceptive. We can require the user to explicitly tell our agent what to do and how to do it. The events that are generated could contain all the information the agent needs to determine the current state and the appropriate action. However, one of the major reasons we want and need intelligent agents is to free the user from having to be so explicit. Spelling out, in gory detail, the sequence of actions necessary for a computer to complete a task is not the user's job (it's programming!). That is the power and pleasure of delegating to others. You can say, "schedule a trip to Raleigh," and your travel agent gets it done.

If perception is the ability to recognize patterns, and our agent receives its inputs as streams of data, then we are entering the realm of machine learning and pattern recognition. Learning is not only useful for adapting behavior, it is also quite handy when we want to recognize changes in our environment. A learning system can associate certain states of the world with certain situations. These situations can be normal and expected, or they can be novel and unexpected. Simply logging the occurrence of events and then computing the likelihood or probability of an event or situation can add useful function to an agent. Building a table or map between these states and the associated action is even better. Supervised learning algorithms, such as neural networks and decision trees, can be used to automatically make these associations. Once again, if we know all of the situations our agent can get into before we send it out into cyberspace, then we can just build this into its knowledge base. But in a complex environment with a large number of possible situations, learning may be the only viable option.

Action

Once our agent has perceptively recognized that a significant event has occurred, the next step is to take some action. This action could be to realize that there is no action to take, or it could be to send a message to another agent to take an action on our behalf. Like people, agents take actions through *effectors*. For people, muscles are effectors when we take physical action in the world. We can take action through speech (using different muscles) or by sending e-mail (different muscles again). By communication with other people, we can cause them to act and change the environment.

But suppose we take an action by giving a command to the operating system or to an application. Delete a file. Send e-mail. Do we assume that the action has completed? Do we change our current model of the state of the world? What if we ask another agent to do something for us? Is it prudent to think that everything will work correctly (the agent is trustworthy and bug-free, the network server is up, the transaction goes across the wire)? Or, do we take the cynical view that Murphy's Law is always in effect? The answer is, "It depends." Just as we know that if we put a book down on our desk, it will be there the next time we walk by, if our agent takes an action directly under its control, we can probably consider it done. But when we are dealing with intermediaries, whether other agents or unknown systems, then some extra precautions and checking are probably in order.

Multiagent Systems

So far in this chapter, we have looked at what a single intelligent agent must be capable of to help a user get her work done. But, just as we have companies where the unique talents of many people are combined to solve problems, we can have multiple intelligent agents working together toward a common goal. Some basic characteristics of multiagent systems are that each agent has a limited view of the state of the world, there is no global control, the data is decentralized, and the computation (agent) is asynchronous [Sycara 1998].

Whenever two autonomous, moderately intelligent beings try to communicate, problems arise. First, they have to speak the same language that uses the same set of tokens or symbols. Then, they must agree on what those symbols mean. They must also develop a way to exchange communications in that language. They can't both talk at the same time. They can't both try writing on the same page at the same time. These are all fundamental problems in communication, and the first AI applications that tried to use multiple agents had to resolve each of these issues. Later, in the next section, we describe blackboard systems, the first multiagent AI application architecture. But for now, let's look at an example of the latest work in multiagent systems, playing soccer using intelligent agents.

The RoboCup soccer competitions (www.robocup.org) have been held annually since the 1997 IJCAI conference in Nagoya Japan. The competitions are held in a variety of formulations, but they essentially involve teams of autonomous agents competing against each other in a game of European football or soccer. The games are played with the aid of a soccer server that coordinates the information concerning the position of the player agents on the field, the position of the ball, and the visual and audio sensor inputs to each player. The sensing and action time scales are between 100 milliseconds and 150 milliseconds, which are realistic in terms of human sensory processing and reaction times. The teams of agents must coordinate all of their actions from movement to passing to shooting. In addition to software agents, the RoboCup has been extended to utilize the Sony robot dogs in competitions involving real robots and balls. While films of these competitions are entertaining and sometimes amusing, they indicate the real advances that have been made in AI and robotics over the past decade.

Soccer is a game played on a rectangular field with 11 players on a team. The winning strategy includes offense (scoring the most goals by putting the ball in the opposing team's net) and defense (preventing the opposing team from putting the ball in your net). A single player is designated as the goalkeeper whose primary job is to protect the goal. In terms of planning, the objective is to have scored the most goals at the end of the game. Each player has to be able to position himself on the field, pass the ball, intercept opposing passes, block shots, dribble the ball, and take shots at the opposing goal.

As an example of how two teams approached this challenge, we will describe the strategies used by the ISIS and CMUnited teams. The ISIS team at the University of Southern California [Tambe 1997] uses a framework called STEAM (a Shell for TEAMwork) implemented in the SOAR inferencing environment [Newell 1990]. The system has built-in operators to explicitly model teamwork using hierarchical role-based assignments. The challenge in a multiagent environment is that planning must occur between agents communicating their intentions and commitments to each other. A joint persistent goal [Cohen and Levesque 1990] is pursued as a mutual goal until one of the agents determines that the goal has been achieved or that it has become unachievable for some reason. The team must then reach consensus that this is the case and agree on a new joint persistent goal. In a dynamic task such as playing soccer, you can see that the need for communications among agents could be substantial. A typical sequence of messages is for an agent to *request* another agent to commit to a joint persistent goal, and that agent would then *confirm*. STEAM develops this basic mechanism into high-level team operators that instantiate joint intentions and goals. In most cases, it is impossible to plan a complete sequence of actions that will achieve a complex goal in a dynamic environment. This is one of the motivations for the development of partial-order planners such as the SharedPlans framework [Grosz and Kraus 1993]. STEAM uses concepts from SharedPlans such as recipes or scripts of actions and partial plans. Planning and replanning is an ongoing activity in changing environments. Trying to do this when tens or hundreds of autonomous software agents are involved, whose actions must be coordinated, is a non-trivial problem to solve.

The CMUnited team from Carnegie Mellon University uses a combination of learning and planning to create a team. They created a team using a layered approach. Each agent has a model of the world that includes visual inputs from the soccer server as well as communications and beliefs concerning other agents on the field. The agents are completely autonomous and support eight unique actions. They contain a mix of neural networks, decision-trees, and reinforcement learning based on Q-learning [Watkins 1989]. The individual agents are trained to know how to position themselves to intercept the ball. They use "locker room agreements" to have some set plays or predetermined team behaviors when certain situations occur in a game. If you've ever played or coached a team sport, you know that this is a realistic approach for coordinating teams in game situations. CMUnited uses a probabilistic approach, *Hidden Markov Models*, to model their opponents' expected behaviors in game situations.

It should be pointed out that both the ISIS and CMUnited teams were successful in the RoboCup tournaments, even though they used very different approaches in terms of the individual agents and their multiagent team strategies. Notice that these complex systems were created using many of the same algorithms presented in Part One. In the next section, we discuss perhaps the oldest multiagent system architecture, blackboards.

Blackboards

While blackboards and chalk are now out of fashion, replaced by whiteboards and dry-erase markers, they are still a useful metaphor for an important AI architecture. The blackboard architecture was first introduced in the Hearsay II speech recognition project [Erman et al. 1980]. It featured a system with multiple *knowledge sources* or independent agents, each with a specific domain of expertise related to speech analysis. The *blackboard* is a data structure that is used as the general communication mechanism for the multiple knowledge sources and is managed and arbitrated by a *controller* [Jagannathan, et al. 1989].

As each agent works on its part of the problem, it looks to the blackboard to pick up new information posted by other agents, and it, in turn, posts its results to the blackboard. So, much like a blackboard in a classroom environment, the blackboard is an information-sharing device, with multiple writers and multiple readers. The agents, like students, each work at their own pace on the problems that are of most interest to them or where they have knowledge to apply, and add information to the blackboard when they can. Other agents use this information to further their own work. Thus, the blackboard architecture allows multiple agents to work independently and cooperate to solve a problem.

The blackboard model is a generalization of the architecture used in Hearsay II. It is an opportunistic problem-solving technique because at each control cycle any kind of reasoning method can be used. An event model is used to signal when changes are made to the blackboard and to notify the knowledge sources or agents that something has changed. An event could trigger the activation of a set of agents or the controller could dynamically determine which agent to start. The controller also limits access to the blackboard so that two agents don't try to write on the same space at the same time.

One final point regarding blackboard systems is that the knowledge sources or agents are very tightly coupled through the blackboard data structure and its interfaces. If you are building a single large application and want to modularize the knowledge bases, then blackboards are a fine communication mechanism. However, if you want an environment where agents with very different structures and with no knowledge of a centralized blackboard can work together, we need more formal interfaces such as those described in the next section.

Communication

When our agents need to talk to each other, they can do this in a variety of ways. They can talk directly to each other, provided they speak the same language. Or they can talk through an interpreter or facilitator, provided they know how to talk to the interpreter, and the interpreter can talk to the other agent.

There is a level of basic language—the syntax and format of the messages—and there is a deeper level—the meaning or semantics. While the syntax is often easily understood, the semantics are not. For example, two English-speaking agents may get confused if one talks about the boot and bonnet, and the other about the trunk and hood of an automobile. They need to have a shared vocabulary of words and their meaning. This shared vocabulary is called an ontology.

Each specific domain might have its own ontology. For example, there might be a medical ontology, an automobile ontology, and a computer components ontology. When agents negotiate about or plan for a task in one of these domains, they use a common ontology to ensure there are no doubts about the semantics of the message terms.

As the eXtensible Markup Language (XML) gains acceptance in industry and across the Internet, it may become the common representation format for messages. In XML, a Data Type Definition (DTD) is used to define a particular ontology. Industry vertical DTDs have been developed for computer components (RosettaNet) and others. A definition of HyperText Markup Language (HTML) has been created using XML. In the next section, we introduce the most widely used agent communication language (ACL).

Knowledge Query and Manipulation Language (KQML)

The KQML provides a framework for programs and agents to exchange information and knowledge. Like KIF, KQML (these acronyms sort of roll off the tongue, don't they?) came out of the DARPA Knowledge Sharing Effort. Whereas KIF deals with knowledge representations, KQML focuses on message formats and message-handling protocols between running agents. But only the message protocols are specified, not the language used to represent the content of the message. KQML defines the operations that agents may attempt on each other's knowledge bases and provides a basic architecture for agents to share knowledge and information through special agents called facilitators. Facilitators act as matchmakers or secretaries for the agents they service.

KQML messages are called *performatives*, which is a term from speech-act theory [Searle 1969]. There are various types of speech acts, including *directives*, which are commands or requests; *representatives*, which state facts or beliefs; and *commissives*, such as promises or threats [Nilsson 1998]. Each message is intended to implicitly perform some specified action. There are a large number of performatives defined in KQML, and most agent-based systems support only a small subset. The performatives, or message types, are reserved words in KQML. Using performatives, agents can ask other agents for information, tell other agents facts, subscribe to the services of agents, and offer their own services.

KQML uses ontologies (explicit specifications of the meaning, concepts, and relationships applicable to some specific domain) to ensure that two agents communicating in the same language can correctly interpret statements in that language. For example, in English, when we say "Java," are we referring to coffee, an island, or a programming language? To eliminate this ambiguity, every KQML message explicitly states what ontology is being used.

KQML messages encode information at three different architectural levels: content, message, and communication. An example of a KQML message from agent *joe* asking about the price of a share of SUN stock might be encoded as:

```
(ask-one
  :sender joe
  :content (real price = sun.price())
  :receiver stock-server
  :reply-with sun-stock
  :language java
  :ontology NYSE-TICKS)
```

The KQML performative is *ask-one*; the receiver of the message is an agent named *stock-server*. The *:content* parameter completely defines the content level. The *:reply-with*, *:sender*, and *:receiver* parameters specify information at the communication level. The performative name, the *:language* specification, and the *:ontology* name are part of the message level. Note that we could send the exact same message with a different language and content piece, or the same language but with different ontology, and thus subtly or dramatically change the meaning of the message. But the performative, *ask-one*, would still be a query from agent *joe* to agent *stock-server*.

Two agents who want to communicate using KQML require the services of a KQML facilitator or matchmaker [Kuokka and Harada 1995]. The agents communicate with the matchmaker using standard KQML messages. They can register themselves as providers of services or information by using the *advertise* performative. Agents can also ask the matchmaker to recommend other agents using the *recommend, recruit*, and *broker* performatives. The matchmaker provides a centralized meeting-place for agents, and establishes a community where agents can interact. Note that the matchmaker cannot vouch for the trustworthiness of the agents that advertise their services, nor can it guarantee that an agent can provide a specific piece of information. Nevertheless, the matchmaker plays an important role in a multiagent system. The alternative would be for every agent to query every other agent whenever it needed to collaborate.

Although KQML has been used in many multiagent systems applications, it does not mean that my KQML agents can talk with your KQML agents. In almost all cases, the implementations of KQML are highly dependent on the performatives used and the exact interaction protocols that are defined [Singh 1998]. Every communication can be viewed from three perspectives: the sender's, the receiver's, and an outside observer's. For the sender and receiver, this is a private communication; from the agent society perspective, it is a public exchange. Singh argues that KQML and most other agent communication languages emphasize the private perspective, primarily the sender's view. This seemingly violates the human discourse literature, which indicates that the sender and receiver should be treated as equally important. Furthermore, if the goal of having a standard agent communication language is to allow interoperability, then you must be able to observe compliance, and this can only be done from a public, or social, perspective.

While not everyone working on multiagent systems believes that KQML is the best model for agent communications, it is still the most widely used technique. In fact, KQML has been extended and modified for use as the basic agent communications language (ACL) in the FIPA standards discussed in the next section. A Java implementation of this framework, called JACKAL, was developed at the University of Maryland, Baltimore County (Finin et al. 1995), and is available at the IBM alphaWorks Web site (www.alphaworks.ibm.com).

Agent Standards

As agents continue to develop and gain use in industrial applications, efforts to standardize their implementation and to ensure interoperability continue. Two major efforts at standardization are the Foundation for Intelligent Physical Agents (FIPA) and the Object Management Group (OMG) Agent Working Group. FIPA is dominated by computer and telecommunications companies and is focused primarily on agent-level issues. OMG is the standards body that created the CORBA distributed object protocol and tends to focus on object-level interoperability and management.

FIPA

The first set of FIPA specifications that led to commercial implementations and limited interoperability demonstrations were the FIPA 97 standards [O'Brien and Nicol 1998]. The three major areas addressed were agent management, agent communications, and agent software integration. The FIPA 97 specifications required CORBA IIOP as the communications protocol, a speech-act based agent communication language, and a set of interaction protocols for defining dialogues between agents (including negotiation). However, there were several major weaknesses in the FIPA 97 specification. The rise of Java RMI and HTTP as alternative communications protocols was a prime factor in the development of a new, more technology-independent specification.

The FIPA 2000 specifications represent several years of work with contributions from major technology companies including Sun, IBM, Fujitsu, and HP. Perhaps the biggest change in FIPA 2000 standards is the definition of an abstract architecture, allowing alternative implementations that will interoperate. Information on the current FIPA standards can be found at www.fipa.org.

As shown in Figure 6.1, the FIPA agent management reference model defines only basic infrastructure. An agent platform provides an Agent Management System (AMS) that controls the agent life-cycle, a Directory Facilitator (DF), which is a yellow-pages lookup service, and a Message Transport System (MTS) which provides internal agent-to-agent communications as well as external messaging with other FIPA-compliant agent platforms.

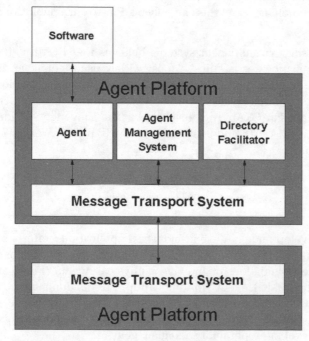

Figure 6.1 The FIPA Agent Platform.

FIPA makes no strong statements about the internal structure of the agents running on the agent platform. However, the FIPA specifications do rely on the BDI agent model, expecting agents to have mental states, beliefs about other agents and the state of the world, and desires and plans for taking actions to change the state of the world. Agents can take actions by interfacing with software outside of the agent platform or via speech acts exchanged with other agents. The FIPA agent communications specification includes interaction protocols, which are tightly scripted sequences of speech acts, for asking questions, sharing knowledge, and participating in various types of auctions and negotiations.

OMG

The Object Management Group has taken the lead in the area of mobile agent systems. The Mobile Agent Systems Interoperability Facilities (MASIF) specification approved in 1998 defines how agents can migrate between agent platforms using CORBA Interface Definition Language (IDL) interfaces and the CORBA security, naming, and life-cycle services. The MASIF specification is largely based on the IBM Aglets mobile agent system design.

Cooperating Agents

The case for having multiple agents cooperate to do a job is compelling. Why have one agent slave away when we can have fifty working together to accomplish the same task? What's more, why have one huge artificial intelligence knowledge base and application if we can solve the same problem by constructing and maintaining a collection of much smaller and simpler agents? Of course, the idea of breaking a problem into smaller pieces is not an AI invention; divide and conquer is an ancient military strategy. In computer science, this was one of the basic tenets of top-down structured design, used in everything from COBOL to Pascal. However, with agents, the advantages of small, independent knowledge sources must be weighed against the considerable disadvantages of introducing a language barrier between them. In several domains, the benefits have far outweighed the costs.

System management is an area in which cooperating agents have been used successfully. As client/server and distributed-computing models have evolved over the last two decades, problems with system management have become apparent. System managers, who were accustomed to performance monitors that provided clear views of the state of the centralized host, had a difficult time handling applications that ran across networks of workstations. The solution was to deploy system monitor agents on each of these distributed systems. A centralized controller could communicate with the remote monitor's agent (usually by polling) to get information on the status of each remote computer. The distributed system management application could integrate that information to provide an overview of the current state of the system. While starting out as very simple agents, these monitor agents have grown more sophisticated over time.

Agents are also useful in electronic commerce (e-commerce), in which intelligent agents represent both consumers and providers of products and services. In a simple form, an agent may represent a traveler who wants to book a flight, querying various airline reservation systems to find the best price and itinerary. In a more complex form, the buying agent must deal with a selling agent, who has its own agenda (to make as much money as possible per transaction for its owner) and strategies. In this marketplace context, the agents are cooperating to serve the interests of both parties. At the same time, there is an undercurrent of competition. The Kasbah system developed at MIT Media Lab is an example of this kind of electronic marketplace [Chavez and Maes 1996].

Multiagent design systems is another area in which multiple independent agents have proven their value [Lander 1997]. In a collaborative design system, many designers must work on overlapping pieces of the design at the same time. A change in one part may impact several others. The entire design system includes the human designers as well as the intelligent agents, so human-computer interactions are important. Often, personal assistant agents are used to provide the interface between the designers and the agents in the system. A important aspect of multiagent design systems is that each intelligent agent has its own perspective on what a "good" or "optimal" design is, depending on its area of expertise. This is not very different from cross-functional development teams. Thus, each agent must be willing to compromise in order to achieve a better overall or global design. This also means that somewhere there is an agent that can provide some measure of the quality of the overall design and can arbitrate conflicts among the more specialized agents.

Multiagent Planning

Coordinating a collection of autonomous agents is not a trivial task, as we illustrated in our earlier discussion of the RoboCup application. The primary approach has been to extend traditional AI planning algorithms by including concepts of joint intentions and commitments among agents.

Early approaches to multiagent planning used a centralized planner whose job was to figure out the complete sequence of actions required for the team to achieve its goals. This centralized planner often played an active role in synchronizing the activities of the various agents in the team. The partial global planning algorithm [Durfee 1988] was one of the first to have autonomous agents communicating and coordinating their local plans while working to achieve group goals.

The next logical development in multiagent planning algorithms was to explicitly model teams, teamwork, and team interactions. The joint-intentions framework models a team's mental state [Cohen and Levesque 1990]. A joint intention means that every team member is committed to achieving some goal while also believing the other team members are pursuing that goal. The team members exchange messages to update their mutual beliefs and synchronize their behavior, establishing what is called a joint commitment.

A somewhat different approach, used by the SHAREDPLAN model, is based on team members intending that an action be performed [Grosz and Sidner 1990]. SHARED-PLAN uses common recipes or scripts of actions as building blocks for creating plans.

This work was extended to include the ability to use partial plans or scripts to deal with planning in dynamic environments [Grosz and Kraus 1996].

Multiagent planning is fairly complex. It requires that agents share substantial amounts of information, incurring significant communication and processing overhead. For large teams of agents, the cost of planning to coordinate and synchronize agent actions could be prohibitive. If the environment changes frequently, then re-planning is required. It is likely that a combination using the team structure and roles to limit communications, along with these distributed planning techniques, will provide the best solution to building multiagent teams.

Competing Agents

As soon as we have agents that do our bidding, other people will have agents to do theirs. Our agent wants to get the best deal for us. Other agents want to get the best deal for their owners. Whose agent wins? Probably the one with the most intelligence, the most specialized knowledge about the task it is trying to perform, the most powerful reasoning system to apply that knowledge to problem-solving in the domain, and, in all likelihood, the one that can learn from experience and get better over time.

This assumes, of course, that we have a level playing field. It wouldn't be fair if your agent was on a server negotiating with another agent that could access a large local database of information while your agent could not. What if your agent was scanned by the server, and information about your negotiating position (prices, strategies, rules, etc.) was placed in the hands of the other agent? Would you send your agent out on the Internet if you thought you could lose or be taken advantage of so easily? Probably not. In our opinion, there will have to be secure agent marketplaces, where agents register and are guaranteed to have equal access to server services and information.

There is also competition between agents at a less direct level. For example, suppose two knowledge workers at competing companies are both trying to finish a project proposal for a customer. If one has a set of intelligent agents that can help him find the information required in half the time of his competitor, that gives him a competitive advantage. This is just an extension of the current use of information technology to help a company win in the marketplace. When everyone has intelligent agents working for them, the winner will be the one with the best agents.

Negotiation

Negotiation protocols such as Contract Net [Smith 1980] are the basis for many multiagent system applications. The basic steps in the Contract Net protocol are as follows:

1. Manager agent calls for bids to complete a task (announcement).
2. Contractor agents evaluate the announcement and optionally respond with their bids.
3. The manager agent selects one of the contractor (bidder) agents.
4. The contractor agent performs the task and returns the results.

One weakness of the original Contract Net protocol is that the contractor agent cannot bid for multiple jobs at the same time. If he later receives a better offer, the contractor can break his commitment to the original manager agent. This forces another cycle of bidding. This protocol is typical of most agent interaction protocols. It defines a strict sequence of actions and messages to be exchanged. Each agent involved in the protocol needs to model the state machine of the exchange. If an agent is engaged in simultaneous conversations with other agents, the bookkeeping and overhead can be prohibitive. Although bidding is useful, it is one of the most basic forms of negotiation that can take place between people or agents.

An auction is another interaction protocol in which the seller initiates the auction and monitors the process while buyers respond with offers to the auctioneer. Auctions typically have strict rules governing the behavior of the auctioneer and the selection of a buyer. Various types of auctions, such as English (increasing price) and Dutch (decreasing price), have different sets of well-known rules [Kumar and Feldman 1998].

Bargaining is the most complicated form of negotiation protocol, because proposals and counter proposals may be offered back and forth until both parties agree or disagree. Bargaining is more complex from an agent point of view, because an offer of $500 as an opening may not be acceptable, but it may be fine if it is the result of several counter offer exchanges that started at $1000.

Negotiation is also a fertile ground for the use of learning, both to identify opponents' bidding strategies and to learn from experience [Zeng and Sycara 1998]. Applications of negotiation are widespread in business, especially in supply chain applications where multiple agents representing businesses can automate business-to-business transactions [Su, Huang, and Hammer 2000]. In Chapter 10, "Marketplace Application," we implement a simple marketplace application in which agents use bargaining to buy and sell goods.

Agent Software Engineering Issues

Designing agents and multiagent systems brings many new issues to the forefront. Over the past three decades, programming techniques have improved because of increasingly powerful abstractions, including procedural abstraction, abstract data types, and object-oriented programming. Now agents may offer the next advancement in software engineering by allowing designers and programmers to think of applications in terms of collections of interacting autonomous agents [Wooldridge and Jennings 1999]. Agent-oriented programming [Shoham 1994] can provide a complementary and natural extension to distributed object-oriented design practices.

As described in the sidebar in Chapter 1, "Introduction," the difference between agents and objects is largely a matter of granularity and level of abstraction. Agents are bigger than objects, so there will be fewer agents than objects. Being able to think at a higher level of abstraction will provide an advantage when designing applications that naturally fall into the agent-oriented paradigm. Wooldridge and Jennings (1999) caution that agents are not likely to be the silver bullet of software engineering [Brooks 1975], which would provide an order of magnitude of improvement in development productivity. Also, remember, that agents are software, just like AI algorithms, not magic. Finally, agents and multiagent systems are usually multithreaded software, which implies they are complex systems that require care to avoid problems with data synchronization and deadlock.

Another issue when designing agent systems is to realize that the AI or intelligent software component will be a small part of the total programming effort. Most of the software will deal with traditional information technology tasks such as communications, resource allocations, database access, and transaction processing. This mistake was one of the reasons that commercial AI companies failed in the late 1980s. They built software systems that were islands separated from the rest of the enterprise applications. Expert systems were often programmed in Lisp and Prolog instead of languages that could be easily integrated with COBOL and C applications running on standard business computers. In the case of multiagent systems, there is no need to create a new distributed computing framework especially for agents when the infrastructure already exists to support distributed object applications.

A well-designed multiagent system makes use of concurrency, both inside individual agents and certainly among different agents. Sequencing control through a set of agents is not making the best use of the agent-oriented programming paradigm. If you want a collection of autonomous agents, then they have to be running simultaneously (via multithreading), not sequentially. You should make use of the existing infrastructure for distributed objects, events, message passing, security, directory services, and so on. Don't develop your own agent communication language when a more standard technique such as KQML will do.

The agent's use of AI must be appropriate for its role [Wooldridge and Jennings 1999]. Using too much AI will create a bloated, heavyweight system, while using no AI at all means you are really designing a distributed object application, not a multiagent system. Yes, agents are a cool marketing buzzword, but labeling an application as having agents when they contain no intelligence, autonomy, or goal-directed behavior is very misleading. Next, we look at some common techniques for designing agents.

Designing Agents

A common approach for designing agents and multiagent systems is to define roles for team members. In the RoboCup team for example, agents play the role of goalie, forwards, midfielders, and defenders. Models such as the AGR (Agent-Group-Role) model [Ferber and Gutknecht 1998] are useful for formulating multiagent system problems in which agents are members of one or more overlapping groups, and can dynamically take on one or more roles in the application. Furthermore, agents may have persistent roles or long-term assignments as well as task-specific, short-term roles [Tambe, et al. 1999]. This is another example of the difference between agents and distributed object-oriented systems. Objects don't usually change roles once the application has been deployed.

While agent applications are becoming increasingly popular, there have not been many proposals for agent-oriented methodologies for analysis, design, and software development [Iglesias, Garijo, and Gonzalez 1998]. There is some feeling that agents are little more than active objects and so existing OO analysis and design methodologies should be applied. But as we pointed out in Chapter 1, "Introduction," agents are not simply objects. Although agents and objects may both employ message-passing (or method invocation), what they do in response to those messages is quite different. Objects do what they are asked (or told) to do. An agent can refuse a request, and a single message may result in a complex series of speech acts between agents, and even a complete reorientation of the agent's goals and behavior. Other aspect of agents that OO modeling does not adequately address are the complex mental states, reasoning, planning, and social aspects of multiagent system applications.

One method that has been proposed is the agent modeling technique for systems of BDI agents [Kinny, Georgeff, and Rao 1996]. This approach looks at the problem from two perspectives, an external and an internal one. The external view breaks the system into two major elements, the agents themselves (the agent model) and their interactions (interaction model). The internal viewpoint uses three models for each BDI agent class: an agent model for defining relationships between agents, a goal model for describing goals and events the agent will respond to, and a plan model for achieving the agent goals.

The up-front analysis requires that agents' roles be identified so they can be arranged in a class hierarchy. Responsibilities are then assigned to each role, along with the services required to meet those responsibilities. Finally, each interaction is defined down to the level of individual speech-acts and the associated data.

Another popular approach is the CoMoMas extension to the CommonKADS knowledge engineering methodology [Glaser 1996]. CommonKADS is a European standard for building knowledge-based systems (expert systems). The CoMoMas approach specifies a collection of models, including the agent model, which defines the agent architecture and knowledge; the expertise model, which differentiates among task, reactive, and problem-solving knowledge; the task model; the cooperation model, which defines communication primitives; and the system model, which defines the organization of the agent society.

Summary

In this chapter, we explored how artificial intelligence techniques are used to build intelligent agents, as well as many issues related to multiagent systems. The main points are as follows:

- There are many alternative *artificial intelligence techniques* for knowledge representation, reasoning, and learning. The specific functions and requirements of an intelligent agent are the prime determinant of which AI techniques should be used.

- The amount of *intelligence* required by an agent, in terms of the size of the knowledge base and sophistication of the reasoning algorithms, is significantly impacted by the degree of *autonomy* and *mobility* the agent has. Mobile agents place special requirements on the security of the knowledge base as it travels through the network.

- *Learning* is most useful when an agent is used in complex environments to perform repetitive tasks, or when the agent must adapt to unknown situations. Personal assistants that model user preferences and collaborative agents will also benefit from learning capabilities.

- Agents must be able to perceive the physical or virtual world around them using *sensors*. A fundamental part of perception is the ability to recognize and filter out the expected events and attend to the unexpected ones. Intelligent agents use *effectors* to take actions either by sending messages to other agents or by calling application programming interfaces or system services directly.

- Multiagent systems are applications in which many autonomous software agents are combined to solve large problems. The RoboCup challenge is an example of the current state-of-the-art of multiagent systems, in which teams of autonomous agents compete in a simulated soccer tournament.

- The *blackboard architecture* allows a group of agents to cooperate to solve problems. The *blackboard* is a centralized data structure used for communication and data sharing among agents. The *controller* manages the blackboard as well as the generation and dispatching of events to the agents in the system.

- *Knowledge Query and Manipulation Language* (*KQML*) provides a framework for a set of independent agents to communicate and cooperate on a problem using messages called *performatives*. KQML specifies information at the *communication level* (sender and receiver), the *message level* (language and ontology), and the *content level* (language-specific sentences).

- Standards are becoming more important as agents become a large part of the electronic commerce infrastructure. The Foundation for Intelligent Physical Agents (FIPA) and the Object Management Group (OMG) have created standards for mobile agents and multiagent systems.

- *Cooperation* among agents allows a community of specialized agents to pool their capabilities to solve large problems, but with the additional cost of communication overhead. Distributed systems management, electronic commerce, and multiagent design systems are three application areas in which cooperating agents have been applied. Planning and coordination is a major technical issue in multiagent teams.

- *Competition* between agents will occur as soon as intelligent agents are deployed by individuals or companies with different agendas, and those agents interact in the e-commerce environment. Intelligent agents will be used to provide competitive advantages for individuals and businesses. Negotiation protocols, such as Contract Net, auctions, and bargaining, are used to allow agents to compete for business.

- Designing multiagent systems is similar to object-oriented design but requires some additional analysis and modeling techniques. Agent roles and social interactions must be clearly understood in order to develop practical multiagent system applications.

Exercises

1. How does artificial intelligence relate to intelligent agents in terms of their perceptiveness and action-taking abilities? Is AI essential or superfluous?

2. What role does the controller play in a blackboard system?

3. What are the strengths and weaknesses of KQML as an agent communication language? Do you think speech-act theory is the correct model to use for agent communication? Why or why not?

4. What infrastructure would be required to set up an auction or marketplace for use by multiple intelligent agents?

5. Many of the agent design methodologies focus on analyzing the roles that agents play in an application. Do you think this approach makes sense? How else could you define the functions each agent must perform in an application?

6. Another important aspect of multiagent system design is specifying the interactions and communications between agents. How is this analysis phase similar to or different from object-oriented design techniques?

7. The planning and coordination of agents in multiagent teams offers many technical challenges. What are the advantages and disadvantages of centralized versus distributed planning? If you were fielding a team in the RoboCup challenge, what approach would you use?

CHAPTER 7

Intelligent Agent Framework

I n this chapter, we develop an intelligent agent architecture using object-oriented design techniques. We start with a generic set of requirements and refine them into a set of specifications. We explicitly state our design philosophy and goals and consider various design and implementation alternatives under those constraints. We explore how intelligent agents can be used to expand the capabilities of traditional applications and how they can serve as the controller for a group of applications. With minor modifications, we reuse the artificial intelligence functions we developed in the first part of this book.

Requirements

The first step in any software development project is the collection of requirements from the intended user community. In our case, this was made difficult because our readers could not provide this kind of feedback until we had already designed and developed the product (this book). In the first edition, we made some obvious decisions concerning the audience and intended purpose of this book, as indicated by the title. In this second edition, we have taken reader feedback into account. We are going to develop intelligent agents using Java. We are also going to provide the ability to add intelligence to new or existing applications written in Java. An additional fundamental requirement is that we should reuse the artificial intelligence code we developed in the first part of this book.

Another requirement is that our intelligent agent framework must be practical. Not practical in the sense that it is product-level code ready to put into production, but in that the basic principles and thrust of our design are applicable to solving real-world problems. While providing a stimulating learning experience is a goal, we are not interested in exploring purely academic or, more accurately, esoteric issues. If you understand what we are doing and why we are doing it, you should be able to use these techniques to develop your own intelligent agent applications.

Focus on the topic at hand is another requirement. This is a book about intelligent agents. We would be doing the reader a disservice if we spent large amounts of time developing communications code, an object-oriented database, or a mechanism for performing remote procedure calls. We will try to maximize the amount of code dealing with intelligent agents, and minimize the code not directly related to the topic. At the same time, because this is a book about Java programming, we want to use the features and capabilities found in Java and the JDK 1.2 development environment.

Having just said all this, we acknowledge that providing a decent user interface is also a requirement. Luckily, with the current Java development environments, providing a usable GUI is not a major problem. We will use the Borland JBuilder tool to create these interfaces. Because most of the GUI code is generated, we will not spend much time or energy discussing this aspect of our applications. There are certainly other visual builder tools that can generate Java code, and they could be used instead of the Borland product.

The next requirement comes from the authors, who also spend much time reading programming books. We will not create a complex design and describe it in minute detail. While this would be an interesting exercise for us, we doubt it would provide value to you, our readers. We'll call this the "keep it simple, stupid" requirement, and hope that explicitly listing it here will shame us into following this maxim when we get too carried away.

The last requirement is that our architecture must be flexible enough to support the applications presented in the next three chapters. As a preview, we will be building agents to plug into a simple agent platform, to handle information filtering over the Internet, and to perform simple multiagent electronic commerce transactions.

To summarize the requirements, we want a simple yet flexible architecture that is focused on intelligent agent issues. It must be practical so it can solve realistic problems and must have a decent user interface so its functions and limitations will be readily apparent to the users. In the next section, we talk about our goals from a technical perspective.

Design Goals

Requirements come from our users and tell us what functions or properties our product must have in order to be successful. Having a validated set of requirements is useful, because it focuses our energy on the important stuff. It is just as important to have a clear set of design goals that we can use to guide the technical decisions that must be made as we develop the solution that meets those requirements. Just as with requirements, we must explicitly state our design goals and assumptions.

There are some fundamental issues that will drive our design. The first is that we can view our intelligent agents either as adding value to a single standalone application, or as a freestanding community of agents that interact with each other and other applications. The first is an application-centric view of agents, where the agents are helpers to the application (and therefore of the users of the application). This approach is the least complex because we can view the agent as a simple extension of the application functionality. By providing our intelligent agent functions as an object-oriented framework, we can easily add intelligent behavior to any Java application.

The second approach is more agent-centric, where the agents monitor and drive the applications. Here our agent manager itself is an application and must interface with other applications that are driven by the agents. The complexity here is that we must define a generic mechanism for application communications through our agent manager. One method is to require every application to modify its code to be "agent-aware." Another is for us to provide a common way to interface with the unique application programming interfaces.

The agent framework we are developing must be easily understood and straightforward to use. The primary aim of developing this framework is to illustrate how intelligent agents and the different AI techniques can be used to enhance applications. Our coding style will be straightforward. Data members will be generally *protected* and accessor functions will be used in the majority of cases. *This is not commercial-level code.* Bullet-proofing code can sometimes make even simple logic seem complex. Our applications will work as designed, but they will not be able to handle all unexpected input data or error conditions.

We will construct the agent framework so that inter-agent communication is supported. It must also be flexible so that support for new applications, AI techniques, and other features can be easily added.

Functional Specifications

In this section, we take the requirements and our design goals, and turn them into a list of functions that satisfy those requirements and goals. This defines what we have to build. The functional specifications are a contract between the development team and the user community. Here is the functionality we need:

1. It must be easy to add an intelligent agent to an existing Java application.

2. A graphical construction tool must be available to compose agents out of other Java components and other agents.

3. The agents must support a relatively sophisticated event-processing capability. Our agent will need to handle events from the outside world or from other agents, and signal events to outside applications.

4. We must be able to add domain knowledge to our agent using if-then rules, and support forward and backward rule-based processing with sensors and effectors.

5. The agents must be able to learn to do classification, clustering, and prediction using learning algorithms.

6. Multiagent applications must be supported using a KQML-like message protocol.

7. The agents must be persistent; once an agent is constructed, there must be a way to save it in a file and reload its state at a later time.

Intelligent Agent Architecture

Now that we have specified the functions that our intelligent agent architecture must provide, we must make our design decisions. We will take the function points in order and discuss the various issues and tradeoffs we must make.

1. It must be easy to add an intelligent agent to an existing Java application.

   The easiest way for us to add an agent to an existing application is to have the application instantiate and configure the agent and then call the agent's methods as service routines. That way the application is always in control, and it can use the intelligent functions as appropriate. This is easy, but this is hardly what we would consider an intelligent agent. It is embedded intelligence, but there is no autonomy. Another possibility is to have the application instantiate and configure the agent and then start it up in a separate thread. This would give the agent some autonomy, although it would be running in the application's process space. The application could yield to the agent when necessary, and the agent would yield when it was done processing so that the application could continue. A third possibility is to have the agent run in a separate thread, but use events rather than direct method invocations to communicate between the application and agent. Because this gives us both autonomy and flexibility, this is the design we will pursue.

2. A graphical construction tool must be available to compose agents out of other Java components and other agents.

   There are graphical development tools such as Borland's JBuilder, WebGain's Visual Café, and IBM's VisualAge for Java that allow you to construct applications using a "construction from parts" metaphor. However, Java provides a basic component capability through its *java.beans* package. JavaBeans is a Java component model that allows software functions to be treated as "parts" which can be put together to construct an application. Each JavaBean has a well-defined interface that allows a visual builder tool to manipulate that object. It also has a defined runtime interface that allows applications comprised of JavaBeans to run.

   Another nice feature of Beans is that they can be nested, meeting our requirement for the ability to compose agents out of other agents. This allows us to develop special-purpose agents that can be reused in other higher-level agents. For example, we can have low-level agents that use neural networks for learning and high-level agents that use rules to determine what actions to take. This function is roughly equivalent to the Composite design pattern as specified by Gamma et al. (1995).

3. The agents must support a relatively sophisticated event-processing capability. Our agent will need to handle events from the outside world or from other agents, and signal events to outside applications.

   The JDK 1.1 release featured a powerful event-processing model called the Delegation Event Model. This event framework design was actually driven by the requirements of the JavaBeans component model. This model is based on event **sources** and event **listeners**. There are many different classes of events with different levels of granularity. The agent can be an **EventListener**, and whenever the agent is notified that an event occurred, it can process the event. We can describe our own event type by subclassing the **EventObject** class.

4. We must be able to add domain knowledge to our agent using if-then rules, and support forward and backward rule-based processing with sensors and effectors.

The **BooleanRuleBase**, **Rule**, and **RuleVariable** classes we developed in Chapter 4, "Reasoning Systems," can be used in our agents to provide forward and backward rule-based inferencing. We will have to extend the functionality to support sensors and effectors. The main reason for providing this functionality is to provide a way for users to specify conditions and actions without programming. If we build a JavaBeans property editor for our **BooleanRuleBase** class, a user could easily construct a set of **RuleVariable**s and **Rule**s to perform the logic behind an intelligent agent's behavior. We provide this functionality, but do not exploit it. That is, the task of developing a property editor for use in a visual JavaBean development environment is left as an exercise for the reader.

5. The agents must be able to learn to do classification, clustering, and prediction using learning algorithms.

In Chapter 5, "Learning Systems," we designed and developed decision tree classifiers, neural clustering, and prediction algorithms in Java. We can use the **DecisionTree**, **BackPropNet**, and **KMapNet** classes to provide these functions to our agents.

6. Multiagent applications must be supported using a KQML-like message protocol.

In order to provide this functionality, we will have to go back to the drawing board and come up with an agent that can handle tasks like a KQML facilitator or matchmaker. We would like to use our existing rule capabilities to help provide this function, if possible. We can use the Java event model to provide the communication mechanism between agents and the facilitator and define our own event objects to hold the message content.

7. The agents must be persistent; once an agent is constructed, there must be a way to save it in a file and reload its state at a later time.

The *java.io* package in the Java run-time supports serialization of Java objects. Simply marking the class as implementing the **Serializable** interface makes saving and loading objects very easy to do. Any data members that are not explicitly declared **transient** will be saved out to a file. This is another advantage of using Java to implement our agent framework.

The CIAgent Framework

While trying not to be too cute, we have selected the name **CIAgent** for our intelligent agent framework, where **CIAgent** stands for "*Constructing Intelligent Agents*." Many other names suggested themselves to us, but this seems like a reasonable choice, given the title of the book. If it really bugs you, we hope it doesn't interfere with your understanding and use of our design.

To summarize the decisions we made in the preceding section, we are going to construct our intelligent agents so they can interact with the JavaBeans component model. This design decision, combined with reuse of code from Part One of this book, allows us to meet most of our functional specifications. We have to make some enhancements to our rule processing, as well as develop a facilitator for our multiagent applications. However, we are well on our way to providing a usable intelligent agent framework.

The next step is to sketch out our class structure and interfaces. Figure 7.1 shows all of the classes in the *ciagent* package. Before we get to the **CIAgent** abstract base class that defines the common interface used by the elements of our architecture, we introduce several utility classes.

The CIAgent Base Classes

CIAgent is the base class that defines a common programming interface and behavior for all the agents in our framework. In terms of design patterns, **CIAgent** uses a composite design. This means that we can use a single **CIAgent** or compose the agents into groups, and still treat the group as if it were a single logical **CIAgent** object. This design pattern is very powerful because it allows us to build up a hierarchy of **CIAgents**, using other specialized **CIAgent** classes in the process.

Figure 7.2 shows the relationship between the classes that make up a functional **CIAgent** instance. In the following paragraphs we describe each class in detail.

The **CIAgent** class uses several helper classes including **CIAgentState**, **CIAgentTimer**, and **CIAgentEventQueue**. **CIAgentState**, shown in Figure 7.3, contains a

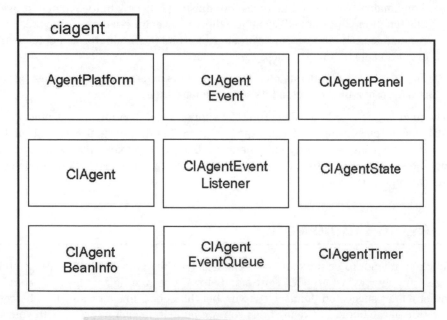

Figure 7.1 The *ciagent* package UML diagram.

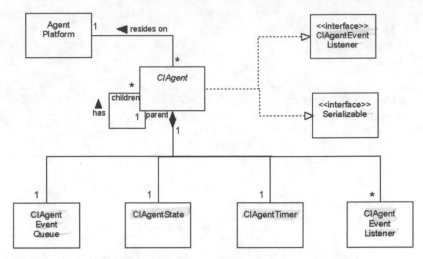

Figure 7.2 The CIAgent UML class diagram.

single data member, the **int** *state*. When a **CIAgentState** object is constructed, its *state* is set to UNINITIATED. Changes can be made using the *setState()* method.

The **CIAgentTimer** class, shown in Figure 7.4, implements the **Runnable** interface, which requires that it implement the *run()* method, which is called by the *runnit* **Thread**. This is the mechanism we use to give our agents autonomy. The **CIAgentTimer** provides two basic functions to our **CIAgents**. The first is the autonomous behavior where the agent's *processTimerPop()* method gets called every *sleepTime* milliseconds. The other is the ability to process events in an asynchronous manner by queueing them up and then processing them every *asyncTime* milliseconds. Both of these behaviors are supported by a single thread. The timer is controlled by the *startTimer()*, *stopTimer()*, and *quitTimer()* methods. The *startTimer()* method creates the thread the first time and starts it if it isn't already running. The *stopTimer()* method simply sets a *timerEnabled* **boolean** to false where the *run()* method will see it and will avoid calling the *processTimerPop()* method. The *quitTimer()* method sets the *quit* flag to true, causing the *run()* method to exit and the *runnit* thread to end. Note that the **CIAgentTimer** class is coded to have a single lifecycle.

Fig 7.7

To communicate with other **CIAgents** and other JavaBeans, we implement the **CIAgent-EventListener** interface, as shown in Figure 7.7. This interface extends the standard Java **EventListener** interface used by all *java.awt* components and JavaBeans. Although we do not extend any JavaBeans class, the **CIAgent** class is a JavaBean, by virtue of our **EventListener** interface and the public, zero-argument default *CIAgent()* constructor. A **Vector** of listeners holds all Java objects which implement the **CIAgentEventListener** interface and which have registered themselves using the *addCIAgentEventListener()* method. Any Java **Object** can be the event source for **CIAgentEvent**s, and any object that implements the **CIAgentEventListener** interface can be a registered listener for those events. The **CIAgent** class provides the *addCIAgentEventListener()* and

```java
package ciagent;

import java.io.*;

public class CIAgentState implements Serializable {
  public static final int UNINITIATED = 0;
  public static final int INITIATED = 1;
  public static final int ACTIVE = 2;
  public static final int SUSPENDED = 3;
  public static final int UNKNOWN = 4;
  private int state;

  public CIAgentState() {
    state = UNINITIATED;
  }

  public synchronized void setState(int state) {
    this.state = state;
  }

  public int getState() {
    return state;
  }

  public String toString() {
    switch(state) {
      case UNINITIATED: {
        return "Uninitiated";
      }
      case INITIATED: {
        return "Initiated";
      }
      case ACTIVE: {
        return "Active";
      }
      case SUSPENDED: {
        return "Suspended";
      }
      case UNKNOWN: {
        return "Unknown";
      }
    }
    return "Unknown";
  }
}
```

Figure 7.3 The CIAgentState class listing.

```
package ciagent;

import java.util.*;
import java.io.*;

public class CIAgentTimer implements Runnable, Serializable {
  private CIAgent agent;
  private int sleepTime = 1000;
  private boolean timerEnabled = true;
  private int asyncTime = 500;
  transient private Thread runnit = new Thread(this);
  private boolean quit = false;
  private boolean debug = false;

  public CIAgentTimer(CIAgent agent) {
    this.agent = agent;
  }

  public void setSleepTime(int sleepTime) {
    this.sleepTime = sleepTime;
  }

  public int getSleepTime() {
    return sleepTime;
  }

  public void setAsyncTime(int asyncTime) {
    this.asyncTime = asyncTime;
  }

  public int getAsyncTime() {
    return asyncTime;
  }

  public void startTimer() {
    timerEnabled = true;
    if(!runnit.isAlive()) {
      runnit.start();
    }
  }

  public void stopTimer() {
    timerEnabled = false;
  }

  public void quitTimer() {
```

(continues)

Figure 7.4 The CIAgentTimer class listing.

```
    quit = true;
}

public void run() {
  long startTime = 0;
  long curTime = 0;

  if(debug) {
    startTime = new Date().getTime();
    curTime = startTime;
  }
  if(sleepTime < asyncTime) {
    asyncTime = sleepTime;
  }
  int numEventChecks = sleepTime / asyncTime;

  if(debug) {
    System.out.println("sleepTime= " + sleepTime + " asyncTime= "
                        + asyncTime + "numEventChecks= "
                        + numEventChecks);
  }
  while(quit == false) {
    try {
      for(int i = 0; i < numEventChecks; i++) {
        Thread.sleep(asyncTime);
        if(debug) {
          curTime = new Date().getTime();
          System.out.println("async events timer at "
                              + (curTime - startTime));
        }
        if(quit) {
          break;
        }
          agent.processAsynchronousEvents();
      }
      if(timerEnabled && (quit == false)) {
        if(debug) {
          curTime = new Date().getTime();
          System.out.println("timer event at " + (curTime -
            startTime));
        }
        agent.processTimerPop();
      }
    } catch(InterruptedException e) {}
  }
}
```

Figure 7.4   The CIAgentTimer class listing (Continued).

```
   private void readObject(ObjectInputStream theObjectInputStream)
       throws ClassNotFoundException, IOException {
     runnit = new Thread(this);
     theObjectInputStream.defaultReadObject();
   }
 }
```

Figure 7.4   Continued.

removeCIAgentEventListener() methods so that other listeners can be added to the multicast event notification list. These methods fully support the JavaBeans event API, so **CIAgent**s can be wired up using any visual builder tool that supports JavaBeans.

The *notifyCIAgentEventListeners()* method is used to send events to registered listeners. Note that the *addCIAgentEventListener()*, *removeCIAgentEventListener()*, and *notifyCIAgentEventListener()* methods must be synchronized to control access to the listener's **Vector** in a multithreaded environment.

Each **CIAgent** has a **String** member or property for its *name*, and we implement the standard JavaBean methods for setting and getting the *name* through the bean's **Customizer** or property editor. We use the JavaBean **PropertyChangeSupport** class to make the *name* a bound property. When the *name* is changed, other property change listeners will be notified. **PropertyChange** events are used in JavaBeans to signal configuration or state changes, while the **CIAgentEvents** are used for agent communication while processing an application.

The other methods we define include the *initialize()* and *reset()* methods for getting the agent to a known state, the *startAgentProcessing()* and *stopAgentProcessing()* methods for starting the agent-processing thread or stopping it. The *suspendAgentProcessing()* and *resumeAgentProcessing()* methods can be used to temporarily stop the autonomous behavior and invocation of the *processTimerPop()* method.

The CIAgents provided in this book could be easily turned into **Applets**, or with subclassing of an **awt.Component**, they could be made into visible JavaBeans. As implemented here, our CIAgents are invisible JavaBeans, meaning that they can be used in the Visual Builder environment, but they do not represent graphical components in the application GUI.

We provide the *addAgent()* and *removeAgent()* methods to build composite **CIAgent**s and the *getChildren()* method to access any contained agents. The **CIAgent** class implements the **Serializable** interface so that we can save and load **CIAgent** objects to files. We have marked several data members as **transient**, meaning that they will not be saved when the object is serialized out to a file. Consequently, we must implement the *readObject()* method, which recreates the transient members when the **CIAgent** is being deserialized. Note that if we didn't do this, serialization would also serialize all objects registered as *listeners* and all events on the *eventQueue*.

```
package ciagent;

import java.util.*;
import java.awt.*;
import javax.swing.*;
import java.beans.*;
import java.io.*;

public abstract class CIAgent
    implements CIAgentEventListener, Serializable {
  public static final int DEFAULT_SLEEPTIME = 15000;
  public static final int DEFAULT_ASYNCTIME = 1000;
  protected String name;
  private CIAgentState state = new CIAgentState();
  private CIAgentTimer timer = new CIAgentTimer(this);
  transient private Vector listeners = new Vector();
  transient private CIAgentEventQueue eventQueue = new
    CIAgentEventQueue();
  transient private PropertyChangeSupport changes =
    new PropertyChangeSupport(this);
  private boolean traceOn = false;
  protected int traceLevel = 0;
  protected AgentPlatform agentPlatform = null;
  protected Vector children = new Vector();
  protected CIAgent parent = null;

  public CIAgent() {
    this("CIAgent");
  }

  public CIAgent(String name) {
    this.name = name;
    timer.setAsyncTime(DEFAULT_ASYNCTIME);
    timer.setSleepTime(DEFAULT_SLEEPTIME);
    state.setState(CIAgentState.UNINITIATED);
  }

  public void setName(String newName) {
    String oldName = name;

    name = newName;
    changes.firePropertyChange("name", oldName, name);
  }

  public String getName() {
    return name;
  }
```

Figure 7.5 The CIAgent class listing.

```
protected void setState(int newState) {
  int oldState = state.getState();

  changes.firePropertyChange("state", oldState, newState);
  this.state.setState(newState);
}

public CIAgentState getState() {
  return state;
}

public void setSleepTime(int sleepTime) {
  timer.setSleepTime(sleepTime);
}

public int getSleepTime() {
  return timer.getSleepTime();
}

public void setAsyncTime(int asyncTime) {
  timer.setAsyncTime(asyncTime);
}

public int getAsyncTime() {
  return timer.getAsyncTime();
}

public void setTraceLevel(int traceLevel) {
  this.traceLevel = traceLevel;
}

public int getTraceLevel() {
  return traceLevel;
}

public void setAgentPlatform(AgentPlatform agentPlatform) {
  this.agentPlatform = agentPlatform;
}

public AgentPlatform getAgentPlatform() {
  return agentPlatform;
}

public Vector getAgents() {
  if(agentPlatform == null) {
    return null;
```

(continues)

Figure 7.5 Continued.

```
    } else {
      return agentPlatform.getAgents();
    }
  }

  public CIAgent getAgent(String name) {
    if(agentPlatform == null) {
      return null;
    } else {
       return agentPlatform.getAgent(name);
    }
  }

  public abstract String getTaskDescription();

  public Vector getChildren() {
    return (Vector) children.clone();
  }

  public void setParent(CIAgent parent) {
    this.parent = parent;
  }

  public CIAgent getParent() {
    return parent;
  }

  public Class getCustomizerClass() {
    Class customizerClass = null;

    try {
      BeanInfo beanInfo = Introspector.getBeanInfo(this.getClass());
      BeanDescriptor beanDescriptor = beanInfo.getBeanDescriptor();

      customizerClass = beanDescriptor.getCustomizerClass();
    } catch(IntrospectionException exc) {
      System.out.println("Can't find customizer bean property " +
        exc);
    }
    return customizerClass;
  }

  public String getDisplayName() {
    String name = null;

    try {
      BeanInfo beanInfo = Introspector.getBeanInfo(this.getClass());
```

Beans

Figure 7.5 The CIAgent class listing (Continued).

```
      BeanDescriptor beanDescriptor = beanInfo.getBeanDescriptor();

    name = (String) beanDescriptor.getValue("DisplayName");
  } catch(IntrospectionException exc) {
    System.out.println("Can't find display name bean property " +
      exc);
  }
  if(name == null) {
    name = this.getClass().getName();
  }
  return name;
}

public void reset() {}

public abstract void initialize();

public synchronized void startAgentProcessing() {
  timer.startTimer();
  setState(CIAgentState.ACTIVE);
}

public synchronized void stopAgentProcessing() {
  timer.quitTimer();
  setState(CIAgentState.UNKNOWN);
}

public void suspendAgentProcessing() {
  timer.stopTimer();
  setState(CIAgentState.SUSPENDED);
}

public void resumeAgentProcessing() {
  timer.startTimer();
  setState(CIAgentState.ACTIVE);
}

public abstract void process();

public abstract void processTimerPop();

public void processAsynchronousEvents() {
  CIAgentEvent event = null;

  while((event = eventQueue.getNextEvent()) != null) {
```

(continues)

Figure 7.5 Continued.

```
      processCIAgentEvent(event);
  }
}

public void processCIAgentEvent(CIAgentEvent event) {}

public void postCIAgentEvent(CIAgentEvent event) {
  eventQueue.addEvent(event);
}

public synchronized void addCIAgentEventListener(
    CIAgentEventListener listener) {
  listeners.addElement(listener);
}

public synchronized void removeCIAgentEventListener(
    CIAgentEventListener listener) {
  listeners.removeElement(listener);
}

protected void notifyCIAgentEventListeners(CIAgentEvent e) {
  Vector l;

  synchronized(this) {
    l = (Vector) listeners.clone();
  }
  for(int i = 0; i < l.size(); i++) {
    ((CIAgentEventListener) l.elementAt(i)).processCIAgentEvent(e);
  }
}

public synchronized void addPropertyChangeListener(
    PropertyChangeListener listener) {
  changes.addPropertyChangeListener(listener);
}

public synchronized void removePropertyChangeListener(
    PropertyChangeListener listener) {
  changes.removePropertyChangeListener(listener);
}

public void trace(String msg) {
  CIAgentEvent event = new CIAgentEvent(this, "trace", msg);

  notifyCIAgentEventListeners(event);
}
```

Figure 7.5   The CIAgent class listing (Continued).

```
public void addAgent(CIAgent child) {
  children.addElement(child);
  child.setParent(this);
}

public void removeAgent(CIAgent child) {
  children.removeElement(child);
}

private void readObject(ObjectInputStream theObjectInputStream)
    throws ClassNotFoundException, IOException {
  changes = new PropertyChangeSupport(this);
  listeners = new Vector();
  eventQueue = new CIAgentEventQueue();
  theObjectInputStream.defaultReadObject();
}
}
```

Figure 7.5   Continued.

CIAgentEvent

The **CIAgentEvent** class, shown in Figure 7.6, is derived from the Java **EventObject** class, as required by the JavaBeans specification. There are three *CIAgentEvent()* constructors defined. The first takes a single parameter, the *source*, which is a reference to the object sending the event. The second constructor creates a notification event, which takes the *source* and an event argument object. The third constructor is used to create an action event and requires the *source* object, an *action* **String** that can be a method name in the target object, and an event argument object. The argument is defined as an **Object** so that subclasses of **CIAgent** can send any object as an argument in a **CIAgentEvent**. We cannot know in advance what will be needed in a subclass. In Chapter 10, "MarketPlace Application," we will use this flexibility to define a KQML-like message object. Getter methods are provided for the action and argument properties.

CIAgentEventListener

The **CIAgentEventListener** interface, in Figure 7.7, extends the **EventListener** interface and requires that two methods be implemented. These are the *postCIAgentEvent()* method which usually would place the event on an **CIAgentEventQueue** for later asynchronous processing, and the *processCIAgentEvent()* method, which usually results in immediate processing of the event on the caller's thread.

```
package ciagent;

import java.util.*;

public class CIAgentEvent extends java.util.EventObject {
  private Object argObject = null;
  private String action = null;

  public CIAgentEvent(Object source) {
    super(source);
  }

  public CIAgentEvent(Object source, Object argObject) {
    this(source);
    this.argObject = argObject;
  }

  public CIAgentEvent(Object source, String action, Object argObject)
{
    this(source);
    this.action = action;
    this.argObject = argObject;
  }

  public Object getArgObject() {
    return argObject;
  }

  public String getAction() {
    return action;
  }

  public String toString() {
    StringBuffer buf = new StringBuffer();

    buf.append("CIAgent ");
    buf.append("source: " + source);
    buf.append("action: " + action);
    buf.append("argObject: " + argObject);
    return buf.toString();
  }
}
```

Figure 7.6 The CIAgentEvent class listing.

```
package ciagent;

import java.util.*;

public interface CIAgentEventListener extends java.util.EventListener
{
    public void processCIAgentEvent(CIAgentEvent e);

    public void postCIAgentEvent(CIAgentEvent e);
}
```

Figure 7.7 CIAgentEventListener interface listing.

introduce a data structure lecture in the Java part using Vectors

CIAgentEventQueue

The **CIAgentEventQueue** class, listed in Figure 7.8, implements a queue of **CIAgentEvents**. Its only data member is the *eventQueue*, a **Vector** instance. The *addEvent()* method is used to add an event to the end of the queue, the *getNextEvent()* method is a non-blocking method that either returns null if the queue is empty, or removes the first event from the queue and then returns it. The *peekEvent()* method is used to test whether the queue is empty. It either returns null, meaning the queue is empty, or it returns the event at the front of the queue without removing it.

The methods provided by the **CIAgent** base class are intended to be used in a specific sequence so that the **CIAgentState** follows a predictable set of transitions. The lifecycle of a **CIAgent** should follow this sequence of states:

1. Construct the **CIAgent** object instance. The state is set to UNINITIATED.
2. Either programmatically or using a **Customizer**, set the JavaBean properties. ?
3. Call the *initialize()* method. The state is set to INITIATED.
4. Call the *startAgentProcessing()* method to start the *eventQueue* thread and any asynchronous event and timer processing. The state is set to ACTIVE.
5. Use the agent in an application by calling the *process()* method directly, or by sending action events to be processed asynchronously. If the *processTimerPop()* method is overridden and the timer *sleepTime* is set, the agent can also perform periodic autonomous processing.
6. Use the *suspendAgentProcessing()* and *resumeAgentProcessing()* methods to temporarily halt the autonomous behavior and the invocation of the *processTimerPop()* method. Note that this does not stop the asynchronous **CIAgentEvent** processing (if enabled). The agent state goes to SUSPENDED

```
package ciagent;

import java.util.*;
import java.io.*;

public class CIAgentEventQueue implements Serializable {
  private Vector eventQueue;

  public CIAgentEventQueue() {
    eventQueue = new Vector();
  }

  public synchronized void addEvent(CIAgentEvent event) {
    eventQueue.addElement(event);
  }

  public synchronized CIAgentEvent getNextEvent() {
    if(eventQueue.size() == 0) {
      return null;
    } else {
      CIAgentEvent event = (CIAgentEvent) eventQueue.elementAt(0);

      eventQueue.removeElementAt(0);
      return event;
    }
  }

  public synchronized CIAgentEvent peekEvent() {
    if(eventQueue.size() == 0) {
      return null;
    } else {
      return (CIAgentEvent) eventQueue.elementAt(0);
    }
  }
}
```

Figure 7.8 CIAgentEventQueue class listing.

after a *suspendAgentProcessing()* call and back to ACTIVE when *resumeAgentProcessing()* is called.

7. Call the *stopCIAgentProcessing()* method to stop the *eventTimer* thread. The state is set to UNKNOWN.

It is up to the implementers of the **CIAgent** subclass to ensure the agent *state* conforms to this expected behavior. The state transitions are illustrated in the UML diagrams in Figure 7.9 and Figure 7.10. Figure 7.9 shows the start-up sequence from creation to initialization. Figure 7.10 presents the interactions for synchronous and asynchronous event processing and autonomous agent behavior.

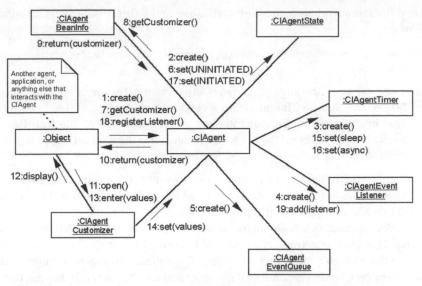

Figure 7.9 The CIAgent start-up collaboration diagram.

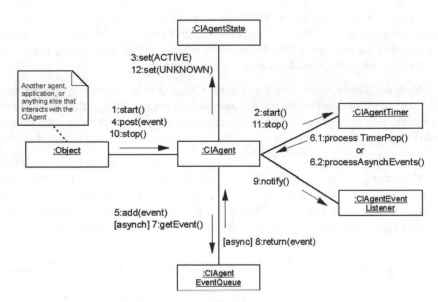

Figure 7.10 The CIAgent action collaboration diagram.

BooleanRuleBase Enhancements

In this section, we describe the enhancements to our **BooleanRuleBase** classes. We include support for sensors and effectors in rules, and for facts as part of the rule base. We define two Java interfaces, **Sensor** and **Effector**, to support this function. We also extend the **Clause** class with a **SensorClause** and **EffectorClause**. Our support is as follows:

```
if sensor(sensorName, RuleVariable) then effector(effectorName,
parameters)
```

where **sensor** is an instance of **SensorClause**, and **effector** is an instance of **EffectorClause**. The **SensorClause** makes a call to a sensor method that is defined by any class that implements the **Sensor** interface and registers it with the **RuleBase**. At runtime the **RuleBase** looks up the *sensorName* and calls the method on the registered sensor object. A similar technique is used for the effectors.

In extending the behavior of the **Rule** class to support the **SensorClause** and **EffectorClause** classes, we uncovered a case in which we broke the rule of encapsulation of knowledge about implementation. In the *Rule.display()* method, the **Clause** was formatted for display. This code included references to an *lhs*, *condition*, and *rhs* in the **Clause**. However, our **SensorClause** and **EffectorClause** do not set these data members, so the *Rule.display()* method failed. The solution to this is to define a *display()* method on the **Clause** class and its subclasses and for *Rule.display()* to use that method. This encapsulates the knowledge about the **Clause** and how it should be formatted for display.

The **Sensor** interface, shown in Figure 7.11, consists of a single method *sensor()* which takes three parameters: the object (**SensorClause**) which called the method, the name of the sensor to use, and a **RuleVariable** in which to store the results, if any. The *sensor()* method returns a **boolean** value.

The **SensorClause** class, listed in Figure 7.12, extends **Clause** by adding an object data member that implements the **Sensor** interface and a **String** that specifies the *sensorName*. A *SensorClause()* takes two parameters: the name of the sensor to test and a **RuleVariable** to hold the truth value. The *check()* method is called by a **Rule** to evaluate the truth value of the **SensorClause**.

The **Effector** interface, shown in Figure 7.13, allows any **Class** to be called as an effector by a **Rule** in a **RuleBase**. It must implement the interface by providing a single *effector()* method that takes an **Object**, an effector name (for cases where the implementing class may support multiple effectors), and a **String** argument parameter. An

```
package rule;

import java.util.*;
import java.io.*;

public abstract interface Sensor {
  public Boolean sensor(Object obj, String sName, RuleVariable lhs);
}
```

Figure 7.11 The Sensor interface listing.

```
package rule;

import java.util.*;
import java.io.*;

public class SensorClause extends Clause {
  Sensor object;
  String sensorName;

  SensorClause(String sName, RuleVariable Lhs) {
    lhs = Lhs;
    cond = new Condition("=");
    rhs = " ";
    lhs.addClauseRef(this);
    ruleRefs = new Vector();
    truth = null;
    consequent = false;
    sensorName = sName;
  }

  public String display() {
    return "sensor(" + sensorName + "," + rhs + ") ";
  }

  public Boolean check() {
    if(consequent == true) {
      return null;
    }
    if(lhs.value == null) {
      BooleanRuleBase rb = ((Rule) ruleRefs.firstElement()).rb;

      object = (Sensor) (rb.getSensorObject(sensorName));
      truth = object.sensor(this, sensorName, lhs);
    }
    return truth;
  }
}
```

Figure 7.12   The SensorClause class listing.

alternate implementation that may be useful would be to support an **Object** as the argument parameter.

The **EffectorClause** class, listed in Figure 7.14, extends **Clause** by adding members for the name of the effector to call, a data member containing a reference to the object which implements the *effector()* method, and a **String** of arguments. The *Effector-Clause()* constructor takes two parameters: the name of the effector to call and the

```
package rule;
import java.util.*;
import java.io.*;

public abstract interface Effector {
  public long effector(Object obj, String eName, String args);
}
```

Figure 7.13 The Effector interface listing.

argument **String**. The *perform()* method is provided to call the *effector()* method on the object that has registered to provide that effector function.

To support facts, we add a new class called **Fact**, shown in Figure 7.15, whose constructor takes a single clause as a parameter. A **Fact** can be an assignment of a value to

```
package rule;

import java.util.*;
import java.io.*;

public class EffectorClause extends Clause {
  Effector object;
  String effectorName;
  String arguments;

  public EffectorClause(String eName, String args) {
    ruleRefs = new Vector();
    truth = new Boolean(true);
    consequent = true;
    effectorName = eName;
    arguments = args;
  }

  public String display() {
    return "effector(" + effectorName + "," + arguments + ") ";
  }

  public Boolean perform(BooleanRuleBase rb) {
    object = (Effector) (rb.getEffectorObject(effectorName));
    object.effector(this, effectorName, arguments);
    return truth;
  }
}
```

Figure 7.14 The EffectorClause class listing.

```
package rule;

import java.util.*;
import java.io.*;
import java.awt.*;
import javax.swing.*;

public class Fact {
  BooleanRuleBase rb;
  String name;
  Clause fact;
  Boolean truth;
  boolean fired = false;

  Fact(BooleanRuleBase Rb, String Name, Clause f) {
    rb = Rb;
    name = Name;
    fact = f;
    rb.addFact(this);
    truth = null;
  }

  public void assert(BooleanRuleBase rb) {
    if(fired == true) {
      return;
    }
    rb.trace("\nAsserting fact " + name);
    truth = new Boolean(true);
    fired = true;
    if(fact.lhs == null) {
      ((EffectorClause) fact).perform(rb);
    } else {
      fact.lhs.setValue(fact.rhs);
    }
  }

  void display(JTextArea textArea) {
    textArea.append(name + ": ");
    textArea.append(fact.toString() + "\n");
  }
}
```

Figure 7.15 The Fact class listing.

a **RuleVariable**, a sensor call, or an effector call. The **Fact**s are defined as part of the **RuleBase** with the other **Rule**s. But the **Fact**s are also registered in the **RuleBase**. The *initializeFacts()* method is called to set the **Fact**s before an inferencing cycle is performed.

The main reason for adding sensors and effectors is to add procedural attachments to our rule-processing capability. Instead of being limited to the variables we have defined in the rule base, we can call outside methods to gather data using sensors, or to take actions when a rule fires using effectors. We use the effectors in the *Marketplace* application in Chapter 10, "MarketPlace Application."

Discussion

Now that we have defined the **CIAgent** framework, what can we do with it? In the next three chapters we explore this question by constructing ten different agents and using them in a variety of applications. As we go through those chapters, we make use of the flexibility in our **CIAgent** design; in some cases we tightly couple the agents to the application, while in others we create an agent platform where our agents exchange **CIAgentEvents** to communicate.

While the **CIAgent** framework is not complex, it still has the basic attributes required of agents and agent applications. Our **CIAgents** can be autonomous and they can handle asynchronous events, so they can act like daemons. This behavior is provided by our **CIAgentTimer** and **CIAgentEventQueue** classes. **CIAgents** can be composed to build a complicated hierarchy of function by virtue of our use of the *Composite* design pattern.

Our agents are JavaBeans, so they can be mixed with other non-agent Java classes and components. With the addition of **BeanInfo** and **Customizer** classes, the **CIAgents** can be used with most Visual Builder development tools. We make use of this flexibility in our first application, described in the next chapter.

Summary

In this chapter we described the **CIAgent** intelligent agent framework. The main points include the following:

- We described our requirements and high-level design goals and translated them into a set of *specifications*. These included:
    1. It must be easy to add an intelligent agent to an existing Java application.
    2. A graphical construction tool must be available to compose agents out of other Java components and other agents.
    3. The agents must support a relatively sophisticated event-processing capability.
    4. We must be able to add domain knowledge to our agent using if-then rules, and support forward and backward rule-based processing with sensors and effectors.
    5. The agents must be able to learn to do classification, clustering, and prediction using learning algorithms.

6. Multiagent applications must be supported using a KQML-like message protocol.

7. The agents must be persistent; once an agent is constructed, there must be a way to save it in a file and reload its state at a later time.

■ We described the **CIAgent** base class, the **CIAgentState**, **CIAgentTimer**, **CIAgentEventQueue**, and **CIAgentEvent** classes and the **CIAgentEventListener** interface to provide support for the intelligent agents used in the applications in the following chapters.

■ We extended our if-then rule processing function by adding the **Facts**, **SensorClause**, and **EffectorClause** classes, and the **Effectors** and **Sensors** interfaces. This allows our rules to call functions to test conditions and perform actions.

Exercises

1. What are some of the design decisions that limit the usefulness or applicability of the **CIAgent** architecture?

2. How could you extend the **CIAgent** architecture to implement an information filtering agent? A personal assistant agent?

3. In the **CIAgent** architecture, we chose to use the JavaBeans delegation event model. How could you provides equivalent function using the Java **Observer/Observable** framework? What are the advantages and disadvantages of this approach compared to using JavaBeans event notification?

4. Compare your design from Exercise 4.3 for adding sensors and effectors to the implementation provided in this chapter. Did you use any Java interfaces in your solution?

5. We chose to use a single thread to implement both asynchronous events and timer processing in a **CIAgent**. What are the advantages and disadvantages of this design? What are the synchronization issues involved?

6. The JavaBean model assumes that methods can be called in any order. However, we define strict ordering in the **CIAgent** start-up sequence. Does this invalidate our use of JavaBeans for agents?

7. The **CIAgentEventListener** interface defines two methods for event processing, *postCIAgentEvent()* for asynchronous messages, and *processCIAgentEvent()* for synchronous messages. What design alternatives are there for implementing this capability?

Personal Agent Manager Application

I n this chapter, we illustrate how we can use the **CIAgent** architecture to construct a personal assistant application that uses several intelligent agents to assist a user with tasks. The application provides an agent platform that serves as the environment in which the agents live and work with one another. One of the agents developed in this chapter watches a file on the local system and alerts the user, executes a command, or signals another agent when a trigger condition is met. This agent is then decomposed into smaller helper agents that handle the simple tasks of scheduling events and notifying the user when events occur. The final agent is another task-based agent that checks airline flights and fares on a Web site and notifies the user about flights matching the user's criteria.

Introduction

The first intelligent agent application we develop is a basic agent platform that allows us to create, configure, and control a set of personal assistant agents that will do tasks on our behalf. Our goal is to provide a flexible base that illustrates the general concepts of a multiagent platform and that can be easily extended by plugging in additional agents. The *PAManager* application provides the graphical user interface for managing the agents and makes use of the agent customizer dialogs to allow interaction with the other **CIAgents** running on the platform. The user can start, suspend, or resume agent execution from within the *PAManager* application or can stop and remove an agent from the platform.

The *PAManager* application classes are **PAManagerApp**, which contains the *main()*, and **PAManagerFrame**, which implements our main window. They were constructed using the Borland/Inprise JBuilder 3.0 Java interactive development environment. The Visual Builder allows us to create the complete GUI using Java Swing components in a drag-and-drop style. JBuilder automatically generates the Java code for creating the GUI controls and action event handlers in the **PAManagerFrame** class. The **PAManagerApp** code that invokes the **PAManagerFrame** is not presented here. It simply instantiates the **PAManagerFrame** class and displays it. Likewise, a substantial amount of the code in the **PAManagerFrame** class deals with GUI control logic, and we will not present that material here. All of the classes discussed in this chapter are in the *pamanager* package, shown in Figure 8.1.

The FileAgent

The first agent we will create to run on the *PAManager* platform is the **FileAgent**, listed in Figure 8.2. A **FileAgent** monitors a file or directory on the current system. When the **FileAgent** detects that a specific file has been changed or deleted, or has grown to a size larger than a given threshold, the **FileAgent** will take some action. The user can specify that the **FileAgent** displays an alert message, executes a command, or sends an event to another agent.

The three conditions that can be checked by the **FileAgent** are: whether the file has been MODIFIED, whether the file has been DELETED (it does not exist in the file system), or whether the file exceeds a THRESHOLD size. The *action* taken by the **FileAgent** when the *condition* occurs can be: ALERT, if the user is to be notified; EXECUTE, if a command should be executed; or EVENT, if a **CIAgentEvent** should be sent to another agent. The name of the file or directory is stored in the *fileName* **String** member, and information about when it was changed is stored in *lastChanged*. The *threshold* contains the size, in bytes, that is being compared against the actual file size.

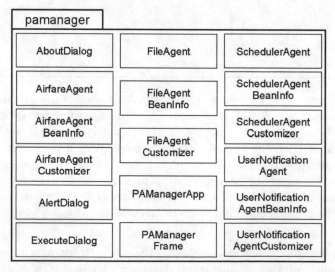

Figure 8.1 The *pamanager* package UML diagram.

```
package pamanager;

import java.io.*;
import java.awt.*;
import javax.swing.*;
import java.util.*;
import ciagent.*;

public class FileAgent extends CIAgent {
  public static final int MODIFIED = 0;
  public static final int DELETED = 1;
  public static final int THRESHOLD = 2;
  public static final int ALERT = 0;
  public static final int EXECUTE = 1;
  public static final int EVENT = 2;
  protected int condition;
  protected int action = EVENT;
  protected String fileName;
  protected File file;
  protected long lastChanged;
  protected int threshold;
  protected JDialog actionDialog;
  protected String actionString;
  protected String parms;

  public FileAgent() {
    name = "Watch";
  }

  public FileAgent(String name) {
    super(name);
  }

  public String getTaskDescription() {
    return "Watching filename=" + fileName + "condition=" + condition;
  }

  public void setFileName(String fileName) {
    this.fileName = fileName;
    file = new File(fileName);
    lastChanged = file.lastModified();
  }

  public String getFileName() {
    return fileName;
  }
```

(continues)

Figure 8.2   The FileAgent class listing.

```
public void setCondition(int cond) {
  condition = cond;
}

public int getCondition() {
  return condition;
}

public void setThreshold(int thresh) {
  threshold = thresh;
}

public int getThreshold() {
  return threshold;
}

public void setAction(int action) {
  this.action = action;
}

public int getAction() {
  return action;
}

public void setActionString(String actionString) {
  this.actionString = actionString;
}

public String getActionString() {
  return actionString;
}

public void setParms(String params) {
  parms = params;
}

public String getParms() {
  return parms;
}

public void setDialog(JDialog dlg) {
  actionDialog = dlg;
}

public void initialize() {
  if(actionDialog != null) {
    actionDialog.dispose();
```

Figure 8.2   The FileAgent class listing (Continued).

```
  }
  JFrame frame = new JFrame();

  if(action == ALERT) {
    actionDialog = new AlertDialog(frame, name + ": Alert", false);
  }
  if(action == EXECUTE) {
    actionDialog = new ExecuteDialog(frame, name + ": Execute",
      false);
  }
  setSleepTime(15 * 1000);
  setState(CIAgentState.INITIATED);
}

public void process() {
  if(checkCondition()) {
    performAction();
  }
}

public void processCIAgentEvent(CIAgentEvent e) {}

public void processTimerPop() {
  process();
}

private boolean checkCondition() {
  boolean truth = false;

  switch(condition) {
    case MODIFIED:
      truth = changed();
      break;
    case DELETED:
      truth = !exists();
      break;
    case THRESHOLD:
      truth = threshold > length();
      break;
  }
  return truth;
}

void performAction() {
  Date time = Calendar.getInstance().getTime();
  String timeStamp = time.toString();
```

(continues)

Figure 8.2 Continued.

```
      switch(action) {
        case ALERT:
          trace(timeStamp + " " + name + ": Alert fired \n");
          ((AlertDialog) actionDialog).appendMsgText(timeStamp + " - "
              + parms);
          actionDialog.show();
          break;
        case EXECUTE:
          trace(name + ": Executing command \n");
          executeCmd(parms);
          break;
        case EVENT:
          notifyCIAgentEventListeners(new CIAgentEvent(this,
            actionString, "Watch condition on " + fileName + " was
            triggered!"));
          break;
      }
    }

    public int executeCmd(String cmd) {
      Process process = null;
      String line;
      String osType = (System.getProperty("os.name")).toUpperCase();

      trace(cmd);
      actionDialog.show();
      try {
        if(osType.equals("WINDOWS 95")) {
          process = Runtime.getRuntime().exec("command.com /c " + cmd
              + "\n");
          BufferedReader data = new BufferedReader(
            new InputStreamReader(process.getInputStream()));

          while((line = data.readLine()) != null) {
            trace(line);
          }
          data.close();
        } else if(osType.equals("AIX") || osType.equals("UNIX")) {
          process = Runtime.getRuntime().exec(cmd + "\n");
          BufferedReader data = new BufferedReader(
            new InputStreamReader(process.getInputStream()));

          while((line = data.readLine()) != null) {
            trace(line);
          }
          data.close();
        } else if(osType.equals("WINDOWS NT")) {
```

Figure 8.2 The FileAgent class listing (Continued).

```
      process = Runtime.getRuntime().exec("cmd /C " + cmd + "\n");
      BufferedReader data = new BufferedReader(
        new InputStreamReader(process.getInputStream()));

      while((line = data.readLine()) != null) {
        trace(line);
      }
      data.close();
    } else if(osType.equals("OS/2")) {
      process = Runtime.getRuntime().exec("cmd.exe /c " + cmd +
        "\n");
      BufferedReader data = new BufferedReader(
        new InputStreamReader(process.getInputStream()));

      while((line = data.readLine()) != null) {
        trace(line);
      }
      data.close();
    } else {
      trace("FileAgent Error -- unsupported OS or run-time
        environment");
    }
  } catch(IOException err) {
    trace("Error: EXEC failed, " + err.toString());
    err.printStackTrace();
    return -1;
  }
  if(((ExecuteDialog) actionDialog).getCancel() == true) {
    stopAgentProcessing();
  }
  if(process != null) {
    return process.exitValue();
  } else {
    return -1;
  }
}

protected boolean exists() {
  return file.exists();
}

protected boolean changed() {
  long changeTime = lastChanged;

  lastChanged = file.lastModified();
  return !(lastChanged == changeTime);
```

(continues)

Figure 8.2 Continued.

```
  }

  protected long length() {
    return file.length();
  }

  protected long lastModified() {
    return file.lastModified();
  }
}
```

Figure 8.2   The FileAgent class listing (Continued).

The *actionDialog* is used to display information for the user when the ALERT or EXE-CUTE action has been chosen. The *parms* member is also used when executing a command. The *actionString* is used as the action parameter on the **CIAgentEvent** created if the EVENT action was chosen.

The *initialize()* method sets up the dialogs for the ALERT or EXECUTE actions. It also sets the sleep timer for the agent to 15 seconds and sets the agent's state to INITIATED. Whenever the sleep timer pops or the agent is called synchronously, the *process()* method gets called and the file *condition* is tested. If the condition is met, then the specified *action* is performed.

In addition to the **FileAgent** class, **FileAgentCustomizer** and **FileAgentBeanInfo** classes are provided for the **FileAgent**. The **FileAgentCustomizer** is shown in Figure 8.3. These classes will be used by the **PAManagerFrame** when instantiating a **File-Agent** bean. Before running the **FileAgent**, let's take a closer look at the *PAManager* platform, where the **FileAgent** will run.

The PAManagerFrame

The **PAManagerApp** instantiates a **PAManagerFrame** object that does the majority of the work in the application. When the **PAManagerFrame** is instantiated, the constructor initializes the GUI controls and then calls the *readPropertiesFile()* method to get the class names of all the **CIAgent**s that can run on the PAManager platform. The properties file is called *pamanager.properties* and must be located in the directory from which the **pamanager.PAManagerApp** is run.

```
private void readPropertiesFile() {
  Properties properties = new Properties();

  try {
    FileInputStream in = new FileInputStream("pamanager.properties");
```

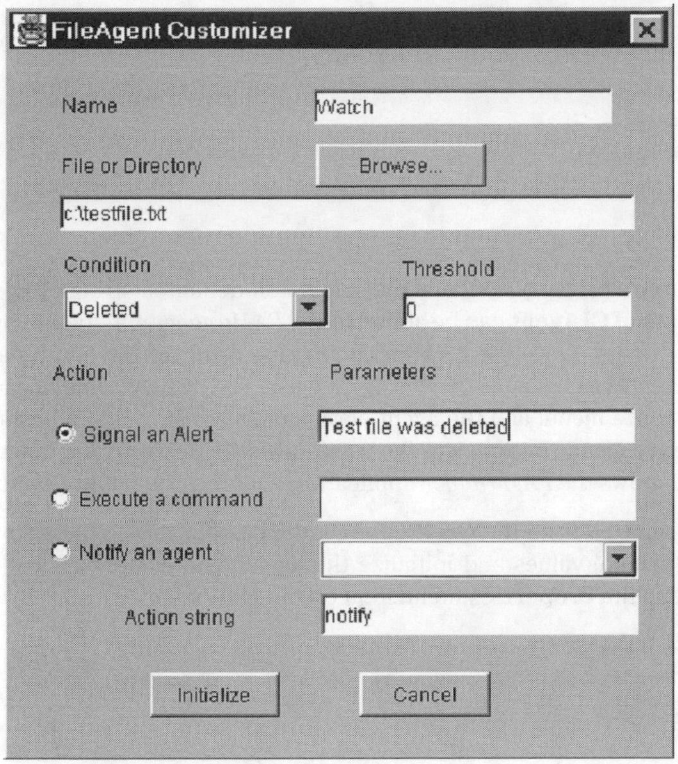

Figure 8.3 The FileAgentCustomizer window.

```
properties.load(new BufferedInputStream(in));
String property;

property = properties.getProperty("AgentClassNames");
StringTokenizer tok = new StringTokenizer(property, ";");
String displayName;

while(tok.hasMoreTokens()) {
  String agentClassName = tok.nextToken();
  CIAgent agent = null;

  try {
    Class klas = Class.forName(agentClassName);

    agent = (CIAgent) klas.newInstance();
    displayName = agent.getDisplayName();
    System.out.println("Adding agent class ... " + displayName);
    addAgentMenuItem(displayName);
    agentClasses.put(displayName, agentClassName);
  } catch(Exception exc) {
```

```
            System.out.println("Error can't instantiate agent: "
                            + agentClassName + " " + exc.toString());
        }
    }
  } catch(Exception e) {
    System.out.println(
      "Error: cannot find or load PAManager properties file");
  }
}
```

The *AgentClassNames* property contains the semicolon-delimited string of agent class names. Any subclass of **CIAgent** can be added to the *PAManager* application by adding the class name to the list. Once the **PAManagerFrame** retrieves the list, it parses the class names and creates an instance of each agent class. The display name of each agent is added to the **Create** menu, and the agent class names are stored in a hashtable for later use. The **Create** menu control gives the user the ability to create and initialize new agents. Figure 8.4 shows the *PAManager* application with the populated **Create** menu.

Once an agent is selected from the **Create** menu, the customizer for the agent is then used to set the attribute values and initialize the agent. The customizer can also be invoked by selecting the **Properties** menu item on the **Edit** menu.

```
void CreateMenuItem_actionPerformed(ActionEvent theEvent) {
  setCursor(Cursor.getPredefinedCursor(Cursor.WAIT_CURSOR));
  CIAgent agentBean = null;
```

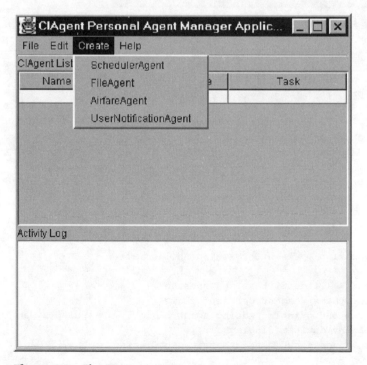

Figure 8.4 The PAManager Create menu.

```
        Object bean = null;
        String beanName = theEvent.getActionCommand();
        String className = (String) agentClasses.get(beanName);

        try {
          Class klas = Class.forName(className);

          bean = klas.newInstance();
          agentBean = (CIAgent) bean;
          agentBean.setAgentPlatform(this);
          agentBean.addCIAgentEventListener(this);
          agentBean.addPropertyChangeListener(this);
          openCustomizer(agentBean, true);
          addAgent(agentBean);
        } catch(Exception e) {
          JOptionPane.showMessageDialog(this, e.toString(),
              "Error: Can't create agent " + beanName,
              JOptionPane.ERROR_MESSAGE);
        }
        setCursor(Cursor.getPredefinedCursor(Cursor.DEFAULT_CURSOR));
        refreshTable();
        this.invalidate();
        this.repaint();
    }

    void propertiesMenuItem_actionPerformed(ActionEvent e) {
        int selectedRow = agentTable.getSelectedRow();

        if((selectedRow < 0) || (selectedRow >= agents.size())) {
          return;
        }
        CIAgent agent = (CIAgent) agents.elementAt(selectedRow);

        openCustomizer(agent, false);
    }
```

Once an agent has been created, it shows up in the **CIAgent** list in the *PAManager* application window. For each agent, the name, type of agent, state, and task are listed. You can select an agent by clicking on the row that contains the information for the agent. Once an agent is selected, the **Edit** menu can be used to change the state of the agent. Figure 8.5 shows the *PAManager* application populated with agents in various states.

When an agent has been initialized, its state changes to INITIATED, and the **Start processing** selection is available on the **Edit** menu. The **Start processing** menu item is used to activate an agent by calling the *startAgentProcessing()* method on the selected **CIAgent**. The agent's state is now ACTIVE, and that is reflected in the *PAManager* window. Once an agent is active, its timer is running and it is processing timer pops and events.

```
    void startProcessingMenuItem_actionPerformed(ActionEvent e) {
        int selectedRow = agentTable.getSelectedRow();
```

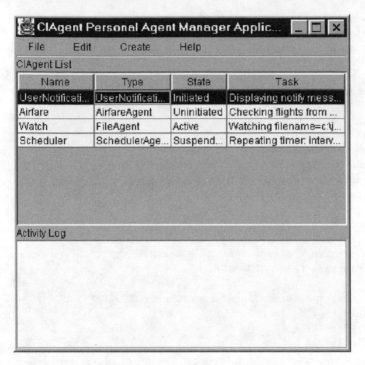

Figure 8.5 The *PAManager* application window.

```
if((selectedRow < 0) || (selectedRow >= agents.size())) {
  return;
}
CIAgent agent = (CIAgent) agents.elementAt(selectedRow);

if(agent.getState().getState() == CIAgentState.INITIATED) {
  agent.startAgentProcessing();
  setEditMenuItemStates();
  updateTable();
}
}
```

An agent's processing can be suspended using the **Suspend processing** menu selection and resumed using the **Resume processing** menu selection. These actions call the corresponding *suspendAgentProcessing()* and *resumeAgentProcessing()* **CIAgent** methods.

```
void suspendProcessingMenuItem_actionPerformed(ActionEvent e) {
  int selectedRow = agentTable.getSelectedRow();

  if((selectedRow < 0) || (selectedRow >= agents.size())) {
    return;
  }
```

```
      CIAgent agent = (CIAgent) agents.elementAt(selectedRow);

    agent.suspendAgentProcessing();
    setEditMenuItemStates();
    updateTable();
  }

  void resumeProcessingMenuItem_actionPerformed(ActionEvent e) {
    int selectedRow = agentTable.getSelectedRow();

    if((selectedRow < 0) || (selectedRow >= agents.size())) {
      return;
    }
    CIAgent agent = (CIAgent) agents.elementAt(selectedRow);

    agent.resumeAgentProcessing();
    setEditMenuItemStates();
    updateTable();
  }
```

The **Cut** menu selection is used to stop an agent by calling the *stopAgentProcessing()* method on the selected agent. It also removes the agent from the platform. The **Clear** menu item in the **File** menu can be used to stop all agents and remove them from the platform.

```
  void Cut_actionPerformed(ActionEvent e) {
    int selectedRow = agentTable.getSelectedRow();

    if((selectedRow < 0) || (selectedRow >= agents.size())) {
      return;
    }
    CIAgent agent = (CIAgent) agents.elementAt(selectedRow);

    agent.stopAgentProcessing();
    agents.removeElementAt(selectedRow);
    refreshTable();
    setEditMenuItemStates();
  }

  void clearMenuItem_actionPerformed(ActionEvent e) {
    int size - agents.size();

    for(int i = 0; i < size; i++) {
      CIAgent agent = (CIAgent) agents.elementAt(0);

      agent.stopAgentProcessing();
      agents.removeElementAt(0);
    }
    refreshTable();
    traceTextArea.setText("");
  }
```

In addition to managing the user interface and the agent lifecycles, the **PAManager-Frame** implements the **CIAgentEventListener** interface and adds itself as a listener to every agent it creates. This enables the **PAManagerFrame** to receive **CIAgentEvents** which are processed by its *processCIAgentEvent()* method. All **CIAgentEvents** are processed by displaying the event information in the text area within the frame.

```java
public void processCIAgentEvent(CIAgentEvent event) {
  Object source = event.getSource();
  String agentName = "";

  if(source instanceof CIAgent) {
    agentName = ((CIAgent) source).getName();
  }
  Object arg = event.getArgObject();
  Object action = event.getAction();

  if(action != null) {
    if(action.equals("trace")) {
      if(((arg != null) && (arg instanceof String))) {
        trace("\n" + (String) arg);
      }
    } else {
      trace("\nPAManager received action event: " + action
            + " from agent " + agentName);
    }
  }
}
```

FileAgent Example

The basic functions provided by the **FileAgent** and the *PAManager* application can be illustrated using a simple example. We will use the **FileAgent** to monitor a file called *testfile.txt* and send an alert message when the file is deleted. The scenario is as follows:

1. Create a file called *testfile.txt* on the local file system.

2. Run the *PAManager* application: *java pamanager.PAManager.*

3. Select **FileAgent** from the **Create** menu. Fill in the customizer as shown in Figure 8.2. Be sure to specify the correct path and filename, depending on the operating system on which you are running this application. Click on the **Initialize** button.

4. Select *Watch* **FileAgent** from the **CIAgent** list in the *PAManager* application window. Select the **Start processing** option in the **Edit** menu.

5. Outside of the *PAManager* application, delete the *testfile.txt* that you created in Step 1.

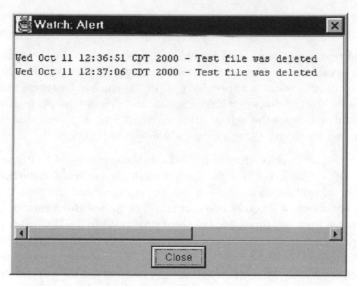

Figure 8.6 The AlertDialog window.

6. Once the **FileAgent**'s timer pops, an **AlertDialog** window will appear and display the message that the file was deleted. The window will look similar to what is shown in Figure 8.6. Note that the agent will send an alert message every 15 seconds, once the file is deleted. Note, too, that trace messages are appearing in the text area at the bottom of the Personal Agent Manager Application window.

7. Use the **Cut** selection on the **Edit** menu to stop the *Watch* **FileAgent** and remove it from the application.

8. At this point you can either leave the *PAManager* running to use later in this chapter, or exit the *PAManager* application by choosing the **Exit** option from the **File** menu.

Now that you've seen the **FileAgent** and the *PAManager* application in action, let's take a look at a few other agents you can run on this platform.

The SchedulerAgent

Our next agent, the **SchedulerAgent**, is not very intelligent but is certainly autonomous and provides an extremely useful function. A **SchedulerAgent** can be used to set one-shot alarms that go off at a specified time, or it can be used for recurrent alarms at specified intervals. When an alarm condition occurs, the **SchedulerAgent** sends a **CIAgentEvent** to all of its registered listeners. In effect, the **SchedulerAgent** can be used to schedule the tasks of other agents by sending events to the agents at a specified time or after a specified interval of time has passed.

The **SchedulerAgent** has several data members. The *interval* holds a value, in milliseconds, for interval alarms. The *oneShot* boolean flag indicates whether this agent will send a single one-shot event at a specified time or if it will send an event every time the *interval* expires. The *time* member holds the date and time for one-shot alarms. The *actionString* member defines the action string for the **CIAgentEvent** that is generated. The customizer for setting these attributes is shown in Figure 8.7.

The *initialize()* method checks whether the **SchedulerAgent** is set to trigger a one-shot alarm or will go off periodically. If the agent is a one-shot scheduler, the *interval* is set to the number of milliseconds between the current time and the time the alarm should go off. Regardless of whether this is a one-shot **SchedulerAgent** or not, the interval is used to set the sleep timer, and the agent state is set to INITIATED. Whenever the sleep timer pops, the *processTimerPop()* method calls the *notifyCIAgentEventListeners()* to send an event to all the registered listeners. If the agent is a one-shot scheduler, its work is done, and the *stopAgentProcessing()* method is called to end the agent. Note that the *process()* and *processCIAgentEvents()* methods are not used in this agent. A listing of the **SchedulerAgent** class is shown in Figure 8.8.

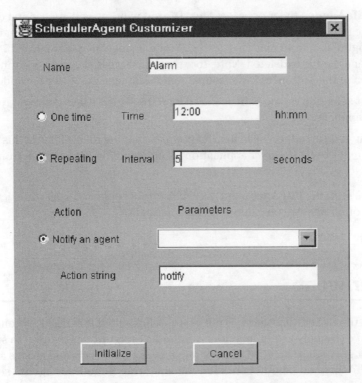

Figure 8.7 The SchedulerAgentCustomizer window.

```
package pamanager;

import java.awt.*;
import javax.swing.*;
import java.io.*;
import java.util.*;
import ciagent.*;

public class SchedulerAgent extends CIAgent implements Serializable {
  protected int interval = 60000;
  protected boolean oneShot = false;
  protected Date time = null;
  protected String actionString = "notify";

  public SchedulerAgent() {
    this("Scheduler");
  }

  public SchedulerAgent(String name) {
    super(name);
  }

  public String getTaskDescription() {
    if(oneShot) {
      return "One-shot timer: time = " + time.toString();
    } else {
      return "Repeating timer: interval = " + (interval / 1000);
    }
  }

  public void setInterval(int secs) {
    interval = secs * 1000;
  }

  public int getInterval() {
    return interval / 1000;
  }

  public void setOneShot(boolean flag) {
    oneShot = flag;
  }

  public boolean getOneShot() {
    return oneShot;
  }
```

(continues)

Figure 8.8   The SchedulerAgent class listing.

```
public void setTime(Date date) {
  time = date;
}

public Date getTime() {
  return time;
}

public void setActionString(String actionString) {
  this.actionString = actionString;
}

public String getActionString() {
  return actionString;
}

public void initialize() {
  if(oneShot) {
    long currentTime = Calendar.getInstance().getTime().getTime();

    interval = (int) (time.getTime() - currentTime);
  }
  setSleepTime(interval);
  setAsyncTime(interval);
  setState(CIAgentState.INITIATED);
}

public void process() {}

public void processTimerPop() {
  String timeStamp = Calendar.getInstance().getTime().toString();

  notifyCIAgentEventListeners(new CIAgentEvent(this, actionString,
      timeStamp));
  if(oneShot) {
    stopAgentProcessing();
  }
}

public void processCIAgentEvent(CIAgentEvent e) {}
}
```

Figure 8.8 The SchedulerAgent class listing (Continued).

The **SchedulerAgent**, while performing a useful task, needs to cooperate with other agents since sending an event serves no useful purpose unless another object is waiting to catch and process the event. Fortunately, the *PAManager* platform listens for events from any agent on the platform. We can use this to illustrate the function of the **Sched-ulerAgent**. The scenario is as follows:

1. Run the**PAManagerApp**, if it is not already running.

2. Select **SchedulerAgent** from the **Create** menu. Fill in the customizer as shown in Figure 8.7. Click on the **Initialize** button.

3. Select the *Alarm* **SchedulerAgent** from the **CIAgent** list in the *PAManager* application window. Select the **Start processing** option in the **Edit** menu.

4. Every 5 seconds, when the **SchedulerAgent**'s timer pops, an event will be displayed in the text area at the bottom of the Personal Agent Manager Application window.

5. Use the **Cut** selection on the **Edit** menu to stop the *Alarm* **SchedulerAgent** and remove it from the application.

6. At this point you can either leave the *PAManager* running to use later in this chapter, or exit the *PAManager* application by choosing the **Exit** option from the **File** menu.

The **PAManagerApp**, as shown in Figure 8.9, is useful for testing the **SchedulerAgent**, but a more realistic scenario would be for the **SchedulerAgent** to notify another agent when its timer pops. Earlier we looked at the **FileAgent** which had the ability to alert the user by displaying a message when a certain file condition occurred. It would be nice if the **SchedulerAgent** had this same capability. In fact, many agents that we develop may need the ability to notify the user. Rather than duplicate this function in all of our

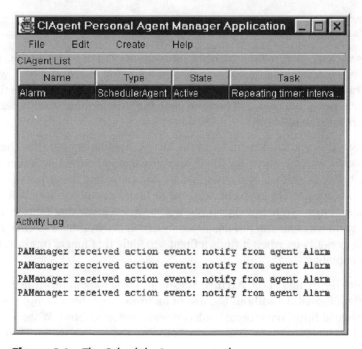

Figure 8.9 The SchedulerAgent example.

agents, we develop one agent, the **UserNotificationAgent**, whose primary function is to notify the user when it receives an event.

The UserNotificationAgent

The **UserNotificationAgent** is a very simple agent, as shown in Figure 8.10. It contains only one unique member, the dialog in which the notification messages are displayed. Its *initialize()* method creates this dialog, using the same **AlertDialog** class we used in the **FileAgent**. The sleep timer is set to five seconds, and the state is set to INITIATED. Once the **UserNotificationAgent** is started, its *processCIAgentEvent()* method is called to process any events it receives. Note that it does not process timer pops or do any synchronous processing. When an event is received, the event action is checked to see if it is a "notify" event. If it is, the message text is retrieved from the event and displayed.

Even though the **UserNotificationAgent** is a very simple agent, it is quite useful. It provides a centralized user interface for the display of notification messages and can be used by multiple agents in a system. This prevents the duplication of function and code as well as provides a nicer user interface, because all messages are displayed in a single window for the user. We are not going to show an example of the **UserNotification-Agent** in action until we demonstrate the final **CIAgent** in this chapter, the **Airfare-Agent**.

The AirfareAgent

All of the agents we have seen so far have been autonomous, but not very intelligent. The **FileAgent** has a few hard-coded conditions that were being checked, but it was not using any rules or inferencing. The final agent we will examine in this chapter is the **AirfareAgent**, which uses a rule base and forward chaining to determine when a published airfare is of interest to the user.

When scheduling a trip, you'll often find that the airfare fluctuates over time, based on the number of seats available, how far in advance the trip is booked, whether a "fare war" is going on between airlines, and other factors known only to the airline. To get the best fares available, you need to keep checking the airline or travel services Web site for flight schedules that meet your travel criteria, waiting for a price that is in your price range. In this section we create an intelligent agent that is programmed to check a Web site for us and only notify us when it finds a flight schedule that meets our criteria at a price we find acceptable.

Before we get into the details of the **AirfareAgent**, let's first look at how one would go about getting the information without the use of an agent. For this example, we have created a Web page at http://www.bigusbooks.com/airfareQuery.html. When you bring this page up in a Web browser, you see a form similar to the one shown in Figure 8.11.

In our example, we want to fly from Rochester, MN to Orlando, FL on July 1st and return on July 8th. After entering the travel dates and the originating and destination cities in

```
package pamanager;

import java.io.*;
import java.awt.*;
import javax.swing.*;
import java.util.*;
import ciagent.*;

public class UserNotificationAgent extends CIAgent
    implements Serializable {
  protected AlertDialog notificationDialog;

  public UserNotificationAgent() {
    name = "UserNotification";
  }

  public UserNotificationAgent(String name) {
    super(name);
  }

  public String getTaskDescription() {
    return "Displaying notify messages";
  }

  public String getMsgText() {
    return notificationDialog.getMsgText();
  }

  public void setMsgText(String text) {
    notificationDialog.setMsgText(text);
  }

  public void appendMsgText(String text) {
    notificationDialog.appendMsgText(text);
  }

  public void setDialog(JDialog dlg) {
    notificationDialog = (AlertDialog) dlg;
  }

  public void initialize() {
    if(notificationDialog != null) {
      notificationDialog.dispose();
    }
    JFrame frame = new JFrame();
```

(continues)

Figure 8.10   The UserNotificationAgent class listing.

```
      notificationDialog = new AlertDialog(frame,
          "CIAgent User Notification Agent: " + name, false);
      setSleepTime(5 * 1000);
      setState(CIAgentState.INITIATED);
    }

    public void process() {}

    public void processCIAgentEvent(CIAgentEvent e) {
      if(e.getAction().equalsIgnoreCase("notify")) {
        Date time = Calendar.getInstance().getTime();
        String timeStamp = time.toString();
        String text = (String) e.getArgObject();
        String source = e.getSource().getClass().toString();

        if(e.getSource() instanceof CIAgent) {
          source = ((CIAgent) e.getSource()).getName();
        }
        notificationDialog.appendMsgText("Event received on " +
          timeStamp
            + " from " + source + ":\n" + text);
        if(!notificationDialog.isVisible()) {
          notificationDialog.show();
        }
      }
    }

    public void processTimerPop() {}
}
```

Figure 8.10 The UserNotificationAgent class listing (Continued).

the form, pressing the **Get Airfare** button would send the entries to the Web server for processing. In this case, the data is sent to a CGI-bin program that processes the request and returns the results. An example results page is shown in Figure 8.12.

Note that the URL displayed by the Web browser contains the name of the CGI-bin program we are invoking and the parameters with the travel information we entered. In our example, the full URL string is http://www.bigusbooks.com/cgi-local/airfare.pl?&dmon=JUL&dday=1&orig=RST&dest=MCO&rmon=JUL&rday=8. In order to minimize network traffic, the HTML code shortens the months to three character abbreviations (JUL for July) and the cities to three character airport codes (MCO for Orlando).

Let's further suppose that it is our desire to fly from Rochester in the evening and catch our return flight either in the morning or the afternoon. We are willing to pay up to $1000.00 for our ideal flight times.

But often, when scheduling a trip, we're willing to settle for less than ideal if the price is right. We may take a flight that departs in the morning and returns in the afternoon, if

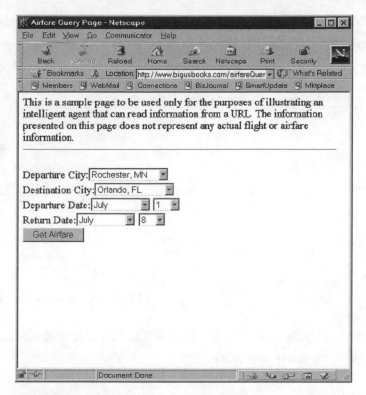

Figure 8.11 The Airfare query html page.

the price is less than $800.00. Or we may be willing to leave in the morning and return in the evening if the price is less than $600.00. Without using an agent, we would periodically go out to the Web site, enter in our dates and cities, and check the flights that were returned to see if any match our flight schedule and pricing criteria. At a time when prices are changing rapidly, as is often the case when a fare war is being waged, we may need to repeat this process quite often in order to get the right flights at the right price. Wouldn't it be nice to have an agent that could check the flights for us and only notify us when it finds something in our price range? The **AirfareAgent** does just that.

The **AirfareAgent** has a number of data members that are used to hold the query parameters sent to the Web page. They are the *departMonth*, *departDay*, *origCity*, *destCity*, *returnMonth*, and *returnDay*. A **String** data member, *actionString,* contains the action for the **CIAgentEvent** sent when a desirable travel itinerary is found. The customizer for setting these attributes is shown in Figure 8.13.

In addition to the attributes set in the customizer, the **AirfareAgent** contains a **BooleanRuleBase**, *rb* , with rules that specify the desired flight times and prices. A few **RuleVariables** (*departs*, *returns*, and *price*) are used to hold time and price information during inferencing.

As shown in the listing in Figure 8.14, the *initialize()* method in the **AirfareAgent** sets up the flight rule base by calling the *initFlightRuleBase()* method. The sleep timer is

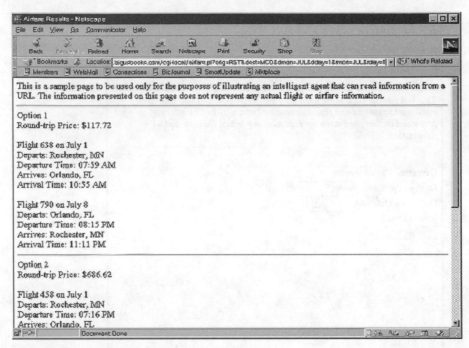

Figure 8.12 The Airfare results html page.

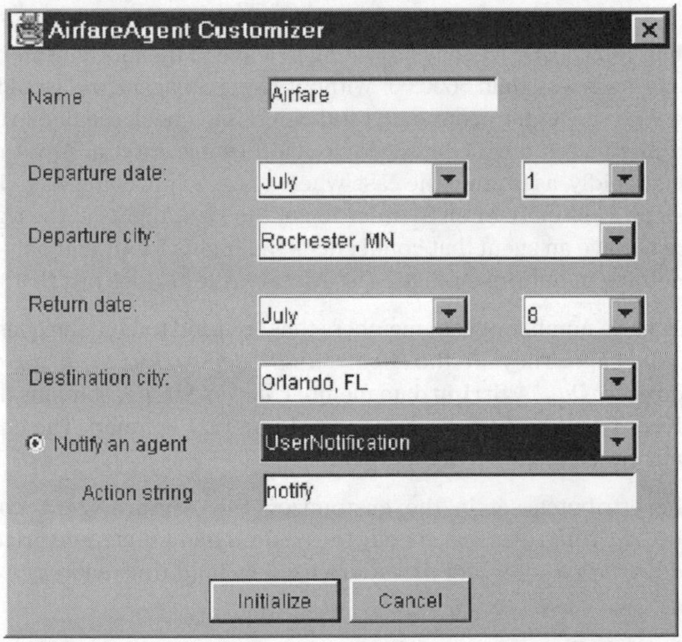

Figure 8.13 The AirfareAgentCustomizer window.

```
package pamanager;

import java.awt.*;
import javax.swing.*;
import java.io.*;
import java.util.*;
import java.text.*;
import java.net.*;
import ciagent.*;
import rule.*;

public class AirfareAgent extends CIAgent implements Serializable {
  protected String departMonth = "JAN";
  protected String departDay = "1";
  protected String origCity = "RST";
  protected String destCity = "MCO";
  protected String returnMonth = "FEB";
  protected String returnDay = "2";
  protected BooleanRuleBase rb = new BooleanRuleBase("Flight");
  protected RuleVariable departs = new RuleVariable(rb, "departs");
  protected RuleVariable returns = new RuleVariable(rb, "returns");
  protected RuleVariable price = new RuleVariable(rb, "price");
  protected String actionString = "notify";

  public AirfareAgent() {
    name = "Airfare";
  }

  public AirfareAgent(String name) {
    super(name);
  }

  public void setDepartMonth(String departMonth) {
    this.departMonth = departMonth;
  }

  public String getDepartMonth() {
    return departMonth;
  }

  public void setDepartDay(String departDay) {
    this.departDay = departDay;
  }

  public String getDepartDay() {
    return departDay;
```

(continues)

Figure 8.14   The AirfareAgent class listing.

```java
}

public void setReturnMonth(String returnMonth) {
  this.returnMonth = returnMonth;
}

public String getReturnMonth() {
  return returnMonth;
}

public void setReturnDay(String returnDay) {
  this.returnDay = returnDay;
}

public String getReturnDay() {
  return returnDay;
}

public void setOrigCity(String origCity) {
  this.origCity = origCity;
}

public String getOrigCity() {
  return origCity;
}

public void setDestCity(String destCity) {
  this.destCity = destCity;
}

public String getDestCity() {
  return destCity;
}

public void setActionString(String actionString) {
  this.actionString = actionString;
}

public String getActionString() {
  return actionString;
}

public String getTaskDescription() {
  return "Checking flights from " + origCity + " to " + destCity;
}

public void initialize() {
```

Figure 8.14 The AirfareAgent class listing (Continued).

```
      initFlightRuleBase();
      setSleepTime(30000);
      setState(CIAgentState.INITIATED);
}

public void process() {
   URL url;
   String parms = "?" + "&dmon=" + departMonth
                      + "&dday=" + departDay
                      + "&orig=" + origCity
                      + "&dest=" + destCity
                      + "&rmon=" + returnMonth
                      + "&rday=" + returnDay;
   HttpURLConnection connection;
   String rank = null;

   try {
      url =
        new URL("http://www.bigusbooks.com/cgi-local/airfare.pl");
      connection = (HttpURLConnection) url.openConnection();
      connection.setDoOutput(true);
      PrintWriter out =
        new PrintWriter(connection.getOutputStream());

      out.println(parms);
      out.close();
      BufferedReader in = new BufferedReader(
        new InputStreamReader(connection.getInputStream()));
      String inputLine;
      int i, j = 0, k = 0;
      int x, y;

      i = 0;
      String prices[] = new String[3];
      String flight[][] = new String[3][2];
      String times[][] = new String[3][2];

      while((inputLine = in.readLine()) != null) {
        x = inputLine.indexOf("Price:");
        if(x != -1) {
          y = inputLine.indexOf('.', x);
          prices[i] = inputLine.substring(x + 8, y + 3);
          i++;
          j = k = 0;
        }
        x = inputLine.indexOf("Flight");
```

(continues)

Figure 8.14 Continued.

```
      if(x != -1) {
        flight[i - 1][j] = inputLine.substring(x);
        j++;
      }
      x = inputLine.indexOf("Departure Time:");
      if(x != -1) {
        y = inputLine.lastIndexOf(':');
        String hours = inputLine.substring(x + 16, y);

        if(inputLine.indexOf("PM") != -1) {
          int hrs = Integer.parseInt(hours) % 12 + 12;

          hours = Integer.toString(hrs);
        }
        times[i - 1][k] = hours + inputLine.substring(y + 1, y + 3);
        k++;
      }
    }
    in.close();
    for(i = 0; i < 3; ++i) {
      rb.reset();
      trace("Checking departure at " + times[i][0] + " return at "
            + times[i][1] + " for a price of " + prices[i]);
      departs.setValue(times[i][0]);
      returns.setValue(times[i][1]);
      price.setValue(prices[i]);
      rb.forwardChain();
      rank = rb.getVariable("flightRank").getValue();
      if(rank != null) {
        String msg = "An iterary was found that meets your \""
                      + rank
                      + "\" flight criteria.\nDeparture from "
                      + origCity
                      + ": " + flight[i][0] + " departs at "
                      + times[i][0].substring(0, 2) + ":"
                      + times[i][0].substring(2)
                      + "\nReturn from "
                      + destCity + ": " + flight[i][1]
                      + " departs at "
                      + times[i][1].substring(0, 2) + ":"
                      + times[i][1].substring(2) + "\nPrice: $"
                      + prices[i];

        notifyCIAgentEventListeners(
          new CIAgentEvent(this, actionString, msg));
      }
    }
```

Figure 8.14 The AirfareAgent class listing (Continued).

```
    } catch(Exception e) {
      String msg =
        "Problems retrieving information from the web site.\n"
        + "Please make sure that you are connected to the Internet\n"
        + "and that the web site is up. To do this, use your
          browser \n"
        + "to go to www.bigusbooks.com/aifareQuery.html and enter
          the\n"
        + "same dates and cities. If it doesn't work, the server \n"
        + "must be having problems and you can try again later.";

      notifyCIAgentEventListeners(new CIAgentEvent(this, actionString,
        msg));
      e.printStackTrace();
    }
  }

  public void processCIAgentEvent(CIAgentEvent e) {
    if(e.getAction().equalsIgnoreCase("process")) {
      process();
    }
  }

  public void processTimerPop() {}

  public void initFlightRuleBase() {
    RuleVariable departureTime =
      new RuleVariable(rb, "departureTime");

    departureTime.setLabels("morning afternoon evening");
    RuleVariable desiredDeparture =
      new RuleVariable(rb, "desiredDeparture");

    desiredDeparture.setLabels("yes no");
    RuleVariable returnTime = new RuleVariable(rb, "returnTime");

    returnTime.setLabels("morning afternoon evening");
    RuleVariable desiredReturn =
      new RuleVariable(rb, "desiredReturn");

    desiredReturn.setLabels("yes no");
    RuleVariable flightRank = new RuleVariable(rb, "flightRank");

    flightRank.setLabels("good better best");
    Condition cEquals = new Condition("=");
```

(continues)

Figure 8.14 Continued.

```
Condition cNotEquals = new Condition("!=");
Condition cGreaterThan = new Condition(">");
Condition cLessThan = new Condition("<");
Rule morningDeparture =
  new Rule(rb, "morningDeparture",
    new Clause(departs, cLessThan, "1200"),
    new Clause(departureTime, cEquals, "morning"));
Rule afternoonDeparture =
  new Rule(rb, "afternoonDeparture",
    new Clause[]{
      new Clause(departs, cGreaterThan, "1159"),
      new Clause(departs, cLessThan, "1700") },
    new Clause(departureTime, cEquals, "afternoon"));
Rule eveningDeparture =
  new Rule(rb, "eveningDeparture",
    new Clause(departs, cGreaterThan, "1659"),
    new Clause(departureTime, cEquals, "evening"));
Rule morningReturn =
  new Rule(rb, "morningReturn",
    new Clause(returns, cLessThan, "1200"),
    new Clause(returnTime, cEquals, "morning"));
Rule afternoonReturn =
  new Rule(rb, "afternoonReturn",
    new Clause[]{
      new Clause(returns, cGreaterThan, "1159"),
      new Clause(returns, cLessThan, "1700") },
    new Clause(returnTime, cEquals, "afternoon"));
Rule eveningReturn =
  new Rule(rb, "eveningReturn",
    new Clause(returns, cGreaterThan, "1659"),
    new Clause(returnTime, cEquals, "evening"));
Rule desireableDeparture =
  new Rule(rb, "desirableDeparture",
    new Clause(departureTime, cEquals, "evening"),
    new Clause(desiredDeparture, cEquals, "yes"));
Rule undesirableDeparture1 =
  new Rule(rb, "undesirableDeparture1",
    new Clause(departureTime, cEquals, "morning"),
    new Clause(desiredDeparture, cEquals, "no"));
Rule undesirableDeparture2 =
  new Rule(rb, "undesirableDeparture2",
    new Clause(departureTime, cEquals, "afternoon"),
    new Clause(desiredDeparture, cEquals, "no"));
Rule undesirableReturn =
  new Rule(rb, "undesirableReturn",
    new Clause(returnTime, cEquals, "evening"),
    new Clause(desiredReturn, cEquals, "no"));
```

Figure 8.14   The AirfareAgent class listing (Continued).

```
Rule desirableReturn1 =
  new Rule(rb, "desirableReturn1",
    new Clause(returnTime, cEquals, "morning"),
    new Clause(desiredReturn, cEquals, "yes"));
Rule desirableReturn2 =
  new Rule(rb, "desirableReturn2",
    new Clause(returnTime, cEquals, "afternoon"),
    new Clause(desiredReturn, cEquals, "yes"));
Rule bestFlight =
  new Rule(rb, "bestFlight",
    new Clause[]{
      new Clause(desiredDeparture, cEquals, "yes"),
      new Clause(desiredReturn, cEquals, "yes"),
      new Clause(price, cLessThan, "1000.00") },
    new Clause(flightRank, cEquals, "best"));
Rule betterFlight1 =
  new Rule(rb, "betterFlight1",
    new Clause[]{
      new Clause(desiredDeparture, cEquals, "yes"),
      new Clause(desiredReturn, cEquals, "no"),
      new Clause(price, cLessThan, "800.00") },
    new Clause(flightRank, cEquals, "better"));
Rule betterFlight2 =
  new Rule(rb, "betterFlight2",
    new Clause[]{
      new Clause(desiredDeparture, cEquals, "no"),
      new Clause(desiredReturn, cEquals, "yes"),
      new Clause(price, cLessThan, "800.00") },
    new Clause(flightRank, cEquals, "better"));
Rule goodFlight =
  new Rule(rb, "goodFlight",
    new Clause[]{
      new Clause(desiredDeparture, cEquals, "no"),
      new Clause(desiredReturn, cEquals, "no"),
      new Clause(price, cLessThan, "600.00") },
    new Clause(flightRank, cEquals, "good"));
  }
}
```

Figure 8.14 Continued.

set to thirty seconds, and the state is set to INITIATED. After the **AirfareAgent** is initialized, the *processCIAgentEvent()* method is called to process any events it receives. The **AirfareAgent** only processes events with the *process* action. All other events are ignored. If a *process* event is received or if the agent is called synchronously, the *process()* method sends the airfare request to the Web page and checks the results to see if the returned flights are of interest to the user.

Let's examine the *initFlightRuleBase()* method in more detail. First, a **RuleVariable** called *departureTime* is defined that can take the value *morning, afternoon,* or *evening.* Another **RuleVariable**, *desiredDeparture*, can take the value *yes* or *no* to indicate whether the departure time falls within the user's preferences. Similar **RuleVariables** are defined for the return time as well. A **RuleVariable** called *rank* is used to rate each set of flight options and can take on the value of *good, better,* or *best.* In addition, **Condition** objects are defined for "=", "!=", ">", and "<".

The first **Rule**, *morningDeparture*, has an antecedent **Clause** defined as the *departs* **RuleVariable** being less than 1200 (noon). The consequent **Clause** of this **Rule** assigns *morning* to the *departureTime.* Rules for *afternoonDeparture, eveningDeparture, morningReturn, afternoonReturn,* and *eveningReturn* are defined in the same way, using the appropriate times and conditions in the antecedent **Clauses**.

The next set of **Rules** defines whether the departure and return times are in the desired range. The *desiredDeparture* is set to *yes* when the *departureTime* is *evening.* The *desiredReturn* is set to *yes* when the *returnTime* is *morning* or *afternoon.*

The last set of **Rules** ranks the flights. If the flight has a desired departure time, a desired return time, and costs less the $1000.00, its flight *rank* is set to *best.* If either the departure time or the return time is undesirable, but the cost is less than $800.00, the flight *rank* is set to *better.* If neither the departure time nor the return time are in the desired time periods, but the cost is less than $600.00, the flight *rank* is set to *good.* Note that if the flight falls outside of these times and prices, the flight *rank* is *null.*

The rule base is actually a little more complex than it needs to be, but it was created that way in order to illustrate rules with antecedent clauses that are dependent on the consequent clauses in other rules. This provides a slightly more interesting forward-chaining scenario because some rules cause new rules to be added to the conflict set as the processing progresses.

The *process()* method provides the bulk of the work done by the **AirfareAgent**. The first thing the *process()* method does is connect to the Web page and CGI-bin program that generates the flight information. The **java.net.URL** class and associated **java. net.HttpURLConnection** are part of the standard Java environment that enables our agent to easily send and retrieve information from the Web. Once the connection is open, a **PrintWriter** is used to send the parameters for the query to the CGI-bin program. After the parameters are sent, the output stream is closed and the input stream is read. A *while()* loop is used to read the HTML that is returned as a result of the airfare request. Each *inputLine* is parsed, and the times and prices for all the flights are stored in their respective arrays. The flight numbers are also stored in an array.

Once the input stream is closed, the flight times and prices are used to set the *departs, returns,* and *price* **RuleVariable**s. The *forwardChain()* method is then called on the *rb* **BooleanRuleBase**. After the inferencing is complete, the *rank* **RuleVariable** is retrieved and if it is set to *good, better,* or *best,* a **CIAgentEvent** is created using the *actionString* and an appropriate message. Finally, the *notifyCIAgentEventListeners()* method is called to send the event to any interested agents.

The HTML Parsing Problem

When we developed the **AirfareAgent**, the original intent was that it would go out to a commercial Web site like *Travelocity*, or one of the airline sites, for its flight and airfare information. We actually implemented the agent and everything worked well until the format of the Web site changed. The problem we encountered was that we needed to retrieve certain content from the Web site, and the only way we could do that was to parse the HTML, looking for certain strings like "Price" or "Flight" to help us determine where the price or flight information was on the page. Unfortunately, with this approach, you are at the mercy of the Web page implementer. When the Web page changes, your parsing no longer works.

This is a big drawback that impedes the development of general-purpose agents that surf the Web, looking for and acting on specific information found in a Web page. It can only use textual cues to help parse the information on the page, and the results of this parsing may not yield the proper results. This is because HTML describes only how the content should be presented. What is needed is a way to describe the meaning or semantics of the page content. This is one of the reasons the eXtensible Markup Language (XML) was developed.

XML is the next generation of Web content markup languages. It is extensible in that it allows you to make up your own XML tags. To insure portability, it also provides a way to communicate what the tags mean so that others can read and process your XML documents. Using Document Type Definitions (DTDs), you can specify the new elements you have introduced, what the elements' attributes are, what values the elements can take, and relationships between elements. The rules specified in the DTD enable others to parse the XML document in an intelligent manner, and writing an XML parser is a fairly simple endeavor.

Unfortunately, XML is still in its fairly early stages of adoption in the industry. Most Web content is specified using only HTML, although a few XML editors and browsers are available. Once XML becomes more prevalent in the industry, writing intelligent agents that can do useful work out on the Web will become a much easier task.

The **AirfareAgent** can be used along with the **SchedulerAgent** and the **UserNotificationAgent** to check airfares periodically and notify the user whenever a flight is found that might be of interest to the user. The major interactions among the agents are illustrated in Figure 8.15.

The agents can be created and started using the *PAManager* application. It is important to create the agents in the correct order so that the event listener agent is created before the agent that generates the event. The scenario is shown on the following page.

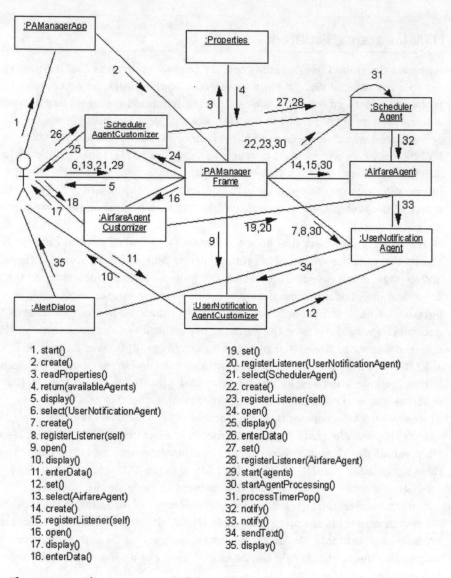

1. start()
2. create()
3. readProperties()
4. return(availableAgents)
5. display()
6. select(UserNotificationAgent)
7. create()
8. registerListener(self)
9. open()
10. display()
11. enterData()
12. set()
13. select(AirfareAgent)
14. create()
15. registerListener(self)
16. open()
17. display()
18. enterData()

19. set()
20. registerListener(UserNotificationAgent)
21. select(SchedulerAgent)
22. create()
23. registerListener(self)
24. open()
25. display()
26. enterData()
27. set()
28. registerListener(AirfareAgent)
29. start(agents)
30. startAgentProcessing()
31. processTimerPop()
32. notify()
33. notify()
34. sendText()
35. display()

Figure 8.15 The PAManager collaboration UML diagram.

1. Run the **PAManagerApp**, if it is not already running.

2. Select **UserNotificationAgent** from the **Create** menu. Set the name and click on the **Initialize** button.

3. Select **AirfareAgent** from the **Create** menu. Fill in the customizer as shown in Figure 8.12. Use the drop-down list to select the **UserNotificationAgent** created in Step 2 as the agent to send an event to when a flight is found that meets the user's criteria. Click on the **Initialize** button.

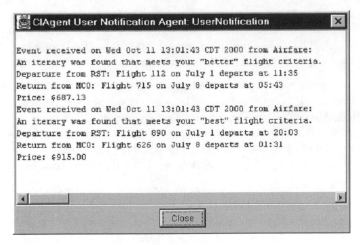

Figure 8.16 The UserNotification Alert dialog.

4. Select **SchedulerAgent** from the **Create** menu. Set the interval to 15 seconds. Use the drop-down list to select the **AirfareAgent** created in Step 3 as the agent to send an event to when its timer pops. Set the **Action string** to *process*. Click on the **Initialize** button.

5. Select each agent in the **CIAgent** list in the *PAManager* application window and use the **Start processing** option in the **Edit** menu to start each agent.

6. Every 15 seconds, when the **SchedulerAgent**'s timer pops, an event will be sent to the **AirfareAgent**. When a flight is found that matches the *good, better,* or *best* criteria, an event will be sent to the **UserNotificationAgent**. Figure 8.16 shows an example of the information displayed by the **UserNotificationAgent**. The text area at the bottom of the Personal Agent Manager Application window can be used to monitor activity as it occurs.

7. Use the **Exit** selection on the **File** menu to stop all the agents and end the application.

Discussion

In this chapter, we have sketched out quite a bit of function. The base *PAManager* application is quite flexible and can be used as a testbed for multiagent experiments. The agents we provided run the gamut from the monolithic and not-very-intelligent **FileAgent** to the more specialized **AirfareAgent**. We introduced the idea of having agents play roles with the **SchedulerAgent** and the **UserNotificationAgent**.

The agent services provided by *PAManager* are basic life-cycle services (create, start, suspend, resume, and stop). A more general implementation would provide a mechanism for agents to register their capabilities and possibly their interests. This function is called directory services. The agent communication facilities are limited to passing **CIAgentEvent**s with action strings and simple arguments. A more general implementation would provide KQML or some other agent communication language. Both of these capabilities are explored in the following two chapters.

However, the use of the agent's JavaBean features added quite a bit to the application. Because we read the list of agent class names from a text properties file, we can easily extend the platform. Also, by relying on the agent's own customizer dialogs, we have no hard dependencies in the **PAManagerFrame** GUI on the individual agents. As long as the agent customizer can talk to the underlying agent, there is no problem. The *PAManager* application makes use of the behaviors defined in the **CIAgent** base class.

An alternate method for creating the **FileAgent** would be to use if-then rules as the engine. From this perspective, the **SchedulerAgent** would be used as the event-generating agent, and the **FileAgent** would be used as a sensor in the antecedent of a rule. Whenever the **SchedulerAgent** sent a **CIAgentEvent** to the **FileAgent**, it would invoke a forward-chaining inference cycle, with rules specifying the various file watch conditions. The three actions currently defined in the **FileAgent** would instead be defined as effector methods in the **BooleanRuleBase**. When a rule fires, the effector method would be called, and the correct action would be taken.

We also could have moved additional function, like the command execution function, out of the **FileAgent** and into a separate agent, much like we did with the alert capabilities in the **UserNotificationAgent**. When designing intelligent agent applications, or object-oriented applications in general, it is not always clear-cut how the function should be partitioned. In many cases, it comes down to a judgment call based on how often the particular function will be reused by other classes. If it has wide applicability, then separating it out is probably the thing to do. The **UserNotificationAgent** can serve as the unifying interface between many agents running on the *PAManager* platform and a user, so it seemed like an obvious choice to break out into a separate agent.

Summary

In this chapter we developed a *Personal Agent Manager* application and four **CIAgents** that run on the *PAManager* platform. The main points include the following:

- The *PAManager* application allows a user to create **CIAgents** that communicate and cooperate with one another to perform useful tasks for the user. Any agent that extends the **CIAgent** class can be run on the *PAManager* platform.

- The **FileAgent** sleeps for 15-second intervals, and when it wakes up, it checks the state of the target file or directory. If a certain file condition is found, it can alert the user, execute a command, or send a **CIAgentEvent** to another agent.

- The **SchedulerAgent** can be used as a one-shot alarm or a repeated, interval alarm. When its timer goes off, it sends a **CIAgentEvent** to its registered listeners.

- The **UserNotificationAgent** receives **CIAgentEvents** and displays the event messages in a dialog for the user.

■ The **AirfareAgent** processes **CIAgentEvent**s by checking flight and airfare information on a Web site, and sends a **CIAgentEvent** if its rule-based inferencing determines that the flight meets a certain set of criteria. The **AirfareAgent** can cooperate with the **SchedulerAgent** and **UserNotificationAgent** to check the Web site periodically and notify the user when flights of interest are available.

Exercises

1. What other functions could the **SchedulerAgent** perform for an application? Implement one.

2. How would you extend the **FileAgent** to handle more complex conditions or watches on multiple files?

3. Sketch out a design for the **FileAgent** using the **BooleanRuleBase** approach described in the Discussion section. Would the agent be bigger or smaller?

4. The *PAManager* agents and their connections go away when the application ends. How could you make the agents in this chapter persistent across invocations of the application? Does the **CIAgent** framework support this function? Do the agents developed in this chapter support this function?

5. The *PAManager* application serves as a simple agent platform. Develop an agent that extends **CIAgent** and add it to the platform through the *pamanager.properties* file. You must include **BeanInfo** and **Customizer** classes with your agent. Design the new agent so that it communicates with one of the existing *PAManager* agents using **CIAgentEvents**.

6. There is no central directory service provided in the *PAManager* application. It would be nice to allow agents to register their capabilities and requirements in this directory service so they can find other agents running on the platform. Would you add this function directly to the agent platform or implement it as an agent? Why?

7. In the **AirfareAgent** we use forward-chaining inferencing. How would you use backward chaining in an agent and still maintain its autonomous behavior? For example, you wouldn't want it prompting the user for values.

8. Modify the **AirfareAgent** to query a commercial travel Web site and parse the results for input to the rule base. Also, allow the user to specify parameters for the *good*, *better*, and *best* criteria used in the rule base.

CHAPTER 9

InfoFilter Application

The Internet is the focus of the intelligent agent application in this chapter. Several agents are designed and implemented, including an Internet news reader agent, a Web page reader agent, and an intelligent agent that assists a user by filtering information. The user can specify a profile of keywords and provide explicit ratings for each article. Three alternate methods are provided for filtering the articles, including keyword match, clustering, and predictive modeling based on the user ratings.

Introduction

The **CIAgent** *InfoFilter* application developed in this chapter provides the basic functionality of a general-purpose information filter. Agents are provided to gather source information from Internet newsgroups and from Internet Web pages. The **NewsReaderAgent** can connect to a specified news server, request the articles from a specific newsgroup (such as *comp.lang.java.api*), and download all or a limited number of articles to a personal computer (PC). The **URLReaderAgent** reads the data from a single specified Web page *Uniform Resource Locator* (URL) and downloads it to the PC. After it is downloaded, each article or Web page is scored against a keyword list and optionally can be scored by using two neural networks. The user can rate each piece of information by using a five-level scale. The subject line from each news article (or URL) is displayed in a table control. The user can browse individual articles or Web page sources by selecting them from the table.

One goal of this application is to help the user deal with all of the electronic noise that is generated in newsgroups. Wouldn't it be great if, when you downloaded a news group, all you saw were the articles that genuinely interested you ? All of the posts from that jerk on the West Coast would disappear. All of the spam postings that offer great

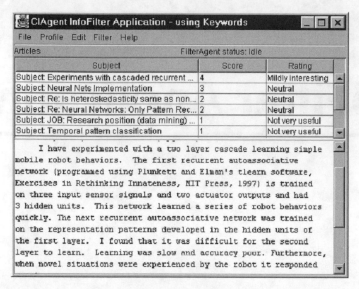

Figure 9.1 CIAgent *InfoFilter* application.

cellular phone service or the greatest software since sliced bread would never waste your time again. On the other hand, you would never miss a news article or post that discusses the topics that interest you. That is the motivation behind the **CIAgent** *InfoFilter* (see Figure 9.1). In the remainder of this chapter, we will show you how to apply intelligent agents to score and filter the unwanted news articles. We will also explore the basic mechanisms for reading Internet newsgroups by using the *Network News Transport Protocol* (NNTP).

Another goal is to show how an agent-based application can be used to intelligently rank Web pages based on their content. While we do not explore this topic in great detail, we provide the basic capability with pointers to how it can be easily enhanced to provide more function.

The main panel of the *InfoFilter* application (shown in Figure 9.1) is implemented by the **InfoFilterFrame** class and consists of two main GUI controls. The top of the frame contains a table control with a list of article subject lines (or the URL of a Web page), their filtering score, and an associated user rating. The bottom text area displays the selected news article and trace information as the articles are scored and the various types of filters are created. A read-only text label in the upper right displays the status of the **FilterAgent** that is used to score the articles.

Under the **File** pull-down menu, the user can download a newsgroup or URL by selecting the menu item. When either action is selected, a corresponding agent (**NewsReaderAgent** or **URLReaderAgent**) is instantiated and its customizer dialog is displayed. The **NewsReaderAgentCustomizer**, shown in Figure 9.2, enables the user to select or specify a News Host (a server that is running NNTP server software) and the name of a newsgroup to download. The user can choose to have every article on the server downloaded or can limit the download to a specified number of articles (the default is to limit

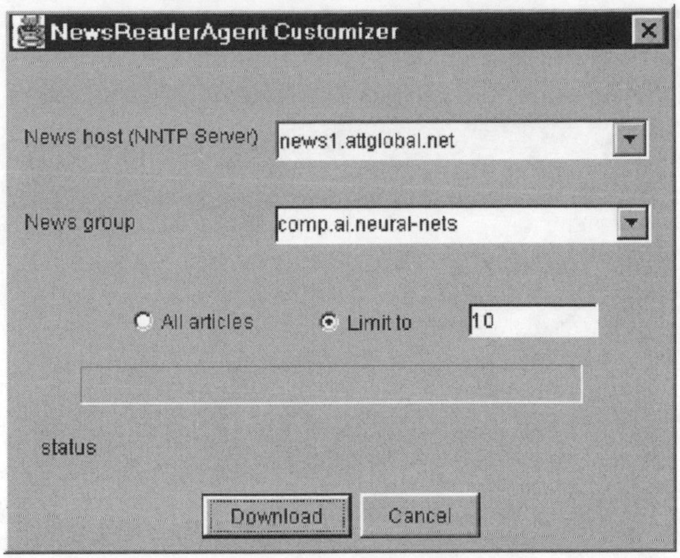

Figure 9.2 The NewsReaderAgent Customizer dialog.

the number of articles to 10). To actually load the newsgroup, the user must press the **Download** button. This action starts the **NewsReaderAgent** running on its own thread to download the articles. As each article is read, the agent sends a **NewsArticle** object as an argument in an *addArticle* **CIAgent** action event to the **InfoFilterFrame** (and to **NewsReaderAgentCustomizer**). The customizer's progress indicator is updated, and the article is added to the **InfoFilterFrame** table of articles.

A similar but simpler sequence occurs when the user selects to download a Web page. The **URLReaderAgent** is instantiated, and its customizer dialog is displayed (shown in Figure 9.3). The user must select or specify a valid *Hypertext Transport Protocol* (HTTP) URL. The agent also optionally supports a parameter to be passed to a CGI-BIN program if one is running at that URL. The data is downloaded and a **NewsArticle** object is sent to the **InfoFilterFrame** in a **CIAgent** *addArticle* action event. The *Info-Filter* application treats information from newsgroups and Web pages identically. The only difference is the subject line.

Individual articles can be **save**d and **load**ed from the *InfoFilter* application. This function is provided primarily as a debugging aid so that selected articles can be scored and added to the user profile data file. Both **Save Article** and **Load Article** options bring up a **FileDialog** so that the user can specify the directory path and file to write or read.

The **Profile** menu contains a list of actions that are related to the maintenance of the user's *InfoFilter* profile. The **Customize ...** option displays the **FilterAgentCustomizer** dialog shown in Figure 9.4. That dialog enables the user to enter a list of words or terms that are of interest to him or her. The dialog enables the user to add or remove keywords from the list. Specifying the keywords is the first thing that a user should do when starting to build a customized user profile. A default set of terms is provided in the **InfoFilter** application. The 10 default keywords are *java, agents, fuzzy, intelligent, neural,*

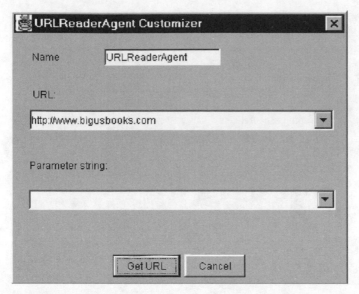

Figure 9.3   The URLReaderAgent Customizer dialog.

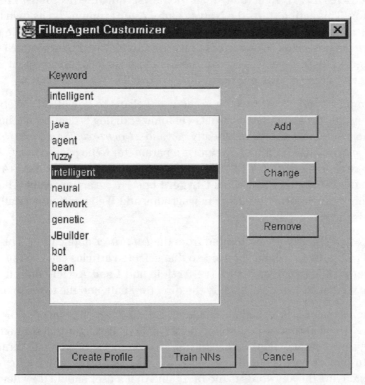

Figure 9.4   The FilterAgent Customizer dialog.

network, *genetic*, *rule*, *learning*, and *inferencing*. Each article or Web page that is loaded into the *InfoFilter* is searched, and the number of times each keyword appears is counted and summed. This total number of keyword hits is used as the raw match score for keyword filtering.

Whenever the keyword list is modified, a new profile must be created. Pressing the **Create Profile** button on the **FilterAgentCustomizer** dialog will destroy the current profile and create a new one by using the keywords that are listed in the dialog. The InfoFilter profile consists of two text files. The first, *infofilter.prf*, contains the **DataSet** definition (as described in Chapter 5, "Learning Systems"), which is a list of data types (in this case, all of them are continuous) and the corresponding field names. This file describes the layout of the data in the *infofilter.dat* file. The user can add records to the *infofilter.dat* file by selecting the **Add article** or **Add all articles** menu item. **Add article** will append a single record containing the match counts and the current rating to *infofilter.dat*. **Add all articles** will append the profile records for all of the articles that are currently loaded in the *InfoFilter* application to the *infofilter.dat* file. The *infofilter.dat* file is used as the input data set for building the neural cluster filter and the neural prediction rating filter.

Selecting the **Train NN Models** menu item from the **Profile** pull-down menu will cause the **FilterAgent** to train the cluster neural network and the prediction ratings neural network on its own thread. You must have added data to the profile in order for the neural networks to train correctly. As training progresses, status messages are displayed in the upper-right text label. The **Keyword filter** simply forces a count of all of the keyword matches in the loaded articles. The **Cluster filter** instantiates a Kohonen map neural network and reads the data in the *infofilter.dat* file to train the network. The neural prediction rating or **Feedback filter** creates and trains a back propagation neural network that uses the user rating data in the *infofilter.dat* file as the target of a prediction model.

The **Filter** menu contains the options for which type of filter is used. Selecting a menu item forces the selected technique to be applied and the articles to be sorted. The default is **using Keywords**, but if the neural networks models have been trained, the user can select **using Clusters** or **using Feedback** as the filter method to be applied.

When the user selects a **Filter** (either **Keyword**, **Cluster**, or **Feedback**), the currently loaded articles are sorted based on their score. For the **Keyword** filter, the score is simply the sum of all keyword matches (as described previously). For the **Cluster** filter, this score is the average of the keyword scores for all articles that fall into that cluster (see Chapter 5, "Learning Systems," for a complete discussion of neural clustering). The score for the **Feedback** filter is the back propagation neural network output unit activation—a value ranging from 0.0 to 1.0. We will discuss this topic in more detail in the next section.

The Ratings column in the **InfoFilterFrame** table shown in Figure 9.5 implements a combo box editor that enables the user to assign a value that corresponds to the usefulness of the article. Each article has a user rating value that is automatically set when the newsgroup is read. This numeric value ranges from 0.0 for articles where there are no matches to 1.0 for articles that have more than five matches. This automatic assignment is provided as a convenience to the user so that a value does not have to be set for each article. The user is allowed to override the automatic value through a ComboBox.

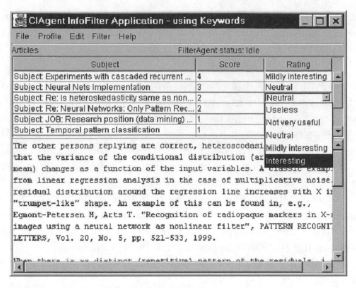

Figure 9.5 InfoFilter user rating editor.

The user rating value is used as the target value when training the back propagation model in the Feedback filter. The label **Useless** maps to a feedback value of 0, **Not very useful** to 0.25, **Neutral** to 0.5, **Mildly Interesting** to 0.75, and **Interesting** to 1.0.

An Example

In this section, we describe the process that is used to create and use the three filters provided by the *InfoFilter* application. To start the application, run the following command:

```
>java infofilter.InfoFilterApp
```

When the *InfoFilter* main panel appears, go to **File** and select the **Download News Group . . .** menu item. The **NewsReaderAgentCustomizer** dialog is displayed showing two combo boxes: one with a default news server and another with a default newsgroup name. You must have an active Internet connection for the following step to succeed. Users should enter the name of their own *Internet Service Provider* (ISP) news server here. When **Download** is clicked, the **NewsReaderAgent** will begin downloading the articles on its own thread and pass them to the customizer dialog and the **InfoFilterFrame** one at a time. When the specified number of articles is downloaded, press **Cancel** to close the dialog. The articles will be listed in the table control in the **InfoFilterFrame** window.

Next, go to the **Profile** menu and select **Customize . . . .** A list of the 10 default keywords that are hard-coded into the **FilterAgent** is displayed. Users can select any keyword they wish (single words only and no phrases). Next, select the **Create Profile** button on the dialog. This action initializes the two profile files, *infofilter.dat* and *infofilter.dfn*. You are now ready to start building your personal filter profile. You cannot train the neural network filters until you add articles to the profile.

The **Newsgroup** list on the **NewsReaderAgentCustomizer** is primed with five default Internet newsgroups: *comp.ai.fuzzy, comp.ai.neural-nets, comp.ai.genetic, comp.ai. shells*, and *comp.ai*. These newsgroups were chosen because they are reasonable places to find news posts or articles containing our default keyword list. To load the first newsgroup, *comp.lang.ai*, select that item in the ComboBox. The **FilterAgent** then begins requesting articles the news host has in the news group. As each article is downloaded, the subject line is parsed from the header and is displayed in the **Subject** column in the **InfoFilterFrame** table as well as on the customizer dialog, and the body or text of the news article is read and displayed in the text area. The subject line and body are stored in a **NewsArticle** object.

Now that a set of news articles is loaded, we can see how well they match our specified keywords. The keyword filter is the default, so the articles are sorted in the table in descending order based on the total number of keywords that are found in the body of the article or the Web page *Hypertext Markup Language* (HTML) source. The top-scoring item is selected, and the body of that article is displayed in the text area.

In order to use either the **Cluster** filter or the **Feedback** filter, profile data must first be saved for a reasonably sized set of articles. By default, the **NewsReaderAgent** reads only 10 articles from each newsgroup (this value is a parameter on the **NewsReader-AgentCustomizer**). If the five default newsgroups are read, that gives 100 article profile records. To store the article profiles in the *infofilter.dat* text file, select the **Add all articles** menu option in the **Profile** menu. Assuming that the news server had 10 articles in the *comp.lang.ai* news group, 10 records would be written.

Continue by downloading each of the next four newsgroups in turn (or selecting your own newsgroups) and selecting **Add all articles** from the **Profile** menu. At this point, there should be approximately 100 records in the *infofilter.dat* file.

Now that there is profile data, we can train the **FilterAgent**'s neural networks. Select the **Customize . . .** menu item from the **Profile** menu to open the **FilterAgentCustomizer**. Next, select the **Train NN Models** button on the customizer. The **FilterAgent** creates a neural network that reads the *infofilter.dat* file and clusters the article profile records into four segments. (The number of segments was an arbitrary decision; it could easily have been 9, 16, or 25.) The keyword score for each article in each cluster is summed, and the cluster average is computed. The score for each article in a particular cluster is set to the cluster average value. This step produces the segmentation model used by the **Cluster** filter. In order to use the **Cluster** filter, however, it must also be selected as the filter type on the **Filter** menu. If the **use Clusters** menu item is checked on the **Filter** menu, the news articles list will be refreshed with the articles from the top-scoring cluster first, the second-best cluster second, and so on.

The last filter that is provided in the *InfoFilter* application is the **Feedback** filter. This filter also uses a neural network model to determine the article scores. The **FilterAgent** creates a back propagation prediction model by using the article profile records as input and the user rating score as the target output value. If none of the default feedback settings were overridden before the articles were added to the profile, the model will predict a score ranging from 0.0 to 1.0, where any articles that have more than five keyword matches will have a value of 1. If different values were provided for selected articles by explicit user feedback using the five levels that are defined in the **Feedback** menu, the results could be slightly different. For example, if articles that contained the word "neural" were rated as more interesting than ones that contained the word "java," they would have higher scores from the **Feedback** filter (although each had an identical raw match score).

After the **Feedback** filter model is built, it must be selected as the desired filter technique by checking the **use Feedback** menu item on the **Filter** menu. The articles in the **InfoFilterFrame** table will be reordered according to the score that they received from the neural prediction model.

InfoFilterFrame Class

The *InfoFilter* application classes, **InfoFilterApp**, which contains our *main()* and **InfoFilterFrame** that implements our main window, were constructed by using the Borland JBuilder 3.0 Java interactive development environment. The Visual Builder enables us to create the complete GUI by using Java Swing components in a drag-and-drop style. JBuilder automatically generates the Java code for creating the GUI controls and action event handlers in the **InfoFilterFrame** class. We then added the logic for creating the **FilterAgent**, **NewsReaderAgent**, and **URLReaderAgent** and for setting up the **InfoFilterFrame** display. The **InfoFilterApp** code that invokes the **InfoFilterFrame** is not presented here. This code simply instantiates the **InfoFilterFrame** instance and displays it. Likewise, a substantial amount of the code in the **InfoFilterFrame** class deals with GUI control logic, and we will not present that material here. Instead, we will highlight only brief sections of the code that demonstrate how to use the underlying agent classes. All of the classes that we discuss in this chapter are in the *infofilter* package (illustrated in Figure 9.6). **InfoFilterFrame** extends **JFrame** and provides a table and a large text area as the main interface elements and presents a menu bar of options in order to enable the user to perform the desired actions.

The **InfoFilterFrame** class instantiates a **FilterAgent**, a **NewsReaderAgent**, and a **URLReaderAgent** for use in the application. The **FilterAgent** is used as an internal helper class, and its customizer is accessed by using the **Profile Customizer . . .** menu item. The **NewsReaderAgent** and **URLReaderAgent** also use their own customizer dialogs to interface with users. The **InfoFilterFrame** is a **CIAgentEventListener**, and it registers as a listener on the agents. These agents communicate with the **InfoFilterFrame** by using **CIAgentEvents**.

Actions that deal with communicating and reading data from the news server are handled by the **NewsReaderAgent** class. Actions that are related to building the user profile, scoring articles, or building the neural network filters are handled by the **FilterAgent**. Most of these method calls are handled asynchronously. In other words, the *InfoFilter* application signals the **FilterAgent** on its main processing thread and control immedi-

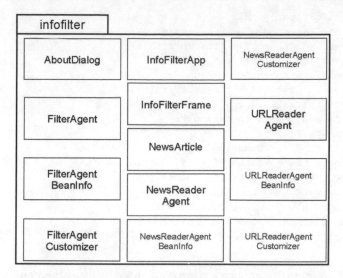

Figure 9.6 The *infofilter* package UML diagram.

ately returns to the GUI while the **FilterAgent** processes on its own autonomous thread. For example, the **Train NN** button in the **FilterAgentCustomizer** calls the *trainClusterNet()* and *trainRatingNet()* methods in the **FilterAgent** that simply turn on boolean switches or flags for the agent to see when it wakes up periodically looking for work. This approach is used because training the neural networks can be a long-running action, and by handling these tasks asynchronously, the *InfoFilter* application is not tied up waiting for these actions to complete. The **FilterAgent** signals when it is done by calling the *clusterNetTrained()* and *ratingNetTrained()* methods. These methods enable the corresponding **Filter** menu options so that **Cluster** and **Feedback** filtering can be selected.

```
Vector articles = new Vector();
FilterAgent filterAgent = new FilterAgent();
NewsReaderAgent newsReaderAgent = new NewsReaderAgent();
URLReaderAgent uRLReaderAgent = new URLReaderAgent();
NewsArticle currentArt;
boolean scored = false;
int filterType = 0;

private void init() {
  try {
    FilterAgent tmpFilterAgent =
      FilterAgent.restoreFromFile(FilterAgent.fileName);

    if(tmpFilterAgent != null) {
      filterAgent = tmpFilterAgent;
    }
  } catch(Exception e) {}
```

```
            filterAgent.infoFilter = this;
            filterAgent.addCIAgentEventListener(this);
            newsReaderAgent.addCIAgentEventListener(this);
            newsReaderAgent.initialize();
            newsReaderAgent.startAgentProcessing();
            uRLReaderAgent.addCIAgentEventListener(this);
            uRLReaderAgent.initialize();
            uRLReaderAgent.startAgentProcessing();
            filterAgent.initialize();
            filterAgent.startAgentProcessing();
            openFileDialog = new java.awt.FileDialog(this);
            openFileDialog.setMode(FileDialog.LOAD);
            openFileDialog.setTitle("Open");
            saveFileDialog = new java.awt.FileDialog(this);
            saveFileDialog.setMode(FileDialog.SAVE);
            saveFileDialog.setTitle("Save");
        }
```

The three **CIAgents** used in this application are configured by using their customizers. In the *downloadNewsGroupsMenuItem_actionPerformed()* method that follows, we give an example of how the **InfoFilterFrame** instantiates and opens these Customizer dialogs. First, the **Customizer** class is retrieved from the agent by using the **CIAgent** *getCustomizerClass()* method. This code is in the **CIAgent** base class and uses the **BeanInfo** class and a bean descriptor to get the customizer class name. This code then creates an instance of the **Customizer** by using the *newInstance()* method. For usability, we position the dialog slightly offset from the **InfoFilterFrame** window. Next, we pass a reference to the agent instance to the **Customizer** by using the *setObject()* method. Finally, we perform a *show()* and open the agent-specific customizer dialog.

```
    void downloadNewsGroupMenuItem_actionPerformed(ActionEvent e) {
        Class customizerClass = newsReaderAgent.getCustomizerClass();

        if(customizerClass == null) {
            trace("Error can't find NewsReaderAgent customizer class");
            return;
        }
        Customizer customizer = null;

        try {
            customizer = (Customizer) customizerClass.newInstance();
        } catch(Exception exc) {
            System.out.println("Error opening customizer - " + exc.toString());
            return;
        }
        Point pos = this.getLocation();
        JDialog dlg = (JDialog) customizer;

        dlg.setLocation(pos.x + 20, pos.y + 20);
        customizer.setObject(newsReaderAgent);
        dlg.show();
    }
```

The two **CIAgentEventListener** methods are as follows. The *postCIAgentEvent()* method just calls the *processCIAgentEvent()* method because the **InfoFilterFrame** does not process asynchronous events. The *processCIAgentEvent()* method handles three types of **CIAgentEvents**. Trace action events are displayed in the text area by calling the *trace()* method. Status action events are displayed in the status text label by using the *setText()* method. Furthermore, *addArticle* action events are passed along to the *addArticle()* method.

```
public void processCIAgentEvent(CIAgentEvent event) {
  Object source = event.getSource();
  Object arg = event.getArgObject();
  Object action = event.getAction();

  if(action != null) {
    if(action.equals("trace")) {
      if(((arg != null) && (arg instanceof String))) {
        trace((String) arg);
      }
    } else if(action.equals("addArticle")) {
      addArticle((NewsArticle) arg);
    } else if(action.equals("status")) {
      filterAgentStatusLabel.setText("FilterAgent status: "
          + (String) arg);
    }
  }
}

public void postCIAgentEvent(CIAgentEvent event) {
  processCIAgentEvent(event);
}
```

The **InfoFilterFrame** *addArticle()* method takes a single **NewsArticle** instance as an input parameter. The article is added to the **Vector** of *articles*. The article is scored using the current *filterType*. We then update the table by using the *refreshTable()* method. The body of the article is displayed in the text area. We enable menu items to make sure that the user can add the article to the profile if desired. Note that this method is called by and runs on the **NewsReaderAgent** or **URLReaderAgent** thread:

```
protected void addArticle(NewsArticle art) {
  articles.addElement(art);
  filterAgent.score(art, filterType);
  refreshTable();
  articleTextArea.setText(art.getBody());
  articleTextArea.setCaretPosition(0);
  addArticleMenuItem.setEnabled(true);
  addAllMenuItem.setEnabled(true);
  saveArticleMenuItem.setEnabled(true);
}
```

The *insertionSort()* method that is used to sort the articles is a standard implementation of the insertion sort algorithm [Sedgewick, 1984] that was adapted for Java. First, the elements in the **Vector** are copied into an array for convenience. Next, starting at the second element in the array, we walk through the array and sort as we go. Once the sort algorithm is complete, the array elements are copied back into a return **Vector**.

The *filterAgent* member holds a reference to the **FilterAgent**, a **CIAgent**-based intelligent agent that handles the user profile maintenance and the scoring and building of models that are used by the **Cluster** and **Feedback** filters. The *filterType* member indicates which filter technique the user wants to use to determine the order in which articles are displayed.

NewsReaderAgent Class

The **NewsReaderAgent** class, listed in Figure 9.7, handles all aspects of reading an Internet newsgroup. This class contains several data members, including a *newsHost*, the *newsgroup*, the *news* **Socket** (which is used to connect and talk to the news server), and the *newsIn* and *newsOut* streams (which are used to send data over the **Socket** connection).

The *connectToNewsHost()* method makes the initial connection to the NNTP news server. The *newsHost* **String** contains the address of the news server supplied by the user (the default is *news1.attglobal.net*). The NNTP specification by Kantor and Lapsley (1986; Internet RFC No. 977) says that NNTP servers should listen on well-known port number 119, so an instance of a **Socket** to the *newsHost* is created by using that port. The *newsIn* and *newsOut* data streams are instantiated. A **DataInputStream** is used for reading, and a **PrintStream** is used for writing. After making the initial socket connection, the news server responds with its status, which is read into the *reply* **String** and displayed in the **InfoFilterFrame** text area by sending a *trace* **CIAgentEvent** to the listener. If anything goes wrong, such as an incorrect news host address or a network communication error, any **Exceptions** that are generated by the *input/output* (I/O) operations are caught and an error message is displayed (again, by using the *trace* event).

The *closeNewsHost()* method shuts down the **Socket** connection to the news server. The NNTP protocol requires the client to send the QUIT string as the closing message. That string is sent to the server and is echoed to the display. The news server does not send any reply message in response to a QUIT.

The *readNewsGroup()* method takes a single parameter (the name of the newsgroup to be read). NNTP requires the GROUP command, followed by the name of the news group using standard string representation (such as *comp.ai.neural-nets*). The news server responds with a return code, the number of articles in the newsgroup that the server holds, the first and last article ID, and an acknowledgment string stating that the newsgroup has been selected. A **StringTokenizer** is used to parse these parameters. Once a newsgroup is selected on the server, an individual article must be selected. The first article ID that is returned by the GROUP command is used with the STAT command to set an internal cursor on the news server so that subsequent articles can be retrieved by using the NEXT command (rather than requiring each article ID to be known beforehand).

```
package infofilter;

import java.awt.*;
import java.awt.event.*;
import javax.swing.*;
import java.io.*;
import java.net.*;
import java.util.*;
import ciagent.*;

public class NewsReaderAgent extends CIAgent {
  String newsHost = "news1.attglobal.net";
  String newsGroup = "comp.ai.neural-nets";
  Socket news;
  PrintWriter newsOut;
  BufferedReader newsIn;
  boolean newsHostConnectionOK = false;
  int numArticles = 20;
  Vector articles = new Vector();
  NewsArticle currentArt;
  Vector newsGroups = new Vector();

  public NewsReaderAgent() {
    this("NewsReaderAgent");
  }

  public NewsReaderAgent(String Name) {
    super(Name);
  }

  public void setNewsHost(String newsHost) {
    this.newsHost = newsHost;
  }

  public String getNewsHost() {
    return newsHost;
  }

  public void setNewsGroup(String newsGroup) {
    this.newsGroup = newsGroup;
  }

  public String getNewsGroup() {
    return newsGroup;
  }
```

(continues)

Figure 9.7 The NewsReaderAgent class listing.

```
public void setNumArticles(int numArticles) {
  this.numArticles = numArticles;
}

public int getNumArticles() {
  return numArticles;
}

public Vector getArticles() {
  return (Vector) articles.clone();
}

public NewsArticle getArticle(int id) {
  return null;
}

public void initialize() {
  setSleepTime(5 * 1000);
  setState(CIAgentState.INITIATED);
}

public String getTaskDescription() {
  return "Download a news group";
}

public void process() {}

public void stop() {
  trace(name + " stopped \n");
  stopAgentProcessing();
}

public void processTimerPop() {}

public void processCIAgentEvent(CIAgentEvent event) {
  Object source = event.getSource();
  Object arg = event.getArgObject();
  Object action = event.getAction();

  trace(name + ":  CIAgentEvent received by " + name + " from "
        + source.getClass());
  if(action != null) {
    if(action.equals("trace")) {
      if(((arg != null) && (arg instanceof String))) {
        trace((String) arg);
      }
    } else if(action.equals("downloadNewsGroup")) {
```

Figure 9.7 The NewsReaderAgent class listing (Continued).

```
      downloadNewsGroup((Vector) arg);
    }
  }
}

private void init() {
  newsHost = "news1.attglobal.net";
}

protected void sendArticleToListeners(NewsArticle art) {
  CIAgentEvent event = new CIAgentEvent(this, "addArticle", art);

  notifyCIAgentEventListeners(event);
}

protected void downloadNewsGroup(Vector args) {
  System.out.println("NewsReaderAgent .. downloading news group");
  String newsHost;
  String newsGroup;

  newsHost = (String) args.elementAt(0);
  newsGroup = (String) args.elementAt(1);
  connectToNewsHost(newsHost);
  if(newsIn != null) {
    readNewsGroup(newsGroup);
  }
  if(newsOut != null) {
    closeNewsHost();
  }
  if((newsIn == null) || (newsOut == null)) {
    trace("FilterAgent Error - could not connect to NewsHost");
  }
}

public void connectToNewsHost(String newsHost) {
  try {
    news = new Socket(newsHost, 119);
    newsIn =
      new BufferedReader(new InputStreamReader(
        news.getInputStream()));
    newsOut = new PrintWriter(news.getOutputStream(), true);
    String reply = newsIn.readLine();

    trace(reply + "\n");
    newsHostConnectionOK = true;
  } catch(Exception e) {
```

(continues)

Figure 9.7 Continued.

```
        trace("FilterAgent connectToNewsHost() exception:" + e);
        newsHostConnectionOK = false;
    }
}

void closeNewsHost() {
    try {
        String cmd = "QUIT \n";

        newsOut.println(cmd);
        trace(cmd + " \n");
        newsIn.close();
    } catch(Exception e) {
        trace("FilterAgent closeNewsHost() exception:" + e);
    }
    newsHostConnectionOK = false;
}

public void readNewsGroup(String newsGroup) {
    int maxArticles = numArticles;
    int numArticlesRead = 0;

    articles.clear();
    boolean exit = false;

    try {
        String cmd = "GROUP " + newsGroup + " \n";

        newsOut.println(cmd);
        String reply = newsIn.readLine();

        trace(cmd + " \n" + reply + "\n");
        StringTokenizer st = new StringTokenizer(reply);
        String s1 = st.nextToken();
        String s2 = st.nextToken();
        String s3 = st.nextToken();
        String s4 = st.nextToken();
        String s5 = st.nextToken();

        if (s1.equals("411")) {
            trace("Error - invalid news group") ;
            System.out.println("Error - invalid news group");
            return ;
        }

        cmd = "STAT " + s3 + "\n";
        newsOut.println(cmd);
```

Figure 9.7 The NewsReaderAgent class listing (Continued).

```
    reply = newsIn.readLine();
    trace(cmd + " \n" + reply + "\n");
    String retCode;

    do {
      cmd = "HEAD \n";
      newsOut.println(cmd);
      reply = newsIn.readLine();
      trace(cmd + " \n" + reply + "\n");
      StringTokenizer tok = new StringTokenizer(reply, " ");

      retCode = tok.nextToken();
      String id = tok.nextToken();
      String msgId = tok.nextToken();

      if(!retCode.equals("221")) {
        continue;
      }
      NewsArticle art = parseHeader(id);

      articles.addElement(art);
      try {
        Thread.sleep(100);
      } catch(InterruptedException e) {}
      cmd = "BODY \n";
      newsOut.println(cmd);
      reply = newsIn.readLine();
      StringTokenizer stok = new StringTokenizer(reply);

      retCode = stok.nextToken();
      if(!retCode.equals("222")) {
        articles.removeElement(art);
        continue;
      }
      trace(cmd + " \n" + reply + "\n");
      StringBuffer bodyText = new StringBuffer();

      do {
        reply = newsIn.readLine();
        bodyText.append(reply + "\n");
      } while(!reply.equals("."));
      art.setBody(bodyText.toString());
      sendArticleToListeners(art);
      numArticlesRead++;
      cmd = "\n NEXT \n";
      newsOut.println(cmd);
```

(continues)

Figure 9.7   Continued.

```
        reply = newsIn.readLine();
        trace(cmd + " \n" + reply + "\n");
        StringTokenizer st2 = new StringTokenizer(reply);

        retCode = st2.nextToken();
        System.out.println("articles.size() = " + articles.size());
      } while(retCode.equals("223") && (numArticlesRead <
      maxArticles));
      currentArt = (NewsArticle) articles.elementAt(0);
      trace(currentArt.body);
    } catch(Exception e) {
      trace("FilterAgent readNewsGroup() exception:" + e);
    }
  }

  public void readSingleArticle(String id) {
    try {
      String cmd = "STAT " + id + "\n";

      newsOut.println(cmd);
      String reply = newsIn.readLine();

      trace(cmd + " \n" + reply + "\n");
      String s10;

      cmd = "BODY \n";
      newsOut.println(cmd);
      reply = newsIn.readLine();
      trace(cmd + " \n" + reply + "\n");
      do {
        reply = newsIn.readLine();
        trace(reply + "\n");
      } while(!reply.equals("."));
    } catch(Exception e) {
      trace("FilterAgent readSingleArticle() exception:" + e);
    }
  }

  protected NewsArticle parseHeader(String id) {
    NewsArticle art = new NewsArticle(id);
    String subject;
    String line;

    try {
      do {
        line = newsIn.readLine();
        if(line.charAt(0) == 'S') {
```

Figure 9.7 The NewsReaderAgent class listing (Continued).

```
        StringTokenizer tagTok = new StringTokenizer(line, " ");

        if(tagTok.nextToken().equals("Subject:")) {
          art.subject = line;
        }
      }
    } while(!line.equals("."));
  } catch(Exception e) {
    trace("Exception:" + e);
  }
  return art;
}
}
```

Figure 9.7   Continued.

The majority of the *readNewsGroup()* method is a *do* loop, where the NEXT command is used to walk through the newsgroup one article at a time. First, the HEAD command is used to download the header for each article. The *parseHeader()* method takes the article ID as a single input parameter. This method instantiates a **NewsArticle** instance and reads each line of the header and parses it, looking for the Subject: line. This method stores the subject in the *subject* member of the **NewsArticle** object and continues reading the header lines until the news server signals that it is done by sending a line that contains only a period character.

In a similar manner, the BODY command is sent to the news server and the lines of the news articles are downloaded. When the period sentinel character is received, the article *body* member is set by calling the *setBody()* method. The *sendArticleToListeners()* method is used to send a **CIAgentEvent** to the **InfoFilterFrame** with the just-read **NewsArticle** instance passed as the event argument.

The NEXT command steps to the next article in the newsgroup. After each NNTP command string is sent, the return codes are verified. During testing, we encountered cases where the server returned the header for an article in response to the HEAD command but then balked when the BODY command was sent for the same article ID. The *do* loop exits when the *maxArticles* limit is reached or if an error return code is received from the server.

Please note that the **NewsReaderAgent** is not a commercial news reader. There is much more error-checking logic that should be added for a general-purpose news reader. This reader, however, does provide the basic mechanism for browsing an Internet newsgroup and enables us to obtain news articles to build the user profile.

URLReaderAgent Class

The **URLReaderAgent** class, shown in Figure 9.8, reads the data from a single Web page that is specified by a URL. This class is relatively simple because much of the function is

```
package infofilter;

import java.awt.*;
import java.awt.event.*;
import javax.swing.*;
import java.io.*;
import java.net.*;
import java.util.*;
import ciagent.*;

public class URLReaderAgent extends CIAgent {
  URL url = null;
  String paramString = null;
  String contents = "";

  public URLReaderAgent() {
    this("URLReaderAgent");
  }

  public URLReaderAgent(String name) {
    super(name);
  }

  public void setURL(URL url) {
    this.url = url;
  }

  public URL getURL() {
    return url;
  }

  public void setParamString(String paramString) {
    this.paramString = paramString;
  }

  public String getParamString() {
    return paramString;
  }

  public String getContents() {
    return contents;
  }

  public String getTaskDescription() {
    return "Read a URL";
  }
```

Figure 9.8 The URLReaderAgent class listing.

```
public void initialize() {
  setSleepTime(5 * 1000);
  setState(CIAgentState.INITIATED);
}

public void process() {}

public void processTimerPop() {}

public void processCIAgentEvent(CIAgentEvent event) {
  Object source = event.getSource();
  Object arg = event.getArgObject();
  Object action = event.getAction();

  trace("\n" + name + ":  CIAgentEvent received by " + name + "
        from " + source.getClass());
  if(action != null) {
    if(action.equals("trace")) {
      if(((arg != null) && (arg instanceof String))) {
        trace((String) arg);
      }
    } else if(action.equals("getURLText")) {
      String text = getURLText();

      if(text != null) {
        NewsArticle article = new NewsArticle("URL");

        article.setSubject("URL: " + url.toString());
        article.setBody(text);
        sendArticleToListeners(article);
      }
    }
  }
}

protected void sendArticleToListeners(NewsArticle article) {
  System.out.println("URLReaderAgent -- sending URL text to
    listeners ");
  CIAgentEvent event = new CIAgentEvent(this, "addArticle",
    article);

  notifyCIAgentEventListeners(event);
}

protected String getURLText() {
  HttpURLConnection connection;
```

(continues)

Figure 9.8   Continued.

```
        StringBuffer body = new StringBuffer();

        System.out.println("URLReaderAgent ... starting to read URL ");
        try {
          connection = (HttpURLConnection) url.openConnection();
          System.out.println("Opened connection");
          BufferedReader in = new BufferedReader(
            new InputStreamReader(connection.getInputStream()));

          if(in == null) {
            trace("Error: URLReaderAgent could not connect to URL");
            return null;
          }
          String inputLine;

          while((inputLine = in.readLine()) != null) {
            body.append(inputLine);
            body.append("\n");
          }
          in.close();
        } catch(Exception e) {
          trace("Error: URLReaderAgent could not connect to URL : "
                + e.toString());
          return null;
        }
        contents = body.toString();
        return contents;
      }
    }
```

Figure 9.8 The URLReaderAgent class listing.

provided by the *java.net* classes. The three data members include the *url*, which is an instance of the URL object, a *paramString* that contains an optional parameter **String** for submission to CGI-BIN programs, and a *contents* **String** that represents the data that is read from the URL or that is returned by the CGI-BIN at that URL. Most of the work is done in the *getURLText()* method. First, an **HttpURLConnection** is created on the *url* and a **Buffered-Reader** is constructed over the connection. In a *while* loop, we read the Web page source data line by line and add it to our **StringBuffer**. The content is returned as a string.

The *processCIAgentEvent* method is implemented to accept *getURLText* action events. When it receives this action event, the *getURLText()* method is invoked, the Web page is read, and a **NewsArticle** instance is created. The content is placed in the article body, and the URL is set as the subject line. This **NewsArticle** instance is then sent back to the **InfoFilterFrame** instance (which is registered as a **CIAgentEvent** listener) in the *sendArticleToListeners()* method.

The **URLReaderAgent** is quite simple but could be easily extended to act as a crawler or spider by invoking search engines and then processing their return lists. Thus, the *InfoFilter* application could be extended to be a quite powerful Web page evaluation- and knowledge-based search engine. You can test the CGI-BIN capability by selecting the *bigusbooks.com* airfare URL and the corresponding parameter string from the **URL-ReaderAgentCustomizer** combo boxes.

NewsArticle Class

The **NewsArticle** class, shown in Figure 9.9, defines all of the information about a single news article or Web page source. The primary piece of information is the NNTP *id*, which is returned by the News Server in response to the NEXT command as all of the articles in the newsgroup are read. The *subject* member contains either the subject line that is parsed out of the header information or the Web page URL. The *body* member is the entire text returned by the server in response to the BODY command, or the HTML contents of the Web page. The remainder of the members are used by the **InfoFilterFrame** functions. The *counts* array holds the raw keyword match scores. The *keywordScore* is the sum of *counts*. The *rating* is used to describe the usefulness of the article to the user (0.0 is useless, and 1.0 is interesting). The *score* is the article's ranking based on the type of filter that is being applied. The *clusterId* holds the segment into which this article falls in the **Cluster** filter, while the *clusterScore* is the average score for all articles in the cluster.

The NewsArticle class provides the *readArticle()* and *writeArticle()* methods in order to enable test postings to be added to the user profile. For example, the user could load some articles that are of particular interest in order to score them, give them a high value by using the **Feedback** option, and then add the profile record to the *infofilter. dat* file. The *subject* and *body* of the text are concatenated, written out, and read as a single block of bytes. Getter and setter methods are provided for the data members.

The *getProfileString()* method formats the contents of the *counts[]* array (along with the *feedback* and *score* values). This string is a space-delimited text representation that the *addArticleToProfile()* method uses (described later in the **FilterAgent** class). This string is appended to the *infofilter.dat* file shown in Figure 9.9.

FilterAgent Class

The **FilterAgent** class, listed in Figure 9.10, is a subclass of **CIAgent**. This class provides all of the functions that are related to the management of the user profile data, the keyword scoring, and the construction of the neural network models that are used for the **Cluster** and **Feedback** filters. The **FilterAgent** class is tightly coupled with the *InfoFilter* application. As such, it could be used simply as an intelligent helper class, with all of its methods simply called directly by the **InfoFilterFrame**. To illustrate how an intelligent agent can be tightly coupled but still run autonomously, however, we add a simple signaling protocol for the application to initiate long-running **FilterAgent** functions.

```
package infofilter;

import java.io.*;

public class NewsArticle {
  protected String id;
  protected String subject;
  protected String body;
  protected int counts[];
  protected int keywordScore;
  protected double predictedRating = 0.5;
  protected String userRating = FilterAgent.NEUTRAL_RATING;
  protected double rating = 0.5;
  protected double score;
  protected int clusterId;
  protected double clusterScore;

  NewsArticle(String id) {
    this.id = id;
  }

  void readArticle(String fileName) {
    File f = new File(fileName);
    int size = (int) f.length();
    int bytesRead = 0;

    try {
      FileInputStream in = new FileInputStream(f);
      byte[] data = new byte[size];

      in.read(data, 0, size);
      subject = "Subject: " + fileName;
      body = new String(data);
      id = fileName;
      in.close();
    } catch(IOException e) {
      System.out.println("Error: couldn't read news article from "
                         + fileName + "\n");
    }
  }

  void writeArticle(String fileName) {
    File f = new File(fileName);
    String dataOut = subject + " " + body;
    int size = (int) dataOut.length();
    int bytesOut = 0;
    byte data[] = new byte[size];
```

Figure 9.9 The NewsArticle class listing.

```
    data = dataOut.getBytes();
    try {
      FileOutputStream out = new FileOutputStream(f);

      out.write(data, 0, size);
      out.flush();
      out.close();
    } catch(IOException e) {
      System.out.println("Error: couldn't write news article to "
                         + fileName + "\n");
    }
}

public String getSubject() {
  return subject;
}

public void setSubject(String subject) {
  this.subject = subject;
}

public String getBody() {
  return body;
}

public void setBody(String body) {
  this.body = body;
}

public int getKeywordScore() {
  return keywordScore;
}

public void setKeywordScore(int keywordScore) {
  this.keywordScore = keywordScore;
}

public double getScore(int filterType) {
  switch(filterType) {
    case FilterAgent.USE_KEYWORDS:
      return keywordScore;
    case FilterAgent.USE_CLUSTERS:
      return clusterScore;
    case FilterAgent.USE_PREDICTED_RATING:
      return predictedRating;
  }
```

(continues)

Figure 9.9   Continued.

```
    return 0.0;
}

public String getUserRating() {
  return userRating;
}

public double getRating() {
  return rating;
}

public void setClusterScore(double clusterScore) {
  this.clusterScore = clusterScore;
}

public double getClusterScore() {
  return clusterScore;
}

public void setClusterId(int clusterId) {
  this.clusterId = clusterId;
}

public int getClusterId() {
  return clusterId;
}

public double getPredictedRating() {
  return predictedRating;
}

public void setPredictedRating(double predictedRating) {
  this.predictedRating = predictedRating;
}

public void setUserRating(String userRating) {
  this.userRating = userRating;
  if(userRating.equals(FilterAgent.USELESS_RATING)) {
    rating = 0.0;
  } else if(userRating.equals(FilterAgent.NOTVERY_RATING)) {
    rating = 0.25;
  } else if(userRating.equals(FilterAgent.NEUTRAL_RATING)) {
    rating = 0.50;
  } else if(userRating.equals(FilterAgent.MILDLY_RATING)) {
    rating = 0.75;
  } else if(userRating.equals(FilterAgent.INTERESTING_RATING)) {
    rating = 1.0;
```

Figure 9.9 The NewsArticle class listing (Continued).

```
    }
  }

  String getProfileString() {
    StringBuffer outString = new StringBuffer("");

    for(int i = 0; i < counts.length; i++) {
      outString.append(counts[i]);
      outString.append(" ");
    }
    outString.append(rating);
    return outString.toString();
  }
}
```

Figure 9.9   Continued.

```
package infofilter;

import java.awt.*;
import java.io.*;
import java.util.*;
import ciagent.*;
import learn.*;

public class FilterAgent extends CIAgent {
  transient InfoFilterFrame infoFilter;
  protected String[] keywords;
  protected KMapNet clusterNet;
  protected BackProp ratingNet;
  protected boolean buildClusterNet = false;
  protected boolean clusterNetTrained = false;
  protected boolean buildRatingNet = false;
  protected boolean ratingNetTrained = false;
  public static final String fileName = "filterAgent.ser";
  public static final int USE_KEYWORDS = 0;
  public static final int USE_CLUSTERS = 1;
  public static final int USE_PREDICTED_RATING = 2;
  public static final String USELESS_RATING = "Useless";
  public static final String NOTVERY_RATING = "Not very useful";
  public static final String NEUTRAL_RATING = "Neutral";
  public static final String MILDLY_RATING = "Mildly interesting";
  public static final String INTERESTING_RATING = "Interesting";
```

(continues)

Figure 9.10   The FilterAgent class listing.

```
public FilterAgent() {
  this("FilterAgent");
}

public FilterAgent(String name) {
  super(name);
  keywords = new String[10];
  keywords[0] = "java";
  keywords[1] = "agent";
  keywords[2] = "fuzzy";
  keywords[3] = "intelligent";
  keywords[4] = "neural";
  keywords[5] = "network";
  keywords[6] = "genetic";
  keywords[7] = "rule";
  keywords[8] = "learning";
  keywords[9] = "inferencing";
}

public String getTaskDescription() {
  return "Filter articles";
}

public void initialize() {
  setSleepTime(5 * 1000);
  setState(CIAgentState.INITIATED);
}

public void process() {}

public void processTimerPop() {
  if(!buildClusterNet &&!buildRatingNet) {
    status("Idle");
    return;
  }
  if(buildClusterNet) {
    try {
      status("Training Cluster network");
      buildClusterNet = false;
      trainClusterNet();
      infoFilter.clusterNetTrained();
      clusterNetTrained = true;
      status("Cluster network trained");
    } catch(Exception e) {
      status("ClusterNet - No data " + e.toString());
    }
  } else if(buildRatingNet) {
```

Figure 9.10 The FilterAgent class listing (Continued).

```
      try {
        status("Training Rating network");
        buildRatingNet = false;
        trainRatingNet();
        infoFilter.ratingNetTrained();
        ratingNetTrained = true;
        status("Rating network trained");
        saveToFile(fileName);
      } catch(Exception e) {
        status("RatingNet - No data " + e.toString());
      }
    } else if(clusterNetTrained && ratingNetTrained) {
      status("Trained, Serialized");
    }
}

public void processCIAgentEvent(CIAgentEvent e) {
  trace(name + ":  CIAgentEvent received by " + name + " from "
        + e.getSource() + " with arg " + e.getArgObject());
  String arg = (String) e.getArgObject();

  if(arg.equals("buildClusterNet")) {
    buildClusterNet = true;
  } else if(arg.equals("buildRatingNet")) {
    buildRatingNet = true;
  }
}

public String[] getKeywords() {
  return keywords;
}

public void setKeywords(String[] keywords) {
  this.keywords = keywords;
}

public void buildClusterNet() {
  buildClusterNet = true;
}

public void buildRatingNet() {
  buildRatingNet = true;
}

public boolean isClusterNetTrained() {
  return clusterNetTrained;
```

(continues)

Figure 9.10 Continued.

```
  }

  public boolean isRatingNetTrained() {
    return ratingNetTrained;
  }

  void score(NewsArticle article, int filterType) {
    article.counts = countWordMultiKeys(keywords, article.body);
    int size = article.counts.length;
    int sum = 0;

    for(int i = 0; i < size; i++) {
      sum += article.counts[i];
    }
    article.setKeywordScore(sum);
    switch(filterType) {
      case USE_KEYWORDS:
        article.setKeywordScore(sum);
        break;
      case USE_CLUSTERS:
        if(clusterNet != null) {
          double[] inputRec = new double[size + 2];

          for(int i = 0; i < size; i++) {
            inputRec[i] = (double) article.counts[i];
          }
          inputRec[size] = article.getKeywordScore();
          inputRec[size + 1] = article.getRating();
          article.setClusterId(clusterNet.getCluster(inputRec));
        }
        break;
      case USE_PREDICTED_RATING:
        if(ratingNet != null) {
          double[] inputRec = new double[size + 2];

          for(int i = 0; i < size; i++) {
            inputRec[i] = article.counts[i];
          }
          inputRec[size] = article.getKeywordScore();
          inputRec[size + 1] = article.getRating();
          article.setPredictedRating(ratingNet.getPrediction(
            inputRec));
        }
        break;
    }
    if(sum == 0) {
      article.setUserRating(USELESS_RATING);
```

Figure 9.10 The FilterAgent class listing (Continued).

```
    } else if(sum < 2) {
    article.setUserRating(NOTVERY_RATING);
    } else if(sum < 4) {
    article.setUserRating(NEUTRAL_RATING);
    } else if(sum < 6) {
    article.setUserRating(MILDLY_RATING);
    } else {
    article.setUserRating(INTERESTING_RATING);
    }
}

void score(Vector articles, int filterType) {
  try {
    String id;
    Enumeration enum = articles.elements();

    while(enum.hasMoreElements()) {
      trace("");
      NewsArticle article = (NewsArticle) enum.nextElement();

      score(article, filterType);
    }
  } catch(Exception e) {
    trace("Exception:" + e);
  }
  if(filterType == USE_CLUSTERS) {
    computeClusterAverages(articles);
  }
}

void computeClusterAverages(Vector articles) {
  int numClusters = 4;
  int sum[] = new int[numClusters];
  int numArticles[] = new int[numClusters];
  double avgs[] = new double[numClusters];
  Enumeration enum = articles.elements();

  while(enum.hasMoreElements()) {
    NewsArticle article = (NewsArticle) enum.nextElement();
    int cluster = article.getClusterId();

    sum[cluster] += article.getKeywordScore();
    numArticles[cluster]++;
  }
  for(int i = 0; i < numClusters; i++) {
    if(numArticles[i] > 0) {
```

(continues)

Figure 9.10 Continued.

```
        avgs[i] = (double) sum[i] / (double) numArticles[i];
      } else {
        avgs[i] = 0.0;
      }
      trace(" cluster " + i + " avg = " + avgs[i] + "\n");
    }
    enum = articles.elements();
    while(enum.hasMoreElements()) {
      NewsArticle article = (NewsArticle) enum.nextElement();

      article.setClusterScore(avgs[article.clusterId]);
    }
  }

  int[] countWordMultiKeys(String[] keys, String text) {
    StringTokenizer tok = new StringTokenizer(text);
    int keyLen = 1;
    int counts[] = new int[keys.length];
    Vector table[] = new Vector[50];
    Hashtable keyHash = new Hashtable();

    trace("Searching for keywords ... \n");
    for(int i = 0; i < keys.length; i++) {
      int len = keys[i].length();

      if(table[len] == null) {
        table[len] = new Vector();
      }
      table[len].addElement(keys[i]);
      keyHash.put(keys[i], new Integer(i));
      counts[i] = 0;
    }
    while(tok.hasMoreTokens()) {
      String token = tok.nextToken();
      int len = token.length();

      if((len < 50) && (table[len] != null)) {
        Vector searchList = table[len];
        Enumeration enum = searchList.elements();

        while(enum.hasMoreElements()) {
          String key = (String) enum.nextElement();

          if(token.equalsIgnoreCase(key)) {
            Integer index = (Integer) keyHash.get(key);

            counts[index.intValue()]++;
```

Figure 9.10   The FilterAgent class listing (Continued).

```
            continue;
          }
        }
      }
    }
    for(int i = 0; i < keys.length; i++) {
      trace("key = " + keys[i] + " count = " + counts[i] + "\n");
    }
    return counts;
}

void writeProfileDataDefinition() {
  try {
    FileWriter writer = new FileWriter("infofilter.dfn");
    BufferedWriter out = new BufferedWriter(writer);

    for(int i = 0; i < keywords.length; i++) {
      out.write("continuous ");
      out.write(keywords[i]);
      out.newLine();
    }
    out.write("continuous ClassField");
    out.newLine();
    out.flush();
    out.close();
  } catch(IOException e) {
    trace("Error: FilterAgent couldn't create 'infofilter.dfn' \n");
  }
}

void addArticleToProfile(NewsArticle currentArt) {
  try {
    FileWriter writer = new FileWriter("infofilter.dat", true);
    BufferedWriter out = new BufferedWriter(writer);

    out.write(currentArt.getProfileString());
    out.newLine();
    out.flush();
    out.close();
  } catch(IOException e) {
    trace("Error: FilterAgent couldn't append article to
      profile \n");
  }
}

void addAllArticlesToProfile(Vector articles) {
```

(continues)

Figure 9.10 Continued.

```
    try {
      FileWriter writer = new FileWriter("infofilter.dat", true);
      BufferedWriter out = new BufferedWriter(writer);
      Enumeration enum = articles.elements();

      while(enum.hasMoreElements()) {
        NewsArticle art = (NewsArticle) enum.nextElement();

        out.write(art.getProfileString());
        out.newLine();
      }
      out.flush();
      out.close();
    } catch(IOException e) {
      trace("Error: FilterAgent couldn't append article to
        profile \n");
    }
  }
}

void trainClusterNet() {
  DataSet dataSet = new DataSet("ProfileData", "infofilter");

  dataSet.loadDataFile();
  clusterNet = new KMapNet("InfoFilter Cluster Profile");
  clusterNet.setDataSet(dataSet);
  clusterNet.setNumRecs(dataSet.getNumRecords());
  clusterNet.setFieldsPerRec(dataSet.getFieldsPerRec());
  clusterNet.setData(dataSet.getNormalizedData());
  clusterNet.createNetwork(clusterNet.getFieldsPerRec(), 2, 2);
  int maxNumPasses = 20;
  int numRecs = clusterNet.getNumRecs();

  for(int i = 0; i < maxNumPasses; i++) {
    for(int j = 0; j < numRecs; j++) {
      clusterNet.cluster();
    }
    Thread.yield();
  }
  clusterNet.setMode(1);
  for(int i = 0; i < clusterNet.getNumRecs(); i++) {
    clusterNet.cluster();
  }
}

void trainRatingNet() {
  DataSet dataSet = new DataSet("ProfileData", "infofilter");
```

Figure 9.10 The FilterAgent class listing (Continued).

```
      dataSet.loadDataFile();
      ratingNet = new BackProp("InfoFilter Score Model");
      ratingNet.setDataSet(dataSet);
      ratingNet.setNumRecs(dataSet.getNumRecords());
      ratingNet.setFieldsPerRec(dataSet.getNormFieldsPerRec());
      ratingNet.setData(dataSet.getNormalizedData());
      int numOutputs = dataSet.getClassFieldSize();
      int numInputs = ratingNet.getFieldsPerRec() - numOutputs;

      ratingNet.createNetwork(numInputs, 2 * numInputs, numOutputs);
      int maxNumPasses = 2500;
      int numRecs = ratingNet.getNumRecs();

      for(int i = 0; i < maxNumPasses; i++) {
        for(int j = 0; j < numRecs; j++) {
          ratingNet.process();
        }
        Thread.yield();
      }
      trace("\n Back Prop Passes Completed: " + maxNumPasses
            + "  RMS Error = " + ratingNet.getAveRMSError() + " \n");
      ratingNet.setMode(1);
      for(int i = 0; i < ratingNet.getNumRecs(); i++) {
        ratingNet.process();
      }
    }

    public void status(String msg) {
      CIAgentEvent event = new CIAgentEvent(this, "status", msg);

      notifyCIAgentEventListeners(event);
    }

    public static FilterAgent restoreFromFile(String fileName)
        throws ClassNotFoundException, IOException {
      FilterAgent restoredBean = null;
      FileInputStream saveFileIn = new FileInputStream(fileName);
      ObjectInputStream inStream = new ObjectInputStream(saveFileIn);

      restoredBean = (FilterAgent) (inStream.readObject());
      System.out.println("Successfully read FilterAgent from " +
        fileName);
      return restoredBean;
    }

    public void saveToFile(String fileName) {
```

(continues)

Figure 9.10 Continued.

```
    try {
      FileOutputStream saveFileOut = new FileOutputStream(fileName);
      ObjectOutputStream outStream = new ObjectOutputStream(
        saveFileOut);

      outStream.writeObject(this);
      System.out.println("Successfully saved FilterAgent to " +
        fileName);
    } catch(IOException e) {
      System.out.println("FilterAgent.saveToFile() error: "
                         + e.toString());
    }
  }
}
```

Figure 9.10 The FilterAgent class listing (Continued).

The **FilterAgent** defines several additional data members over the **CIAgent** class, a reference to the owning **InfoFilterFrame** instance, an array of **Strings** to hold the *keywords*, the *clusterNet* that holds the **KMapNet** instance for clustering, and the *ratingNet* member that holds the **BackProp** instance for predictive scoring. The two boolean flags—*buildClusterNet* and *buildRatingNet*—are set by the **FilterAgentCustomizer** dialog when the user selects the **Train NN Models** button. When either of these flags are set, the **FilterAgent** will notice when it wakes up from its periodic sleep in the *processTimerPop()* method. This approach enables the agent to autonomously and asynchronously train the neural networks. When the training is complete, the **FilterAgent** signals the completion by using the **InfoFilterFrame** *clusterNetTrained()* and *ratingNetTrained()* methods and sets the corresponding **boolean**s that give the signal that the networks have been trained.

Remember that the **CIAgent** class implements the **CIAgentEventListener** interface, which requires the *processCIAgentEvent()* and *postCIAgentEvent()* methods. These methods have been overridden in the **FilterAgent** to allow other **CIAgents** to initiate the training of the neural networks through the **CIAgentEvent** action mechanism.

The *score()* method takes a single **NewsArticle** and the currently selected *filterType* as inputs. The first task is to count the occurrence of each keyword in the article and then compute the *sum*. Processing continues based on the filter type. For the keyword filter, the *score* is simply the sum of keyword matches. If the **Cluster** filter has been created, the article profile data is passed through the Kohonen map neural network to determine the cluster identifier (which is stored in the article object). The actual **Cluster** filter score cannot be computed in this method, however, because it relies on the computation of the average score of all articles that have the same *clusterId*. These scores are set only in the second *score()* method that takes the entire *articles* **Vector** as a parameter.

A similar approach is taken when **Feedback** filtering is enabled and the back propagation model has been built. But in the **Feedback** case, the neural network output *is* the feedback score. Thus it is immediately assigned using the *setPredictedRating()* method.

One last function performed in this method is the automatic assignment of *rating* or feedback values. A simple threshold ladder determines this value based on the raw match score. If user-specific values were set before *score()* was called, that information would be lost.

The second *score()* method takes a **Vector** of **NewsArticle** objects and the currently selected *filterType* as inputs. This method calls the first *score()* method for each **NewsArticle** in the **Vector**. Because the single *article score()* method takes care of the unique aspects of each filter type, no filter-specific processing is required in this loop. The **Cluster** filter does require some special processing after the *clusterIds* have been set, however. For this reason, there is a call to *computeClusterAverages()* at the end of this *score()* method.

As indicated by its name, *computeClusterAverages()* walks through the **NewsArticles** and computes the raw match score sum and the number of articles in each cluster. The average match score for each cluster is computed by dividing the sum by the number of articles in the cluster. Once these average scores are computed, another pass over the **NewsArticles** is required to set the article score to the corresponding average value.

The *countMultiWordKeys()* method is the workhorse in the **FilterAgent** class. This method takes an array of keyword **Strings** and the article text as parameters and performs a crude but effective search for complete keyword matches. First, an array of **Vectors** is populated with each key with each keyword of length N stored at the nth index of the array. For example, the **Vector** at *table[5]* would contain every key of length 5. During the same pass over the keywords, the *keyHash* **Hashtable** is populated with the keyword as the **Hashtable** key and the length of the keyword (and therefore its index in the *table[]*) as the **Hashtable** value. This setup provides a mapping from the keyword to its index in the keys array. Each element in the *counts[]* array is also initialized to 0.

The method searches the text one word at a time by using a **StringTokenizer** to perform the parsing. The length of each word is used to limit the search to keywords of the same length. A linear search is performed at this point. When a case-insensitive match is found, the *keyHash* is used to find the index of the keyword. This index is used to increment the corresponding element in the *counts[]* array. The result of the *countMultWordKeys()* is an array of integers in which each element represents the total number of hits for each keyword in the text.

The *writeProfileDataDefinition()* method generates the *infofilter.dfn* text file, which defines the layout of the user profile data file. The DataSet class reads a *.dfn* file when it loads a file for training neural networks or decision trees. The file contains pairs of data types and field names. Every keyword has an entry for the number of times that it appears in the article text. The article feedback value is also written out.

The *addArticleToProfile()* method takes a single **NewsArticle** as a parameter and appends its filter profile record to the *infofilter.dat* file. The *NewsArticle.getProfileString()* method formats this information. The *addAllArticlesToProfile()* method calls the *addArticleToProfile()* method for each **NewsArticle** in the *articles* **Vector**.

The *trainClusterNet()* method builds the Kohonen feature map used by the **Cluster** filter. First, a **DataSet** object is instantiated and loaded by using the *infofilter.dat* file. Then, a **KMapNet** object is created and configured to have as many inputs as are defined in the *infofilter.dfn* file and to have four outputs or clusters. The **KMapNet** object is trained for 20 passes over the data; the network weights are locked by setting the mode to 1; and a single pass is used to check the results. Notice that after each training pass, the **FilterAgent** thread yields. This feature enables the *InfoFilter* application to continue its processing.

The *trainRatingNet()* method is used to build the back propagation regression model that is used by the **Feedback** filter. The *infofilter.dat* file is used as the training data. A neural network is created and trained for 2,500 passes over the data (this value might be excessive for large training sets). After each training pass, the thread yields to the *InfoFilter* application. When training completes, the network is locked and a single test pass goes over the data. The trained network uses the article profile (the keyword matches and the score) to predict expected usefulness as represented by the feedback value that is assigned to the article. The output value ranges from 0.0 to 1.0, so articles are sorted in descending order with the score that is closest to 1.0 at the top of the list and the score that is closest to 0.0 at the bottom.

Discussion

Perhaps the main issue in this application is the relationship between the application code and the intelligent agents. One can easily imagine an implementation in which the **FilterAgent** does not exist and its functions are performed by the **InfoFilterFrame** class itself. By maintaining the distinct nature of the **FilterAgent** functions, however, we are in a position to reuse it in a composite agent or multiagent system. While the **FilterAgent** is not as autonomous as the **NewsReaderAgent** or the **URLReaderAgent**, it asynchronously trains the neural network models. With just a little additional work, the **CIAgent**-based **FilterAgent** could be modified to build neural network models against any data set (rather than using the hard-coded InfoFilter data).

In this application, we have developed a modest data-mining capability [Bigus, 1996]. By providing other **CIAgent**s that can access databases or other data sources (the *InfoFilter* application provides Internet news sources and Web pages), an autonomous data-mining system could be built. The **SchedulerAgent** developed in Chapter 8, "Personal Agent Manager Application," can be used to automatically mine data at set times. The **FileAgent** also can be used to trigger data mining when files are modified.

Another design issue for this application is the way in which keyword matching is performed. In the **FilterAgent** class, only complete keyword matches are counted. There are algorithms for performing partial matches so that both singular and plural tenses are counted for each term. The simple whole-word approach used here also misses cases where punctuation marks are adjacent to the word in the text. Obviously, the better the match information, the more accurately we can filter the articles for the user.

The last issue is the compilation of the user profile data. The **Cluster** filter and **Feedback** filter will only perform as well as the profile data used to train the underlying neural network models. With many of the new groups that we tested, only a few of the 20 articles had raw keyword matches that were greater than zero. One solution to this problem is to generate a few canned profile records that are hand constructed with a representative number of keyword matches and feedback values. This training set could be used as the base data, and selected article profiles could be added.

Summary

In this chapter, we developed an information filter for Internet newsgroups by using a tightly coupled **CIAgent**-based intelligent agent. The main points of this chapter include the following:

- **The NewsReaderAgent** uses the underlying protocol for accessing an Internet news server, the *Network News Transport Protocol* (NNTP). News servers listen at port 119. The basic command strings include GROUP for selecting a newsgroup, STAT to set the cursor on a specific article, NEXT to walk through the newsgroup articles, and HEAD and BODY to retrieve data from the individual articles.

- The *InfoFilter* application class provides three types of filtering for newsgroup articles: *Keyword filtering* based on the number of keyword matches, *Cluster filtering* based on grouping similar articles by using neural clustering, and *Feedback filtering* by using a neural prediction model to score articles based on relevance.

- The **FilterAgent** extends the **CIAgent** class by providing methods for keyword scoring and for autonomously training Kohonen map and back propagation neural networks. The **FilterAgent** also maintains the user profile text files *infofilter.dat* and *infofilter.dfn*, which are used for training the neural networks.

- The **URLReaderAgent** reads a single Web page specified by a URL. This agent can also pass a parameter string to a CGI-BIN that can be used to send queries to search engines.

Exercises

1. The *InfoFilter* application currently uses two agents to provide information to be filtered. What other information sources would you add to this application? Assuming that you implement this function as a **CIAgent**, what would you need to change in order to add it to the *InfoFilter* application GUI?

2. While browsing a set of newsgroups, build your own user profile—selecting representative articles across the *Useless* to *Interesting* spectrum. Be sure to set the rating levels appropriately. Train the NN models, then use the **Feedback** filter and see how it performs. Add 20 hand-constructed profile records to the *infofilter.dat* file and rebuild the **Feedback** filter. Did the filtering improve?

3. Enhance or replace the *countWordMultiKeys()* method to improve the keyword match accuracy of the *InfoFilter*. Will the *int counts[]* array still work for your new approach? Will it still work if you add partial-word match capabilities?

4. The **URLReaderAgent** can send parameter strings to any URL. This function could be used to pass queries to an Internet search engine and then retrieve the results. Enhance the **URLReaderAgent** or create a new agent to parse these results, download each URL, and rank them for the user to provide a customized Internet search capability.

5. How would the use of *eXtensible Markup Language* (XML) simplify or complicate the functions that this application provides?

6. The user ratings combo box requires the user to provide explicit feedback on each article. What other techniques could be used to indicate the user's interest (or lack thereof) in specific articles?

7. Could the agents developed in this chapter be used in the *PAManager* application? What would it take to make this happen? What additional function would you gain by having the **URLReaderAgent**, **NewsReaderAgent**, and **FilterAgent** interoperate with the *PAManager* agents?

CHAPTER 10

MarketPlace Application

T his chapter focuses on the issues that are involved when multiple, autonomous agents interact in multiagent systems. The application is an intelligent agent marketplace in which Buyer and Seller agents cooperate and compete to process sales transactions for their owners. A facilitator agent is developed to act as a manager for the marketplace. The Buyer and Seller agents range from using hard-coded logic to rule-based inferencing in their negotiation strategies.

Introduction

Multiagent systems provide a complex and interesting environment for evaluating intelligent agent behavior. While computer-aided design applications take advantage of multiagent systems, the domain knowledge that is required to understand those applications is quite specialized. In this chapter, we will build a multiagent system for an electronic marketplace (because everyone is familiar with buying and selling things, no specialized domain knowledge is necessary). We will develop a **FacilitatorAgent** that manages the marketplace, and we will include several kinds of **BuyerAgents** and **SellerAgents** to interact within that marketplace. All of these intelligent agents are derived from the **CIAgent** base class presented in Chapter 7, "Intelligent Agent Framework." The Buyer and Seller agents are differentiated primarily by the sophistication of their negotiation strategies, ranging from simple, hard-coded logic to forward-chaining rule inferencing.

The **FacilitatorAgent** is the go-between (or matchmaker) between the Buyers and Sellers. All agents must register with the Facilitator before they can interact with any other agents in the marketplace. Sellers advertise their desire to sell products or services with the **FacilitatorAgent**, while Buyers ask the Facilitator to recommend a

325

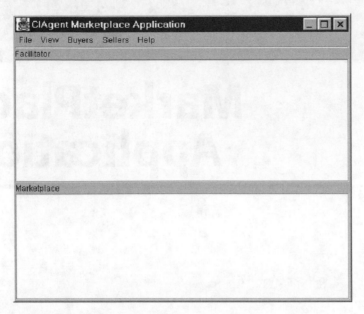

Figure 10.1   CIAgent MarketPlace application.

prospective Seller. Once the Buyer and Seller agents have been introduced by the Facilitator, they continue to communicate indirectly through the **FacilitatorAgent**. Figure 10.1 shows the main panel of the **CIAgent** *MarketPlace* application.

The two text area controls are used to display messages from the Facilitator and the **BuyerAgents** and **SellerAgents** in the marketplace. The **File** pull-down menu items include **Start** and **Stop**; the **View** pull-down menu provides a choice of the **Detail** or **Summary** message content; and the **Buyers** and **Sellers** menus provide three types of Buyers and Sellers to place in the marketplace. These agents can be selected in any combination of Basic, Intermediate, and Advanced Buyers and Sellers. The default setting is for a single, basic **BuyerAgent** and basic **SellerAgent** to be in the marketplace. Up to six independent and autonomous agents can be placed in the marketplace at one time.

When the user selects two to six agents and selects the **Start** option from the **File** menu, a single **FacilitatorAgent** is created along with the selected Buyer and Seller agents. The **SellerAgents** advertise the items that they have to sell by sending messages to the Facilitator and initializing their internal inventory of items. The **BuyerAgents** initialize their own shopping lists. At this point, the marketplace is open for business.

All of the agents are running their own threads and awaken at specified intervals. The first sales negotiation takes place when one of the **BuyerAgents** wakes up and takes an item from its *wishList*. The BuyerAgent then asks the Facilitator to recommend a **SellerAgent** who has advertised its ability to sell that item. If more than one Seller has advertised an item, the Facilitator randomly selects a Seller and returns the name of this **SellerAgent** to the Buyer. This action starts the communication between Buyer and Seller as they try to agree on a price and close the deal. The Facilitator acts as an intermediary between all Buyer and Seller communications, which enables us to watch the exchange of messages between Buyer and Seller agents as the Facilitator displays a trace of these interactions in the top text area.

All of the communications among Buyers, Sellers, and the Facilitator use the **CIAgent-Event** and **CIAgentEventListener** interface described in Chapter 7. The argument object that is passed with the **CIAgentEvent**s is a new object called a **BuySellMessage**, which is modeled after a standard KQML message. Although we are not parsing KQML messages in this application, the use of the **BuySellMessage** class should give you a good feel for what a KQML agent application would look like (refer to Chapter 6, "Agents and Multiagent Systems," for a description of KQML). Remember that KQML uses performatives to indicate the action that it wants another agent to take on its behalf. While KQML specifies the format and some of the content of these interactions, the nitty-gritty details of the Buyer-Seller negotiation are up to the application to define. We describe the sales negotiation convention that the *MarketPlace* application uses in the following list.

After all agents are registered with the Facilitator and the Sellers advertise their wares, the following **BuySellMessage**s are exchanged:

1. The Buyer asks the Facilitator to *recommend-one* Seller for an item, P.

2. The Facilitator *tells* the Buyer the name of the Seller.

3. The Buyer *asks* the Seller (through the facilitator) if the Seller has an item P for sale.

4. The Seller either performs a *make-offer* to the Buyer (passing the item P, a unique item ID, and an initial asking price) or will *deny* that it has item P for sale.

5. The Buyer then can either *accept* the offer by echoing the offer back to the Seller or make a counter offer (with a different price) to the Seller.

6. The Seller can either *accept* the offer, make a counter offer, or *reject* the offer.

7. If the Seller *accepts* the offer, it will send a *tell* message to the Buyer. Then, the sales transaction will be complete.

8. If the Seller *reject*s the offer, the negotiation is over.

Note that the Buyer and Seller never communicate directly but always use the Facilitator as a go-between in a sales negotiation. (Note that a facilitator agent that stays in the middle is sometimes called a broker agent. We will use the name Facilitator, however, because that is the basic role that the agent plays in this application. The **Facilitator-Agent** stays in the middle purely as a convenience for tracing and would otherwise step aside and let the agents interact directly.)

An Example

The following example illustrates the interactions between a single basic **BuyerAgent** and a single basic **SellerAgent**. The application is started by entering the following command:

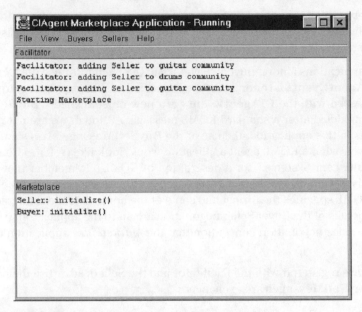

Figure 10.2 MarketPlace Example 1.

```
> java marketplace.MarketplaceApp
```

When the *MarketPlace* main window comes up, the application is started by selecting the **Start** option in the **File** menu. Figure 10.2 shows the main window right after Start is selected but before any sales transactions begin.

The **BuyerAgent** goes to sleep for approximately five seconds before it wakes up and picks the first item from its shopping list. This pause between negotiations makes it easier to follow the messages exchanged between agents. The Buyer has a short list of items to buy: a guitar for $100, a set of drums for $200, and another guitar for $100 (must be starting a power trio?). As it turns out, the **SellerAgent** just happens to have two guitars and one set of drums in his inventory. As described previously, the **Buyer-Agent** asks the Facilitator to recommend the name of a **SellerAgent** who has a guitar to sell. Because there is only one **SellerAgent**, the Facilitator returns the name of the **SellerAgent** to the **BuyerAgent**, and things progress from that point. When the first item is sold, the **BuyerAgent** goes back to sleep for another five seconds. When the **BuyerAgent** wakes up, it pulls the next item off the shopping list, and another set of communications occurs. This sequence continues until the **BuyerAgent** has exhausted its shopping list. When the marketplace has become quiescent, and no activity remains other than the Buyer proudly proclaiming its purchases, the *MarketPlace* application run can be halted by selecting the **Stop** menu option under the **File** menu.

When a **SellerAgent** sells an item, it sends an unadvertise message to the Facilitator, and the **SellerAgent** is removed from the list. Note that if a Seller has multiple items of the same type, it advertises multiple times. As a result, for each sale and each corre-

```
Facilitator: adding Seller to guitar community
Facilitator: adding Seller to drums community
Facilitator: adding Seller to guitar community
Starting Marketplace
Facilitator: Recommended Seller to Buyer for guitar
Facilitator: routing ask message from Buyer to Seller
Facilitator: routing make-offer message from Seller to Buyer
Facilitator: routing make-offer message from Buyer to Seller
Facilitator: routing accept-offer message from Seller to Buyer
Facilitator: routing tell message from Buyer to Seller
Facilitator: removing Seller from guitar community
Facilitator: Recommended Seller to Buyer for drums
Facilitator: routing ask message from Buyer to Seller
Facilitator: routing make-offer message from Seller to Buyer
Facilitator: routing make-offer message from Buyer to Seller
Facilitator: routing accept-offer message from Seller to Buyer
Facilitator: routing tell message from Buyer to Seller
Facilitator: removing Seller from drums community
Facilitator: Recommended Seller to Buyer for guitar
Facilitator: routing ask message from Buyer to Seller
Facilitator: routing make-offer message from Seller to Buyer
Facilitator: routing make-offer message from Buyer to Seller
Facilitator: routing accept-offer message from Seller to Buyer
Facilitator: routing tell message from Buyer to Seller
Facilitator: removing Seller from guitar community
Ending Marketplace
```

Figure 10.3 Facilitator trace log from Example 1.

sponding unadvertise message, the Facilitator always has an up-to-date list of Sellers and items that are available.

Figure 10.3 contains the trace messages from the Facilitator that appear in the top text area. You can see that the **FacilitatorAgent** is started when the *startAgentProcessing()* method is called and is halted when the *stopAgentProcessing()* method is called. Lines 5 through 11 reflect the first transaction between the Buyer and the Seller. Figure 10.4 contains the trace messages from the agents in the *MarketPlace*. The *startAgentProcessing()* method starts both agents. When the **BuyerAgent** wakes up, it announces that it wants to buy a guitar. The exchange of offers follows, and the transaction completes. Note that this level is the default **Summary** level of trace messages. If the **Details** option was selected, additional information would be displayed, including the contents of the **BuySellMessages**.

As you can see, the basic **BuyerAgent** and basic **SellerAgent** came to a price of $175 for the guitars and $300 for the drums. These prices are much higher than the Buyer's goal prices. Similar runs can be done for the Intermediate Buyer and Intermediate Seller, or the Best Buyer can be matched against the Basic Seller. In this case, the Buyer

```
Seller: initialize()
Buyer: initialize()
Buyer is looking to buy guitar
Buyer has purchased 0 items for 0
Buyer: Offer from Seller: content is guitar Seller1 200
Seller: Offer from Buyer: content is guitar Seller1 175
Buyer: Offer from Seller: content is guitar Seller1 175
Buyer: OK -- sale of item guitar with id Seller1 at price of 175 is
  complete
Buyer: guitar purchased!
Seller: Offer from Buyer: content is guitar Seller1 175
Buyer is looking to buy drums
Buyer has purchased 1 items for 175
Buyer: Offer from Seller: content is drums Seller2 325
Seller: Offer from Buyer: content is drums Seller2 300
Buyer: Offer from Seller: content is drums Seller2 300
Buyer: OK -- sale of item drums with id Seller2 at price of 300 is
  complete
Buyer: drums purchased!
Seller: Offer from Buyer: content is drums Seller2 300
Seller has 1 items in inventory.
Seller has earned 475.
Buyer is looking to buy guitar
Buyer has purchased 2 items for 475
Buyer: Offer from Seller: content is guitar Seller3 200
Seller: Offer from Buyer: content is guitar Seller3 175
Buyer: Offer from Seller: content is guitar Seller3 175
Buyer: OK -- sale of item guitar with id Seller3 at price of 175 is
  complete
Buyer: guitar purchased!
Seller: Offer from Buyer: content is guitar Seller3 175
Buyer has purchased 3 items for 650
Buyer has purchased 3 items for 650
Ending Marketplace
```

Figure 10.4 MarketPlace trace log from Example 1.

does much better, as shown in Figure 10.5. The Buyer purchases the three musical instruments for $500.

The last example presents the negotiations between the **BestBuyerAgent** and the **BestSellerAgent**. Figure 10.6 shows this exchange. There is much more haggling going on because the strategies that are implemented in the rule-bases of these agents are more complex. The **BestBuyerAgent** gets the better of the **BestSellerAgent**, completing its three purchases for only $470.

These examples show the basic operation and interactions among agents in *Market-Place*. In the following sections, we describe the design and implementation details of

```
Seller: initialize()
BestBuyer: initialize()
BestBuyer is looking to buy guitar
BestBuyer has purchased 0 items for 0
BestBuyer: Offer from Seller: content is guitar Seller1 200
Seller: Offer from BestBuyer: content is guitar Seller1 125
BestBuyer: Offer from Seller: content is guitar Seller1 125
BestBuyer: OK -- sale of item guitar with id Seller1 at price of 125
  is complete
BestBuyer: guitar purchased!
Seller: Offer from BestBuyer: content is guitar Seller1 125
BestBuyer is looking to buy drums
BestBuyer has purchased 1 items for 125
BestBuyer: Offer from Seller: content is drums Seller2 325
Seller: Offer from BestBuyer: content is drums Seller2 250
BestBuyer: Offer from Seller: content is drums Seller2 250
BestBuyer: OK -- sale of item drums with id Seller2 at price of 250 is
  complete
BestBuyer: drums purchased!
Seller: Offer from BestBuyer: content is drums Seller2 250
Seller has 1 items in inventory.
Seller has earned 375.
BestBuyer is looking to buy guitar
BestBuyer has purchased 2 items for 375
BestBuyer: Offer from Seller: content is guitar Seller3 200
Seller: Offer from BestBuyer: content is guitar Seller3 125
BestBuyer: Offer from Seller: content is guitar Seller3 125
BestBuyer: OK -- sale of item guitar with id Seller3 at price of 125
  is complete
BestBuyer: guitar purchased!
Seller: Offer from BestBuyer: content is guitar Seller3 125
BestBuyer has purchased 3 items for 500
BestBuyer has purchased 3 items for 500
Seller has 0 items in inventory.
Seller has earned 500.
BestBuyer has purchased 3 items for 500
BestBuyer has purchased 3 items for 500
Ending Marketplace
```

Figure 10.5   MarketPlace trace log from Example 2.

```
BestSeller: initialize()
BestBuyer: initialize()
BestBuyer is looking to buy guitar
```

(continues)

Figure 10.6   MarketPlace trace log from Example 3.

```
BestBuyer has purchased 0 items for 0
BestBuyer: Offer from BestSeller: content is guitar BestSeller1 200
BestSeller: Offer from BestBuyer: content is guitar BestSeller1 125
BestBuyer: Offer from BestSeller: content is guitar BestSeller1 175
BestSeller: Offer from BestBuyer: content is guitar BestSeller1 125
BestBuyer: Offer from BestSeller: content is guitar BestSeller1 165
BestSeller: Offer from BestBuyer: content is guitar BestSeller1 115
BestBuyer: Offer from BestSeller: content is guitar BestSeller1 115
BestBuyer: OK -- sale of item guitar with id BestSeller1 at price of
   115 is complete
BestBuyer: guitar purchased!
BestBuyer is looking to buy drums
BestBuyer has purchased 1 items for 115
BestSeller: Offer from BestBuyer: content is guitar BestSeller1 115
BestBuyer: Offer from BestSeller: content is drums BestSeller2 325
BestSeller: Offer from BestBuyer: content is drums BestSeller2 250
BestBuyer: Offer from BestSeller: content is drums BestSeller2 300
BestSeller: Offer from BestBuyer: content is drums BestSeller2 250
BestBuyer: Offer from BestSeller: content is drums BestSeller2 290
BestSeller: Offer from BestBuyer: content is drums BestSeller2 240
BestSeller has 1 items in inventory.
BestSeller has earned 115.
BestBuyer: Offer from BestSeller: content is drums BestSeller2 240
BestBuyer: OK -- sale of item drums with id BestSeller2 at price of
   240 is complete
BestBuyer: drums purchased!
BestBuyer is looking to buy guitar
BestBuyer has purchased 2 items for 355
BestSeller: Offer from BestBuyer: content is drums BestSeller2 240
BestBuyer: Offer from BestSeller: content is guitar BestSeller3 200
BestSeller: Offer from BestBuyer: content is guitar BestSeller3 125
BestBuyer: Offer from BestSeller: content is guitar BestSeller3 175
BestSeller: Offer from BestBuyer: content is guitar BestSeller3 125
BestBuyer: Offer from BestSeller: content is guitar BestSeller3 165
BestSeller: Offer from BestBuyer: content is guitar BestSeller3 115
BestBuyer: Offer from BestSeller: content is guitar BestSeller3 115
BestBuyer: OK -- sale of item guitar with id BestSeller3 at price of
   115 is complete
BestBuyer: guitar purchased!
BestBuyer has purchased 3 items for 470
BestSeller: Offer from BestBuyer: content is guitar BestSeller3 115
BestBuyer has purchased 3 items for 470
BestSeller has 0 items in inventory.
BestSeller has earned 470.
BestBuyer has purchased 3 items for 470
BestBuyer has purchased 3 items for 470
Ending Marketplace
```

Figure 10.6 MarketPlace trace log from Example 3 (Continued).

the **FacilitatorAgent**, **BuyerAgent**, **SellerAgent**, the enhanced Buyer and Seller agents, and the *MarketPlace* main application itself.

FacilitatorAgent

The **FacilitatorAgent**, listed in Figure 10.7, uses the Singleton design pattern ([Gamma et al. 1995]), which ensures that only a single instance of **FacilitatorAgent** exists at one time. This feature prevents an impostor Facilitator from redirecting sales traffic to its own favorite agents and ensures that all Buyers and Sellers can find the marketplace through the global **FacilitatorAgent** instance. We favor a model-view-controller design, where the agents in the marketplace represent the model and the **MarketPlaceFrame** Graphical User Interface (GUI) represents the view and the controller. The **MarketplaceFrame** class implements the **CIAgentEventListener** interface and receives all trace and message events that the Buyer and Seller agents send.

```
package marketplace;

import java.util.*;
import javax.swing.*;
import ciagent.*;

public class FacilitatorAgent extends CIAgent {
  private static FacilitatorAgent instance = null;
  protected Random random = new Random();
  protected Hashtable allAgents = new Hashtable();
  protected Hashtable communities = new Hashtable();
  protected BuySellMessage msg;

  protected FacilitatorAgent() {
    this("Facilitator");
  }

  protected FacilitatorAgent(String name) {
    super(name);
  }

  public void initialize() {
    setSleepTime(10 * 1000);
    setState(CIAgentState.INITIATED);
  }

  public void reset() {
```

(continues)

Figure 10.7 The **FacilitatorAgent** class listing.

```
    allAgents = new Hashtable();
    communities = new Hashtable();
  }

  public String getTaskDescription() {
    return null;
  }

  public void process() {}

  public void processTimerPop() {
    if(traceLevel > 0) {
      trace("Facilitator: active \n");
    }
  }

  public void processCIAgentEvent(CIAgentEvent e) {
    if(traceLevel > 0) {
      trace("Facilitator:  CIAgentEvent received by " + name + "
        from "
            + e.getSource() + " with args " + e.getArgObject()
              + "\n");
    }
    Object arg = e.getArgObject();
    Object action = e.getAction();

    if((action != null) && (action.equals("processMessage"))) {
      msg = (BuySellMessage) arg;
      if(traceLevel > 0) {
        msg.display();
      }
      route(msg);
    }
  }

  static public FacilitatorAgent getInstance() {
    if(instance == null) {
      instance = new FacilitatorAgent("Facilitator");
    }
    return instance;
  }

  public static synchronized void register(CIAgentEvent e) {
    if(instance == null) {
      instance = new FacilitatorAgent();
    }
    instance.allAgents.put(((CIAgent) e.getSource()).getName(),
```

Figure 10.7 The **FacilitatorAgent** class listing (Continued).

```
            e.getSource());
    ((CIAgent) e.getSource()).addCIAgentEventListener(instance);
    instance.addCIAgentEventListener((CIAgent) e.getSource());
}

public synchronized void route(BuySellMessage msg) {
    CIAgent sender = (CIAgent) allAgents.get(msg.sender);

    if(msg.performative.equals("advertise")) {
        trace("Facilitator: adding " + msg.sender + " to " + msg.content
            + " community \n");
        if(communities.containsKey(msg.content)) {
            Vector agents = (Vector) communities.get(msg.content);

            agents.addElement(sender);
        } else {
            Vector agents = new Vector();

            communities.put(msg.content, agents);
            agents.addElement(sender);
        }
        return;
    }
    if(msg.performative.equals("unadvertise")) {
        trace("Facilitator: removing " + msg.sender + " from " +
            msg.content
            + " community \n");
        if(communities.containsKey(msg.content)) {
            Vector agents = (Vector) communities.get(msg.content);

            agents.removeElement(sender);
            if(agents.size() == 0) {
                communities.remove(msg.content);
            }
        }
        return;
    }
    if(msg.performative.equals("recommend-one")) {
        String item = msg.content;

        if(communities.containsKey(msg.content)) {
            Vector agents = (Vector) communities.get(msg.content);
            int num = agents.size();
            int index;

            if(num > 1) {
```

(continues)

Figure 10.7 Continued.

```
            double rand = random.nextDouble();

            index = (int) (rand * num);
        } else {
          index = 0;
        }
        CIAgent agent = (CIAgent) agents.elementAt(index);

        msg.performative = "tell";
        msg.content = agent.getName();
        msg.receiver = msg.sender;
        msg.sender = name;
        trace("Facilitator: Recommended " + agent.getName() + " to "
              + msg.receiver + " for " + item + "\n");
        sender.postCIAgentEvent(new CIAgentEvent(this,
          "processMessage",
            msg));
      } else {
        trace("Facilitator: there are no agents advertising "
              + msg.content + "\n");
      }
      return;
    }
    trace("Facilitator: routing " + msg.performative + " message
      from "
          + msg.sender + " to " + msg.receiver + "\n");
    CIAgent receiver = (CIAgent) allAgents.get(msg.receiver);

    if(receiver != null) {
      receiver.postCIAgentEvent(new CIAgentEvent(this,
        "processMessage",
          msg));
    } else {
      trace("Facilitator: receiver " + msg.receiver + " is
        unknown! \n");
    }
  }
}
```

Figure 10.7 The **FacilitatorAgent** class listing (Continued).

The Facilitator contains two **Hashtables**—one that is a registry for all agents in the marketplace and one that contains the communities that are of interest in the marketplace. For example, there might be a set of **SellerAgents** that sells musical instruments and another set that sells airplane tickets. These sets are grouped into communities or domains. **SellerAgents** are added to these communities by advertising their willingness or ability to sell a product in that domain. Just because an agent advertises something, however, does not mean that it can really deliver that product or service. Besides the obvious case where deviousness is involved, a sincere Seller might advertise a one-of-a-kind item. A Buyer might then ask the Facilitator to recommend a Seller for this item. Negotiations could proceed between the Seller and the Buyer, resulting in a sale. Meanwhile, another Buyer could ask the Facilitator to recommend a Seller, and when it contacts the Seller and asks for a price, the Seller will deny that it has such an item. This scenario can be prevented if the Seller always retracts its advertisements. This application provides this capability. If multiple transactions are going on at the same time, however, one Buyer will have to be disappointed (or the Seller could sell the same item to two Buyers, which is unethical but very profitable in the short term).

As a subclass of **CIAgent**, the **FacilitatorAgent** contains a **CIAgentTimer** instance that is **Runnable**. The **CIAgent** *startAgentProcessing()* method is used to start its thread. This method sleeps for 10 seconds (as specified in the *initialize()* method) and then wakes up to see whether anything exciting is happening. Note that this function is not strictly necessary for this application. The **FacilitatorAgent** alternately runs on the Buyer and Seller agent threads by synchronously handling their **CIAgentEvent** messages. This function enables us to simplify the logic in the Buyer and Seller agents. An alternative design for long-running transactions would be to spin a new thread in the **FacilitatorAgent** whenever an event needs to be processed.

The **CIAgentEventListener** interface requires the *processCIAgentEvent()* method. The **CIAgentEvent** object contains the source object that fired the event (retrieved by using the *getSource()* method on the **CIAgentEvent** object) and the argument object that is retrieved by using the *getArgObject()* method. In all cases in the *MarketPlace* application, this argument object is a **BuySellMessage** object, which is roughly equivalent to a KQML message packet. Once the **BuySellMessage** is extracted from the **CIAgentEvent**, the *route()* method is called to process the message.

The *route()* method takes a **BuySellMessage** as a parameter. The method gets a reference to the sending **CIAgent** from the **Hashtable** of registered agents. In addition to its message routing function, the Facilitator handles three types of performatives in this method: *advertise*, *unadvertise*, and *recommend-one*. The *advertise* and *unadvertise* performatives either add or remove the sending agent from a community. Special logic is needed in order to handle the cases in which the agent is the first to be added or the last to be removed from a community.

First, the *recommend-one* performative determines whether there are any agents in the community of interest. If so, the Facilitator determines how many agents have advertised and then generates a random number in order to select an agent to recommend to the **BuyerAgent**. The case in which a **BuyerAgent** asks for a **SellerAgent** and none have advertised results in an undefined state in the sample application. The **BuyerAgent** is expecting a *tell* response from the Facilitator (which never comes). A reasonable solution here would be to send a *deny* message back to the **BuyerAgent**. The **BuyerAgent** state logic would have to be updated, however, in order to deal with this situation correctly.

BuySellMessage

We use the **BuySellMessage** class in Figure 10.8 as the argument object in a **CIAgent-Event**. This class is basically a collection of data that corresponds to the major slots of a KQML message. The class has two constructors, with the only difference being that one enables the specification of the language and ontology and the other does not. Each **Buy-SellMessage** must specify a *performative*, a *content* string, the *sender* agent's name, and the *receiver* agent's name. In a buyer/seller transaction, these would be the names of the Buyer and Seller agents (although the messages are routed through the **FacilitatorAgent**). The *replyWith* parameter tells the **receiver** object to use that **String** in the *inReplyTo* slot in the reply message. All of the parameters are protected but are still visible to other classes in the *marketplace* package. **EventObjects** are usually immutable, so this approach would be desired in a real application.

```java
package marketplace;

import java.io.*;
import java.util.*;

public class BuySellMessage {
  protected String performative;
  protected String content;
  protected String inReplyTo;
  protected String language;
  protected String ontology;
  protected String receiver;
  protected String replyWith;
  protected String sender;

  BuySellMessage(String Performative, String Content, String
                 InReplyTo, String Language, String Ontology, String
                 Receiver,String ReplyWith, String Sender) {
    performative = Performative;
    content = Content;
    inReplyTo = InReplyTo;
    language = Language;
    ontology = Ontology;
    receiver = Receiver;
    replyWith = ReplyWith;
    sender = Sender;
  }
```

Figure 10.8 The **BuySellMessage** class listing.

```
BuySellMessage(String Performative, String Content, String
            InReplyTo,String Receiver, String ReplyWith, String
            Sender) {
  performative = Performative;
  content = Content;
  inReplyTo = InReplyTo;
  receiver = Receiver;
  replyWith = ReplyWith;
  sender = Sender;
}

public void display() {
  System.out.println("performative: " + performative + "\n"
                + "content: " + content + "\n" + "inReplyTo: "
                + inReplyTo + "\n" + "language: " + language
                + "\n"+ "ontology: " + ontology + "\n"
                + "receiver: " + receiver + "\n"
                + "replyWith: " + replyWith + "\n" + "sender: "
                + sender + "\n");

}
}
```

Figure 10.8 Continued.

BuyerAgent

The **BuyerAgent** class, shown in Figure 10.9, contains the base functionality for all of the Buyers. The major data members include the *wishList*, which is a **Vector** of items that the agent wants to buy and desired purchase prices; the *inventory*, which contains all of the items that the **BuyerAgent** has purchased; and the *negotiations*, which are a **Hashtable** of negotiations that are in progress. The *initialize()* method registers the **BuyerAgent** with the global Facilitator, initializes the *wishList* with instances of **Basic-Negotiation** objects, and starts the agent's **Thread** running. The *processTimerPop()* method provides the body of the agent's thread. This method goes to sleep for five seconds, and then if it still has items on its *wishList* and no negotiation is in progress, it takes the first item off the *wishList* and kicks off a negotiation by asking the Facilitator to recommend a Seller for the item. This method performs this function by first instantiating a **BuySellMessage** object and setting the slots appropriately and then using it as the argument for a new **CIAgentEvent** object. When the **BuyerAgent** registered with the Facilitator, the Facilitator added itself to the **BuyerAgent**'s **CIAgentEventListener** list. So, calling the *notifyCIAgentEventListener()* method results in the Facilitator receiving a copy of the **BuySellMessage**.

The Facilitator will reply to the **BuyerAgent** by sending a **BuySellMessage**. All such messages are received through the *processCIAgentEvent()* method, which is the **Buyer-Agent's** method for receiving messages from other agents in the marketplace. The

```
package marketplace;

import java.util.*;
import ciagent.*;

public class BuyerAgent extends CIAgent {
  protected BuySellMessage msg;
  protected BasicNegotiation current;
  protected Vector wishList = new Vector();
  protected BasicNegotiation pending = null;
  protected Hashtable inventory = new Hashtable();
  protected long totalSpent = 0;
  protected Hashtable negotiations = new Hashtable();

  public BuyerAgent() {
    this("Buyer");
  }

  public BuyerAgent(String Name) {
    super(Name);
  }

  public void initialize() {
    trace(name + ": initialize() \n");
    msg = new BuySellMessage("register:", name, null, null, null,
      null);
    CIAgentEvent e = new CIAgentEvent(this, "processMessage", msg);

    FacilitatorAgent.register(e);
    wishList.addElement(new BasicNegotiation("guitar", 100));
    wishList.addElement(new BasicNegotiation("drums", 200));
    wishList.addElement(new BasicNegotiation("guitar", 100));
    setSleepTime(5 * 1000);
    setState(CIAgentState.INITIATED);
  }

  public String getTaskDescription() {
    return "Buying stuff...";
  }

  public void process() {}

  public void processTimerPop() {
    if((wishList.size() > 0) && (pending == null)) {
      current = (BasicNegotiation) wishList.firstElement();
      pending = current;
      wishList.removeElementAt(0);
```

Figure 10.9 The **BuyerAgent** class listing.

```
      trace(name + " is looking to buy " + current.offer.item + "\n");
      msg = new BuySellMessage("recommend-one", current.offer.item,
          null, "Seller", current.offer.item, name);
      CIAgentEvent e = new CIAgentEvent(this, "processMessage", msg);

      notifyCIAgentEventListeners(e);
    }
    trace(name + " has purchased " + inventory.size() + " items for "
        + totalSpent + "\n");
  }

  public void processCIAgentEvent(CIAgentEvent e) {
    if(traceLevel > 0) {
      trace(name + ":  CIAgentEvent received by " + name + " from "
          + e.getSource() + " with args " + e.getArgObject());
    }
    Object arg = e.getArgObject();
    Object action = e.getAction();

    if((action != null) && (action.equals("processMessage"))) {
      msg = (BuySellMessage) arg;
      if(traceLevel > 0) {
        msg.display();
      }
      processMessage(msg);
    }
  }

  public void processMessage(BuySellMessage msg) {
    if(msg.sender.equals("Facilitator")) {
      if(msg.performative.equals("tell")) {
        BuySellMessage answer = new BuySellMessage("ask",
                              pending.offer.item, msg.replyWith,
                              msg.content, pending.offer.item,
                              name);
        CIAgentEvent e = new CIAgentEvent(this, "processMessage",
          answer);

        notifyCIAgentEventListeners(e);
        return;
      }
    }
    if(msg.performative.equals("deny")) {
      trace(name + ": Seller denied our 'ask' about " + msg.content
          + "\n");
      wishList.addElement(pending);
```

(continues)

Figure 10.9 Continued.

```
      pending = null;
      return;
   }
   Offer offer = new Offer(msg);

   trace(name + ": Offer from " + offer.sender + ": content is "
         + offer.item + " " + offer.id + " " + offer.price + "\n");
   if(negotiations.containsKey(offer.id)) {
     current = (BasicNegotiation) negotiations.get(offer.id);
   } else {
     current = pending;
     pending = null;
     negotiations.put(offer.id, current);
   }
   current.newOffer(offer);
   if(msg.performative.equals("accept-offer")) {
     trace(name + ": OK -- sale of item " + offer.item + " with id "
           + offer.id + " at price of " + offer.price
           + " is complete \n");
     BuySellMessage answer = new BuySellMessage("tell", msg.content,
                              msg.replyWith, msg.sender, offer.item,
                              name);

     trace(name + ": " + offer.item + " purchased! \n");
     inventory.put(offer.id, current);
     negotiations.remove(offer.id);
     totalSpent += offer.price;
     CIAgentEvent e = new CIAgentEvent(this, "processMessage",
       answer);

     notifyCIAgentEventListeners(e);
   }
   if(msg.performative.equals("make-offer")) {
     negotiate(offer, msg);
   }
   if(msg.performative.equals("reject-offer")) {
     trace(name + ": " + msg.sender + " rejected our last offer ");
     negotiations.remove(offer.id);
     wishList.addElement(current);
   }
}

void negotiate(Offer offer, BuySellMessage msg) {
   if(offer.price < current.strikePrice) {
     BuySellMessage answer = new BuySellMessage("make-offer",
                              msg.content, msg.replyWith,
                              msg.sender,
```

Figure 10.9   The **BuyerAgent** class listing (Continued).

```
                                        offer.item, name);
        CIAgentEvent e = new CIAgentEvent(this, "processMessage",
          answer);

        notifyCIAgentEventListeners(e);
      } else {
        current.lastOffer = offer.price - 25;
        BuySellMessage answer = new BuySellMessage("make-offer",
                              offer.item + " " + offer.id + " "
                              + current.lastOffer, offer.item,
                                                   msg.sender,
                                                   offer.item,
                                                   name);
        CIAgentEvent e = new CIAgentEvent(this, "processMessage",
          answer);

        notifyCIAgentEventListeners(e);
      }
    }
  }
```

Figure 10.9   Continued.

MarketPlace application supports two levels of tracing information: a *Summary* level of 0 and a *Details* level of 1. If details are desired, a trace message is displayed. Next, the **BuySellMessage** is extracted from the **CIAgentEvent** and the *processMessage( )* method is called, passing the message as a parameter.

The *processMessage( )* method is the workhorse of the **BuyerAgent**. There are several conditions that it must detect and handle. The first is when the Facilitator responds to the recommend request. This message is a *tell* performative, and the *content* is the name of a **SellerAgent** that has advertised the desired item. In this case, the Seller is asked (through the Facilitator) how much it wants for the item.

Otherwise, the message must contain an offer or counter-offer from a Seller. First, an instance of an **Offer** is created. An **Offer**, as shown in Figure 10.10, contains a triplet of item name, item identifier, and offer price along with the name of the Seller who is making the offer. The **Offer** constructor takes the **BuySellMessage** as a parameter and extracts the information from the sender and content slots of the message. Now that an **Offer** exists, we need to determine whether this offer is the first of a new negotiation or whether this offer is a counter-offer in an ongoing negotiation. If a **BasicNegotiation** object exists in the *negotiations* **Hashtable** with the same item identifier that is contained in the **Offer**, the **BasicNegotiation** object is updated by passing the latest **Offer** by using the *newOffer( )* method. If the item ID is not in the **Hashtable**, it must be the first offer from the **SellerAgent**. The **BuyerAgent** takes the *pending* negotiation, makes it the *current* one, sets *pending* to null, and places the negotiation on the active list.

```
package marketplace;

import java.util.*;

public class Offer {
  protected String sender;
  protected String item;
  protected String id;
  protected long price;

  Offer(String item) {
    sender = "";
    this.item = item;
    id = "";
    price = 0;
  }

  Offer(String sender, String item, String id, long price) {
    this.sender = sender;
    this.item = item;
    this.id = id;
    this.price = price;
  }

  Offer(BuySellMessage msg) {
    StringTokenizer s = new StringTokenizer(msg.content, " ");
    int num = s.countTokens();

    item = s.nextToken();
    id = s.nextToken();
    price = new Long(s.nextToken()).longValue();
    sender = msg.sender;
  }
}
```

Figure 10.10 The **Offer** class listing.

The **Offer** can contain one of three performatives: *make-offer*, *accept-offer*, or *reject-offer*. If the message is an *accept-offer*, the sale is acknowledged by sending a *tell* message back to the Seller. The item is put in the *inventory* of purchases; the *negotiation* is removed from the active list; the money that is spent is added to the tab; and the message is sent. The *pending* negotiation is also set to null so that the next time the **Buyer-Agent** wakes up, it can start a new negotiation if there are still items on its *wishList*. This behavior is an arbitrary design decision. We could just as easily have decided to immediately pull another negotiation off the *wishList*, but we chose this design to enable the transactions to be more spread out in time.

Another alternative is that the Seller rejects the last offer. In our design, this action ends the negotiations. Once again, this is an arbitrary decision, but we wanted to make explicit when the Seller decides to end a negotiation and not have the **BuyerAgent** try to make counter-offers to extend the negotiation. The **BuyerAgent** cleans up the negotiation from the active list and places it back on the *wishList* so that it can try again by asking the Facilitator to recommend another Seller for the item.

The third alternative is that the Seller makes an offer and the **BuyerAgent** needs to negotiate by using the (what else?) *negotiate( )* method. The sophistication of the processing logic in this method is the primary point of differentiation between our basic **BuyerAgent**, the **BetterBuyerAgent**, and the **BestBuyerAgent** classes.

The basic **BuyerAgent** checks whether the Seller's offer price is lower than the *strikePrice*, which is the desired maximum price. If it is, the BuyerAgent accepts the offer by echoing the message back to the Seller, assuming that the **SellerAgent** will accept the offer that it just made. If the offer price is higher than the Buyer is willing to pay, the **BuyerAgent** must make a counter-offer (remember that in this design, only the Seller can reject an offer). The basic agent simply takes $25 off the Seller's price and makes an offer in the hopes that the Seller will accept. Later in this chapter, we will explore the more sophisticated strategies that our **BetterBuyerAgent** and **BestBuyerAgent** use.

SellerAgent

The **SellerAgent** class, listed in Figure 10.11, contains the base functionality for all Sellers. The major data members include the *inventory*, which is a **Hashtable** of items that the agent wants to sell and desired sales prices, and the *negotiations*, which are a **Hashtable** of negotiations that are in progress. The *initialize( )* method registers the **SellerAgent** with the global Facilitator, initializes the *inventory* with instances of **BasicNegotiation** objects, advertises the items to the Facilitator, and starts the agent's **Thread** running. The *processTimerPop( )* method provides the body of the agent's thread. This method goes to sleep for 15 seconds and then reports the status of its inventory.

After the **SellerAgent** advertises its wares to the Facilitator, it must wait for a prospective **BuyerAgent** to contact the Facilitator (looking for a recommendation of a likely Seller). When the Facilitator passes the **SellerAgent**'s name to the **BuyerAgent**, the Buyer sends an *ask* message to start the negotiations. Like the **BuyerAgent** that we described previously, the **SellerAgent** receives any message as an argument from a **CIAgentEvent** through the *processCIAgentEvent( )* method. The *processMessage( )* method interprets the message and determines the appropriate response.

The *processMessage( )* method must take care of two basic situations. First, the method must respond to an initial *ask* from a **BuyerAgent.** It also must respond to an offer. In the first case, there is a lot of housekeeping to do when a **BuyerAgent** asks about an item. First, the method must check to determine whether it still has any of the desired items in inventory (as described previously, it could have just sold the last one). Assuming that it has the item, the method then generates a unique item identifier by calling the *genID( )* method. The item identifier is the **SellerAgent**'s name concatenated with a

```
package marketplace;

import java.util.*;
import ciagent.*;

public class SellerAgent extends CIAgent {
  private long seed = 0;
  protected BuySellMessage msg;
  protected BasicNegotiation current;
  protected long income = 0;
  protected Vector inventory = new Vector();
  protected Hashtable negotiations = new Hashtable();

  public SellerAgent() {
    this("Seller");
  }

  public SellerAgent(String Name) {
    super(Name);
  }

  public String getTaskDescription() {
    return "Selling stuff...";
  }

  public void initialize() {
    trace(name + ": initialize() \n");
    msg = new BuySellMessage("register:", name, null, null, null,
      null);
    CIAgentEvent e = new CIAgentEvent(this, "processMessage", msg);

    FacilitatorAgent.register(e);
    inventory.addElement(new BasicNegotiation("guitar", 100));
    inventory.addElement(new BasicNegotiation("drums", 225));
    inventory.addElement(new BasicNegotiation("guitar", 100));
    Enumeration enum = inventory.elements();

    while(enum.hasMoreElements()) {
      current = (BasicNegotiation) enum.nextElement();
      msg = new BuySellMessage("advertise", current.offer.item, null,
          null, current.offer.item, name);
      e = new CIAgentEvent(this, "processMessage", msg);
      notifyCIAgentEventListeners(e);
    }
    setSleepTime(15 * 1000);
    setState(CIAgentState.INITIATED);
  }
```

Figure 10.11   The **SellerAgent** class listing.

```
public void process() {}

public void processTimerPop() {
  trace(name + " has " + inventory.size() + " items in inventory.
    \n");
  trace(name + " has earned " + income + ".\n");
}

public void processCIAgentEvent(CIAgentEvent e) {
  if(traceLevel > 0) {
    trace(name + ":  CIAgentEvent received by " + name + " from "
          + e.getSource() + " with args " + e.getArgObject());
  }
  Object arg = e.getArgObject();
  Object action = e.getAction();

  if((action != null) && (action.equals("processMessage"))) {
    msg = (BuySellMessage) arg;
    if(traceLevel > 0) {
      msg.display();
    }
    processMessage(msg);
  }
}

String genId() {
  seed++;
  return name + seed;
}

public void processMessage(BuySellMessage msg) {
  if(msg.performative.equals("ask")) {
    String item = msg.content;

    if(itemInInventory(item)) {
      String id = genId();

      current = removeItemFromInventory(item);
      current.offer = new Offer(msg.sender, item, id, 0);
      current.lastOffer = current.strikePrice + 100;
      negotiations.put(id, current);
      BuySellMessage answer = new BuySellMessage("make-offer",
                              item + " " + id + " "
                              + current.lastOffer, msg.replyWith,
                                                   msg.sender,
                                                   item, name);
```

(continues)

Figure 10.11   Continued.

```
          CIAgentEvent e = new CIAgentEvent(this, "processMessage",
            answer);

          notifyCIAgentEventListeners(e);
        } else {
          BuySellMessage answer = new BuySellMessage("deny", item,
                                  msg.replyWith, msg.sender, item,
                                  name);
          CIAgentEvent e = new CIAgentEvent(this, "processMessage",
            answer);

          trace(name + ": deny we have any " + item + " to sell to "
              + msg.sender + "\n");
          notifyCIAgentEventListeners(e);
        }
        return;
      }
      Offer offer = new Offer(msg);

      trace(name + ": Offer from " + offer.sender + ": content is "
          + offer.item + " " + offer.id + " " + offer.price + "\n");
      current = (BasicNegotiation) negotiations.get(offer.id);
      if(current == null) {
        BuySellMessage answer = new BuySellMessage("reject-offer",
                                  msg.content, msg.replyWith,
                                  msg.sender, offer.item, name);
        CIAgentEvent e = new CIAgentEvent(this, "processMessage",
          answer);

        notifyCIAgentEventListeners(e);
        return;
      }
      current.newOffer(offer);
      if(msg.performative.equals("make-offer")) {
        negotiate(offer, msg);
      }
      if(msg.performative.equals("tell")) {
        negotiations.remove(offer.id);
        income += offer.price;
        BuySellMessage msg2 = new BuySellMessage("unadvertise",
                                current.offer.item, null, null,
                                current.offer.item, name);
        CIAgentEvent e = new CIAgentEvent(this, "processMessage", msg2);

        notifyCIAgentEventListeners(e);
      }
    }
```

Figure 10.11   The **SellerAgent** class listing (Continued).

```
void negotiate(Offer offer, BuySellMessage msg) {
  if(offer.price > current.strikePrice) {
    BuySellMessage answer = new BuySellMessage("accept-offer",
                            msg.content, msg.replyWith,
                            msg.sender, offer.item, name);
    CIAgentEvent e = new CIAgentEvent(this, "processMessage",
      answer);

    notifyCIAgentEventListeners(e);
    return;
  }
  if(offer.price < current.strikePrice) {
    rejectOffer(offer);
    return;
  }
  BuySellMessage answer = new BuySellMessage("make-offer",
                          offer.item + " " + offer.id + " "
                          + current.lastOffer, msg.replyWith,
                                              msg.sender,
                                              offer.item, name);
  CIAgentEvent e = new CIAgentEvent(this, "processMessage", answer);

  notifyCIAgentEventListeners(e);
}

void rejectOffer(Offer offer) {
  BuySellMessage answer = new BuySellMessage("reject-offer",
                          msg.content, msg.replyWith, msg.sender,
                          offer.item, name);
  CIAgentEvent e = new CIAgentEvent(this, "processMessage", answer);

  notifyCIAgentEventListeners(e);
  negotiations.remove(offer.id);
  current.offer.id = null;
  inventory.addElement(current);
}

boolean itemInInventory(String item) {
  Enumeration enum = inventory.elements();
  boolean haveItem = false;

  while(enum.hasMoreElements()) {
    BasicNegotiation stockItem = (BasicNegotiation)
      enum.nextElement();

    if(stockItem.getItem().equals(item)) {
```

(continues)

Figure 10.11 Continued.

```
          haveItem = true;
          break;
        } else {
          continue;
        }
      }
    }
    return haveItem;
  }

  BasicNegotiation removeItemFromInventory(String item) {
    Enumeration enum = inventory.elements();
    BasicNegotiation stockItem = null;

    while(enum.hasMoreElements()) {
      stockItem = (BasicNegotiation) enum.nextElement();
      if(stockItem.getItem().equals(item)) {
        inventory.removeElement(stockItem);
        break;
      } else {
        stockItem = null;
        continue;
      }
    }
    return stockItem;
  }
}
```

Figure 10.11 The **SellerAgent** class listing (Continued).

non-repeating integer (for example, Seller1 or BetterSeller3). This item identifier is then used as the **Hashtable** key for both the Buyer and Seller negotiation objects. The item's **BasicNegotiation** object is removed from the inventory list; the item *id* member is set; and the *lastOffer* field is initialized to the minimum selling price plus $100. The **Seller-Agent** then places the **BasicNegotiation** on the active negotiations list and sends a *make-offer* message back to the **BuyerAgent** through the Facilitator that is a registered **CIAgentEventListener**.

In the second case, there is a negotiation in progress. The **SellerAgent** instantiates an **Offer** from the **BuySellMessage** and retrieves the negotiation from the active negotiations list by using the item ID as the **Hashtable** key. If there is no **BasicNegotiation** object with that item *id*, the item must have just been sold. Therefore, the **SellerAgent** sends a *reject-offer* message to the **BuyerAgent**. Otherwise, it will update the **BasicNegotiation** with the current offer. Next, it determines whether the Buyer is making a counter-offer or is simply acknowledging a previous *accept-offer* message. If the offer is a *tell*, it must be the latter case (an item was just sold). The **BasicNegotiation** is removed from the active negotiations list, and the purchase price is added to the sales total.

If the performative is a *make-offer*, the *negotiate()* method is called in order to come up with an appropriate response. As in our **BuyerAgent**, subclasses override this method in order to introduce increasing levels of sophistication.

In the basic **SellerAgent**, if the Buyer's offer price is higher than the desired minimum selling price, the offer is immediately accepted and a message is sent back to the **Buyer-Agent**. The **BuyerAgent** must acknowledge the offer with a *tell* message before the item can be removed from inventory. If the **BuyerAgent** is offering less than the **Seller-Agent** is willing to take for the item, the **Offer** is rejected and the negotiations are closed by placing the item back in inventory (remember, this agent is the basic agent).

The *processMessage()* method calls the *itemInInventory()* method in response to an *ask* message from a Buyer in order to determine whether any items of that type are available to sell. An **Enumeration** is used to walk through the **Vector** to examine each item in *inventory*. A boolean *true* is returned when a match is found. The *removeItemFromInventory()* method has a similar structure to *itemInInventory()*. In this case, though, the found item is removed from the *inventory* **Vector** and the **BasicNegotiation** object is returned to the caller. The **BasicNegotiation** is used as a convenient holder for *inventory* items.

Enhanced Buyers and Sellers

In this section, we will describe improvements to our basic **BuyerAgent** and **SellerAgent**. These enhanced agents extend the **BuyerAgent** and **SellerAgent** classes primarily by overriding the *negotiate()* methods and by utilizing additional information about the negotiation process. The **BetterBuyerAgent** and **BetterSellerAgent** use hard-coded logic with a slightly more aggressive negotiation strategy and warrant no further discussion. The **BestBuyerAgent** and **BestSellerAgent** make use of the **BooleanRuleBase** class and if-then rules in order to determine their prices and actions during the negotiations.

We first focus on the **BestBuyerAgent** class, shown in Figure 10.12. As a subclass of **BuyerAgent**, it inherits all of the basic sales transaction behavior. **BestBuyerAgents** have the same *wishList* items and prices as the **BuyerAgents**. However, they make use of additional information in the **BasicNegotiation** object and also use a set of rules to determine what action to take in the negotiation process.

Several additional data members are added to the **BestBuyerAgent** class. These include *rb*, the **BooleanRuleBase** instance that is initialized in the overridden *initialize()* method, and several **RuleVariables** used in the **BooleanRuleBase**. The *initializeBest-BuyerRuleBase()* method defines the *offerDelta*, an intermediate output variable, and *spread* and *firstOffer*, which are antecedent variables. The *spread* variable is the difference between the current offered price and the asking or *strikePrice*. The *firstOffer* variable is a boolean value that is used to signal when a negotiation is just starting.

In addition to rules that compute the value of *offerDelta*, there are a couple of action rules. These rules have **EffectorClauses** as their consequence. When they fire, they call the *effector()* method that is defined in **BestBuyerAgent**. As described previously, the **Buyer Agent**s can only make offers to the **SellerAgent**s. If the forward-chaining

```
package marketplace;

import java.util.*;
import ciagent.*;
import rule.*;

public class BestBuyerAgent extends BuyerAgent implements Effector {
  protected BooleanRuleBase rb = new BooleanRuleBase("BestBuyer");
  protected RuleVariable offerDelta;
  protected RuleVariable spread;
  protected RuleVariable firstOffer;
  protected Offer offer;

  public BestBuyerAgent() {
    this("BestBuyer");
  }

  public BestBuyerAgent(String Name) {
    super(Name);
  }

  public void initialize() {
    initBestBuyerRuleBase();
    super.initialize();
  }

  public long effector(Object obj, String eName, String args) {
    if(eName.equals("make-offer")) {
      long delta = (new Long(offerDelta.getValue())).longValue();

      current.lastOffer = offer.price - delta;
      BuySellMessage answer = new BuySellMessage("make-offer",
                           offer.item + " " + offer.id + " "
                         + current.lastOffer, offer.item,
                                           msg.sender,
                                           offer.item,
                                           name);

      CIAgentEvent e = new CIAgentEvent(this, "processMessage",
        answer);

      notifyCIAgentEventListeners(e);
      return 0;
    }
    if(eName.equals("accept-offer")) {
      BuySellMessage answer = new BuySellMessage("make-offer",
                           msg.content, msg.replyWith,
                           msg.sender,  offer.item, name);
```

Figure 10.12 The **BestBuyerAgent** class listing.

```
        CIAgentEvent e = new CIAgentEvent(this, "processMessage",
            answer);

        notifyCIAgentEventListeners(e);
        return 0;
    }
    return 1;
}

void negotiate(Offer offer, BuySellMessage msg) {
    rb.reset();
    this.offer = offer;
    if(offer.price >= current.strikePrice) {
        long delta = offer.price - current.strikePrice;

        if(delta < 25) {
            spread.setValue("<25");
        } else if(delta < 50) {
            spread.setValue("25-50");
        } else if(delta >= 50) {
            spread.setValue(">50");
        }
    } else {
        spread.setValue("0");
    }
    if(current.prevOffer.id.equals("")) {
        firstOffer.setValue("yes");
    } else {
        firstOffer.setValue("no");
    }
    offerDelta.setValue(null);
    rb.forwardChain();
    if(offerDelta.getValue() == null) {
        trace(name + " rule base couldn't decide what to do.\n");
    }
}

public void initBestBuyerRuleBase() {
    offerDelta = new RuleVariable(rb, "offerDelta");
    offerDelta.setLabels("0 25 50 100");
    firstOffer = new RuleVariable(rb, "firstOffer");
    firstOffer.setLabels("yes no");
    spread = new RuleVariable(rb, "spread");
    spread.setLabels("<25 25-50 >50");
    Condition cEquals = new Condition("=");
    Condition cNotEquals = new Condition("!=");
```

(continues)

Figure 10.12 Continued.

```
        Rule first =
          new Rule(rb, "first",
            new Clause(firstOffer, cEquals, "yes"),
            new Clause(offerDelta, cEquals, "75"));
        Rule second1 =
          new Rule(rb, "second1",
            new Clause[]{ new Clause(firstOffer, cEquals, "no"),
              new Clause(spread, cEquals, ">50") },
            new Clause(offerDelta, cEquals, "50"));
        Rule second2 =
          new Rule(rb, "second2",
            new Clause[]{ new Clause(firstOffer, cEquals, "no"),
              new Clause(spread, cEquals, "25-50") },
            new Clause(offerDelta, cEquals, "25"));
        Rule second3 =
          new Rule(rb, "second3",
            new Clause[]{ new Clause(firstOffer, cEquals, "no"),
              new Clause(spread, cEquals, "<25") },
            new Clause(offerDelta, cEquals, "0"));
        Rule accept =
          new Rule(rb, "accept",
            new Clause(offerDelta, cEquals, "0"),
            new EffectorClause("accept-offer", "0"));
        Rule counter =
          new Rule(rb, "counter",
            new Clause(offerDelta, cNotEquals, "0"),
            new EffectorClause("make-offer", null));

        rb.addEffector(this, "make-offer");
        rb.addEffector(this, "accept-offer");
      }
    }
```

Figure 10.12 The **BestBuyerAgent** class listing (Continued).

inferencing decides to make a counter-offer or accept, the action rule calls the *effector()* method and the message is sent directly as a consequence (pun intended) of the rule firing. If the **BooleanRuleBase** did not support effector or action rules, an alternative design would be to compute the *offerDelta* and have hard-coded logic examine the value and determine what action to perform.

The negotiating strategy is more complex than in the **BuyerAgent** and **BetterBuyerAgent**, but it is not a masterpiece of haggling by any stretch of the imagination. If the Seller's offer is within $25 of the *strikePrice*, the offer is accepted. Otherwise, depending on the spread size, increasing amounts are deducted from the Seller's offer and a counter-offer is made. The intent is to show how domain knowledge in the form of rules could be integrated into an intelligent agent marketplace. In a commercial application, a more sophisticated rule base would be used.

Next, we focus on the **BestSellerAgent** class, shown in Figure 10.13. Much of its structure mirrors the changes to **BestBuyerAgent**. As a subclass of **SellerAgent**, it inherits all of the basic sales transaction behaviors. **BestSellerAgents** have the same inventory items and prices as the **SellerAgents**.

```java
package marketplace;

import java.util.*;
import ciagent.*;
import rule.*;

public class BestSellerAgent extends SellerAgent implements Effector {
  protected BooleanRuleBase rb = new BooleanRuleBase("BestSeller");
  protected RuleVariable offerDelta;
  protected RuleVariable spread;
  protected RuleVariable firstOffer;
  protected Offer offer;

  public BestSellerAgent() {
    this("BestSeller");
  }

  public BestSellerAgent(String Name) {
    super(Name);
  }

  public void initialize() {
    initBestSellerRuleBase();
    super.initialize();
  }

  public long effector(Object obj, String eName, String args) {
    if(eName.equals("make-offer")) {
      long delta = (new Long(offerDelta.getValue())).longValue();

      if(delta == -100) {
        current.lastOffer = current.strikePrice;
      } else {
        current.lastOffer = offer.price + delta;
      }
      BuySellMessage answer = new BuySellMessage("make-offer",
                          offer.item + " " + offer.id + " "
                        + current.lastOffer, offer.item,
                                              msg.sender,
                                              offer.item,
                                              name);
                                                 (continues)
```

Figure 10.13 The **BestSellerAgent** class listing.

```
      CIAgentEvent e = new CIAgentEvent(this, "processMessage",
        answer);

      notifyCIAgentEventListeners(e);
      return 0;
    }
    if(eName.equals("reject-offer")) {
      rejectOffer(offer);
      return 0;
    }
    if(eName.equals("accept-offer")) {
      BuySellMessage answer = new BuySellMessage("accept-offer",
                             msg.content, msg.replyWith,
                             msg.sender, offer.item, name);
      CIAgentEvent e = new CIAgentEvent(this, "processMessage",
        answer);

      notifyCIAgentEventListeners(e);
      return 0;
    }
    return 1;
}

void negotiate(Offer offer, BuySellMessage msg) {
    rb.reset();
    this.offer = offer;
    if(offer.price < current.strikePrice) {
      spread.setValue("<0");
    } else {
      long delta = offer.price - current.strikePrice;

      if(delta < 25) {
        spread.setValue("0-25");
      } else if(delta < 50) {
        spread.setValue("25-50");
      } else if(delta >= 50) {
        spread.setValue(">50");
      }
    }
    if(offer.price == current.lastOffer) {
      spread.setValue(">50");
    }
    if(current.iteration == 0) {
      firstOffer.setValue("yes");
    } else {
      firstOffer.setValue("no");
```

Figure 10.13 The **BestSellerAgent** class listing (Continued).

```
      }
    current.iteration++;
    if(current.iteration > 10) {
      rejectOffer(offer);
      return;
    }
    rb.forwardChain();
    if(offerDelta.getValue() == null) {
      trace(name
            + " rule base couldn't decide what to do -- so reject
              it.\n");
      rejectOffer(offer);
    }
  }
}

public void initBestSellerRuleBase() {
  offerDelta = new RuleVariable(rb, "offerDelta");
  offerDelta.setLabels("-100 0 30 60 100");
  firstOffer = new RuleVariable(rb, "firstOffer");
  firstOffer.setLabels("yes no");
  spread = new RuleVariable(rb, "spread");
  spread.setLabels("<0 0-25 25-50 >50");
  Condition cEquals = new Condition("=");
  Condition cNotEquals = new Condition("!=");
  Rule first =
    new Rule(rb, "first",
      new Clause(firstOffer, cEquals, "yes"),
      new Clause(offerDelta, cEquals, "50"));
  Rule second1 =
    new Rule(rb, "second1",
      new Clause[]{ new Clause(firstOffer, cEquals, "no"),
        new Clause(spread, cEquals, "25-50") },
      new Clause(offerDelta, cEquals, "40"));
  Rule second2 =
    new Rule(rb, "second2",
      new Clause[]{ new Clause(firstOffer, cEquals, "no"),
        new Clause(spread, cEquals, "0-25") },
      new Clause(offerDelta, cEquals, "0"));
  Rule second3 =
    new Rule(rb, "second3",
      new Clause[]{ new Clause(firstOffer, cEquals, "no"),
        new Clause(spread, cEquals, ">50") },
      new Clause(offerDelta, cEquals, "0"));
  Rule second4 =
    new Rule(rb, "second4",
      new Clause[]{ new Clause(firstOffer, cEquals, "no"),
```

(continues)

Figure 10.13 Continued.

```
            new Clause(spread, cEquals, "<0") },
        new Clause(offerDelta, cEquals, "-100"));
    Rule accept =
      new Rule(rb, "accept",
        new Clause(offerDelta, cEquals, "0"),
        new EffectorClause("accept-offer", "0"));
    Rule reject =
      new Rule(rb, "reject",
        new Clause[]{ new Clause(firstOffer, cEquals, "no"),
          new Clause(offerDelta, cEquals, "-100") },
        new EffectorClause("reject-offer", "0"));
    Rule counter =
      new Rule(rb, "counter",
        new Clause(offerDelta, cNotEquals, "0"),
        new EffectorClause("make-offer", null));

    rb.addEffector(this, "make-offer");
    rb.addEffector(this, "reject-offer");
    rb.addEffector(this, "accept-offer");
  }
}
```

Figure 10.13   The **BestSellerAgent** class listing (Continued).

Additional data members are added to the **BestSellerAgent** class. These members include *rb*, a **BooleanRuleBase** instance, and several **RuleVariables** used in the **BooleanRuleBase**. The *initializeBestSellerRuleBase()* method defines the *offerDelta*, an intermediate output variable, and *spread* and *firstOffer*, which are antecedent variables. *Spread* is the difference between the current offered price and the asking or *strikePrice*. The *firstOffer* boolean signals when a negotiation is just starting.

Like the **BestBuyerAgent**, the **BestSellerAgent** uses action rules to directly send responses. As described previously, the **SellerAgent**s control the negotiations and can decide to accept an offer, make a counter-offer, or reject the offer and break off negotiations with the **BuyerAgents**. The **BooleanRuleBase** in the **BestSellerAgent** is more complex than the **BestBuyerAgent** so that it can handle these additional cases and associated actions.

The *negotiate()* method first resets the rule base and then computes and sets the *spread* value. A special test is added to determine whether the previous and the current offers are identical. If so, that means the Buyer has accepted the offer and the spread value is set to greater than 50 in order to force an accept-offer action. Obviously, accept could have been called directly, but in this case, we want to demonstrate the **BooleanRuleBase** action mechanism.

In testing with the rule-based **BestBuyerAgent** and **BestSellerAgent**, we found that the agents could get into infinite loops bargaining back and forth. The iteration member was added to the **BasicNegotiation** class to keep track of this situation and to short-circuit these loops when they occur. In real multiagent systems, however, there is always the possibility of producing message storms or deadlocks between agents. Failsafe mechanisms to detect and avoid these conditions must be included in commercial implementations.

A forward-chaining inference cycle is performed. The amount of the counter-offer (if any) is computed, and the action or *effector()* methods are called during the inferencing process. (The *effector()* method contains logic for interpreting the value of the *offerDelta* **RuleVariable**, depending on which effector was invoked.)

MarketPlace Application

In this section, we develop a Java application to illustrate the behavior of an electronic markeplace where our facilitator and Buyer and Seller agents interact. The *MarketPlace* application classes **MarketplaceApp**, which contains the *main()* method, and **MarketplaceFrame**, which implements our main window, were constructed using the Borland/Inprise JBuilder 3.0 Java interactive development environment. The visual builder enables us to create the complete GUI by using Java Swing components in a drag-and-drop style. JBuilder automatically generates the Java code for creating the GUI controls and action event handlers in the **MarketplaceFrame** class. We then added the logic for creating the **Facilitator** and Buyer and Seller agents and for setting up the marketplace infrastructure. The **MarketplaceApp** code that invokes the **MarketplaceFrame** is not presented here. This code simply instantiates the **MarketplaceFrame** class and displays it. Likewise, a substantial amount of the code in the **MarketplaceFrame** class deals with GUI control logic, and we will not present that material here. Instead, we will highlight only brief code sections that demonstrate how to use the underlying agent classes. All of the classes that we discuss in this chapter are in the *marketplace* package, as shown in Figure 10.14.

Figure 10.14 The marketplace package UML diagram.

We point out some of the unique application logic that is required to implement the **CIAgent** *MarketPlace*. The seven **CIAgents**—the **FacilitatorAgent** and the three types of Buyer and Seller agents—are data members of the **MarketplaceFrame** class:

```
FacilitatorAgent facilitator;
BuyerAgent basicBuyerAgent;
BetterBuyerAgent intermedBuyerAgent;
BestBuyerAgent advancedBuyerAgent;
SellerAgent basicSellerAgent;
BetterSellerAgent intermedSellerAgent;
BestSellerAgent advancedSellerAgent;
```

The *startMenuItem_actionPerformed( )* method is called when the user selects **Start** from the **File** menu. We first clear both text areas and get the singleton **Facilitator-Agent** instance. We *reset( )* the facilitator, add the **MarketPlaceFrame** instance as a listener, *initialize( )* the facilitator, and then run it. Next, we check the menu item that is associated with each of the six Buyer and Seller agents. If the corresponding menu item is checked, we instantiate the agent, set the trace level (summary or detail), add the listener, initialize it, and then run it.

```
void startMenuItem_actionPerformed(ActionEvent e) {
  topTextArea.setText("");
  traceTextArea.setText("");
  this.setTitle("CIAgent Marketplace Application - Running");
  int traceLevel = SUMMARY;

  if(detailsCheckBoxMenuItem.isSelected()) {
    traceLevel = DETAILS;
  }
  facilitator = FacilitatorAgent.getInstance();
  facilitator.reset();
  facilitator.setTraceLevel(traceLevel);
  facilitator.addCIAgentEventListener(this);
  facilitator.initialize();
  facilitator.startAgentProcessing();
  if(basicSellerCheckBoxMenuItem.isSelected()) {
    basicSellerAgent = new SellerAgent();
    basicSellerAgent.setTraceLevel(traceLevel);
    basicSellerAgent.addCIAgentEventListener(this);
    basicSellerAgent.initialize();
    basicSellerAgent.startAgentProcessing();
  }
  if(intermediateSellerCheckBoxMenuItem.isSelected()) {
    intermedSellerAgent = new BetterSellerAgent();
    intermedSellerAgent.setTraceLevel(traceLevel);
    intermedSellerAgent.addCIAgentEventListener(this);
    intermedSellerAgent.initialize();
    intermedSellerAgent.startAgentProcessing();
  }
  if(advancedSellerCheckBoxMenuItem.isSelected()) {
    advancedSellerAgent = new BestSellerAgent();
```

```
      advancedSellerAgent.setTraceLevel(traceLevel);
      advancedSellerAgent.addCIAgentEventListener(this);
      advancedSellerAgent.initialize();
      advancedSellerAgent.startAgentProcessing();
    }
    if(basicBuyerCheckBoxMenuItem.isSelected()) {
      basicBuyerAgent = new BuyerAgent();
      basicBuyerAgent.setTraceLevel(traceLevel);
      basicBuyerAgent.addCIAgentEventListener(this);
      basicBuyerAgent.initialize();
      basicBuyerAgent.startAgentProcessing();
    }
    if(intermediateBuyerCheckBoxMenuItem.isSelected()) {
      intermedBuyerAgent = new BetterBuyerAgent();
      intermedBuyerAgent.setTraceLevel(traceLevel);
      intermedBuyerAgent.addCIAgentEventListener(this);
      intermedBuyerAgent.initialize();
      intermedBuyerAgent.startAgentProcessing();
    }
    if(advancedBuyerCheckBoxMenuItem.isSelected()) {
      advancedBuyerAgent = new BestBuyerAgent();
      advancedBuyerAgent.setTraceLevel(traceLevel);
      advancedBuyerAgent.addCIAgentEventListener(this);
      advancedBuyerAgent.initialize();
      advancedBuyerAgent.startAgentProcessing();
    }
    topTextArea.append("Starting Marketplace \n");
    startMenuItem.setEnabled(false);
    stopMenuItem.setEnabled(true);
  }
```

The *stopMenuItem_actionPerformed()* method is called when the user selects the **Stop** menu item from the **File** menu. The facilitator agent is not stopped, because that would kill its thread. We simply remove the **MarketPlaceFrame** object as a listener on the thread. For all of the Buyer and Seller agents, if they exist, we call their *stopAgentProcessing()* method (which forces them to exit their *eventQueue* thread and go to the UNKNOWN state). For this reason, each time **Start** is pressed, new Buyer and Seller agents are created:

```
  void stopMenuItem_actionPerformed(ActionEvent e) {
    if(facilitator != null) {
      facilitator.removeCIAgentEventListener(this);
    }
    if(basicSellerAgent != null) {
      basicSellerAgent.stopAgentProcessing();
    }
    if(intermedSellerAgent != null) {
      intermedSellerAgent.stopAgentProcessing();
    }
    if(advancedSellerAgent != null) {
      advancedSellerAgent.stopAgentProcessing();
    }
```

```
      if(basicBuyerAgent != null) {
        basicBuyerAgent.stopAgentProcessing();
      }
      if(intermedBuyerAgent != null) {
        intermedBuyerAgent.stopAgentProcessing();
      }
      if(advancedBuyerAgent != null) {
        advancedBuyerAgent.stopAgentProcessing();
      }
      topTextArea.append("Ending Marketplace \n");
      traceTextArea.append("Ending Marketplace \n");
      this.setTitle("CIAgent Marketplace Application");
      startMenuItem.setEnabled(true);
      stopMenuItem.setEnabled(false);
    }
```

The **CIAgentEventListener** methods are implemented to always have agents process events synchronously on the caller's thread. Even if a caller requested for an event to be processed asynchronously by calling *postCIAgentEvent()*, our implementation of the *postCIAgentEvent()* method simply calls the *processCIAgentEvent()*. The *processCIAgentEvent()* method only listens for *trace* action events and then displays the argument **String** either in the top text area if the event comes from the **FacilitatorAgent** or in the bottom text area if the event source is any other agent:

```
    public void processCIAgentEvent(CIAgentEvent event) {
      Object source = event.getSource();
      Object arg = event.getArgObject();
      Object action = event.getAction();

      if((action != null) && (action.equals("trace"))) {
        if(((arg != null) && (arg instanceof String))) {
          if(source instanceof FacilitatorAgent) {
            traceFacilitator((String) arg);
          } else {
            trace((String) arg);
          }
        }
      }
    }

    public void postCIAgentEvent(CIAgentEvent event) {
      processCIAgentEvent(event);
    }
```

Discussion

In this section, we describe the reasoning behind some of the design decisions that we made while developing the *MarketPlace* application.

Perhaps the first decision that we made was using the KQML-like **BuySellMessage** instead of parsing "real" KQML messages. Our feeling was that we could explore many issues of the agent communications by using the **BuySellMessage** class without getting bogged down by the intricacies of parsing KQML statements. We dealt with the issues that are related to the use of KQML performatives and the maintenance of the conversation states among the Facilitator, Buyer, and Seller agents.

Our next decision was to design our own matchmaker or Facilitator. There are several KQML facilitators in the literature and some in fielded applications and products. Our relatively simple Facilitator provided all of the functions needed for this application without getting too complex. Having the Facilitator stay "in the loop" between the Buyer and the Seller was another design decision that could easily have gone the other way. We felt that the trace logs provided by a centralized Facilitator would be useful. In a system that has many agents, however, having the Facilitator act as the middleman would be a performance bottleneck. As a matchmaker or broker who introduces the agents and then gets out of the way, the Facilitator would provide most of the function while not being a performance liability.

Another fundamental design choice was using the **BuyerAgent** and **SellerAgent** threads to kick off transactions but not to handle event processing. In a commercial multiagent application, it would be better to have the message signaling happen synchronously and the message processing to happen asynchronously. This design is more complicated, however, because you have to worry about signaling end-of-event-processing events. But this design would enable higher throughput with a large number of agents and also would improve the robustness of the overall system, because a single slow agent would not gum up the works. The **CIAgent** framework supports this more complex design, but for simplicity, we chose not to use it.

Also, as may have been apparent, we did not spend a lot of time developing optimal negotiation strategies for the **BuyerAgent** and **SellerAgent**. As we stated, our goal was to show the progress of agents from simple, hard-coded agents to more complex, rule-based agents and to show the benefits of the increased sophistication in the bottom-line performance of the algorithms. One could easily imagine hard-coding a better strategy than we used in the **BestBuyerAgent** and **BestSellerAgent**. But the point was to illustrate the power and flexibility of using a rule-based engine to control the negotiations and to directly invoke actions by using the *effector()* methods.

A simplification that we used in the negotiation strategy was that the **SellerAgent** removed the item from inventory as soon as a Buyer asked about it. This action prevented two negotiations for the same item occurring at the same time. While in a real marketplace this sort of thing occurs all of the time, the added complexity of this approach seems to outweigh the benefits.

Summary

In this chapter, we developed an electronic marketplace application by using seven **CIAgent**-based intelligent agents. The main points include the following:

- The *MarketPlace* application consisted of a single **FacilitatorAgent**, one or more **BuyerAgent**s, and one or more **SellerAgent**s. There were three types of Buyer and Seller agents that used increasingly better negotiating strategies.

- All communications between the Buyers and Sellers went through the Facilitator by using KQML-like objects called **BuySellMessages**. These messages include KQML-performatives such as *register, advertise, unadvertise, recommend-one, ask,* and *tell*. Application-specific performatives included *make-offer, accept-offer,* and *reject-offer*.

- We defined the sales negotiation protocol, giving the **SellerAgent** more control over the process. The **BasicNegotiation** class was introduced to encapsulate the details of each transaction. An **Offer** consists of the agent name, the item, a unique item ID that is generated by the **SellerAgent** at the start of a negotiation, and the offer price.

- The **BestBuyerAgent** and **BestSellerAgent** used the **BooleanRuleBase**, **Rule**, and **Clause** classes from Chapter 4, "Reasoning Systems," along with enhancements such as **EffectorClauses** to represent the negotiation strategy in rule form and directly send the reply messages by using action rules.

Exercises

1. Write a simple KQML parser for the subset of the language that the **BuySellMessage** class supports.

2. Modify or extend the **FacilitatorAgent** behavior so that the Buyers and Sellers directly communicate with each other after a match is made. What are the benefits and drawbacks of this approach?

3. What domain knowledge would be needed to develop a **BuyerAgent** that you would trust with your money? What reasoning skills would be required? How difficult would it be to build this **BuyerAgent**?

4. Agents can be used in both business-to-consumer and business-to-business marketplaces. What are the issues that enable or prevent their use in these marketplaces (security, data formats, ontologies, and so on)?

5. The interaction logic between buyers and sellers in the *MarketPlace* application is hard-coded. What would be required to change this setup to a more flexible architecture? Is this a design flaw or a natural consequence of the KQML speech-act communication model?

6. Online auctions are increasingly popular. Sketch a design for an agent that would do your bidding on a commercial auction site. What data formats would you require? Would you need to use secure sockets? What other requirements would be placed on the agent design and implementation?

Java-Based Agent Environments

W̲e conclude with an examination of several Java-based agent environments. While this list is not an exhaustive compilation of Java-based agents, it provides an overview of what is happening in academia and industry, where the focus is, and what more needs to be done to bring Java intelligent agents to their full potential.

Agent Building and Learning Environment *(ABLE)*

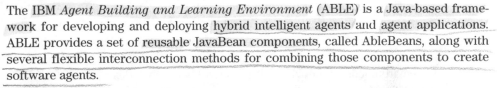

The IBM *Agent Building and Learning Environment* (ABLE) is a Java-based framework for developing and deploying hybrid intelligent agents and agent applications. ABLE provides a set of reusable JavaBean components, called AbleBeans, along with several flexible interconnection methods for combining those components to create software agents.

AbleBeans implement data access, filtering and transformation, learning, and reasoning capabilities. Function-specific AbleAgents are provided for classification, clustering, prediction, and genetic search. Application-specific agents can be constructed by using one or more of these AbleBeans. AbleAgents are situated in their environment through the use of sensors and effectors, which provide a generic mechanism for linking them to Java applications. A *Graphical User Interface* (GUI)-based interactive development environment, the AbleAgent Editor, is provided to assist with the construction of AbleAgents by using AbleBean components.

ABLE is included on the CD-ROM that accompanies this book. You can obtain additional information about ABLE at www.alphaWorks.ibm.com/tech/able.

AgentBuilder

AgentBuilder, from Reticular Systems, Inc., is an integrated software development toolkit for constructing agents in Java. This toolkit uses a high-level, agent-oriented programming language and provides a suite of graphical programming tools for configuring agents and specifying their behaviors. AgentBuilder is intended to enable developers who have no *artificial intelligence* (AI) background to build intelligent agent applications.

Agents in AgentBuilder are *belief-desire-intention* (BDI) agents that use *Knowledge Query and Manipulation Language* (KQML) performatives to communicate. The *Reticular Agent Definition Language* (RADL) is an extension of Shoham's AGENT-0 model and uses behavior rules to define the agent's mental model state changes and actions when given a set of conditions. An agent interpreter monitors incoming messages and processes the agent's behavioral rules.

In addition to agent-level development and debugging tools, AgentBuilder provides a set of graphical project management and domain analysis tools (including an ontology manager, a protocol or dialog manager, and a rule editor). You can find additional information on AgentBuilder's Web site at www.agentbuilder.com.

Aglets

Aglets are Java-based autonomous agents developed by IBM. They provide the basic capabilities that are required for mobility. Each aglet has a globally unique name. A travel itinerary specifies the destinations to which the agent must travel and what actions it must take at each location. In order for an aglet to run on a particular system, that system must be running an aglet host application. This application provides a platform-neutral execution environment for the aglet. The aglet workbench includes a configurable Java security manager that can restrict the activity of an aglet on the system in the same way that the default security manager restricts the activities of an applet.

Aglets can communicate by using a whiteboard that enables agents to collaborate and share information asynchronously. Synchronous and asynchronous message passing is also supported for aglet communication. Aglets are streamed using standard Java serialization or externalization. A network agent class loader is also supplied, which enables an aglet's bytecode stream and state to travel across a network.

While aglets are not inherently intelligent, they are written in Java and can be extended with any of the intelligent Java code that we have provided in previous chapters of this book. IBM has recently turned over the source code to the open source community. For more information about aglets, refer to www.trl.ibm.co.jp/aglets.

FIPA-OS

FIPA Open Source (FIPA-OS), originally developed at Nortel Networks, is an open-agent platform that supports communication by using the FIPA agent communication language standards [Poslad, Buckle, and Hadingham 1999]. As indicated by its name, the platform is distributed under an open-source license and is designed as a set of loosely coupled parts in order to enable the open-source development community to make enhancements.

FIPA-OS provides the set of platform services that are specified in the FIPA agent standards, including an agent management system for life-cycle management, a directory facilitator or yellow pages service, and an agent communication channel for FIPA-compliant messaging and interaction protocols. FIPA-OS includes several agent shells that are base classes that make use of the platform services and that can be extended to add customized behaviors. A visualization tool gives a graphical interface to the FIPA-OS platform. The latest open-source code is found at http://fipa-os.sourceforge.net/.

Gossip

Gossip is a demonstration application of Tryllian, Inc.'s mobile agent software. Tryllian's agents use learning technology to profile their users' preferences and to perform automated actions on behalf of their users. The Tryllian system uses Java to implement a secure, distributed multiagent environment. Their agents use a sense-reason-act loop to control the interaction between the agent and the outside world. Part of the Tryllian infrastructure is an agent platform called the Home Base. Multiple agent Marketplaces are provided so that the mobile agents can meet and interact. Each Marketplace can specify different access privileges so that only certain agents can participate.

Tryllian overcomes some of the security concerns that are associated with mobile agents by providing three levels of protection. First, *Secure Sockets Layer* (SSL) connections are used to transmit the agent code and data. Second, the agent code is signed by using a data encryption algorithm. Third, each user has a digital key to ensure that others cannot access the agent.

The Agent Development Kit is used to create the Tryllian mobile intelligent agents. The core agent (body) can be configured by defining the knowledge (data) and behavior (actions). The Marketplace software, called the Agent RunTime Environment, enables user databases, messaging, and agent-matching software to be incorporated as part of the application. For more information about Gossip, refer to www.tryllian.com/gossip.

JADE

The *Java Development* (JADE) framework, developed at CSELT S.p.A. in Torino, Italy, is a FIPA-compliant toolkit for creating multiagent systems applications. JADE provides a set of tools for debugging and deploying distributed agents.

JADE provides a set of agent services including an agent-naming service, yellow pages service, transport protocols, and interaction protocols that are FIPA compliant. The agent platform can be distributed between several host systems, requiring a single *Java Virtual Machine* (JVM) on each to serve as the agent container. The communication infrastructure enables agents to access private message queues and provides support for FIPA envelopes, encoding schemes, and ontologies. JADE supports *Remote Method Invocation* (RMI), *Common Object Request Broker Architecture Internet Inter-ORB Protocol* (CORBA IIOP), and event notification transport protocols.

Each JADE agent has a single thread by default but can use Java's multi-threading capability if necessary. JADE also supports the complex scheduling of agent tasks as well as integration with the *Java Expert System Shell* (JESS) reasoning engine. A GUI is provided for remote monitoring and control of agents that are running on the JADE agent platform. The source code is available under the *Lesser General Public License* (LGPL) at http://sharon.cselt.it/projects/jade/home.htm.

JATLite

Java Agent Template Lite (JATLite) is a set of lightweight Java packages being developed at Stanford University that can be used to build multiagent systems. JATLite is a layered architecture that provides a different communication protocol at each layer. The bottom-most layer provides only abstract classes that can be implemented to support any communication protocol. The base layer uses the *Transmission Control Protocol/Internet Protocol* (TCP/IP) as the communication mechanism and enables the agent implementers to define the message protocol. The KQML layer provides support for agents that use KQML messages. The Router layer adds message routing that enables messages to be queued for agents that are not active when the Router layer receives the message.

The JATLite framework is intended for developing typed-message, autonomous agents that communicate by using a peer-to-peer protocol. The framework supports both synchronous and asynchronous message passing. Messages can be delivered through polling or message queuing. The framework provides additional security that checks the agent name and password for a more secure connection.

The focus of JATLite is obviously on communication. Like many of the other agent environments that we discuss in this chapter, any intelligence would have to be provided by the agent implementers by using techniques described previously in this book. For more information about JATLite (and its predecessor, JAT), refer to http://java.stanford.edu/java_agent/html.

Jess

Jess, the Java Expert System Shell, is not an agent environment *per se* but is an implementation of the *C Language Integrated Production System* (CLIPS) expert system shell that is written in Java. Ernest Friedman-Hill developed Jess at the Sandia National Laboratories. Jess can be used to give Java applications and agents the capability to reason by using a CLIPS rule base.

NASA's Johnson Space Center developed CLIPS, and more than 4,000 public and private institutions have licensed the application. CLIPS is a forward-chaining rule-based system based on the Rete algorithm. Jess can run code that is written in the CLIPS language, so it acts like a standalone rule engine. But the Jess language has been extended well beyond CLIPS so that it is a general-purpose programming language that can create and manipulate Java objects as well as perform backward chaining inferencing.

Given its heritage, the Jess language syntax looks much like Lisp code. This syntax provides a console for interactive input and dynamic evaluation of rules and functions in addition to using Java reflection (run-time type information) to enable users to access Java objects and methods. The Jess knowledge base contains a set of facts that come in three flavors: *ordered, unordered,* and *definstance* facts. Ordered facts are lists of terms in which the first term is used as a category label. Unordered facts are used to represent Java objects with data members that are accessible as slots. Jess provides the *definstance* fact to represent a specific instance of a JavaBean, while class properties are defined in a *defclass* statement. Facts can be added to the knowledge base by using an *assert* command and removed by using a *retract* command. Each fact is assigned a unique index or ID when it is asserted, which can then be used to reference the fact.

Jess is a Java application that can be run from the command line like any other Java application. It can also be embedded in your own Java programs or agents. Jess can even handle Java events. A rather large user community has formed around this tool. For information about Jess, refer to http://herzberg.ca.sandia.gov/jess/.

Voyager   *mobile agents*

Voyager, from ObjectSpace, Inc., is an agent-enhanced *Object Request Broker* (ORB) that is written entirely in Java. An ORB provides the capability to create objects on a remote system and to invoke methods on those objects. Voyager augments the traditional ORB with agent capabilities.

Voyager agents have mobility and autonomy that is provided in the base class, Agent. An Agent can move itself from one location to another and can leave behind a forwarding address with a secretary so that future messages can be forwarded to its new location. Specialized agents called Messengers are used to deliver messages. Messages can be synchronous, one-way (similar to asynchronous), or future, which are asynchronous but return a placeholder that can be use to retrieve a return value at a later time.

Like aglets, an agent's itinerary instructs the agent as to what operations it needs to perform at each location. Also, similar to aglets, Voyager uses serialization to stream the agent's state as the agent moves from location to location. Voyager also includes a security manager that can be used to restrict the operations that an agent can perform. In the future, Voyager will be enhanced with a rule-based security model that supplements the standard Java security mechanism.

Voyager agents themselves are not inherently intelligent. They do not contain an inference engine, neural networks, or any other artificial intelligence technology. But, like aglets, they can be augmented with any of the artificial intelligence techniques that we have described in this book. You can find additional information about Voyager at www.objectspace.com.

ZEUS *collaborative agents*

The ZEUS agent-building toolkit, developed by British Telecom, is a framework for the development of collaborative agent systems that are constructed by using large, coarse-grained agents that emphasize autonomy and cooperation. The agents cooperate because they have limited resources and knowledge, and they combine their capabilities to solve larger problems than could be solved by working alone. ZEUS was built using Java because of its portability and multi-threading support.

There are three major groups of classes in the ZEUS toolkit: an agent component library, a set of visualization tools, and the agent building software. The agent component library includes a KQML-based agent communication language, a socket-based messaging system, a planning and scheduling system, a coordination engine, and a library of interaction protocols.

A ZEUS agent is logically composed of three layers: a definition layer, an organizational layer, and a coordination layer. The definition layer represents the base agent's BDI capabilities. The organization layer defines the relationships with other agents. The coordination layer models each agent as a social entity. ZEUS agents use multiple threads to implement a mailbox and associated message handler, a coordination engine, an acquaintance model, a planning engine, and local databases.

The agent-building tools are meant to complement and support a six-stage development methodology. A relatively high-level definition of the agent is used as the input to agent-generator software, which automatically produces Java source code for the agent. Because ZEUS was designed for distributed, collaborative multiagent systems, it also provides a set of visualization tools for controlling, monitoring, and debugging agent interactions on the platform. You can find additional information about the ZEUS agent toolkit at www.labs.bt.com/projects/agents.htm.

Discussion

As in the first edition of this book, most of the research for this chapter was conducted on the Web. During the course of our search for information about Java-based tools and products, it was clear that there is much activity in this area. In 1997, many of the agent tools focused more on agent mobility than on artificial intelligence. In 2001, there seems to be much more emphasis on agent intelligence and reasoning.

We tried to select the set of what appeared to be the most popular or complete Java agent environments. We did not download and try all of the tools that we mention in this chapter. But from the systems that we did examine, we could identify some clear patterns. KQML, and the closely related FIPA ACL, were used as the inter-agent communication protocol in several environments. KIF seems to be less popular as a content format. In the systems in which artificial intelligence was included, rule-based processing was a fairly standard feature (while learning is becoming increasingly common).

As with other new technology areas, it seems that intelligent agents will not be a market by themselves. Instead, they will be embedded into business applications where they can provide the most immediate value and slowly will evolve into must-have features in commercial software. Autonomy is now a given for intelligent agents. Mobility clearly has appeal, but it is not clear whether mobility appeals to the developers or to the potential users. The security and infrastructure that is required for mobile agents to easily move around the Internet is slowly being put in place for mobile agents to be useful and secure.

Intelligence is used in agents where the application domain requires this functionality. For many applications today, it seems that hard-coded logic is sufficient. Where more flexibility is required, rule-based inferencing is included. Typically, these are fairly lightweight inference engines as far as traditional AI function is concerned. In many applications (such as e-mail automation), simple rule processing is all that is required.

Learning will probably follow this same pattern. The computational overhead of common learning algorithms makes their use a luxury for most applications. For intelligent agents that reside on Internet servers, however, where their capability to interpret data and patterns in transactions would add significant value, learning might quickly become a necessity. Web page personalization is one application in which this situation is certainly the case.

As far as Java and intelligent agents go, it seems like a match made in heaven. Java's built-in threading support enables autonomy to be easily added to any Java class. Its serialization support and remote-method invocation capabilities make mobility far less daunting than with other programming languages. Finally, its down-to-the-core, object-oriented programming support enables artificial intelligence algorithms to be easily implemented (as we hope we have demonstrated in this book). Three years after writing the first edition of this book, we had no trouble finding Java-based agents and agent platforms.

Our last comment relates to JavaBeans and how the Beans software component model will affect intelligent agents. As we mentioned in Chapter 7, "Intelligent Agent Framework," the sophisticated event model, serialization, and visual construction tools make JavaBeans an ideal way to develop intelligent agents in Java. Depending on how quickly good visual development tools for Beans get to the market (as well as how quickly Beans are accepted in the marketplace), they might become *the* architecture for agents. A JavaBean is a standard, encapsulated software component that every computer that has a JVM can run. Add mobility to Beans, and you have an unbeatable environment for intelligent agent development and deployment.

Summary

In this chapter, we surveyed several Java intelligent agent environments and tools. These include the following:

- The IBM *Agent Building and Learning Environment* (ABLE) is a Java-based framework for developing and deploying hybrid intelligent agents and agent applications. ABLE provides a set of reusable JavaBean components, called AbleBeans, along with several flexible interconnection methods for combining those components to create software agents.

- *AgentBuilder*, from Reticular Systems, Inc., is an integrated software development toolkit for constructing agents in Java. This toolkit uses a high-level, agent-oriented programming language and provides a suite of graphical programming tools for configuring agents and specifying their behaviors.

- *Aglets* are IBM's autonomous and mobile Java agent framework. Aglets are free to roam between servers running the aglet host software and can follow a predefined travel itinerary. An aglet process can be suspended, shipped to another aglet host system, and resume as if it was never stopped.

- *FIPA-OS* is an open-source implementation of the FIPA agent specifications in Java.

- *Gossip* (from Tryllian Systems, Inc.) is a demonstration application of Tryllian's mobile agent software. Gossip agents use learning technology to profile their users' preferences and to perform automated actions on their users' behalf.

- The *Java Development* (JADE) framework, developed at CSELT S.p.A. in Torino, Italy, is a FIPA-compliant toolkit for creating multiagent systems applications. JADE provides a set of tools for debugging and deploying distributed agents.

- *Java Agent Template Lite* (JATLite) is a set of lightweight Java packages that was developed at Stanford University. JATLite provides a layered architecture for building multiagent systems.

- *Java Expert System Shell* (Jess) is a Java implementation of the standard CLIPS rule-base environment that was developed at Sandia National Lab. While not an agent environment, Jess provides rule-based inferencing support in Java.

- The *Voyager* system from ObjectSpace, Inc., is an agent-enhanced *Object Request Broker* (ORB) that is written in Java. Voyager agents are autonomous and mobile but not intelligent.

- The *ZEUS* agent building toolkit from British Telcom is a framework for the development of collaborative agent systems that are constructed by using large, coarse-grained agents that emphasize autonomy and cooperation.

- The state of the art of Java intelligent agents is that they are autonomous, somewhat mobile, and increasingly intelligent. Most often artificial intelligence is utilized through rule-based inferencing and neural learning. The future for Java and intelligent agents looks bright.

Bugs and Plants Rule Bases

This appendix contains the Java implementation of the bugs and plants rule bases provided with the *Rule* application discussed in Chapter 4, "Reasoning Systems." The bugs rule base was the first expert system Joe encountered in graduate school at Lehigh University. It was provided with IBM's Expert System Environment (ESE) on their mainframes. The plants rule base first appeared in an article by Beverly and William Thompson in *Byte* magazine (1985).

The Bugs Rule Base Implementation

```
public void initBugsRuleBase(BooleanRuleBase rb) {
  RuleVariable bugClass = new RuleVariable(rb, "bugClass");

  bugClass.setLabels("arachnid insect");
  bugClass.setPromptText("What is the bug class?");
  RuleVariable insectType = new RuleVariable(rb, "insectType");

  insectType.setLabels("beetle orthoptera");
  insectType.setPromptText("What is the insect type?");
  RuleVariable species = new RuleVariable(rb, "species");

  species.setLabels(
    "Spider Tick Ladybug Japanese_Beetle Cricket Praying_Mantis");
  species.setPromptText("What is the species?");
  RuleVariable color = new RuleVariable(rb, "color");
```

```java
color.setLabels("orange_and_black green_and_black black");
color.setPromptText("What color is the bug?");
RuleVariable size = new RuleVariable(rb, "size");

size.setLabels("small large");
size.setPromptText("What size is the bug?");
RuleVariable leg_length = new RuleVariable(rb, "leg_length");

leg_length.setLabels("short long");
leg_length.setPromptText("What is the leg length?");
RuleVariable antennae = new RuleVariable(rb, "antennae");

antennae.setLabels("0 2");
antennae.setPromptText("How many antennae does it have?");
RuleVariable shape = new RuleVariable(rb, "shape");

shape.setLabels("round elongated");
shape.setPromptText("What shape is the bug's body?");
RuleVariable legs = new RuleVariable(rb, "legs");

legs.setLabels("6 8");
legs.setPromptText("How many legs does it have?");
RuleVariable wings = new RuleVariable(rb, "wings");

wings.setLabels("0 2");
wings.setPromptText("How many wings does it have?");
Condition cEquals = new Condition("=");
Condition cNotEquals = new Condition("!=");
Rule Spider =
  new Rule(rb, "spider",
    new Clause[]{
      new Clause(bugClass, cEquals, "arachnid"),
      new Clause(leg_length, cEquals, "long") },
    new Clause(species, cEquals, "Spider"));
Rule Tick =
  new Rule(rb, "tick",
    new Clause[]{
      new Clause(bugClass, cEquals, "arachnid"),
      new Clause(leg_length, cEquals, "short") },
    new Clause(species, cEquals, "Tick"));
Rule Ladybug =
  new Rule(rb, "ladybug",
    new Clause[]{
      new Clause(insectType, cEquals, "beetle"),
      new Clause(color, cEquals, "orange_and_black") },
    new Clause(species, cEquals, "Ladybug"));
Rule JapaneseBeetle =
  new Rule(rb, "Japanese_Beetle",
    new Clause[]{
      new Clause(insectType, cEquals, "beetle"),
```

```
                new Clause(color, cEquals,"green_and_black") },
              new Clause(species, cEquals, "Japanese_Beetle"));
    Rule Cricket =
      new Rule(rb, "cricket",
        new Clause[]{
          new Clause(insectType, cEquals, "orthoptera"),
          new Clause(color, cEquals, "black") },
        new Clause(species, cEquals, "Cricket"));
    Rule PrayingMantis =
      new Rule(rb, "praying_mantis",
        new Clause[]{
          new Clause(insectType, cEquals, "orthoptera"),
          new Clause(color, cEquals, "green"),
          new Clause(size, cEquals, "large") },
        new Clause(species, cEquals, "Praying_Mantis"));
    Rule ClassArachnid1 =
      new Rule(rb, "class_is_Arachnid1",
        new Clause[]{
          new Clause(antennae, cEquals, "0"),
          new Clause(legs, cEquals, "8") },
        new Clause(bugClass, cEquals, "arachnid"));
    Rule ClassArachnid2 =
      new Rule(rb, "class_is_Arachnid2",
        new Clause(wings, cEquals, "0"),
        new Clause(bugClass, cEquals, "arachnid"));
    Rule ClassInsect1 =
      new Rule(rb, "class_is_Insect1",
        new Clause[]{
          new Clause(antennae, cEquals, "2"),
          new Clause(legs, cEquals, "6") },
        new Clause(bugClass, cEquals, "insect"));
    Rule ClassInsect2 =
      new Rule(rb, "class_is_Insect2",
        new Clause(wings, cEquals, "2"),
        new Clause(bugClass, cEquals, "insect"));
    Rule TypeBeetle =
      new Rule(rb, "typeBeetle",
        new Clause[]{
          new Clause(bugClass, cEquals, "insect"),
          new Clause(size, cEquals, "small"),
          new Clause(shape, cEquals, "round") }
        new Clause(insectType, cEquals, "beetle"));
    Rule TypeOrthoptera =
      new Rule(rb, "typeOrthoptera",
        new Clause[]{
          new Clause(bugClass, cEquals, "insect"),
          new Clause(size, cNotEquals, "small"),
          new Clause(shape, cEquals, "elongated")},
        new Clause(insectType, cEquals, "orthoptera"));
}
```

```
public void demoBugsBC(BooleanRuleBase rb) {
  traceTextArea.append(
    "\n — Setting Values for Bugs BackwardChain Demo —");
  rb.setVariableValue("wings", "2");
  rb.setVariableValue("legs", "6");
  rb.setVariableValue("shape", "round");
  rb.setVariableValue("antennae", "2");
  rb.setVariableValue("color", "orange_and_black");
  rb.setVariableValue("leg_length", "long");
  rb.setVariableValue("size", "small");
  rb.displayVariables(traceTextArea);
}

public void demoBugsFC(BooleanRuleBase rb) {
  traceTextArea.append(
    "\n — Setting Values for Bugs ForwardChain Demo —\n");
  rb.setVariableValue("bugClass", null);
  rb.setVariableValue("insectType", null);
  rb.setVariableValue("wings", "2");
  rb.setVariableValue("legs", "6");
  rb.setVariableValue("shape", "round");
  rb.setVariableValue("antennae", "2");
  rb.setVariableValue("color", "orange_and_black");
  rb.setVariableValue("leg_length", "long");
  rb.setVariableValue("size", "small");
  rb.displayVariables(traceTextArea);
}
```

The Plants Rule Base Implementation

```
public void initPlantsRuleBase(BooleanRuleBase rb) {
  RuleVariable family = new RuleVariable(rb, "family");

  family.setLabels("cypress pine bald_cypress ");
  family.setPromptText("What family is it?");
  RuleVariable treeClass = new RuleVariable(rb, "treeClass");

  treeClass.setLabels("angiosperm gymnosperm");
  treeClass.setPromptText("What tree class is it?");
  RuleVariable plantType = new RuleVariable(rb, "plantType");

  plantType.setLabels("herb vine tree shrub");
  plantType.setPromptText("What type of plant is it?");
  RuleVariable stem = new RuleVariable(rb, "stem");

  stem.setLabels("woody green");
  stem.setPromptText("What type of stem does it have?");
  RuleVariable stemPosition = new RuleVariable(rb, "stemPosition");
```

```
stemPosition.setLabels("upright creeping");
stemPosition.setPromptText("What is the stem position?");
RuleVariable one_main_trunk = new RuleVariable(rb, "one_main_trunk");

one_main_trunk.setLabels("yes no");
one_main_trunk.setPromptText("Does it have one main trunk?");
RuleVariable broad_and_flat_leaves = new RuleVariable(rb,
                                    "broad_and_flat_leaves");

broad_and_flat_leaves.setLabels("yes no");
broad_and_flat_leaves.setPromptText("Are the leaves broad and flat?");
RuleVariable leaf_shape = new RuleVariable(rb, "leaf_shape");

leaf_shape.setLabels("needlelike scalelike");
leaf_shape.setPromptText("What shape are the leaves?");
RuleVariable needle_pattern = new RuleVariable(rb, "needle_pattern");

needle_pattern.setLabels("random even");
needle_pattern.setPromptText("What is the needle pattern?");
RuleVariable silver_bands = new RuleVariable(rb, "silver_bands");

silver_bands.setLabels("yes no");
silver_bands.setPromptText("Does it have silver bands?");
Condition cEquals = new Condition("=");
Condition cNotEquals = new Condition("!=");
Rule Cypress =
  new Rule(rb, "cypress",
    new Clause[]{
      new Clause(treeClass, cEquals, "gymnosperm"),
      new Clause(leaf_shape, cEquals, "scalelike")},
    new Clause(family, cEquals, "cypress"));
Rule Pine1 =
  new Rule(rb, "pine1",
    new Clause[]{
      new Clause(treeClass, cEquals, "gymnosperm"),
      new Clause(leaf_shape, cEquals, "needlelike"),
      new Clause(needle_pattern, cEquals, "random")},
    new Clause(family, cEquals, "pine"));
Rule Pine2 =
  new Rule(rb, "pine2",
    new Clause[]{
      new Clause(treeClass, cEquals, "gymnosperm"),
      new Clause(leaf_shape, cEquals, "needlelike"),
      new Clause(needle_pattern, cEquals, "even"),
      new Clause(silver_bands, cEquals, "yes") },
    new Clause(family, cEquals, "pine"));
Rule BaldCypress =
  new Rule(rb, "baldCypress",
    new Clause[]{
      new Clause(treeClass, cEquals, "gymnosperm"),
```

```
                  new Clause(leaf_shape, cEquals, "needlelike"),
                  new Clause(needle_pattern, cEquals, "even"),
                  new Clause(silver_bands, cEquals, "no") },
              new Clause(family, cEquals, "bald_cypress"));
      Rule Angiosperm =
        new Rule(rb, "angiosperm",
          new Clause[]{
            new Clause(plantType, cEquals, "tree"),
            new Clause(broad_and_flat_leaves, cEquals,"yes") },
          new Clause(treeClass, cEquals, "angiosperm"));
      Rule Gymnosperm =
        new Rule(rb, "gymnosperm",
          new Clause[]{
            new Clause(plantType, cEquals, "tree"),
            new Clause(broad_and_flat_leaves, cEquals, "no") },
          new Clause(treeClass, cEquals, "gymnosperm"));
      Rule Herb =
        new Rule(rb, "herb",
          new Clause(stem, cEquals, "green"),
          new Clause(plantType, cEquals, "herb"));
      Rule Vine =
        new Rule(rb, "vine",
          new Clause[]{
            new Clause(stem, cEquals, "woody"),
            new Clause(stemPosition, cEquals, "creeping") },
          new Clause(plantType, cEquals, "vine"));
      Rule Tree =
        new Rule(rb, "tree",
          new Clause[]{
            new Clause(stem, cEquals, "woody"),
            new Clause(stemPosition, cEquals, "upright"),
            new Clause(one_main_trunk, cEquals, "yes") },
          new Clause(plantType, cEquals, "tree"));
      Rule Shrub =
        new Rule(rb, "shrub",
          new Clause[]{
            new Clause(stem, cEquals, "woody"),
            new Clause(stemPosition, cEquals, "upright"),
            new Clause(one_main_trunk, cEquals, "no") },
          new Clause(plantType, cEquals, "shrub"));
  }

  public void demoPlantsBC(BooleanRuleBase rb) {
    traceTextArea.append(
      "\n — Setting Values for Plants BackwardChain Demo —\n ");
    rb.setVariableValue("stem", "woody");
    rb.setVariableValue("stemPosition", "upright");
    rb.setVariableValue("one_main_trunk", "yes");
    rb.setVariableValue("broad_and_flat_leaves", "no");
    rb.setVariableValue("leaf_shape", "needlelike");
    rb.setVariableValue("needle_pattern", "random");
```

```
      rb.displayVariables(traceTextArea);
}

public void demoPlantsFC(BooleanRuleBase rb) {
    traceTextArea.append(
        "\n — Setting Values for Plants ForwardChain Demo — \n ");
    rb.setVariableValue("stem", "woody");
    rb.setVariableValue("stemPosition", "upright");
    rb.setVariableValue("one_main_trunk", "yes");
    rb.setVariableValue("broad_and_flat_leaves", "no");
    rb.setVariableValue("leaf_shape", "needlelike");
    rb.setVariableValue("needle_pattern", "random");
    rb.displayVariables(traceTextArea);
}
```

Training Data Sets

This appendix contains listings of the training data sets provided with the *Learn* application discussed in Chapter 5, "Learning Systems." Each section shows the data definition file (.dfn) and the corresponding data (.dat) file.

Vehicles Data

The vehicles data set was used as the primary example in Chapter 4, "Reasoning Systems." It is included in Chapter 5 to show how neural networks and decision trees can classify this data.

Vehicles.dfn

```
discrete motor
discrete num_wheels
discrete num_doors
discrete size
discrete vehicleType
discrete ClassField
```

Vehicles.dat

```
no 2 0 small cycle bicycle
no 3 0 small cycle tricycle
yes 2 0 small cycle motorcycle
yes 4 2 small automobile sportsCar
```

```
yes 4 3 medium automobile miniVan
yes 4 4 medium automobile sedan
yes 4 4 large automobile SUV
```

Xor Data

This data set is the standard test for back-propagation networks, because it is not a linearly separable classification problem.

Xor.dfn

```
continuous input1
continuous input2
continuous ClassField
```

Xor.dat

```
0.0 0.0 0.0
1.0 0.0 1.0
0.0 1.0 1.0
1.0 1.0 0.0
```

XorTree Data

This data set can be used with the decision tree, because it defines the binary inputs as discrete variables.

XorTree.dfn

```
discrete input1
discrete input2
discrete ClassField
```

XorTree.dat

```
0.0 0.0 0.0
1.0 0.0 1.0
0.0 1.0 1.0
1.0 1.0 0.0
```

Animal Data

This data set was shipped with the IBM Neural Network Utility, version 3. It is a simple classification problem with a mix of discrete and continuous input data.

Animal.dfn

```
discrete field1
discrete field2
discrete field3
discrete field4
discrete field5
continuous field6
continuous field7
discrete ClassField
```

Animal.dat

```
no   no no  mammal black        4  80000 panther
no   no no  mammal brown        4 100000 lion
no   no yes mammal silver       0  80000 dolphin
yes  no no  mammal black/white  4 150000 zebra
yes  no no  mammal brown        4  80000 deer
yes  no no  bird   black/white  2  60000 ostrich
no   no yes bird   black/white  2  60000 penguin
```

Ramp2 Data

This data set is used to demonstrate the prediction capabilities of back-propagation networks.

Ramp2.dfn

```
continuous input1
continuous input2
continuous ClassField
```

Ramp2.dat

```
0.0 0.1 0.1
0.0 0.2 0.2
```

```
0.0 0.3 0.3
0.0 0.4 0.4
0.0 0.5 0.5
0.0 0.6 0.6
0.0 0.7 0.7
0.0 0.8 0.8
0.0 0.9 0.9
```

Restaurant Data

This data set is used to test the Decision Tree algorithm. It first appeared in Russell and Norvig's artificial intelligence textbook (1995).

Resttree.dfn

```
discrete alternate
discrete bar
discrete FriSat
discrete hungry
discrete patrons
discrete price
discrete raining
discrete reservation
discrete rtype
discrete waitEstimate
discrete ClassField
```

Resttree.dat

```
yes no  no  yes some $$$ no  yes French  0-10  yes
yes no  no  yes full $   no  no  Thai    30-60 no
no  yes no  no  some $   no  no  Burger  0-10  yes
yes no  yes yes full $   no  no  Thai    10-30 yes
yes no  yes no  full $$$ no  yes French  >60   no
no  yes no  yes some $$  yes yes Italian 0-10  yes
no  yes no  no  none $   yes no  Burger  0-10  no
no  no  no  yes some $$  yes yes Thai    0-10  yes
no  yes yes no  full $   yes no  Burger  >60   no
yes yes yes yes full $$$ no  yes Italian 10-30 no
no  no  no  no  none $   no  no  Thai    0-10  no
yes yes yes yes full $   no  no  Burger  30-60 yes
```

Kmap1 Data

This simple data set is used to test the Kohonen map neural network. It contains points in four corners of a three-dimensional space.

Kmap1.dfn

```
continuous input1
continuous input2
continuous input3
```

Kmap1.dat

```
0.1 0.1 0.1
0.1 0.09 0.1
0.1 0.12 0.11
0.1 0.11 0.13
0.5 0.4 0.4
0.5 0.4 0.4
0.5 0.4 0.39
0.5 0.4 0.4
0.6 0.6 0.7
0.59 0.6 0.7
0.61 0.59 0.7
0.61 0.6 0.7
0.9 0.9 0.9
0.9 0.9 0.91
0.9 0.89 0.9
0.9 0.9 0.89
```

ColorTree Data

This simple data set is used to test the Decision Tree learning algorithm. The color field completely identifies the class.

ColorTree.dfn

```
discrete color
discrete fruits3
discrete fruits2
discrete ClassField
```

ColorTree.dat

```
red apples apples red
red banana apples red
red carrots apples red
blue apples apples blue
blue banana apples blue
blue carrots banana blue
```

```
green apples banana green
green banana banana green
green carrots banana green
```

The CD-ROM

The CD-ROM contains the complete Java code with JavaDocs for the examples that appear in the book, as well as some software you might find useful.

- IBM Agent Building and Learning Environment (ABLE)
- Sun Microsystems Inc. Java Run-Time Environment (JRE) 1.3

User Assistance and Information

The software accompanying this book is being provided without warranty or support of any kind. Should you require basic installation assistance, or if your media is defective, please call our product support number at (212) 850-6194, on weekdays between 9 A.M. and 4 P.M., Eastern Standard Time. Or, we can be reached via e-mail at wprtus@wiley.com.

To place additional orders or to request information about other Wiley products, please call (800) 879-4539.

You may contact the authors of this book through their Web site at http://www.bigusbooks.com, or via e-mail at support@bigusbooks.com.

Bibliography

Bigus, J. P. (1996). *Data Mining with Neural Networks.* New York: McGraw-Hill.

Bigus, J. P. and Goolsbey, K. (1990). Combining Neural Networks and Expert Systems in a Commercial Environment. In *Proceedings of the International Joint Conference on Neural Networks*, Washington, D.C.: IEEE Press.

Bigus, J. P. (2000). Agent Building and Learning Environment. In *Proceedings of the International Conference on Autonomous Agents 2000*, Association for Computing Machinery, 108–109. Barcelona, Spain.

Bigus, J. P., Hellerstein, J. L., Jayram, T. S., Squillante, M. S. (2000). AutoTune: A Generic Agent for Automated Performance Tuning. In *Practical Applications of Intelligent Agents and Multi-Agent Systems (PAAM 2000)*, Manchester, UK: The Practical Application Company.

Bratko, I. (1986). *Prolog Programming for Artificial Intelligence.* Reading, MA: Addison-Wesley.

Bratman, M. E. (1987). *Intentions, Plans, and Practical Reasons.* Cambridge, MA: Harvard University Press.

Brooks, F. (1975). *The Mythical Man-Month.* Reading, MA: Addison-Wesley.

Brooks, R. A. (1986). A robust layered control system for a mobile robot. *IEEE Journal of Robotics and Automation* 2:14–23.

Caglayan, A., Snorrason, M., Jacoby, J., Mazzu, J., Jones, R., and Kumar, K. (1997). Learn Sesame: a learning agent. *Applied Artificial Intelligence* 11(5): 393–412.

Caglayan, A., and Harrison, C. (1997) Agent Sourcebook. New York: Wiley.

Chavez, A. and Maes, P. (1996). Kasbah, An Agent Marketplace for Buying and Selling Goods. In *Proceedings of the First International Conference on the Practical Application of Intelligent Agents and Multi-Agent Technology*, London, UK: The Practical Application Company.

Clocksin, W. F. and Mellish, C. S. (1981). *Programming in Prolog.* Berlin: Springer-Verlag.

Cohen, P. R., and Levesque, H. J. (1990). Intention is choice with commitment. *Artificial Intelligence* 42(2–3): 213–261.

Collis, J. C., Ndumu, D. T., Nwana, H. S., and Lee, L. C. (1998). The ZEUS agent building tool-kit. *British Telecom Technology Journal* 16(3): 60–68.

Copeland, B. J., and Proudfoot, D. (1999). Alan Turing's forgotten ideas in computer science. *Scientific American* 280(4): 98–103.

Cornell, G., and Hortsmann, C. S. (1996). *Core Java*. Upper Saddle River, NJ: Prentice Hall.

Cox, E. (1994). *The Fuzzy Systems Handbook: A Practioner's Guide to Building, Using, and Maintaining Fuzzy Systems*. Boston, MA: Academic Press.

Duda, R., Hart, P. E., Nillson, N. J., Reboh, R., Slocum, J., and Sutherland, G. (1977). Development of a computer-based consultant for mineral exploration. In *SRI Report*. Menlo Park, CA: Stanford Research Institute.

Durfee, E. H. (1988). *Coordination of Distributed Problem Solvers*. Boston, MA: Kluwer Academic.

Erman, L. D., Hayes-Roth, F., Lesser, V. R., and Reddy, D. R. (1980). The HEARSAY-II speech-understanding system: Integrating knowledge to resolve uncertainty. *Computing Surveys* 12(2): 213–253.

Ferber, J., and Gutknecht, O. (1998). A meta-model for the analysis and design of organizations in multi-agent systems. In *Proceedings of the International Conference on Multi-Agent Systems '98*. Paris, France: IEEE Press.

Finin, T., Labrou, Y., and Mayfield, J. (1995). KQML as an agent communication language. In *Software Agents*, ed. J. Bradshaw. Cambridge, MA: MIT Press.

Flanagan, D. (1996). *Java in a Nutshell*. Sebastopol, CA: O'Reilly & Associates.

Forgy, C. L. (1982). Rete: A fast algorithm for the many pattern/many object pattern match problem. *Artificial Intelligence* 19:17–37.

Gamma, E., Helm, R., Johnson, R., and Vlissides, J. (1995). *Design Patterns: Elements of Reusable Object-Oriented Software*. Reading, MA: Addison-Wesley.

Gensereth, M. R. and Fikes, R. E. (1992). *Knowledge Interchange Format, version 3.0 Reference Manual*. Stanford University.

Glaser, N. (1996). *Contribution to Knowledge Modelling in a Multi-Agent Framework (the CoMoMAS Approach)*, Ph.D. Thesis, l'Université Henri Poincaré, France.

Grosz, B. and Kraus, S. (1993). Collaborative plans for group activities. In *Proceedings of the Thirteenth International Joint Conference on Artificial Intelligence (IJCAI-93)*, 367–373. Chambery, France: Morgan Kaufman.

Grosz, B. and Sidner, C. (1990). Plans for Discourse. In *Intentions in Communication*, ed. P. Cohen, J. Morgan, and M. Pollak, 417–444. Cambridge, MA: MIT Press.

Hodges, A. (1983). *Alan Turing: The Enigma*. New York: Simon and Schuster.

Holland, J. H., Holyoak, K. J., Nisbett, R. E., and Thagard, P. R. (1986). *Induction: Processes of Inference, Learning, and Discovery*. Cambridge, MA: MIT Press.

IBM (1996). *Intelligent Agent Resource Manager*, Open Blueprint, G325-6592-0.

Iglesias, C. A., Garijo, M., Gonzalez, J. C. (1998). A survey of agent oriented methodologies. In *Proceedings of Intelligent Agents V: Agent Theories, Architectures, and Languages (ATAL '98)*, v. 1555, Springer-Verlag's lecture notes, 317–330.

Jagannathan, V., Dodhiawala, R., Baum, L. S., eds. (1989). *Blackboard Architectures and Applications*. San Diego, CA: Academic Press.

JavaSoft (1996). JavaBeans 1.0 API Specification. http://java.sun.com/beans.

Kantor, B. and Lapsley, P. (1986). *Network News Transport Protocol: A Proposed Standard for the Stream-Based Transmission of News.* RFC 997, Network Working Group.

Kinny, D., Georgeff, M., and Rao, A. (1996). A methodology and modeling technique for systems of BDI agents. In *Agents Breaking Away: Proceedings of the Seventh European Workshop on Modelling Autonomous Agents in a Multi-Agent World (MAA-MAW '96).* Berlin: Springer-Verlag.

Kirkpatrick, S., Gelatt, C. D., and Vecchi, M. P. (1983). Optimization by simulated annealing. *Science* 220:671–680.

Kohonen, T. (1990). The self-organizing map. *Proceedings of the IEEE* 78:1464–1479.

Kumar, M., and Feldman, S. I., (1998). Business negotiation on the Internet. *IBM Institute for Advanced Commerce (IAC) Report.* http://www.ibm.com/iac/reports-technical/reports-bus-neg-internet.html.

Kuokka, D. and Harada, L. (1995). On using KQML for matchmaking. In *Proceedings of the First International Conference on Multiagent Systems.* Menlo Park, CA: AAAI Press.

Lander, S. E. (1997). Issues in multiagent design systems. *IEEE Expert* 12(2): 18–26.

Lange, D. B. (1998). Mobile agents: environments, technologies, and applications. In *Proceedings of the Third International Conference on the Practical Application of Intelligent Agents and Multi-Agent Technology,* 11–14. The Practical Application Company.

Levesque, H. J., Cohen, P. R., and Nunes, J. H. T. (1990). On acting together. *Proceedings of the Eighth National Conference on Artificial Intelligence (AAAI-90),* 94–99. Boston, MA: AAAI Press.

Maes, P. (1991). *Designing Autonomous Agents: Theory and Practice from Biology to Engineering and Back.* Cambridge, MA: MIT Press.

Maes, P. (1994). Agents that reduce work and information overload. *Communications of the ACM* 7:31–40.

Maglio, P. P., Barrett, R., Campbell, C. S., Selker T. (2000). SUITOR: An attentive information system. *Proceedings of the International Conference on Intelligent User Interfaces (IUI 2000),* 169–176. New York: ACM.

McDermott, J. (1982). R1: A rule-based configurer of computer systems. *Artificial Intelligence* 19(1): 39–88.

Merriam-Webster, (1988). *Webster's Ninth New Collegiate Dictionary.* Springfield, MA: Merriam-Webster.

Minsky, M. L. (1980). *The Society of Mind.* New York: Simon and Schuster.

Newell, A. (1980). Physical symbol systems. *Cognitive Science* 4:185–203.

Newell, A. and Simon, H. A. (1963) GPS, a program that simulates human thought. In *Computers and Thought,* ed. E. A. Feigenbaum and J. Feldman. New York: McGraw Hill.

Newell, A. (1990). *Unified Theories of Cognition.* Cambridge, MA: Harvard University Press.

Nilsson, N. J. (1998). *Artificial Intelligence: A New Synthesis.* San Francisco: Morgan Kaufmann.

Nwana, H. S. (1996). Software agents: An overview. *Knowledge Engineering Review* 11(3): 205–244.

O'Brien, P. D., and Nicol, R. C. (1998). FIPA—towards a stance for software agents. *British Telecom Technology Journal* 16(3): 51–59.

Poslad, S., Buckle, P., Hadingham, R. (2000). The FIPA-OS Agent Platform: Open Source for Open Standards, *Practical Applications of Intelligent Agents and Multi-Agent*

Systems (PAAM 2000), Manchester, UK, The Practical Application Company. Quillian, M. R. (1968). Semantic memory. In *Semantic Information Processing*, ed. M. L. Minsky, 216–270. Cambridge, MA: MIT Press. Quinlan, J. R. (1986). Induction of decision trees. *Machine Learning* 1:81–106.

Quinlan, J. R. (1993). *C4.5: Programs for Machine Learning*. San Francisco: Morgan Kaufmann.

Rich, C. and Sidner, C. (1997). COLLAGEN: When Agents Collaborate with People. *Proceedings of the First International Conference on Autonomous Agents (Agents '97)*, Association for Computing Machinery, 284–291.

Rich, E. and Knight, K. (1991). *Artificial Intelligence*. New York: McGraw-Hill.

Robinson, A. J. (1965). A machine-oriented logic based on the resolution principle. *JACM* 12:23–41.

Rumelhart, D. E., Hinton, G. E., and Williams, R. J. (1986). Learning internal representations by error propagation. In *Parallel Distributed Processing*, Vol. 1. Cambridge, MA: MIT Press.

Russell, S. and Norvig, P. (1995). *Artificial Intelligence: A Modern Approach*. Englewood Cliffs, NJ: Prentice Hall.

Sacerdoti, E. D. (1974). Planning in a hierarchy of abstraction spaces. *Artificial Intelligence* 5(2): 155.

Searle, J. (1969). *Speech Acts: An Essay in the Philosophy of Language*. Cambridge, MA: Cambridge University Press.

Sedgewick, R. (1984). *Algorithms*. Reading, MA: Addison-Wesley.

Shannon, C. E. and Weaver, W. (1949). *The Mathematical Theory of Communication*. Urbana, IL: University of Illinois Press.

Shortliffe, E. H. (1976). *Computer-Based Medical Consultations: MYCIN*. New York: Elsevier.

Shoham, Y. (1994). Agent-oriented programming: an overview of the framework and summary of recent research. In *Knowledge representation and reasoning under uncertainty: Logic at work*, ed. Masuch, M. and Polos, L. Berlin: Spinger-Verlag.

Singh, M. (1998). Agent communication languages: Rethinking the principles. *IEEE Computer Magazine* 31(12): 40–47.

Smith, R. G. (1980). The Contract Net Protocol: High-level communication and control in a distributed problem solver. In *Readings in Distributed Artificial Intelligence*, ed. A. Bond and L. Gasser. San Mateo, CA: Morgan Kaufmann.

Stefik, M. J. (1981). Planning and meta-planning. *Artificial Intelligence* 16:141–169.

Stone, P. and Veloso, M. (2000). Multiagent systems: A survey from a machine learning perspective. *Autonomous Robots* 8(3): 345–383.

Su, S. Y. W., Huang, C., and Hammer, J. (2000). A replicable web-based negotiation server for e-commerce. In *Proceedings of the 33rd Hawaii International Conference on Systems Science (HICSS-33)*, Wailea, Maui, Hawaii: IEEE Press.

Sutton, R. (1988). Learning to predict by the methods of temporal differences. *Machine Learning*, 3:9–44.

Sycara, K. (1998). Multiagent systems. *AI Magazine* 19(2): 79–92.

Tambe, M. (1997). Towards flexible teamwork. *Journal of Artificial Intelligence Research* 7:83–124.

Tambe, M., Adibi, J., Al-Onaizan, U., Erdem, A., Kaminka, G. A., Marsella, S. C., and Muslea, I. (1999). Building agent teams using an explicit teamwork model and learning. *Artificial Intelligence* 110(2): 215–239.

Thompson, B. and Thompson, W. (1985). Inside an expert system. *Byte* (April).

Veloso, M., Carbonell, J., Perez, A., Borrajo, D., Fink, E., and Blythe, J. (1995). Integrating Planning and Learning: The PRODIGY Architecture. *Journal of Experimental and Theoretical Artificial Intelligence* 7(1).

Waterman, D. A. (1985). *A Guide to Expert Systems*. Reading, MA: Addison-Wesley.

Watkins, C. J. (1989). *Models of Delayed Reinforcement Learning*, Ph.D. thesis, Psychology Department, Cambridge University, Cambridge, UK.

Williams, J. (1996). *Bots and Other Internet Beasties*. Indianapolis: Sams Net.

Winston, P. H. (1993). *Artificial Intelligence*, third edition. Reading, MA: Addison-Wesley.

Wooldridge, M. J., and Jennings, N. R. (1999). Software engineering with agents: Pitfalls and Pratfalls. *IEEE Internet Computing*, 3(3): 20–27.

Yu, B., Venkatraman, M. and Singh, M. P. (2000) The MARS adaptive social network for information access: architecture and experimental results. In *Applied Artificial Intelligence*. Forthcoming.

Zadeh, L. A. (1994) Fuzzy logic, neural networks and soft computing. *Communications of the ACM* 3:78–84.

Zeng, D., and Sycara, K. (1998). Bayesian learning in negotiation. *International Journal of Human Computer Systems* 48:125–141.

Index

To use this CD-Rom, your system must meet the following requirements:

System Requirements. To run the Java examples, you must have a Java 2 SDK or Java Runtime Environment (JRE) installed on your machine. The Java 2 platform requires at least a 166 MHz Pentium processor. The Sun Java 2 Platform requires 64MB of RAM running Windows 98/NT.

Hard Drive Space. The CIAgent code requires 5MB of disk space. The Sun Java Runtime Environment Version 1.3.0 requires 16MB of disk space. The IBM Agent Building and Learning Environment requires 25MB of disk space.

Peripherals. A CD-ROM drive and a Web browser are required for navigation through the CD and viewing the CIAgent Javadocs. Internet access is required to run several of the CIAgent example applications.

Running the Software. The software must be copied from the CD-ROM to your computer to run. Installation procedures are provided in the index.html file in the root of the CD-ROM. For your convenience, the CIAgent and IBM ABLE software is provided unzipped on this CD-ROM.